Ayu
Watanabe

L♥DK

エルディーケー

1

L♥DK
Ayu Watanabe
1

c o n t e n t s

#1 The Prince's Neighbor 3

#2 Cohabitation Starts 47

#3 True Feelings 89

#4 A Day Off Together 129

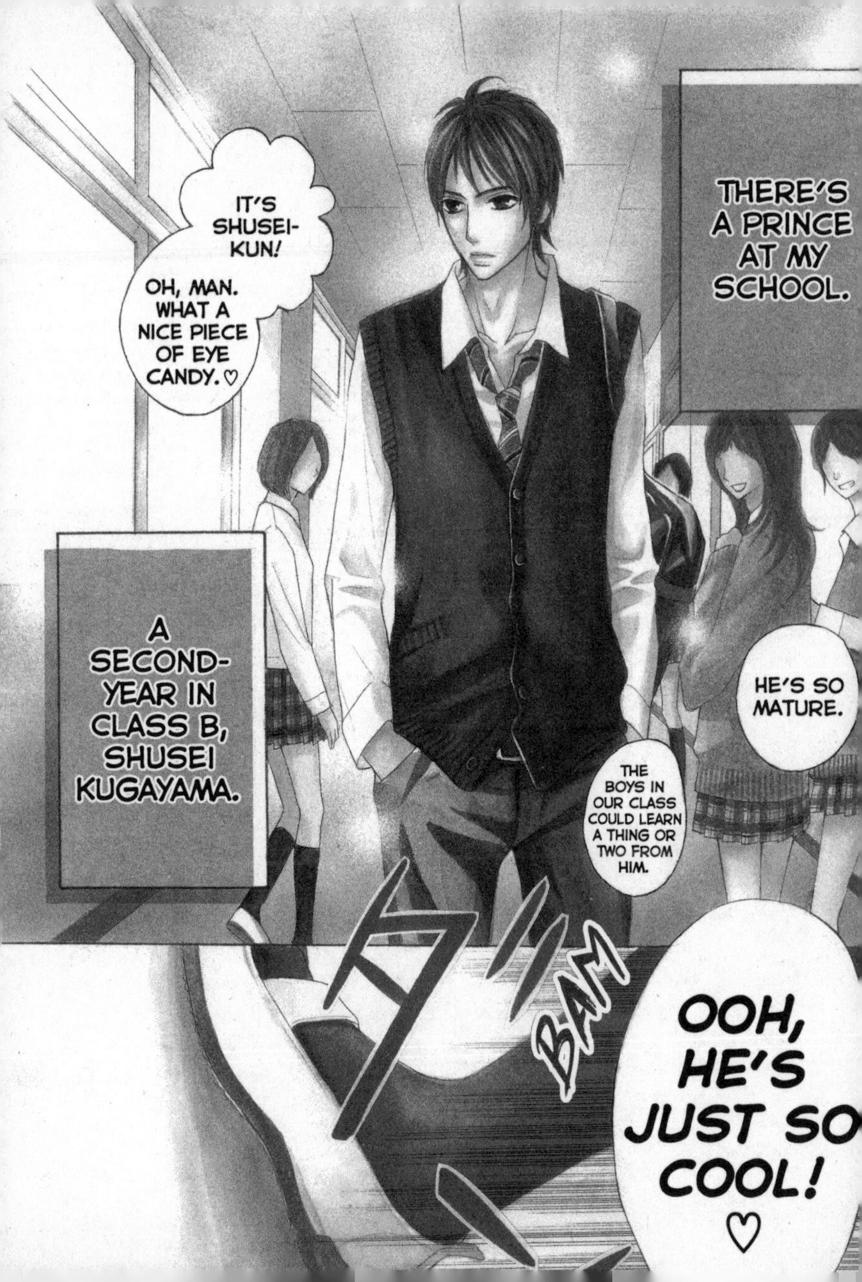
THERE'S A PRINCE AT MY SCHOOL.
IT'S SHUSEI-KUN!
OH, MAN. WHAT A NICE PIECE OF EYE CANDY. ♡
A SECOND-YEAR IN CLASS B, SHUSEI KUGAYAMA.
HE'S SO MATURE.
THE BOYS IN OUR CLASS COULD LEARN A THING OR TWO FROM HIM.
OOH, HE'S JUST SO COOL! ♡
BAM

#1
The Prince's Neighbor

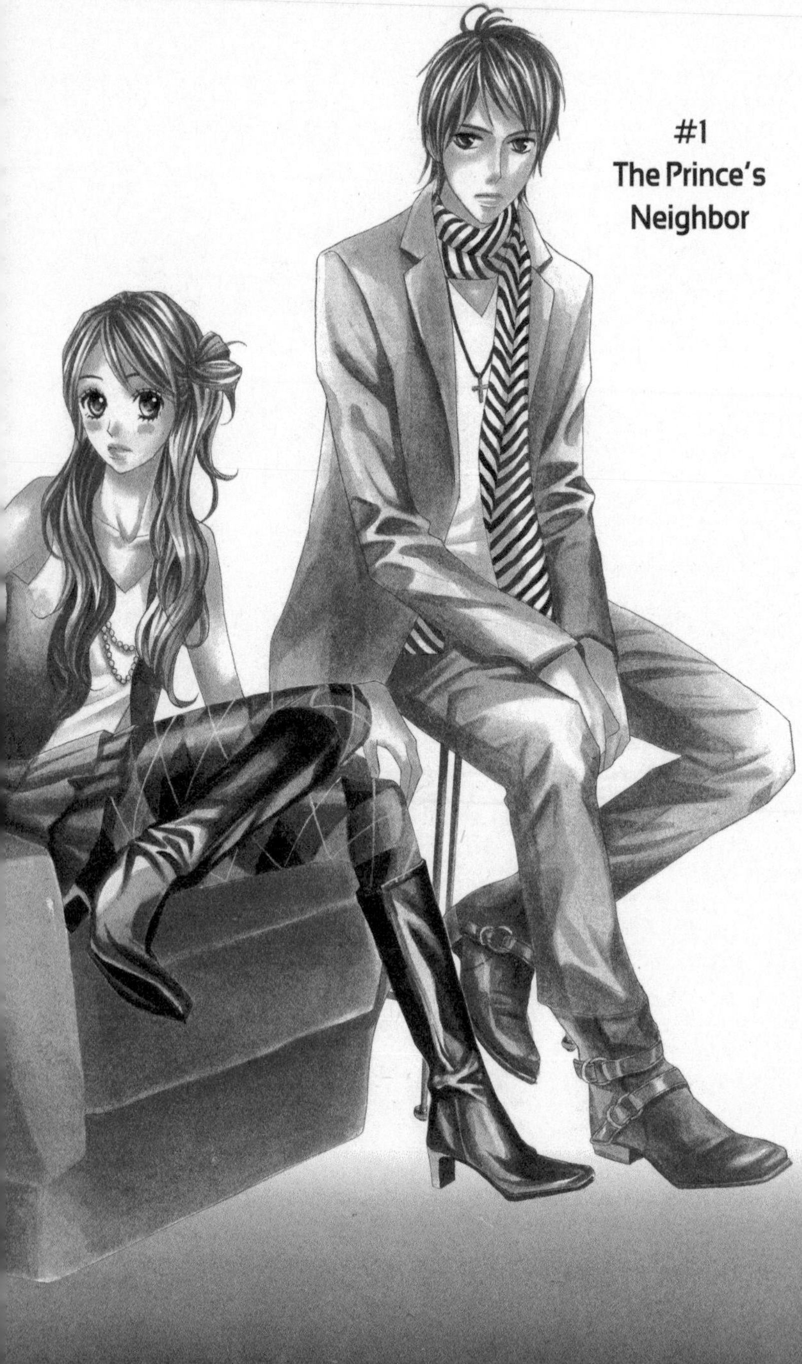

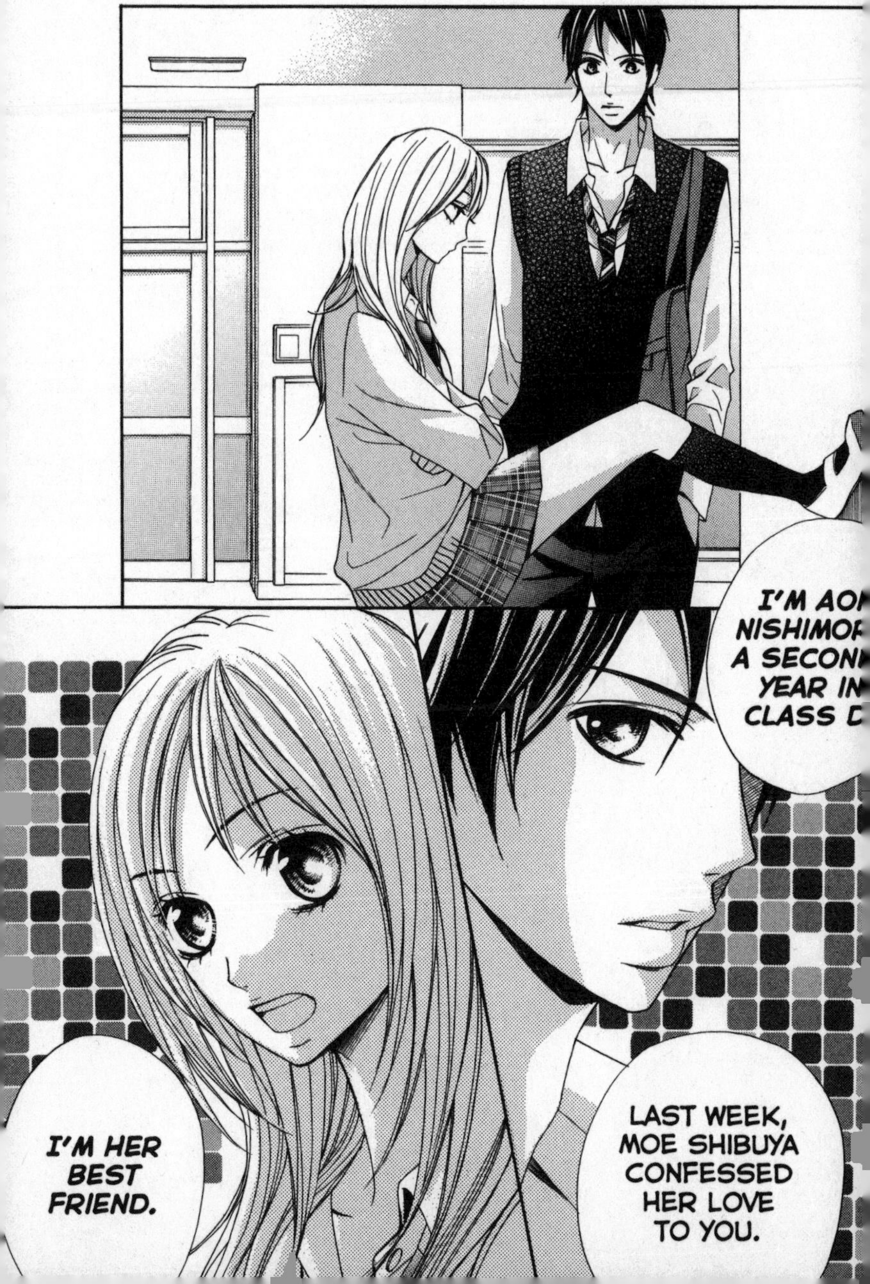
I'M AO
NISHIMOR
A SECON
YEAR IN
CLASS D
LAST WEEK, MOE SHIBUYA CONFESSED HER LOVE TO YOU.
I'M HER BEST FRIEND.

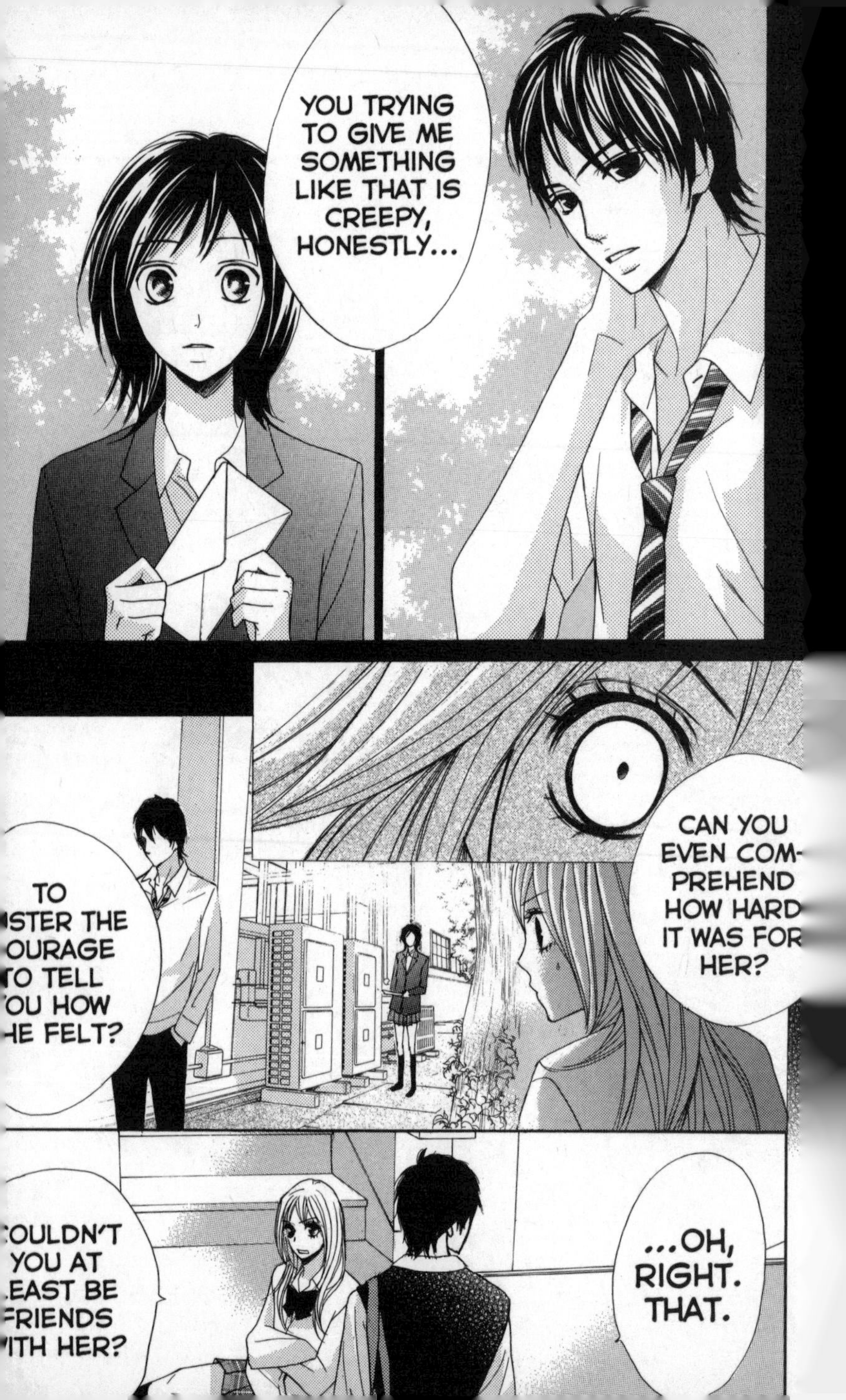
YOU TRYING TO GIVE ME SOMETHING LIKE THAT IS CREEPY, HONESTLY...
CAN YOU EVEN COM-PREHEND HOW HARD IT WAS FOR HER?
TO STER THE OURAGE TO TELL OU HOW HE FELT?
...OH, RIGHT. THAT.
OULDN'T YOU AT EAST BE FRIENDS ITH HER?

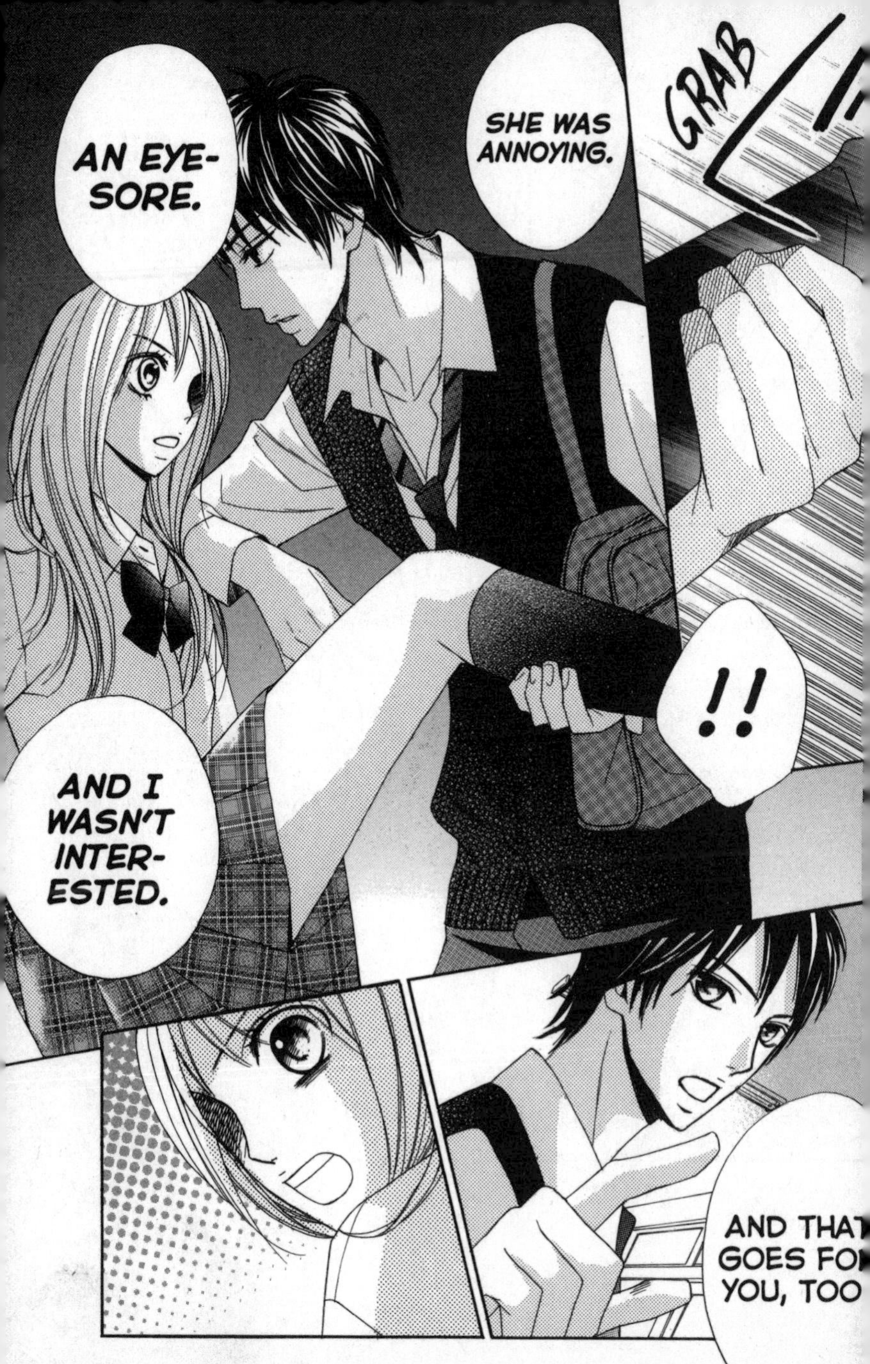
GRAB
!!
SHE WAS ANNOYING.
AN EYE-SORE.
AND I WASN'T INTER-ESTED.
AND THAT GOES FO YOU, TOO

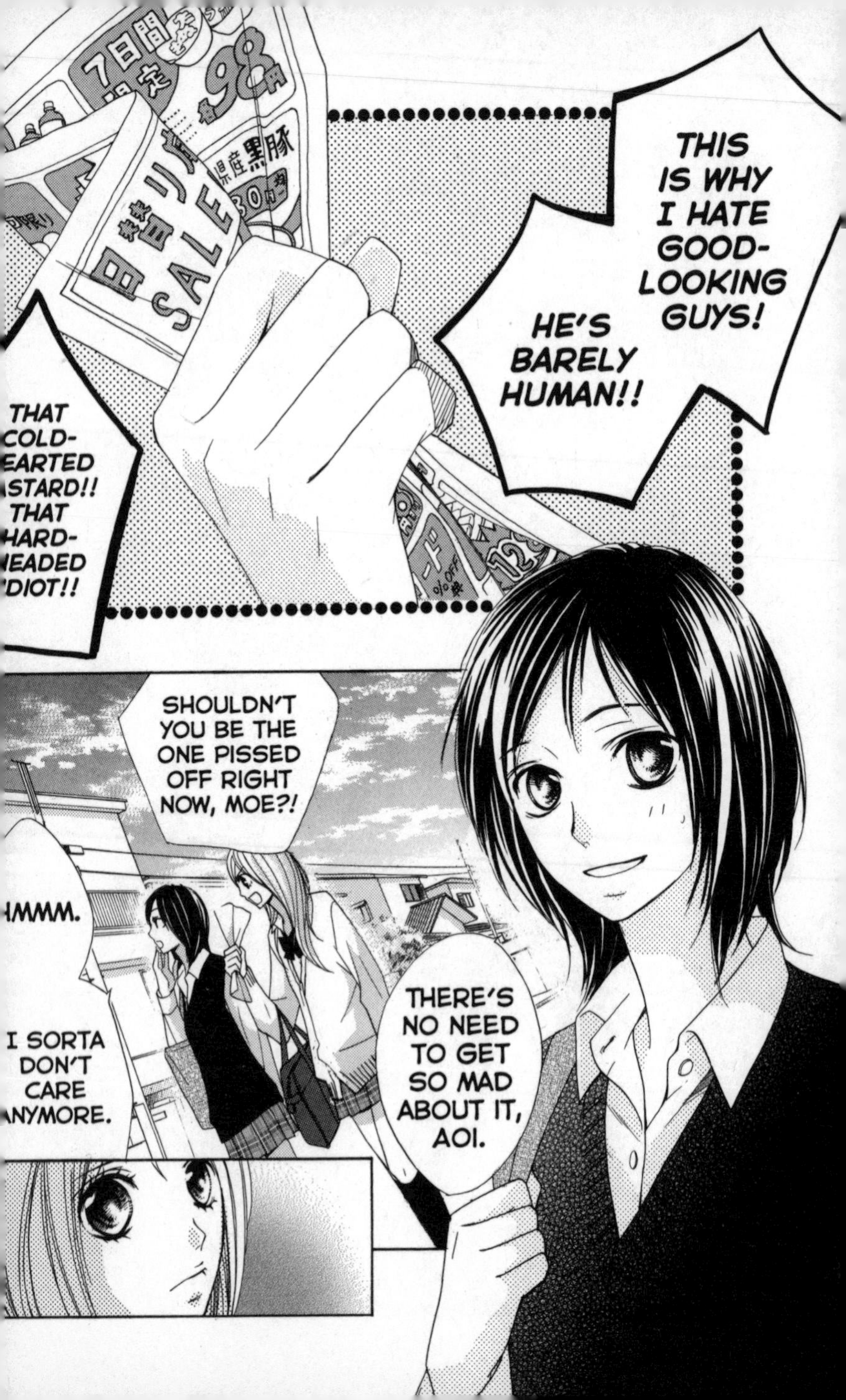
THIS IS WHY I HATE GOOD-LOOKING GUYS!
HE'S BARELY HUMAN!!
THAT COLD-EARTED ASTARD!! THAT HARD-EADED DIOT!!
THERE'S NO NEED TO GET SO MAD ABOUT IT, AOI.
SHOULDN'T YOU BE THE ONE PISSED OFF RIGHT NOW, MOE?!
HMMM.
I SORTA DON'T CARE NYMORE.

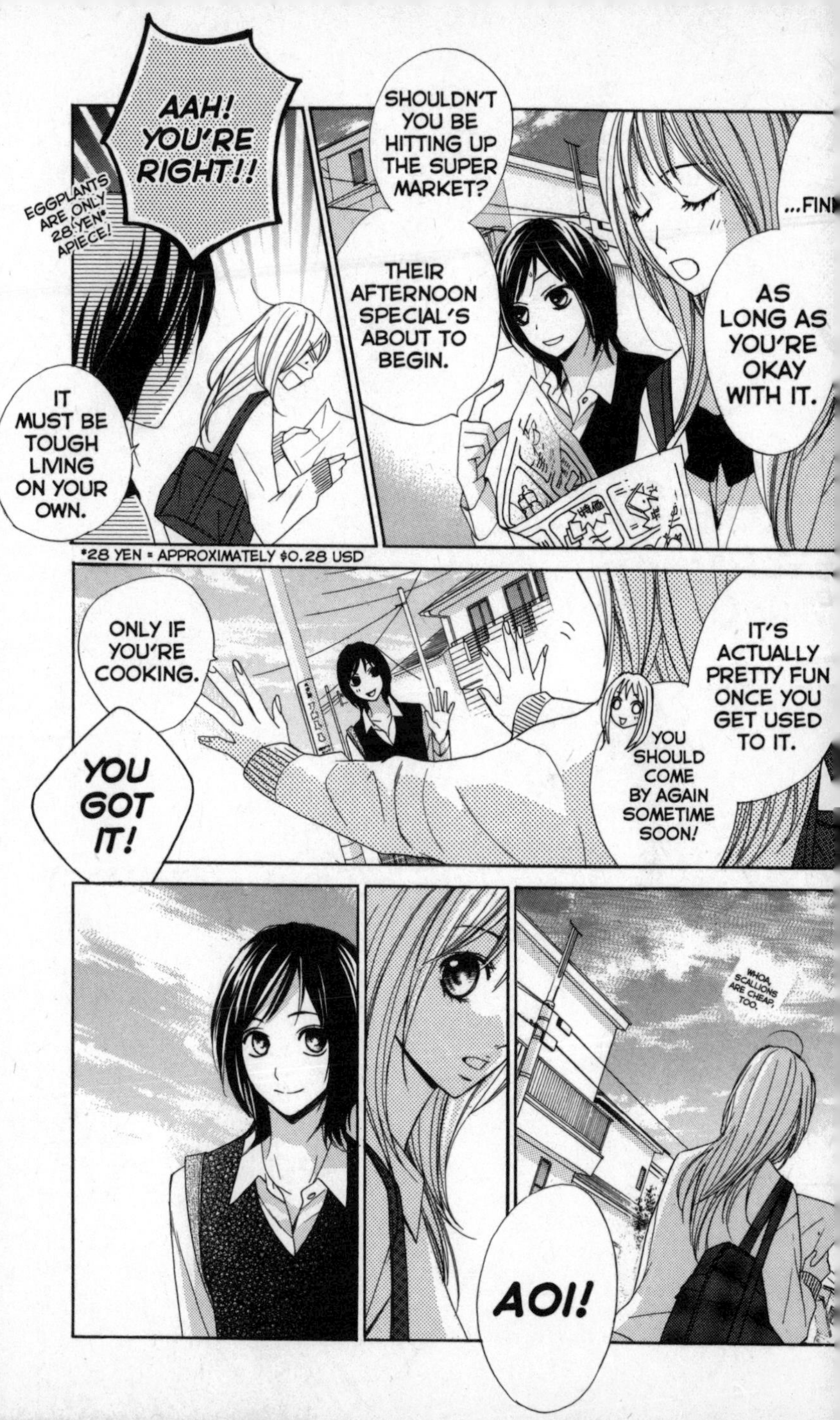
...FIN
AS LONG AS YOU'RE OKAY WITH IT.
SHOULDN'T YOU BE HITTING UP THE SUPER MARKET?
THEIR AFTERNOON SPECIAL'S ABOUT TO BEGIN.
AAH! YOU'RE RIGHT!!
EGGPLANTS ARE ONLY 28 YEN* APIECE!
IT MUST BE TOUGH LIVING ON YOUR OWN.
IT'S ACTUALLY PRETTY FUN ONCE YOU GET USED TO IT.
YOU SHOULD COME BY AGAIN SOMETIME SOON!
ONLY IF YOU'RE COOKING.
YOU GOT IT!
WHOA, SCALLIONS ARE CHEAP, TOO.
AOI!
*28 YEN = APPROXIMATELY $0.28 USD

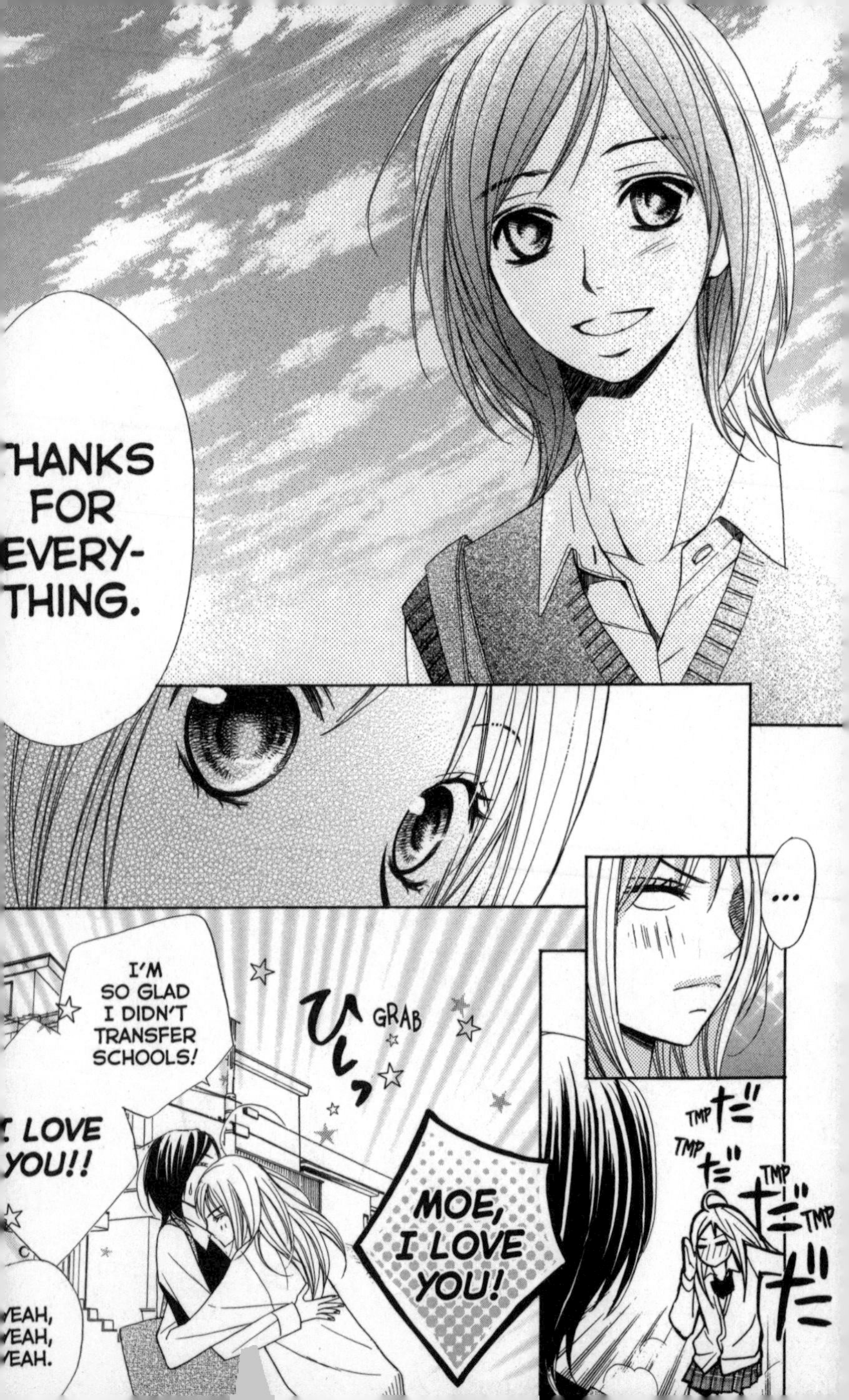
THANKS FOR EVERY-THING.
...
TMP だ TMP だ TMP だ TMP だ
MOE, I LOVE YOU!
I'M SO GLAD I DIDN'T TRANSFER SCHOOLS!
ひしっ GRAB
I LOVE YOU!!
YEAH, YEAH, YEAH.

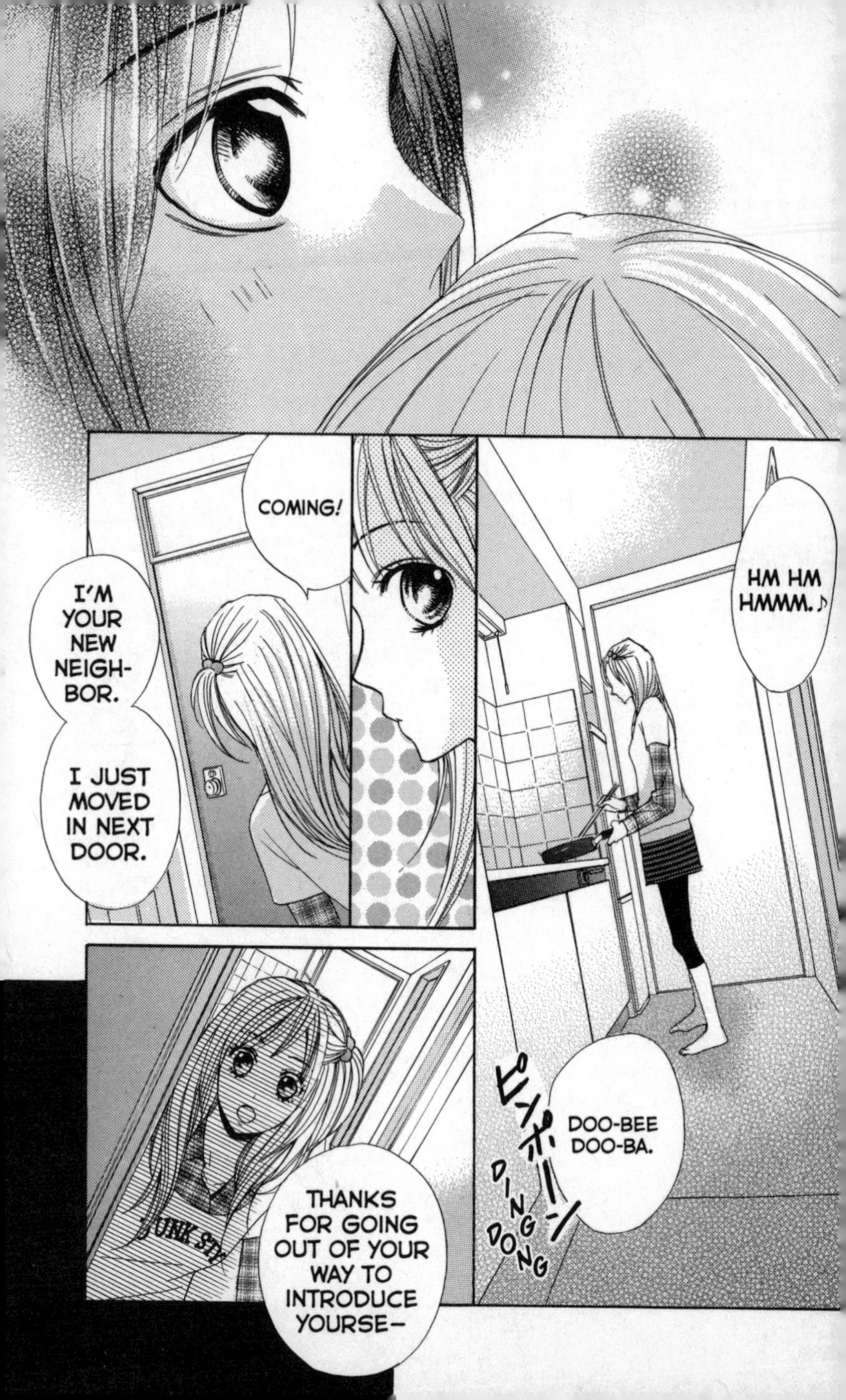
HM HM HMMM.♪
DOO-BEE DOO-BA.
ピンポーン
DING DONG
COMING!
I'M YOUR NEW NEIGHBOR.
I JUST MOVED IN NEXT DOOR.
THANKS FOR GOING OUT OF YOUR WAY TO INTRODUCE YOURSE–

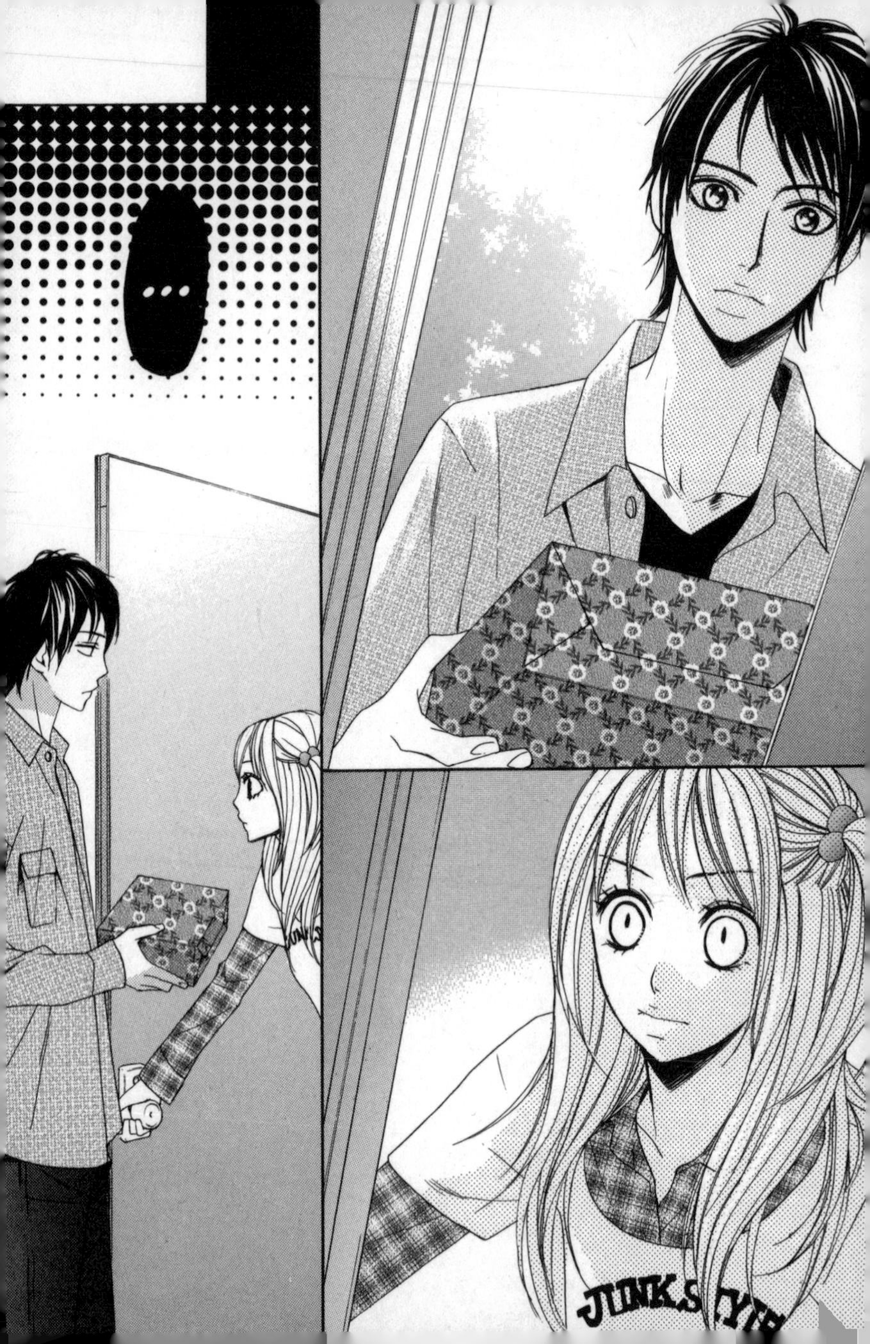
...

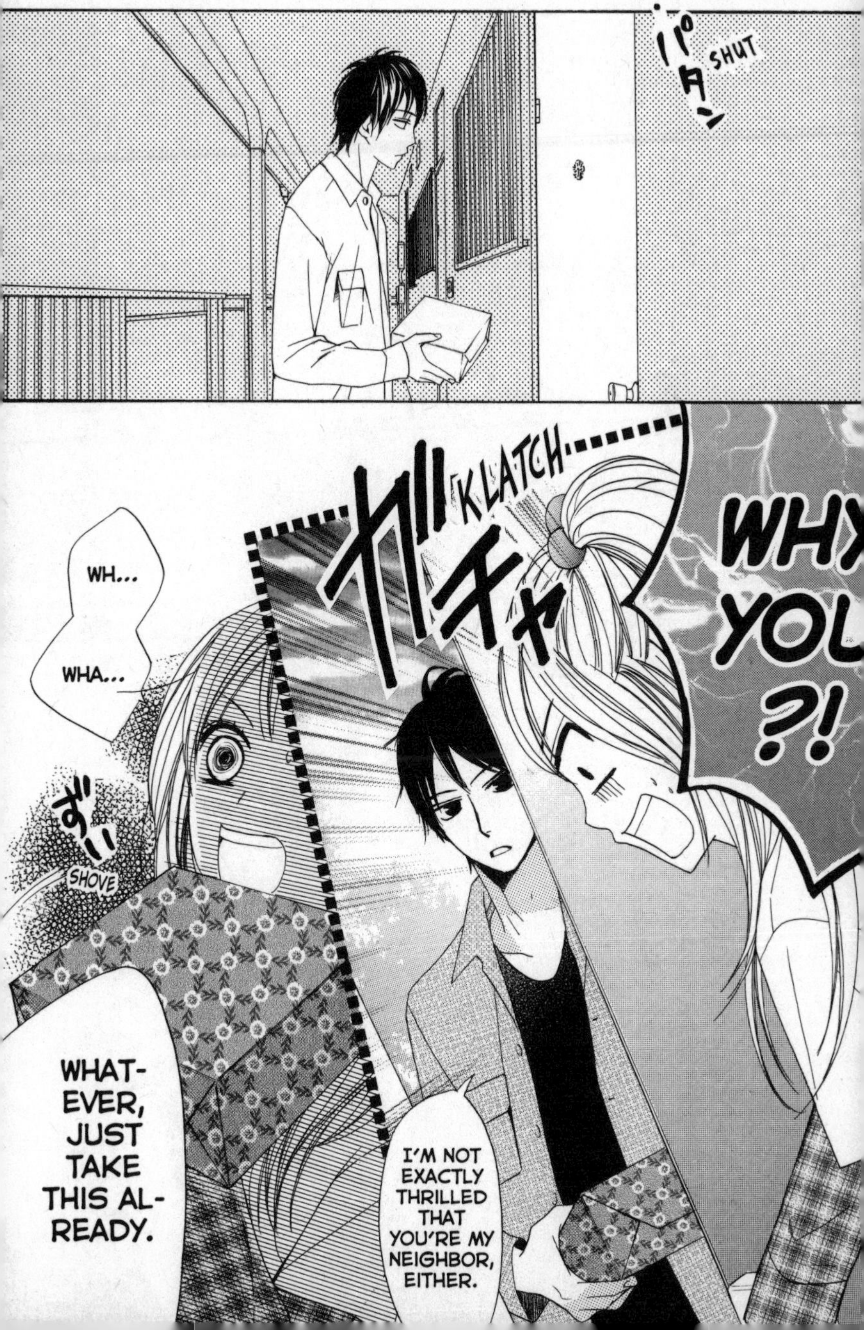
…パタン
SHUT
ガチャ
KLATCH
WHY YOU?!
I'M NOT EXACTLY THRILLED THAT YOU'RE MY NEIGHBOR, EITHER.
WH…
WHA…
ずい
SHOVE
WHAT-EVER, JUST TAKE THIS AL-READY.

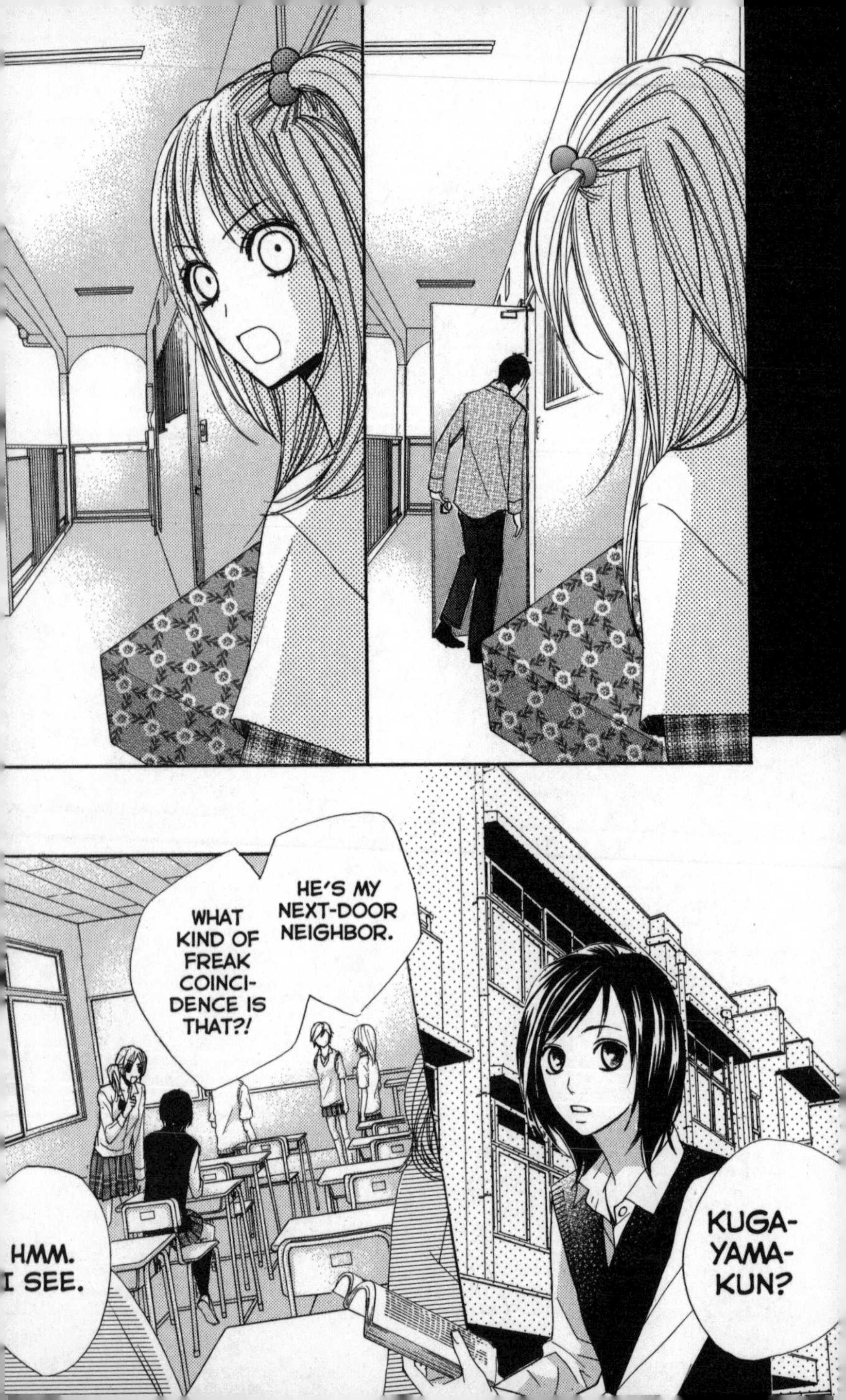
KUGA-YAMA-KUN?
HE'S MY NEXT-DOOR NEIGHBOR.
WHAT KIND OF FREAK COINCI-DENCE IS THAT?!
HMM. I SEE.

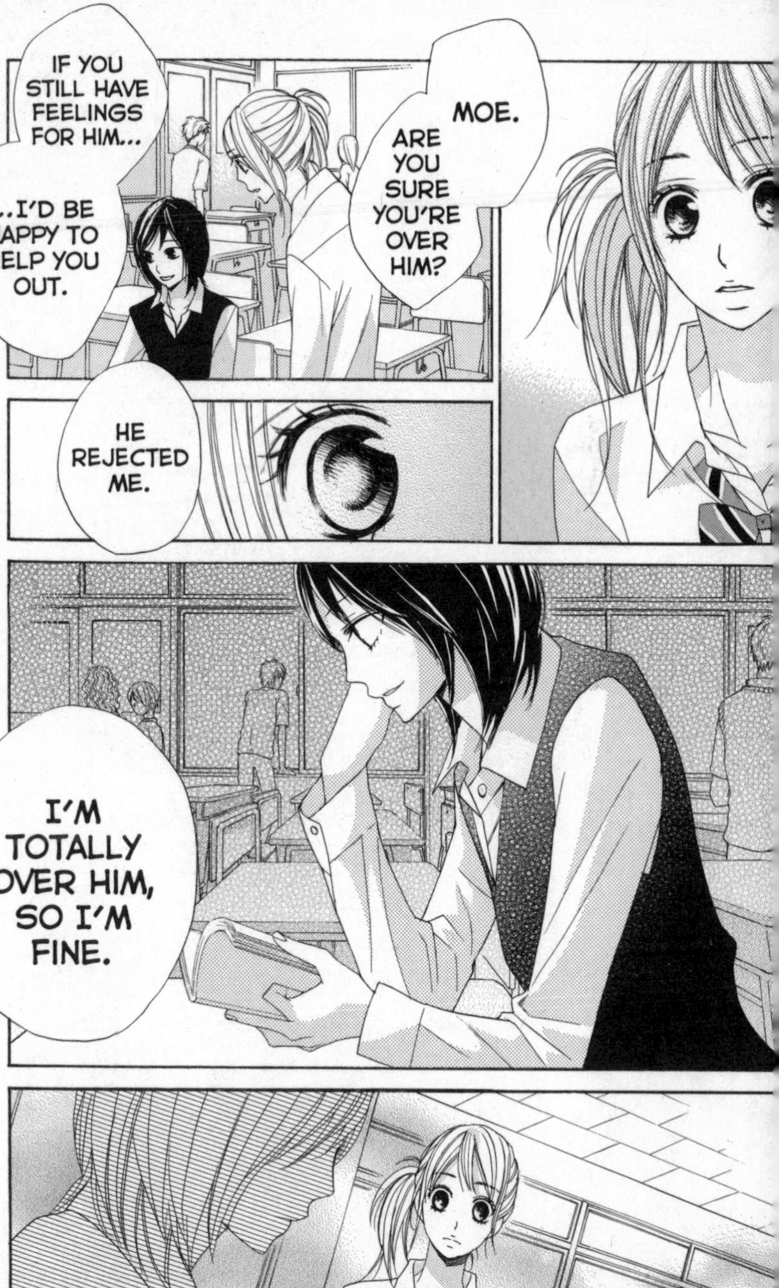
MOE.
ARE YOU SURE YOU'RE OVER HIM?
IF YOU STILL HAVE FEELINGS FOR HIM...
...I'D BE HAPPY TO HELP YOU OUT.
HE REJECTED ME.
I'M TOTALLY OVER HIM, SO I'M FINE.

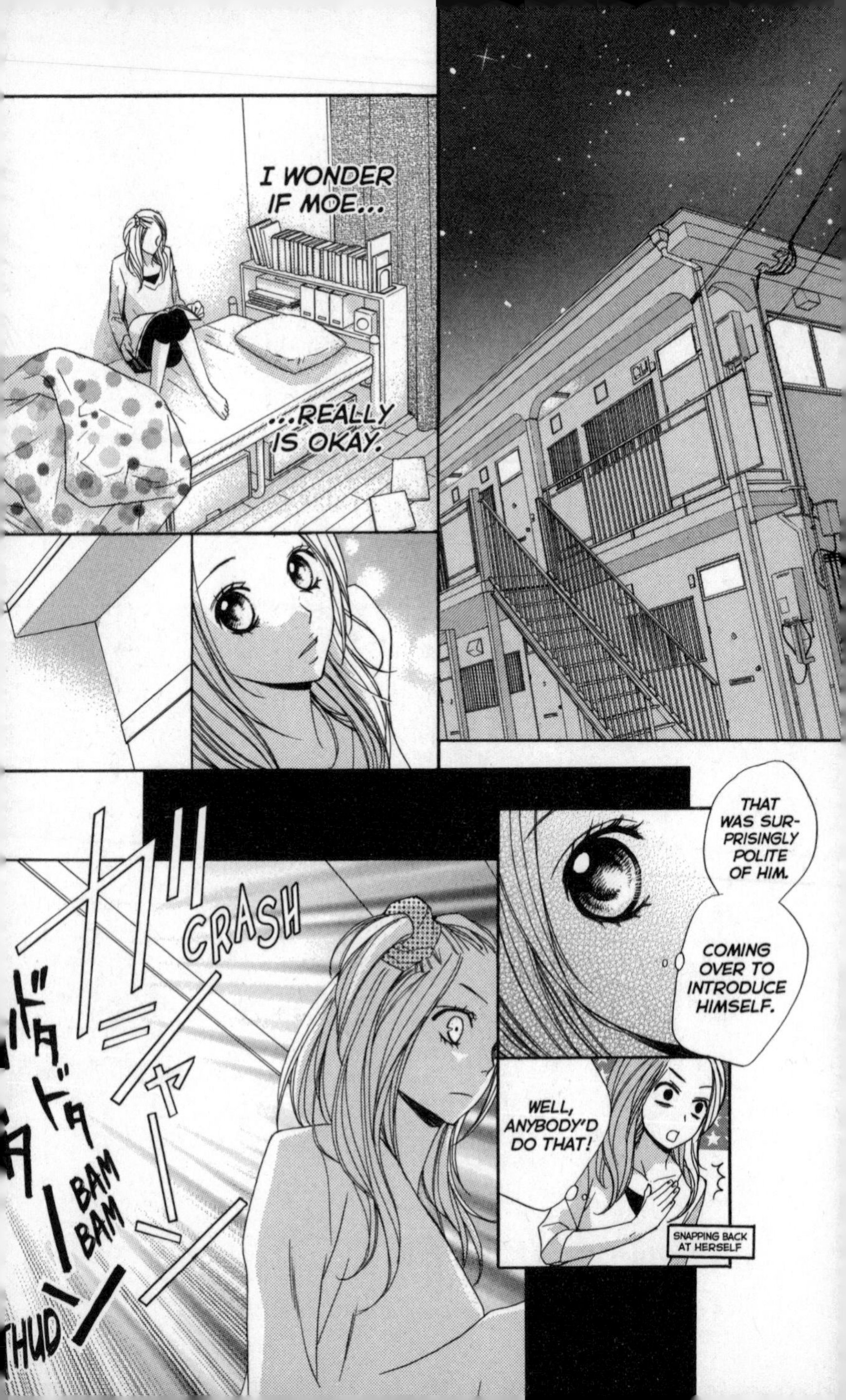
I WONDER IF MOE...
...REALLY IS OKAY.
THAT WAS SURPRISINGLY POLITE OF HIM.
COMING OVER TO INTRODUCE HIMSELF.
WELL, ANYBODY'D DO THAT!
SNAPPING BACK AT HERSELF
CRASH
BAM BAM
THUD

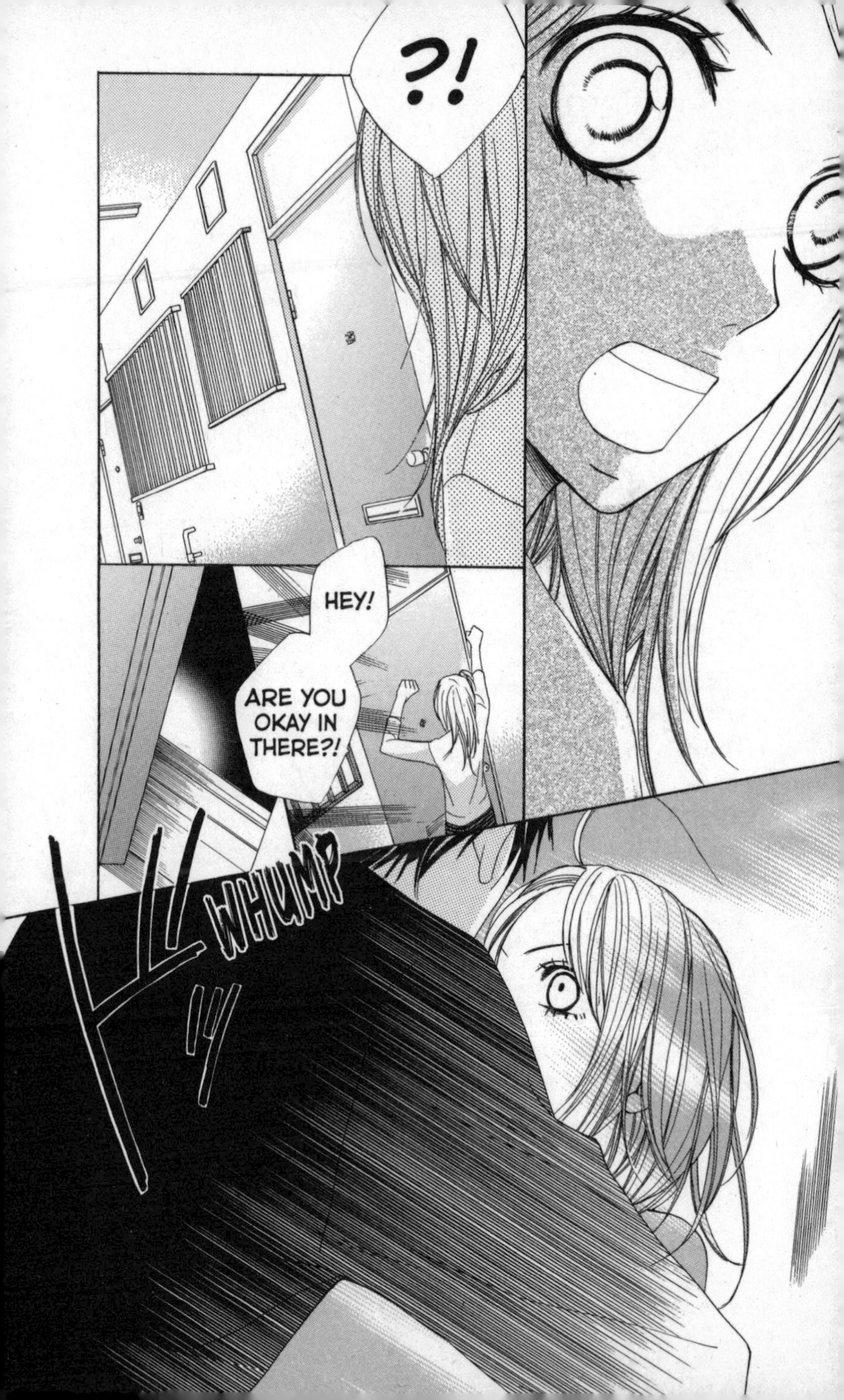
?!
HEY!
ARE YOU OKAY IN THERE?!
WHUMP

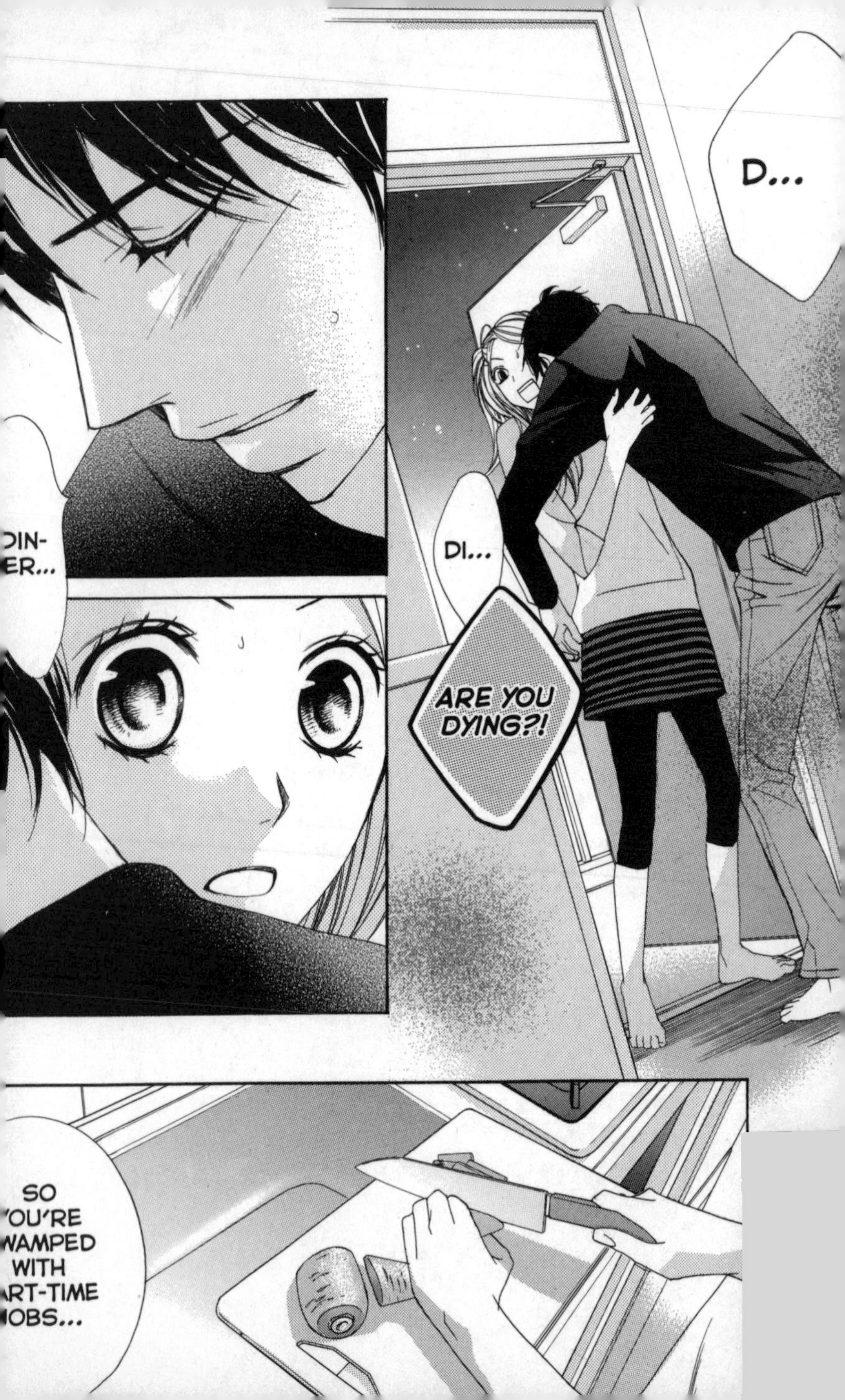
D...
DI...
ARE YOU DYING?!
DIN-ER...
SO OU'RE WAMPED WITH ART-TIME OBS...

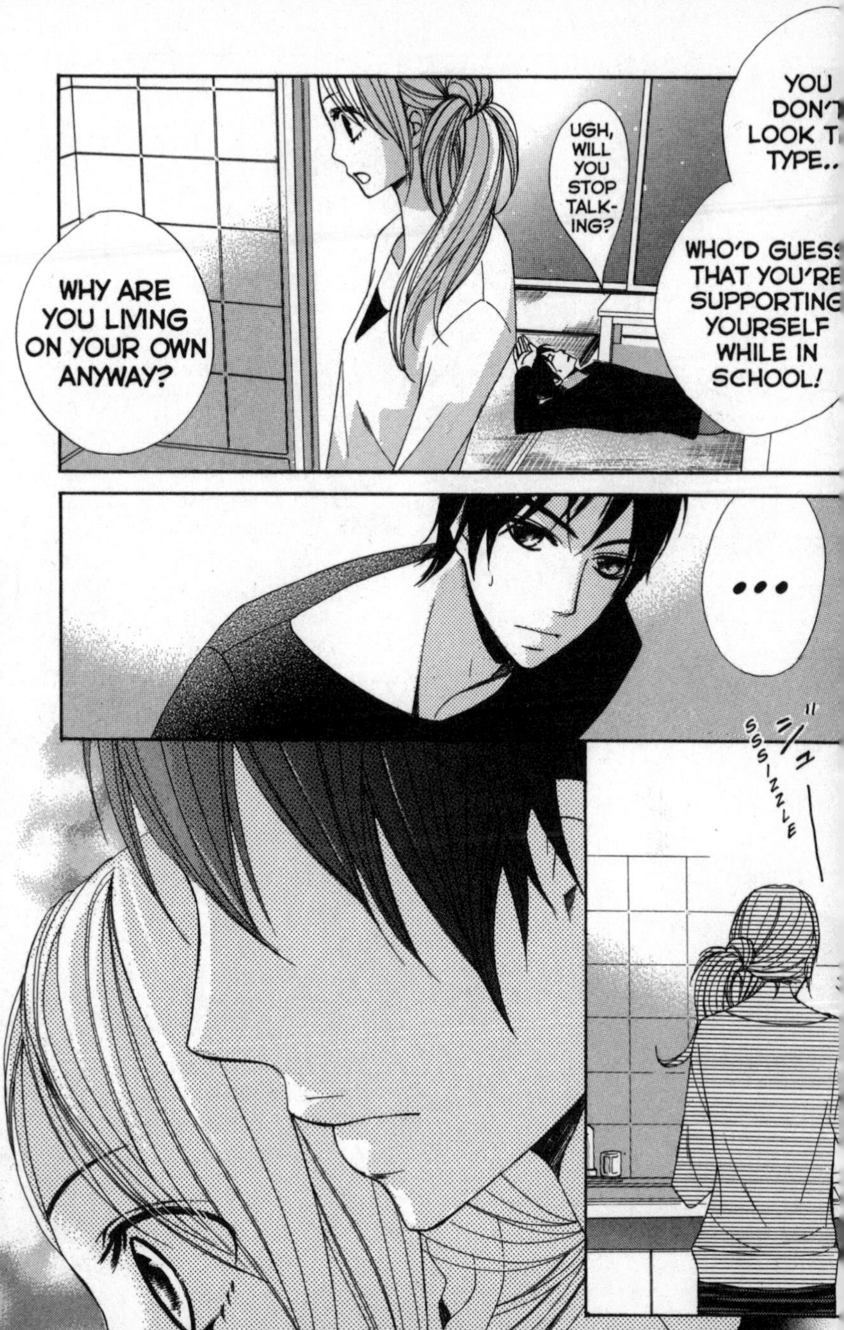
YOU DON'T LOOK T TYPE..
WHO'D GUESS THAT YOU'RE SUPPORTING YOURSELF WHILE IN SCHOOL!
UGH, WILL YOU STOP TALKING?
WHY ARE YOU LIVING ON YOUR OWN ANYWAY?
...
SSSIZZLE

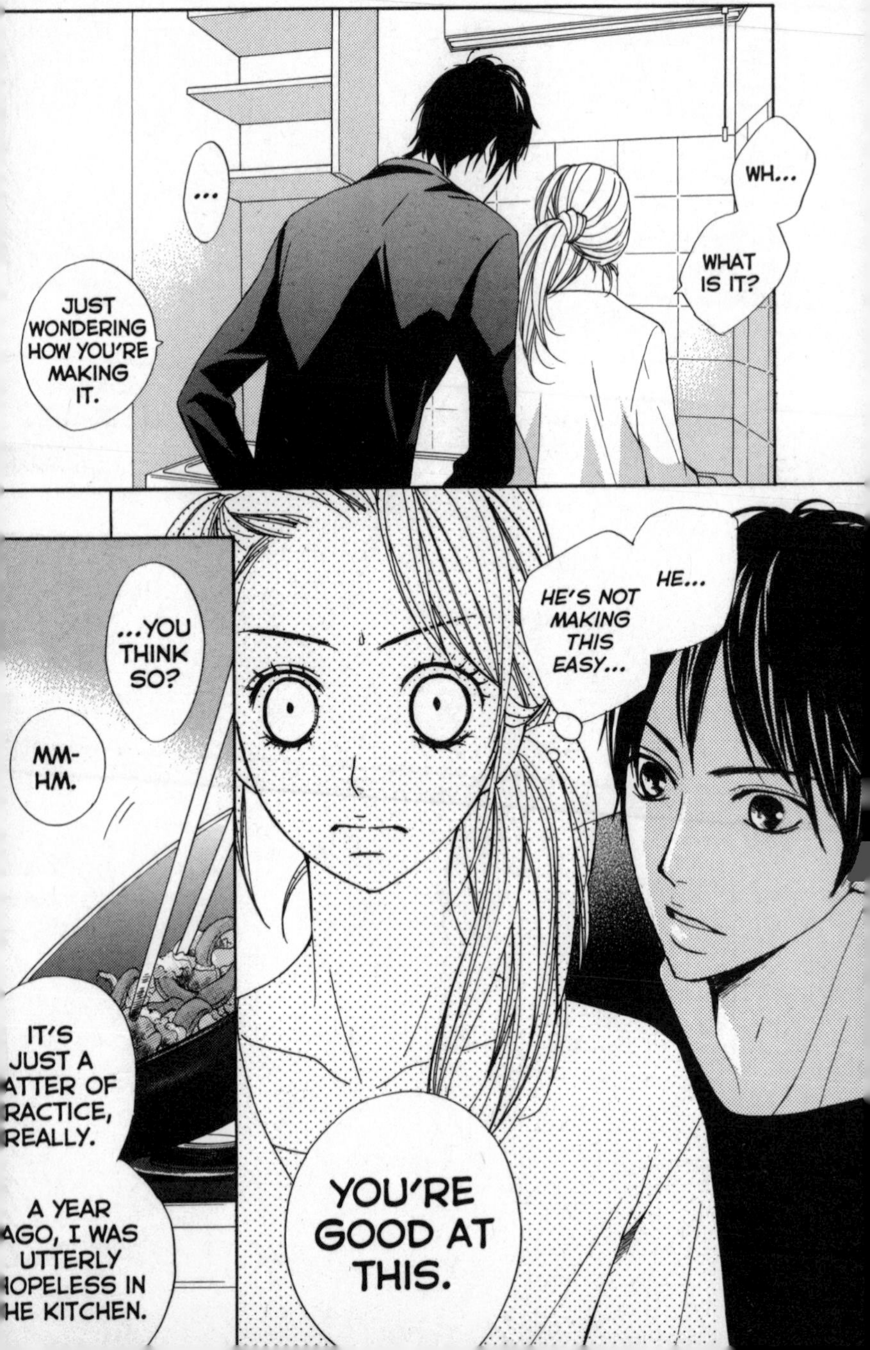
WH...
WHAT IS IT?
...
JUST WONDERING HOW YOU'RE MAKING IT.
HE...
HE'S NOT MAKING THIS EASY...
YOU'RE GOOD AT THIS.
...YOU THINK SO?
MM-HM.
IT'S JUST A ATTER OF RACTICE, REALLY.
A YEAR AGO, I WAS UTTERLY OPELESS IN HE KITCHEN.

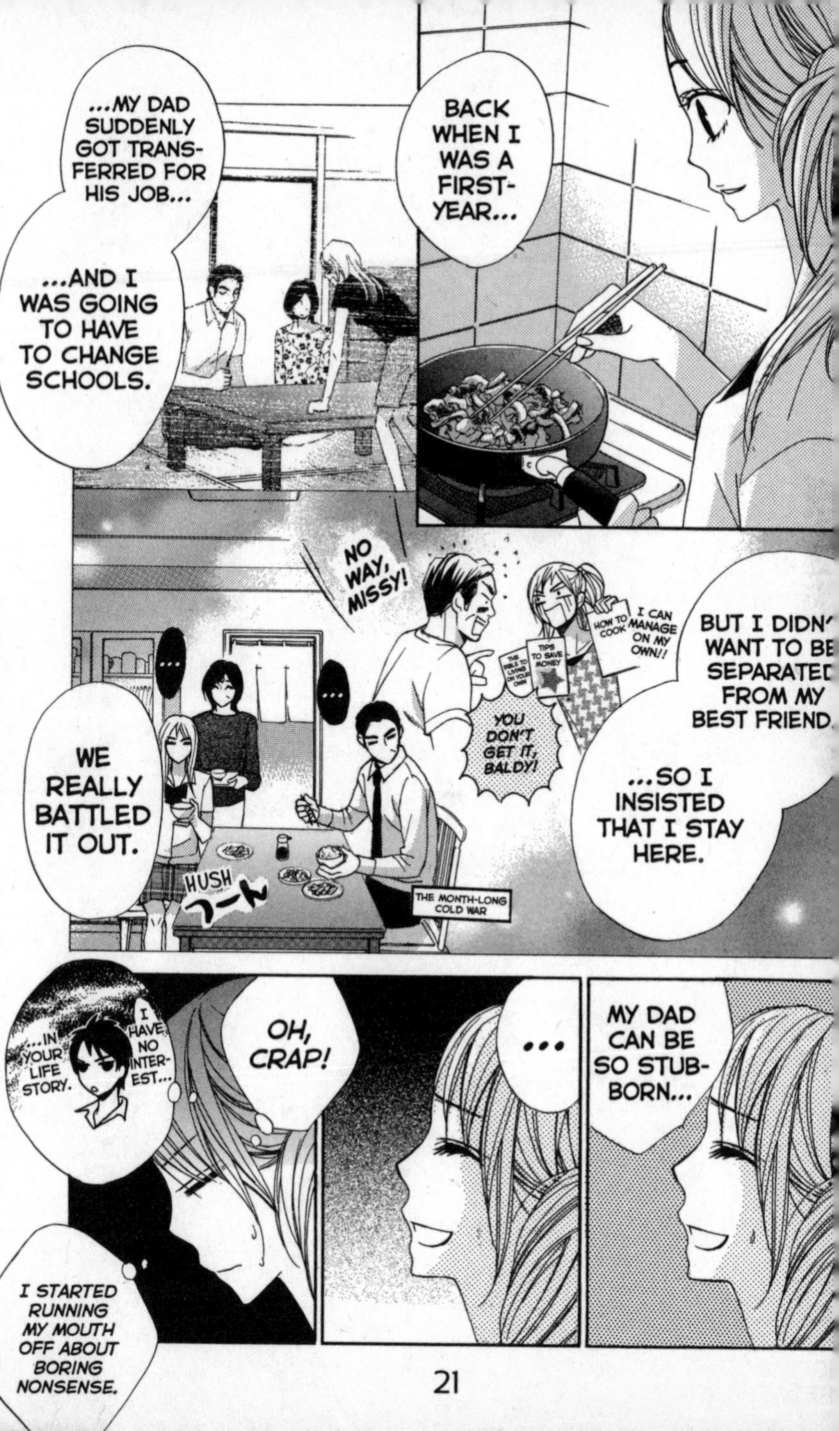
BACK WHEN I WAS A FIRST-YEAR...
...MY DAD SUDDENLY GOT TRANSFERRED FOR HIS JOB...
...AND I WAS GOING TO HAVE TO CHANGE SCHOOLS.
BUT I DIDN'T WANT TO BE SEPARATED FROM MY BEST FRIEND.
...SO I INSISTED THAT I STAY HERE.
I CAN MANAGE ON MY OWN!!
HOW TO COOK
TIPS TO SAVE MONEY
THE BIBLE TO LIVING ON YOUR OWN
NO WAY, MISSY!
YOU DON'T GET IT, BALDY!
...
...
WE REALLY BATTLED IT OUT.
HUSH
THE MONTH-LONG COLD WAR
MY DAD CAN BE SO STUBBORN...
...
OH, CRAP!
I HAVE NO INTEREST...
...IN YOUR LIFE STORY.
I STARTED RUNNING MY MOUTH OFF ABOUT BORING NONSENSE.

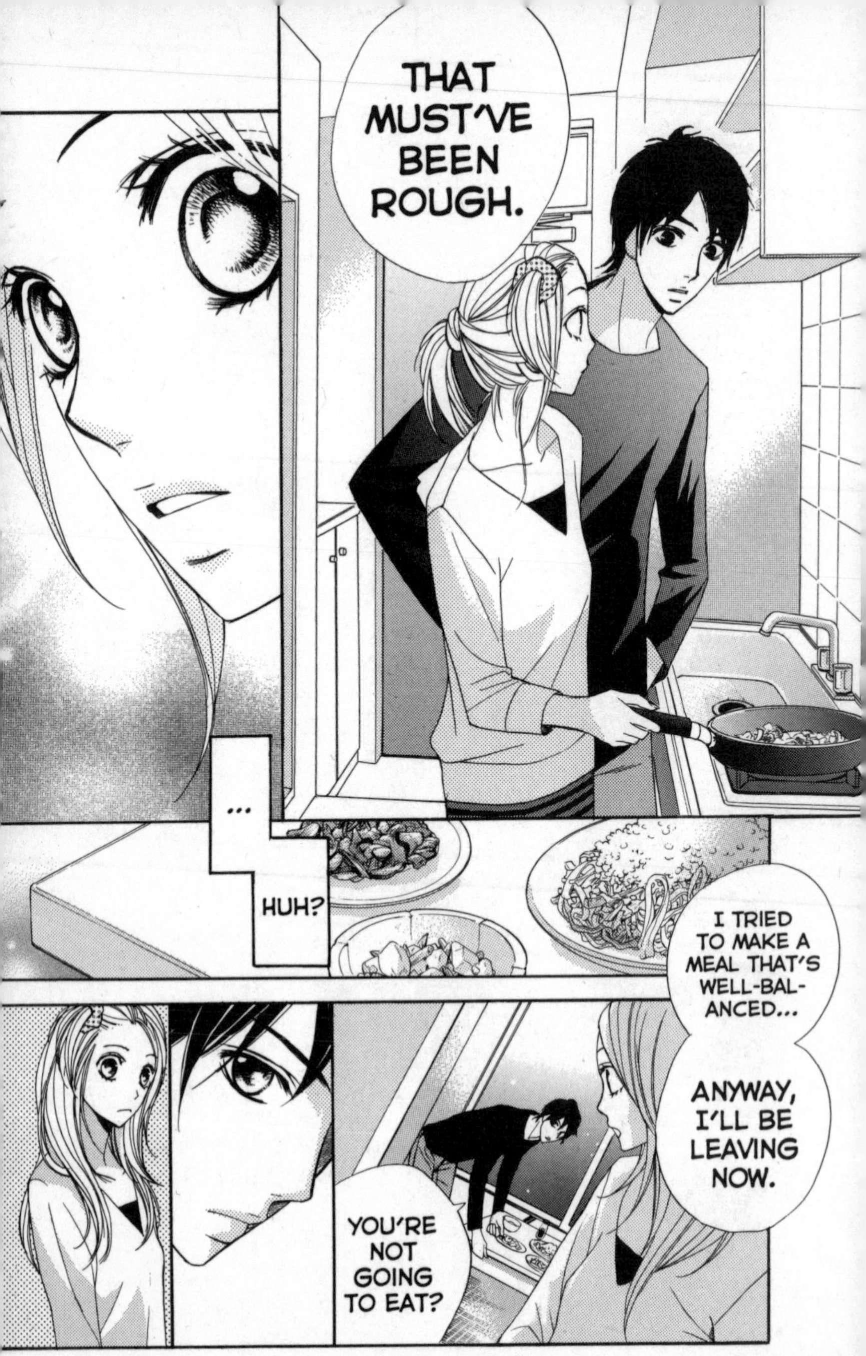
THAT MUST'VE BEEN ROUGH.
...
HUH?
I TRIED TO MAKE A MEAL THAT'S WELL-BAL-ANCED...
ANYWAY, I'LL BE LEAVING NOW.
YOU'RE NOT GOING TO EAT?

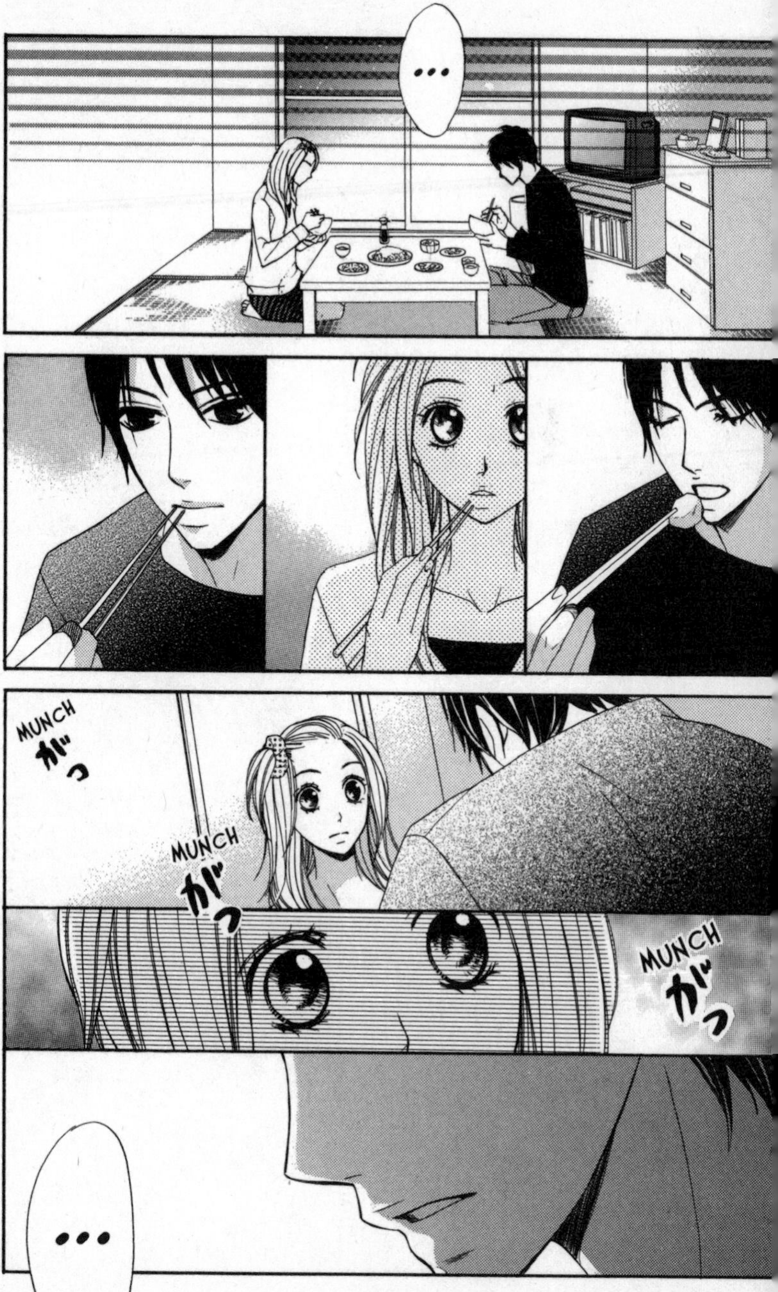
...
MUNCH
がっ
MUNCH
がっ
MUNCH
がっ
...

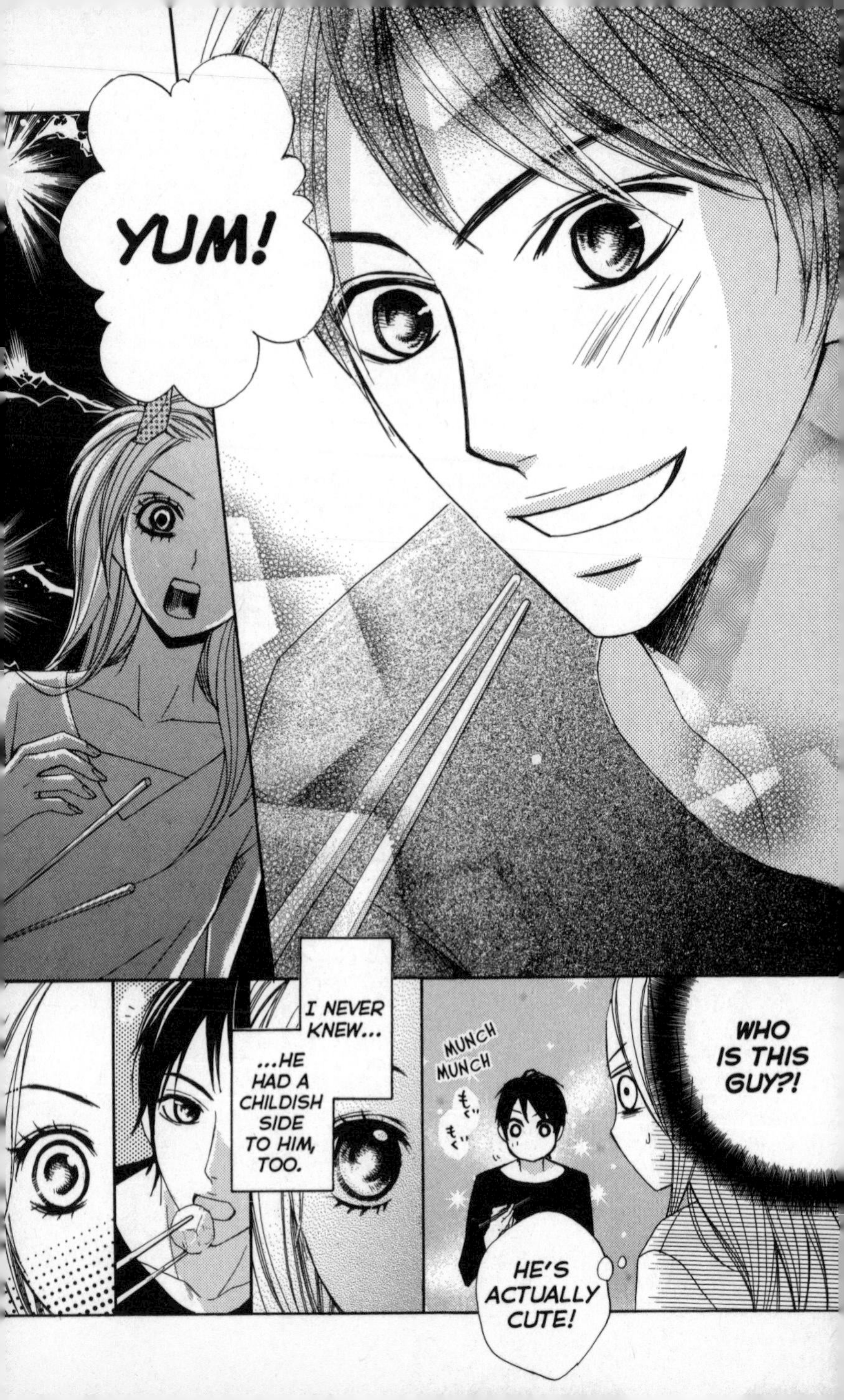
YUM!
WHO IS THIS GUY?!
MUNCH MUNCH
もぐもぐ
HE'S ACTUALLY CUTE!
I NEVER KNEW...
...HE HAD A CHILDISH SIDE TO HIM, TOO.

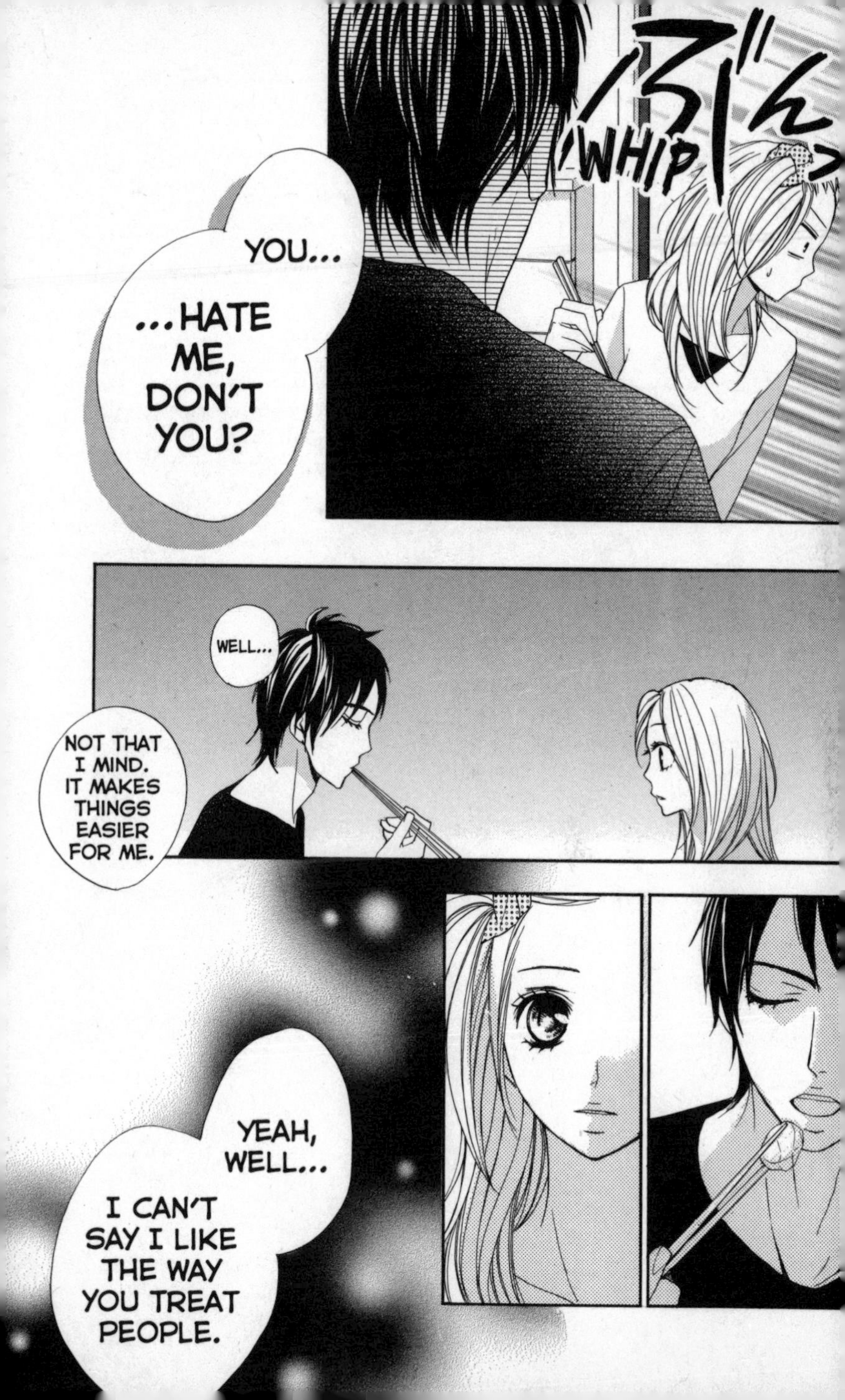
WHIP
YOU... ...HATE ME, DON'T YOU?
WELL...
NOT THAT I MIND. IT MAKES THINGS EASIER FOR ME.
YEAH, WELL...
I CAN'T SAY I LIKE THE WAY YOU TREAT PEOPLE.

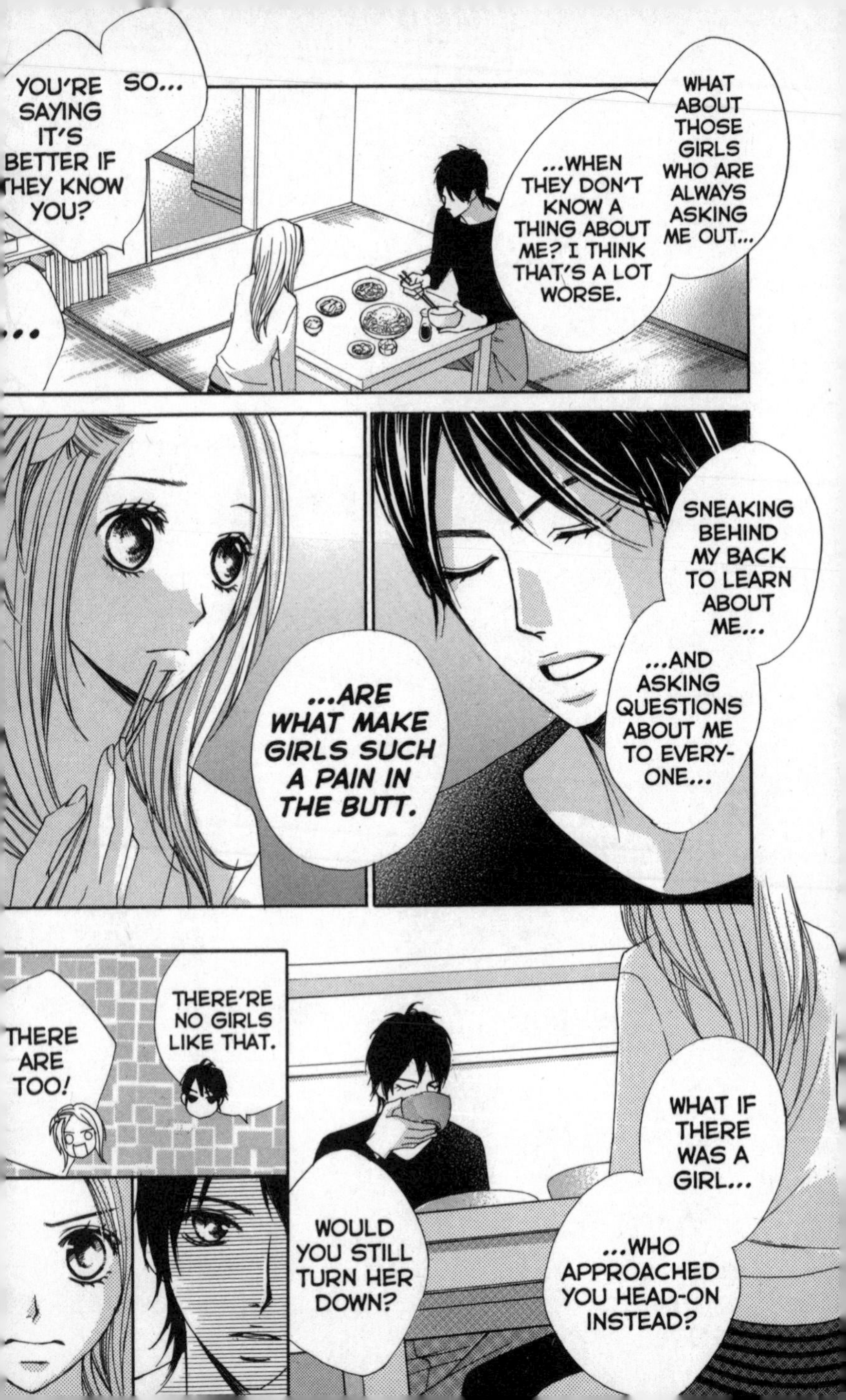
WHAT ABOUT THOSE GIRLS WHO ARE ALWAYS ASKING ME OUT...
...WHEN THEY DON'T KNOW A THING ABOUT ME? I THINK THAT'S A LOT WORSE.
SO... YOU'RE SAYING IT'S BETTER IF THEY KNOW YOU?
...
SNEAKING BEHIND MY BACK TO LEARN ABOUT ME...
...AND ASKING QUESTIONS ABOUT ME TO EVERY-ONE...
...ARE WHAT MAKE GIRLS SUCH A PAIN IN THE BUTT.
WHAT IF THERE WAS A GIRL...
...WHO APPROACHED YOU HEAD-ON INSTEAD?
WOULD YOU STILL TURN HER DOWN?
THERE'RE NO GIRLS LIKE THAT.
THERE ARE TOO!

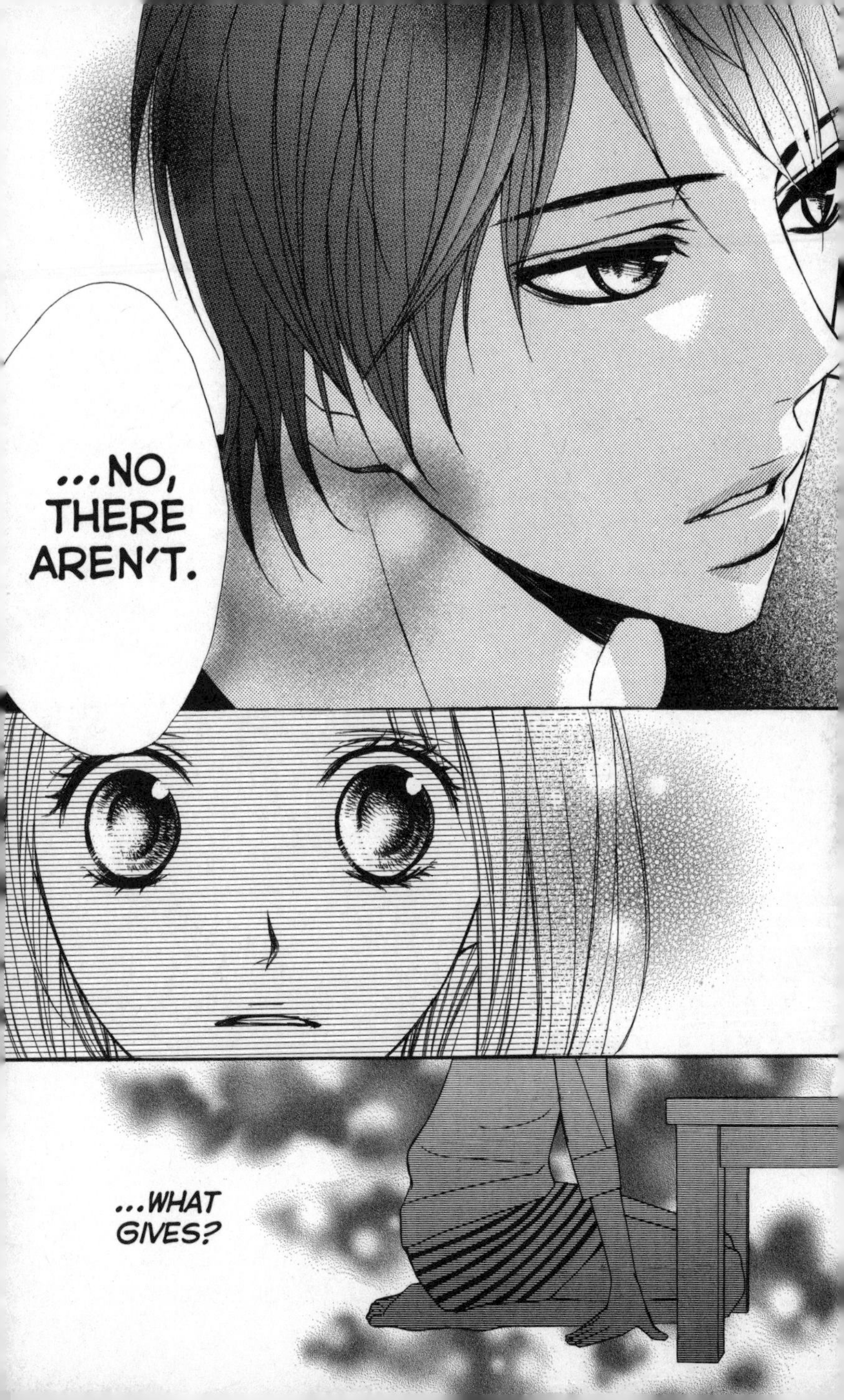
...NO, THERE AREN'T.
...WHAT GIVES?

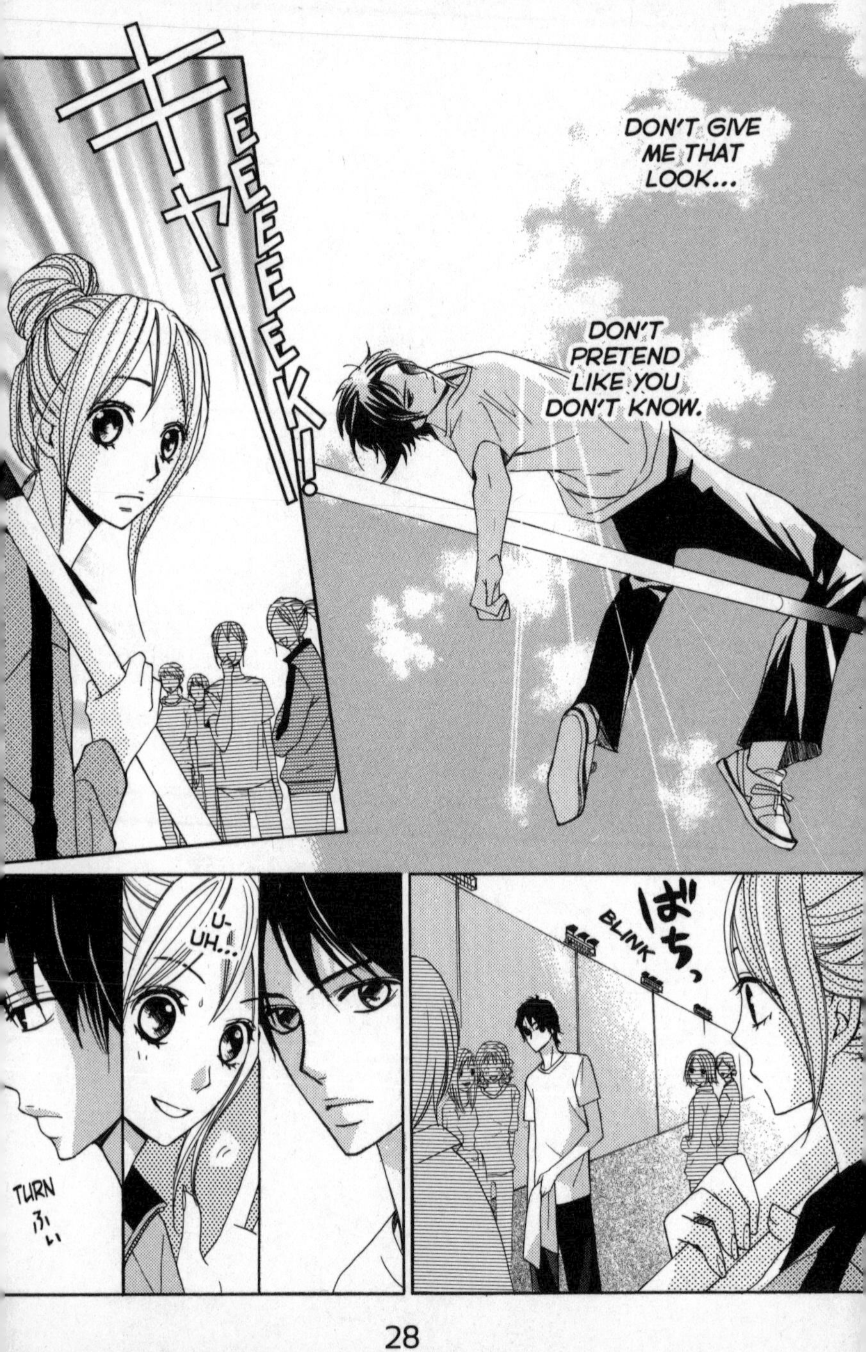
DON'T GIVE ME THAT LOOK...
DON'T PRETEND LIKE YOU DON'T KNOW.
キャー
EEEEEEK!
ぱちっ
BLINK
U-UH...
TURN
ふい

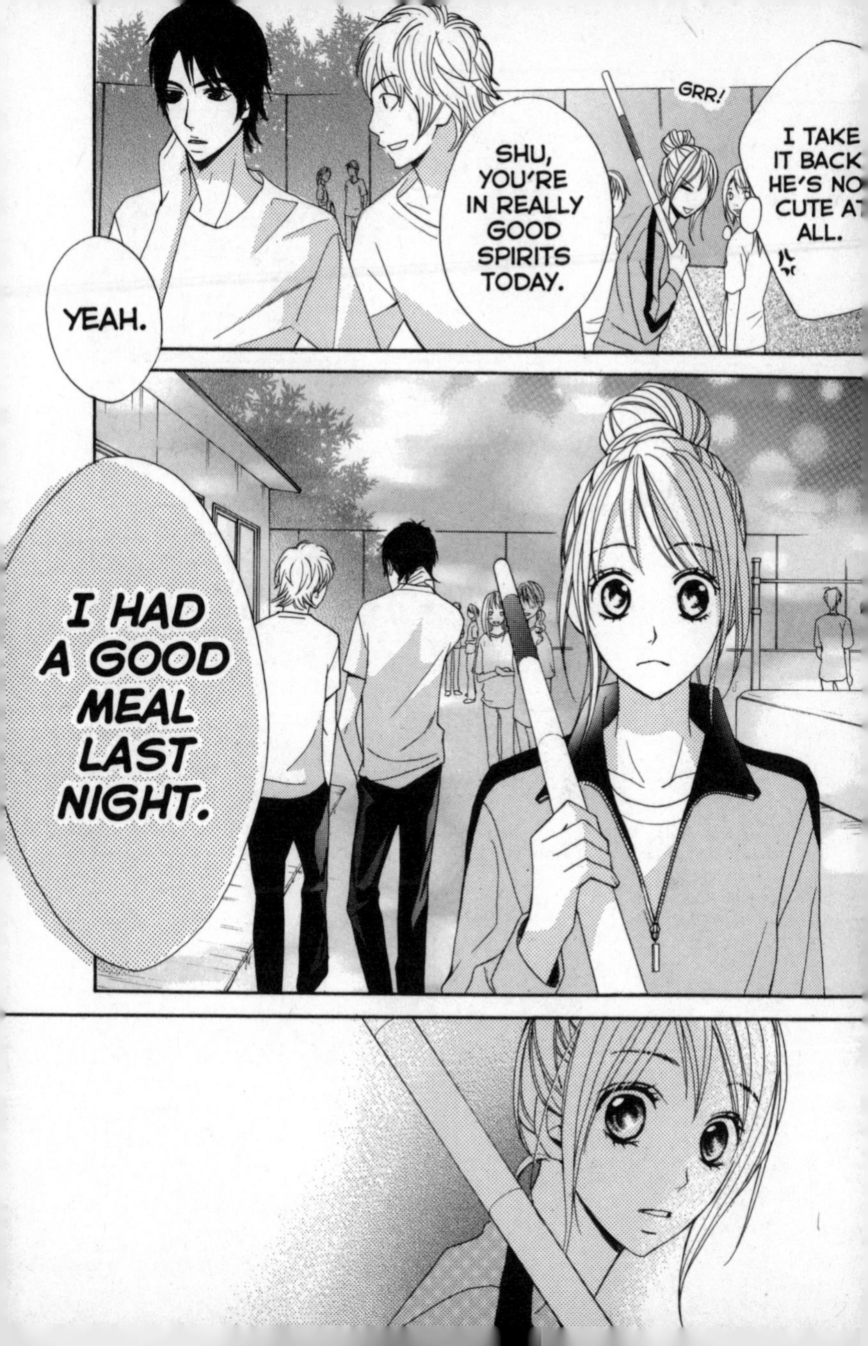
GRR!
I TAKE IT BACK HE'S NO CUTE AT ALL.
SHU, YOU'RE IN REALLY GOOD SPIRITS TODAY.
YEAH.
I HAD A GOOD MEAL LAST NIGHT.

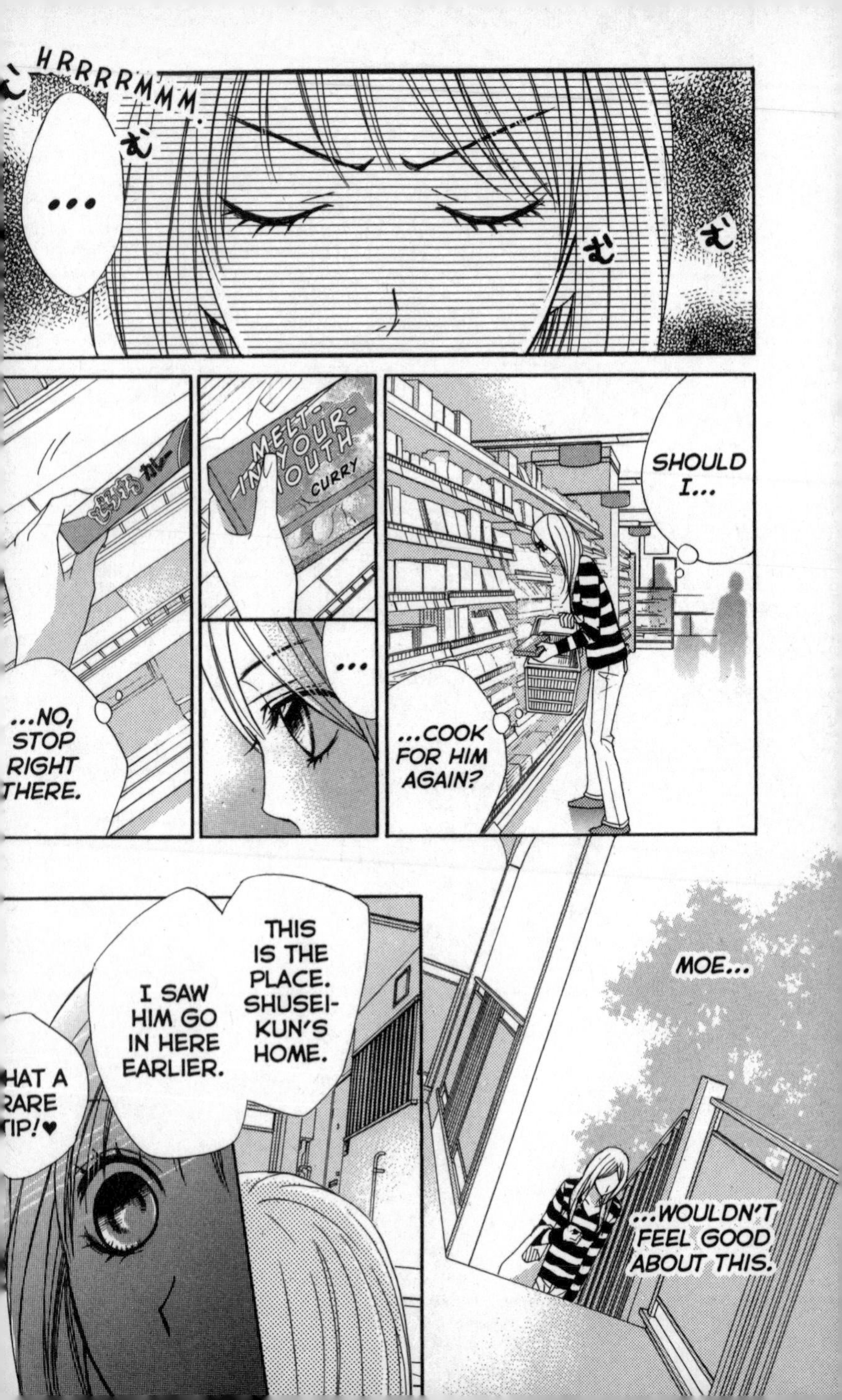
HRRRRMMM.
むむむ
...
SHOULD I...
...COOK FOR HIM AGAIN?
MELT-IN-YOUR-MOUTH CURRY
...
...NO, STOP RIGHT THERE.
MOE...
...WOULDN'T FEEL GOOD ABOUT THIS.
THIS IS THE PLACE. SHUSEI-KUN'S HOME.
I SAW HIM GO IN HERE EARLIER.
HAT A RARE TIP!♥

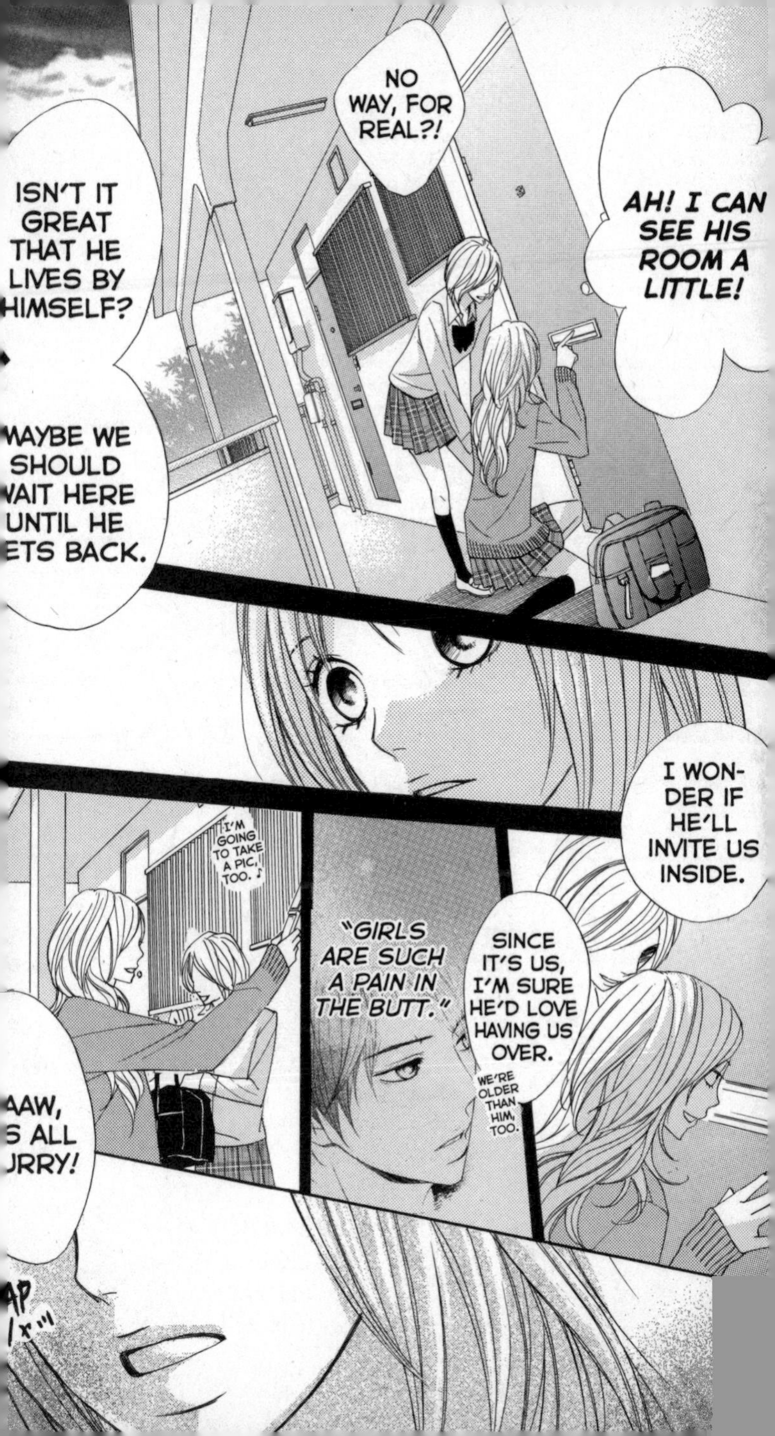
AH! I CAN SEE HIS ROOM A LITTLE!
NO WAY, FOR REAL?!
ISN'T IT GREAT THAT HE LIVES BY HIMSELF?
MAYBE WE SHOULD WAIT HERE UNTIL HE ETS BACK.
I WON-DER IF HE'LL INVITE US INSIDE.
SINCE IT'S US, I'M SURE HE'D LOVE HAVING US OVER.
WE'RE OLDER THAN HIM, TOO.
"GIRLS ARE SUCH A PAIN IN THE BUTT."
I'M GOING TO TAKE A PIC, TOO. ♪
AAW, S ALL URRY!

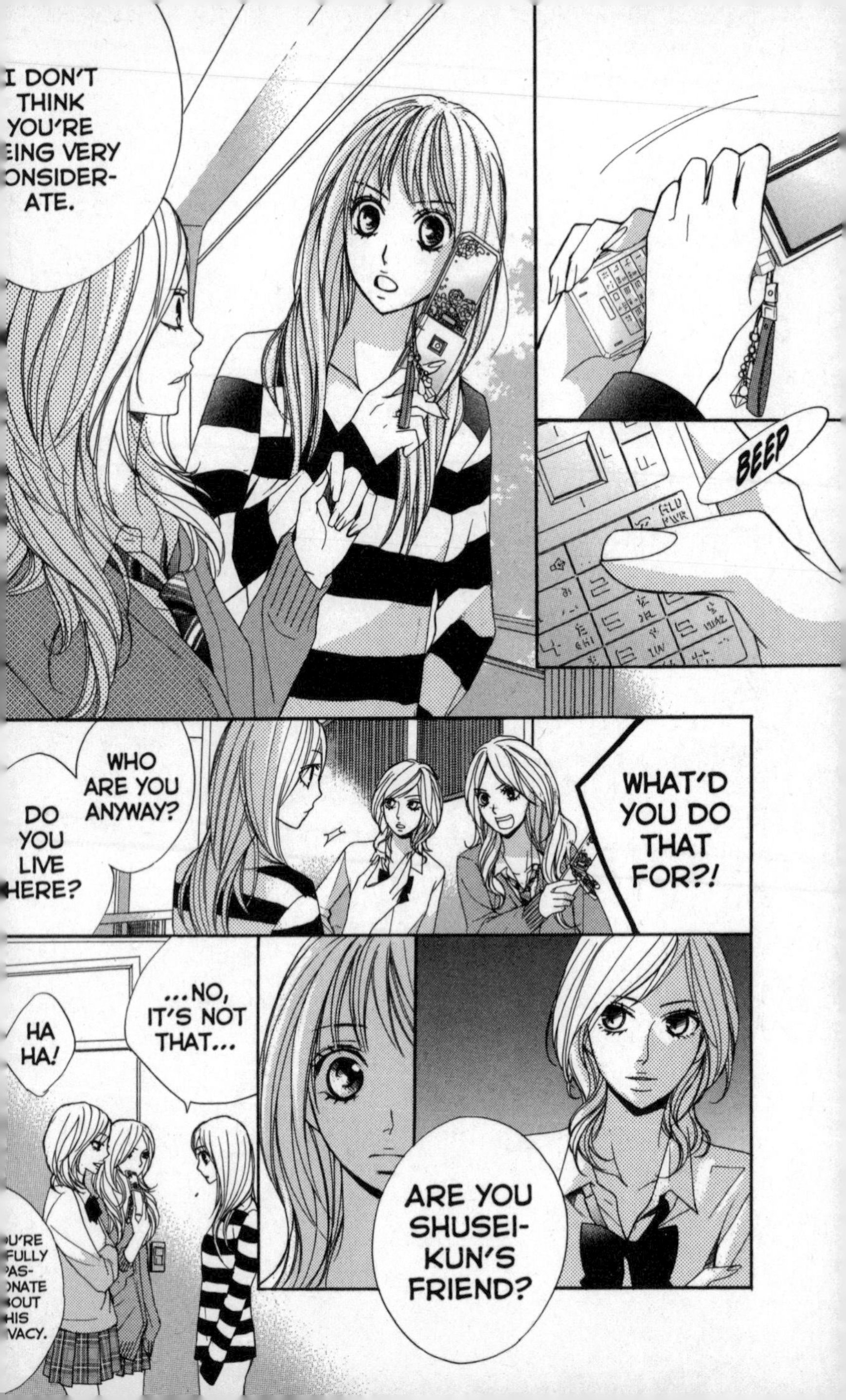
BEEP
I DON'T THINK YOU'RE EING VERY ONSIDER-ATE.
WHAT'D YOU DO THAT FOR?!
WHO ARE YOU ANYWAY?
DO YOU LIVE HERE?
ARE YOU SHUSEI-KUN'S FRIEND?
...NO, IT'S NOT THAT...
HA HA!
U'RE FULLY PAS-ONATE BOUT HIS VACY.

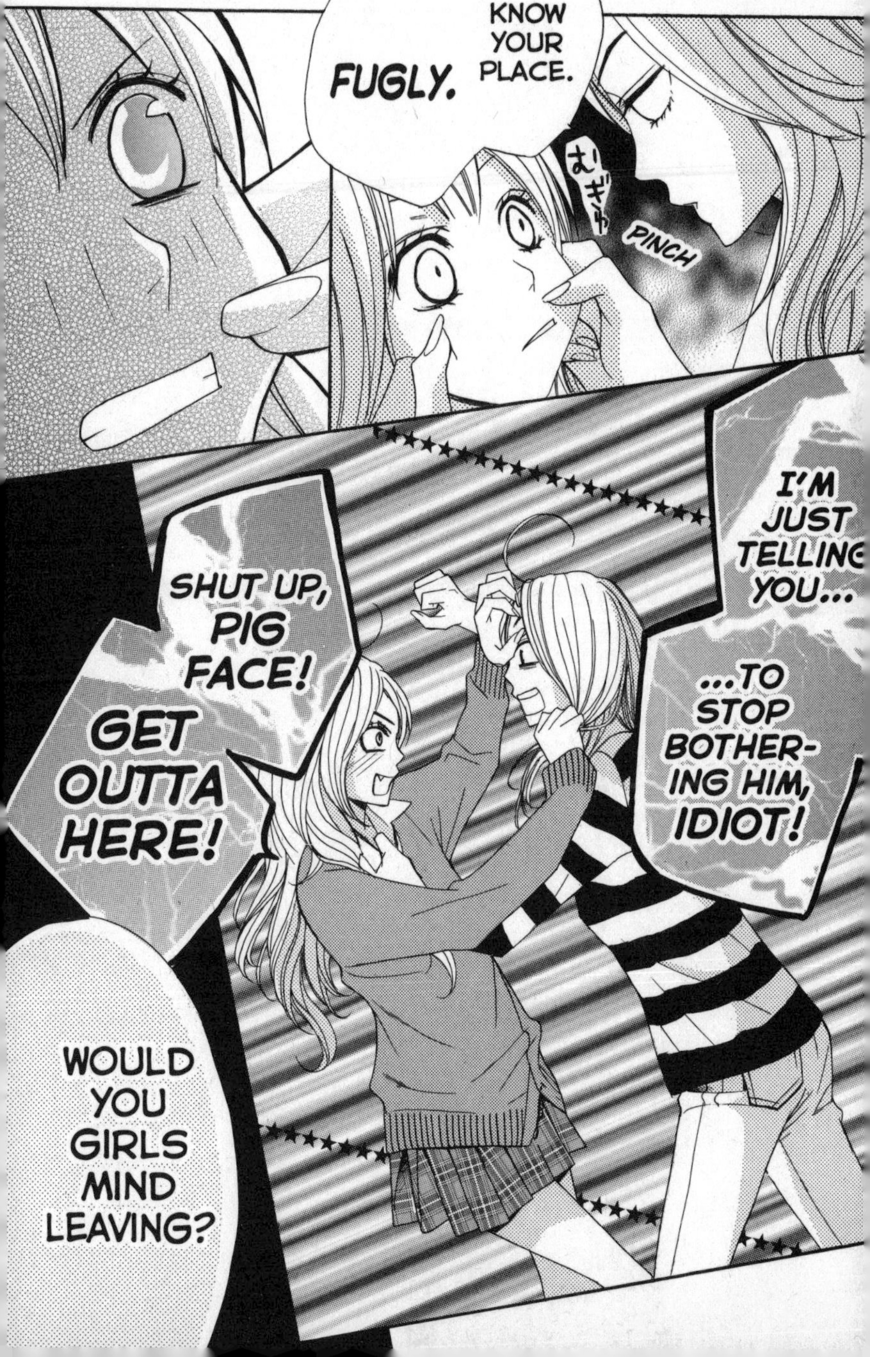
KNOW YOUR PLACE.
FUGLY.
むぎゅ
PINCH
I'M JUST TELLING YOU...
...TO STOP BOTHER-ING HIM, IDIOT!
SHUT UP, PIG FACE!
GET OUTTA HERE!
WOULD YOU GIRLS MIND LEAVING?

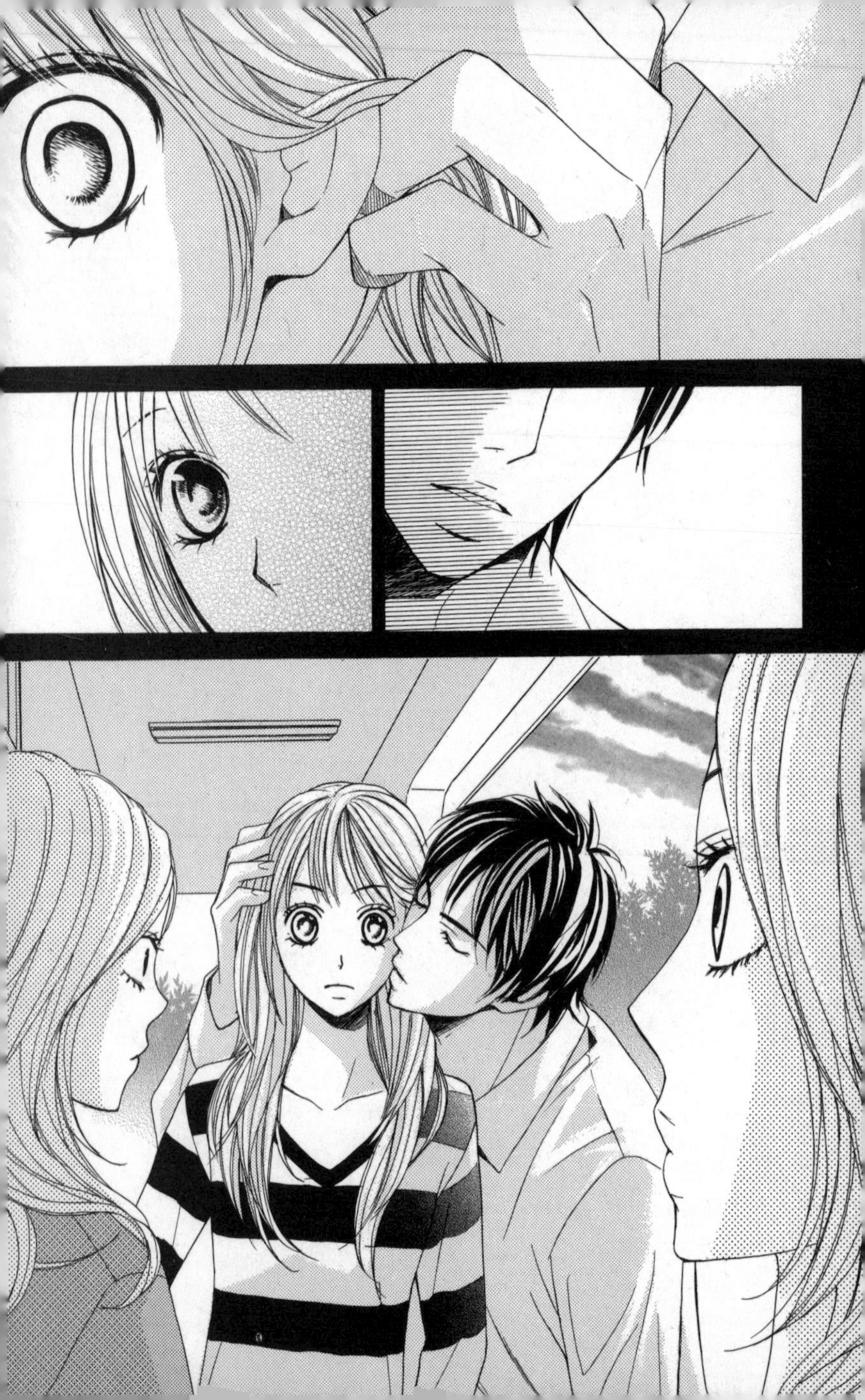

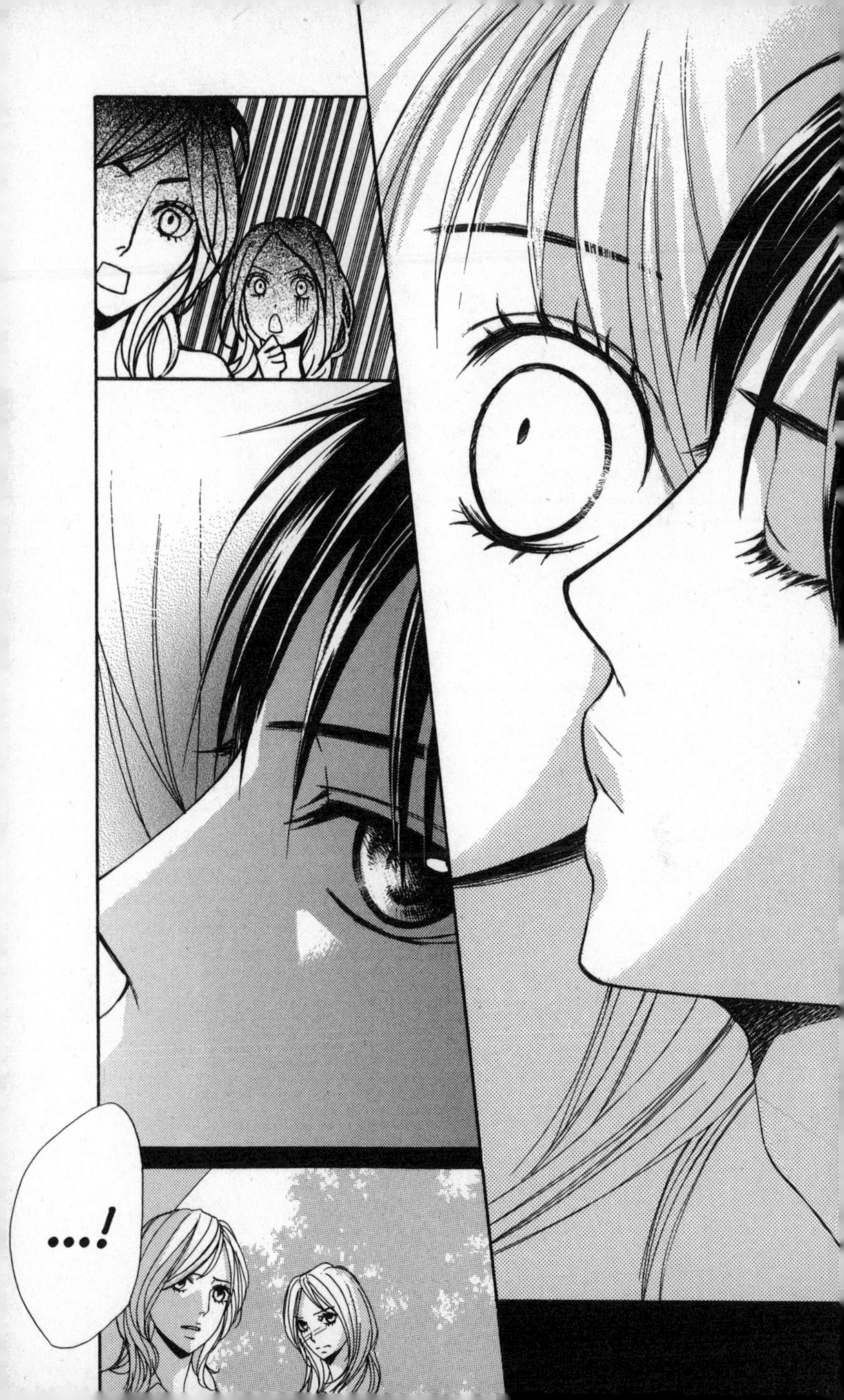
...!

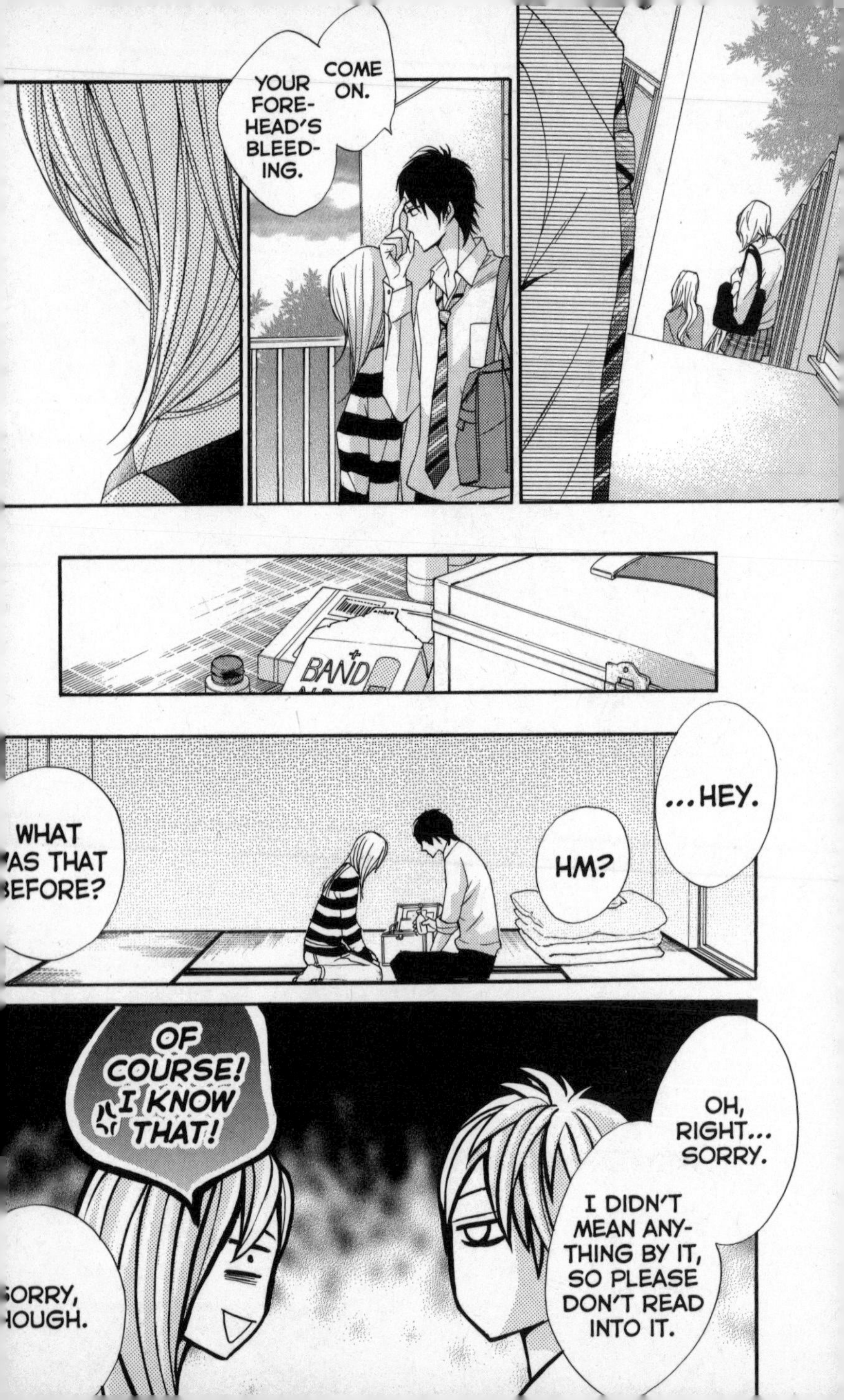
COME ON.
YOUR FOREHEAD'S BLEEDING.
BAND
...HEY.
HM?
WHAT
AS THAT
EFORE?
OH, RIGHT... SORRY.
I DIDN'T MEAN ANYTHING BY IT, SO PLEASE DON'T READ INTO IT.
OF COURSE! I KNOW THAT!
ORRY,
HOUGH.

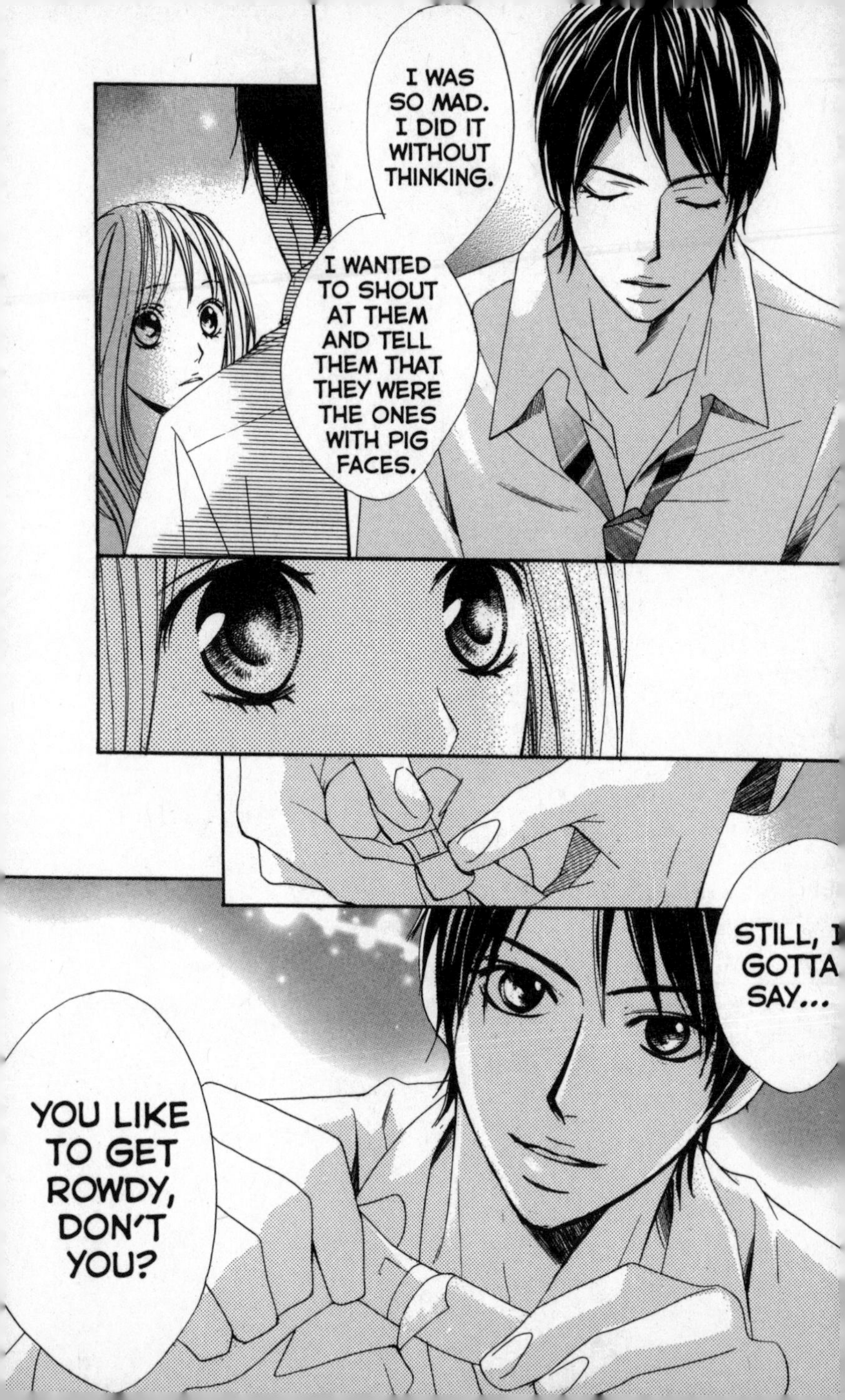
I WAS SO MAD. I DID IT WITHOUT THINKING.
I WANTED TO SHOUT AT THEM AND TELL THEM THAT THEY WERE THE ONES WITH PIG FACES.
STILL, I GOTTA SAY...
YOU LIKE TO GET ROWDY, DON'T YOU?

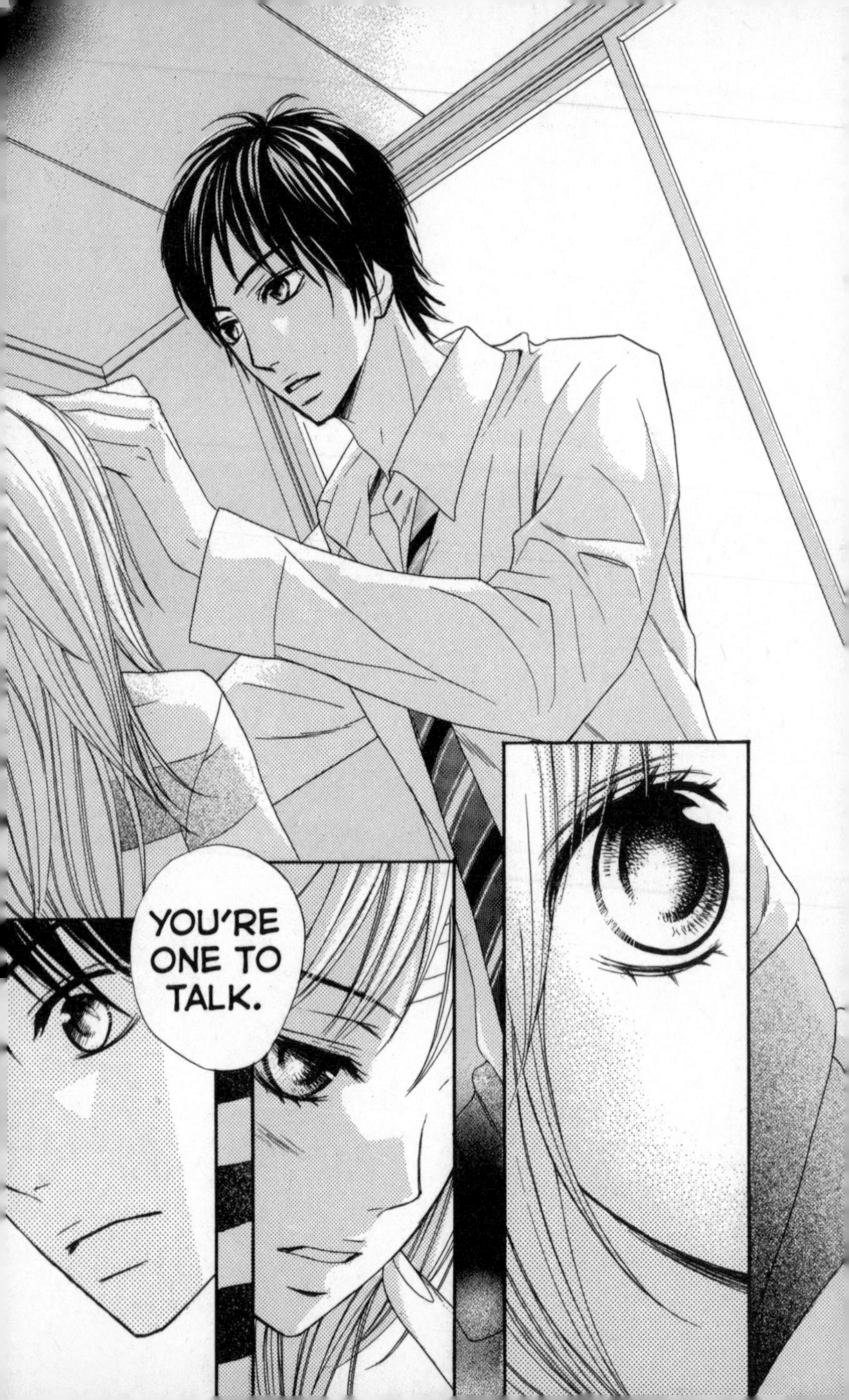
YOU'RE ONE TO TALK.

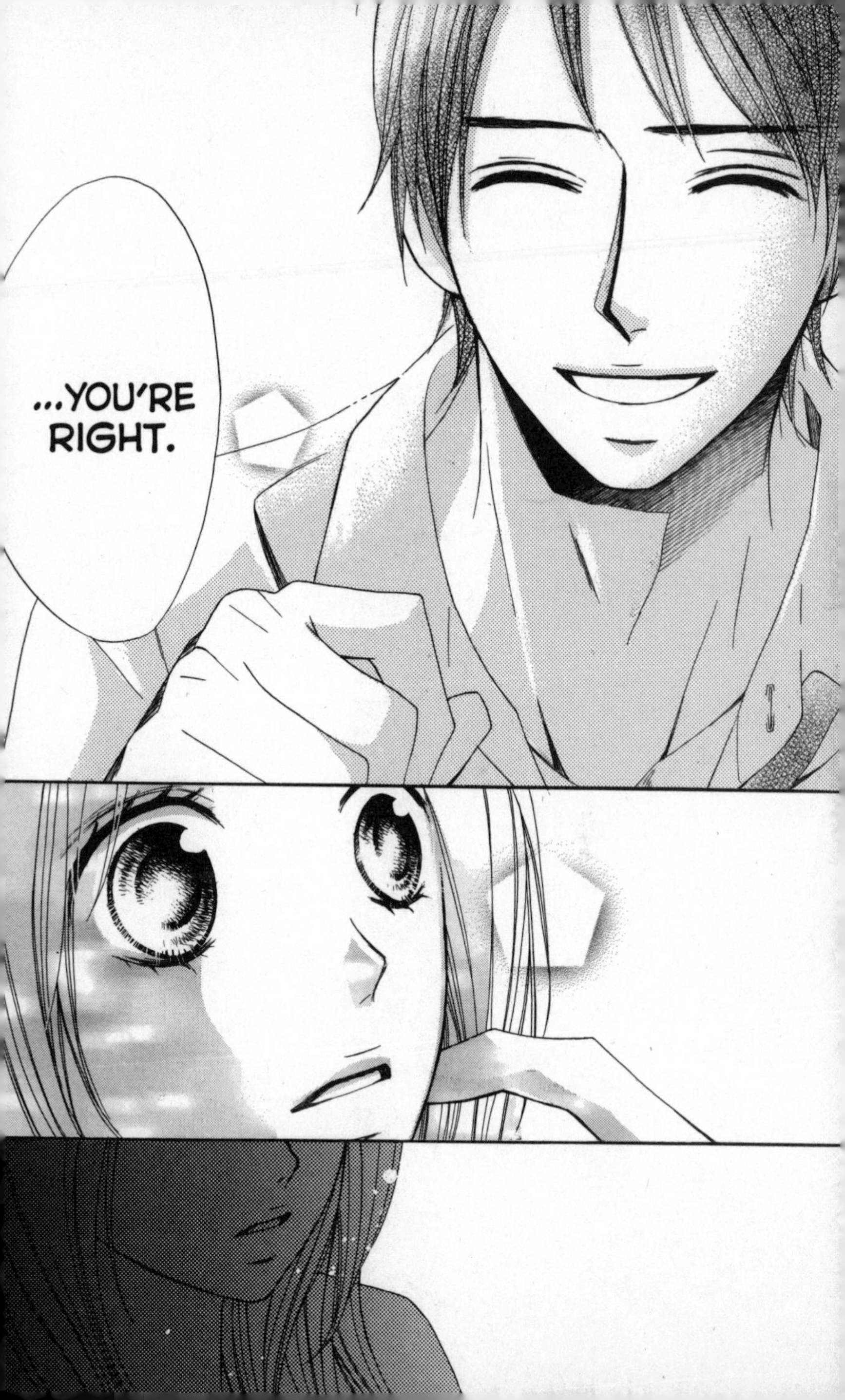
...YOU'RE RIGHT.

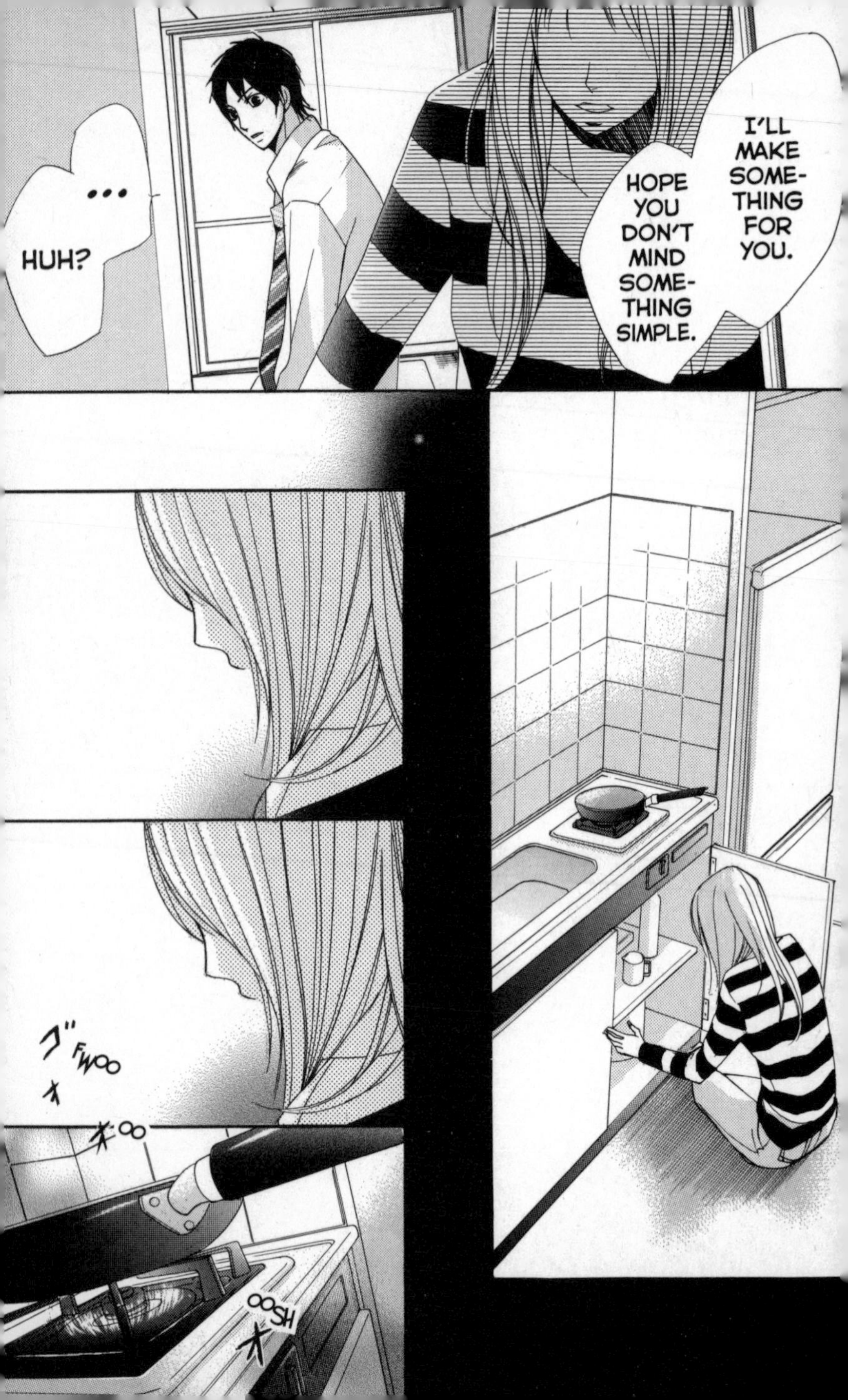
I'LL MAKE SOMETHING FOR YOU.
HOPE YOU DON'T MIND SOMETHING SIMPLE.
... HUH?
ゴォ FWOO
OO
OOSH

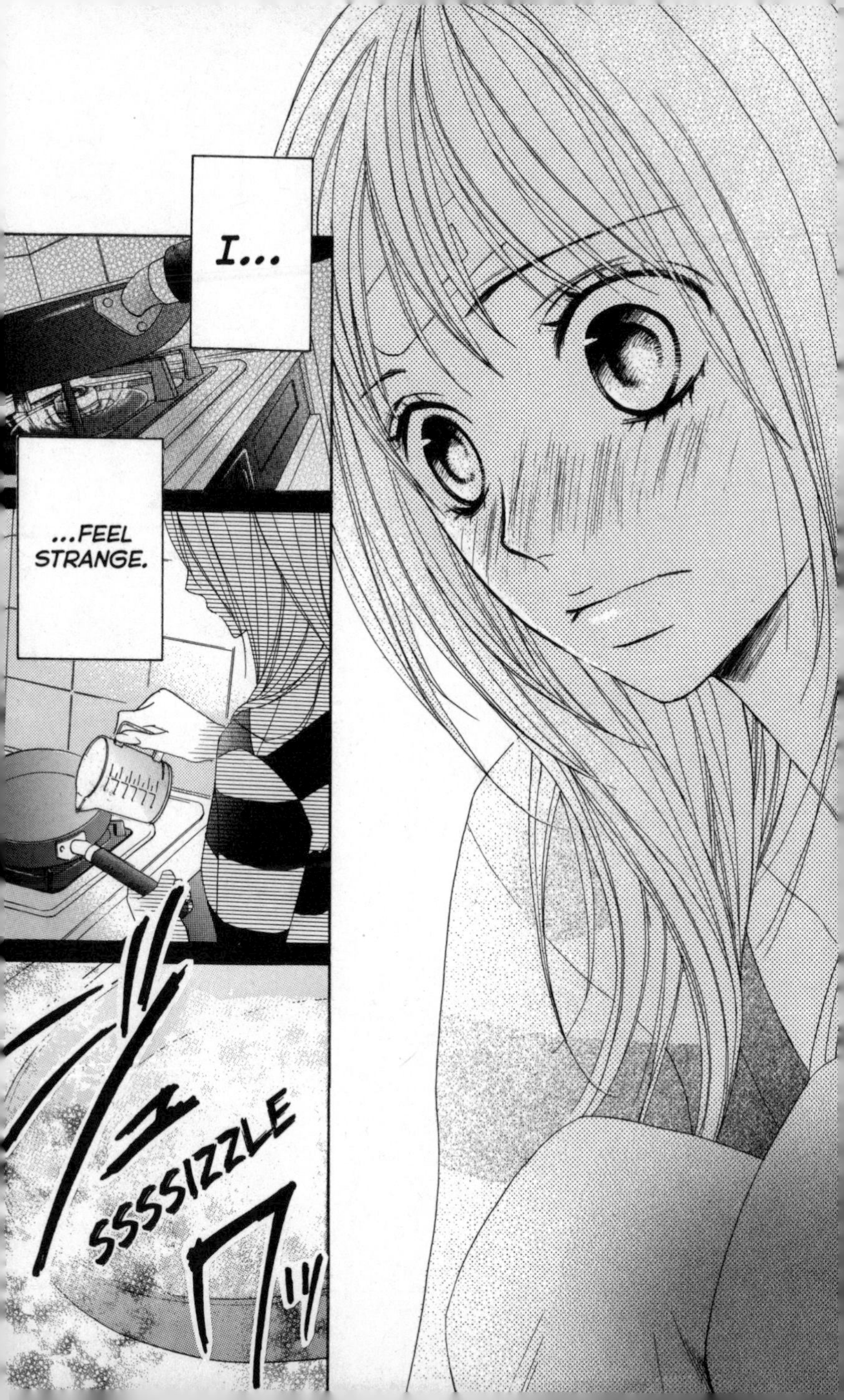
I...
...FEEL STRANGE.
SSSSIZZLE

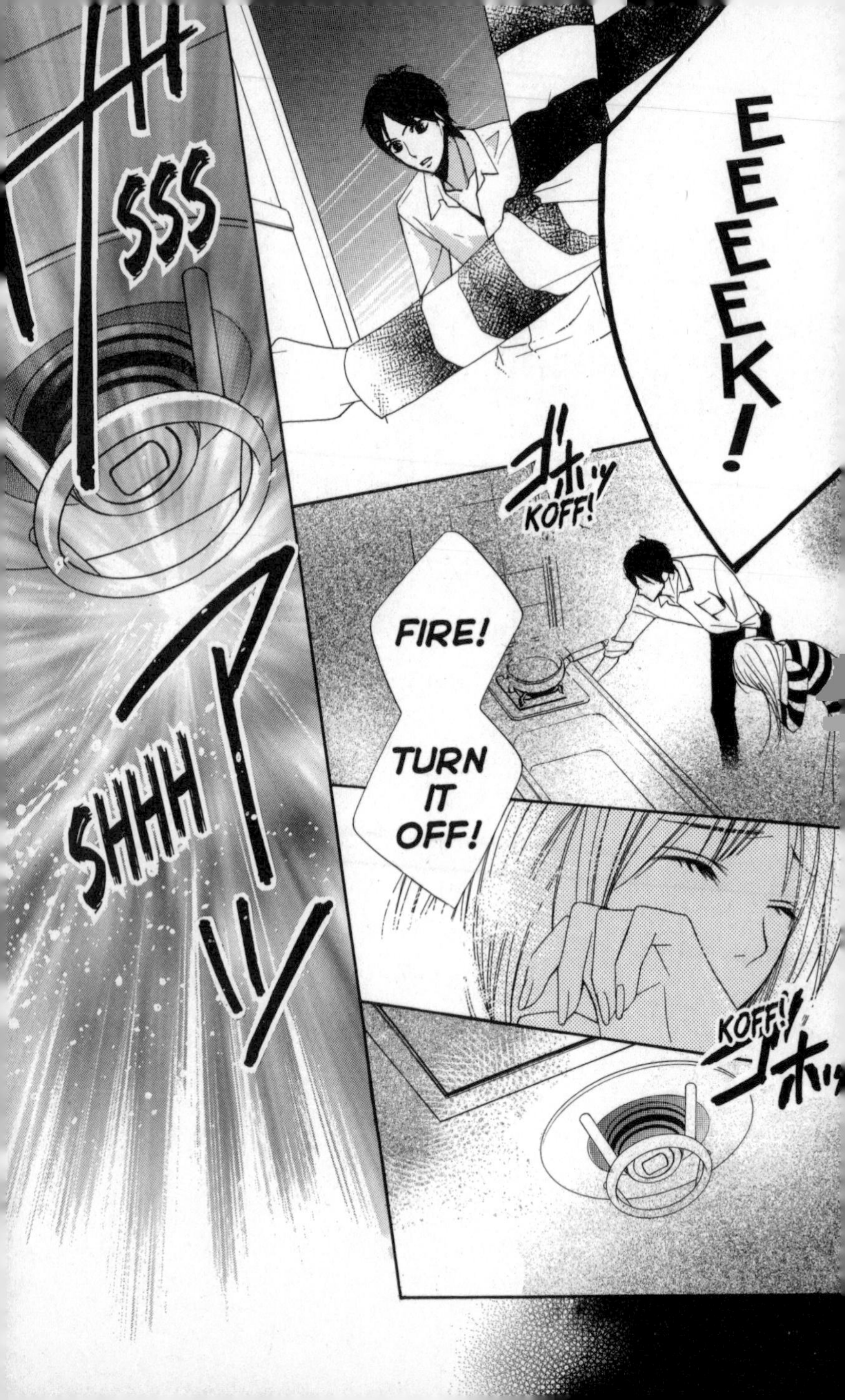
EEEK!
ゴホッ KOFF!
FIRE!
TURN IT OFF!
KOFF! ゴホッ
SSS
SHHH

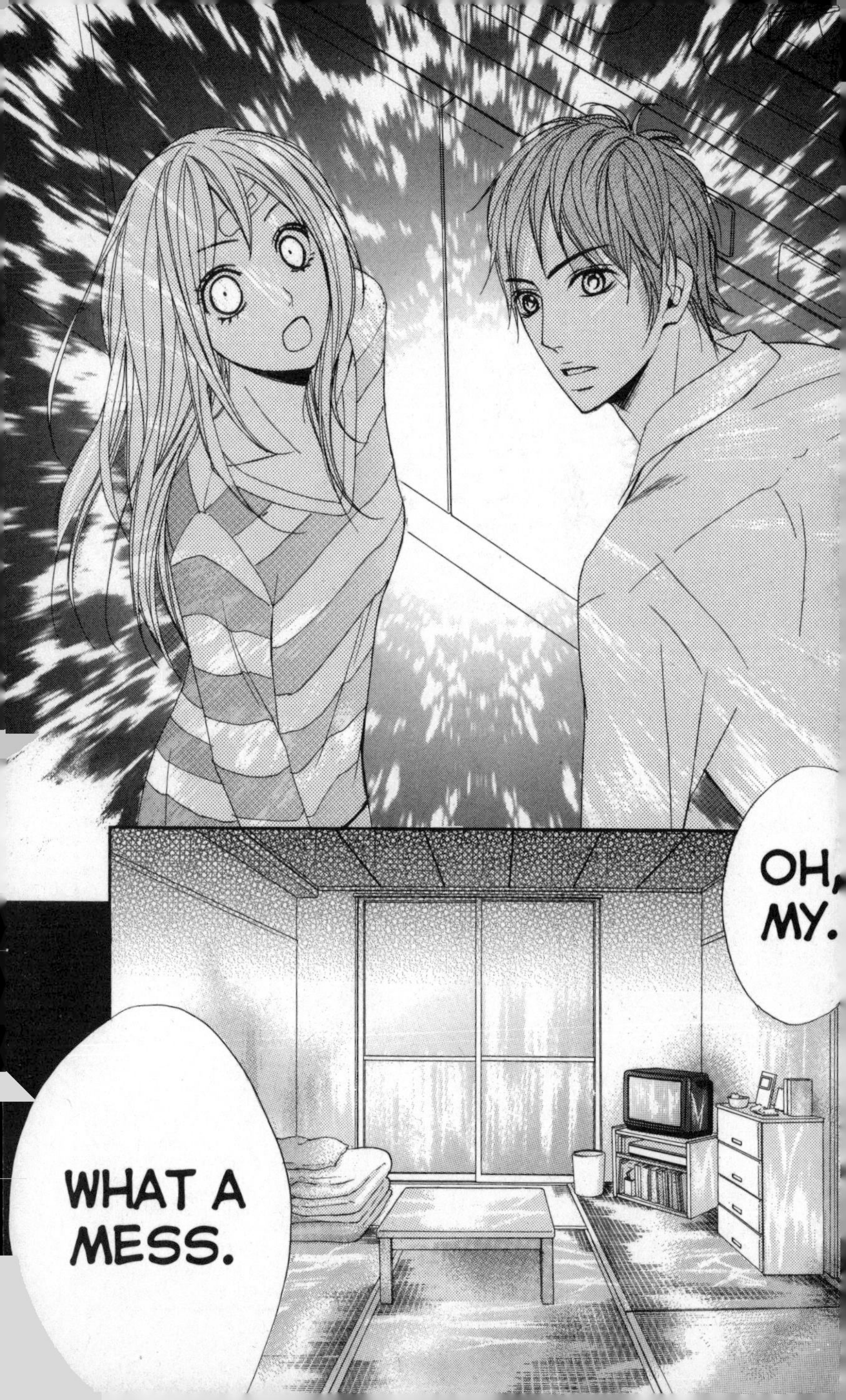
OH, MY.
WHAT A MESS.

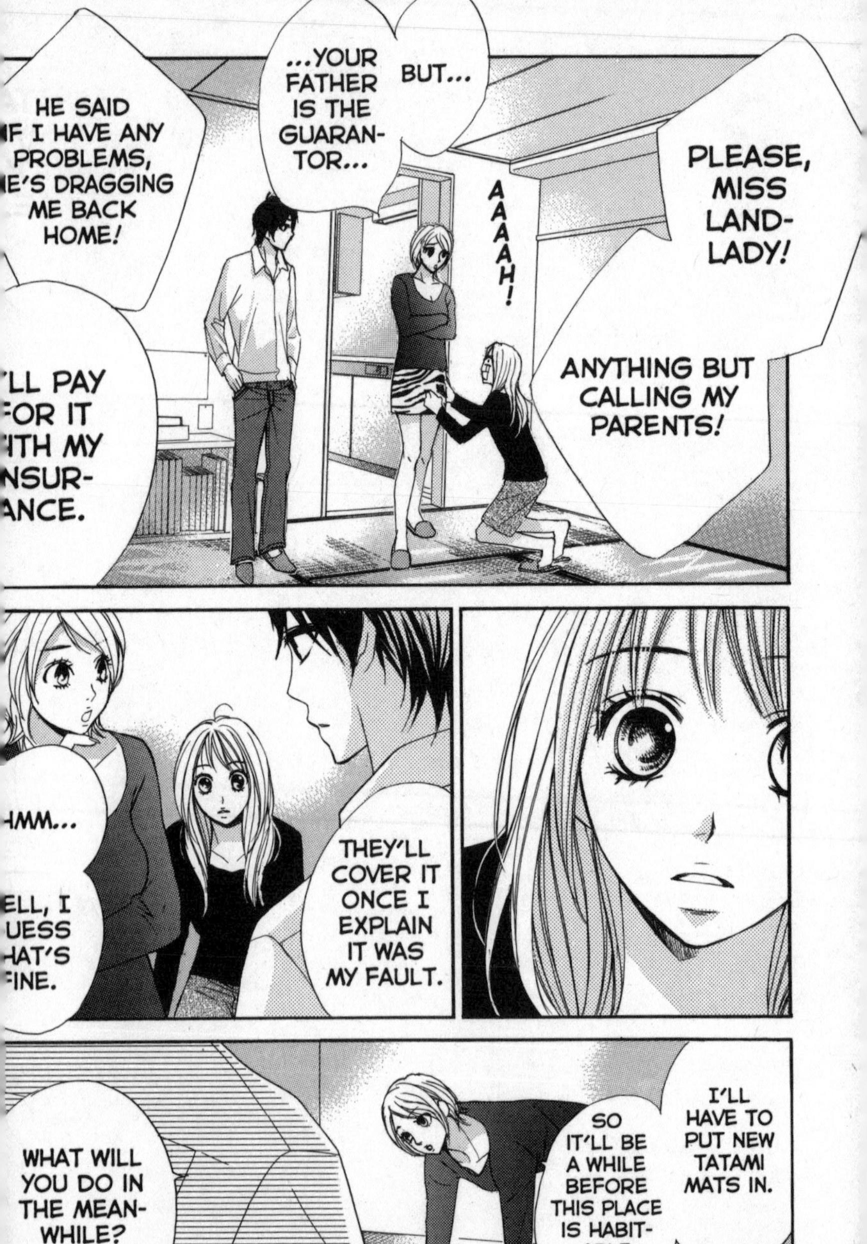
PLEASE, MISS LANDLADY!
ANYTHING BUT CALLING MY PARENTS!
AAAAH!
BUT... ...YOUR FATHER IS THE GUARANTOR...
HE SAID F I HAVE ANY PROBLEMS, E'S DRAGGING ME BACK HOME!
'LL PAY FOR IT ITH MY NSURANCE.
THEY'LL COVER IT ONCE I EXPLAIN IT WAS MY FAULT.
HMM...
ELL, I UESS HAT'S INE.
I'LL HAVE TO PUT NEW TATAMI MATS IN.
SO IT'LL BE A WHILE BEFORE THIS PLACE IS HABITABLE AGAIN.
WHAT WILL YOU DO IN THE MEANWHILE?

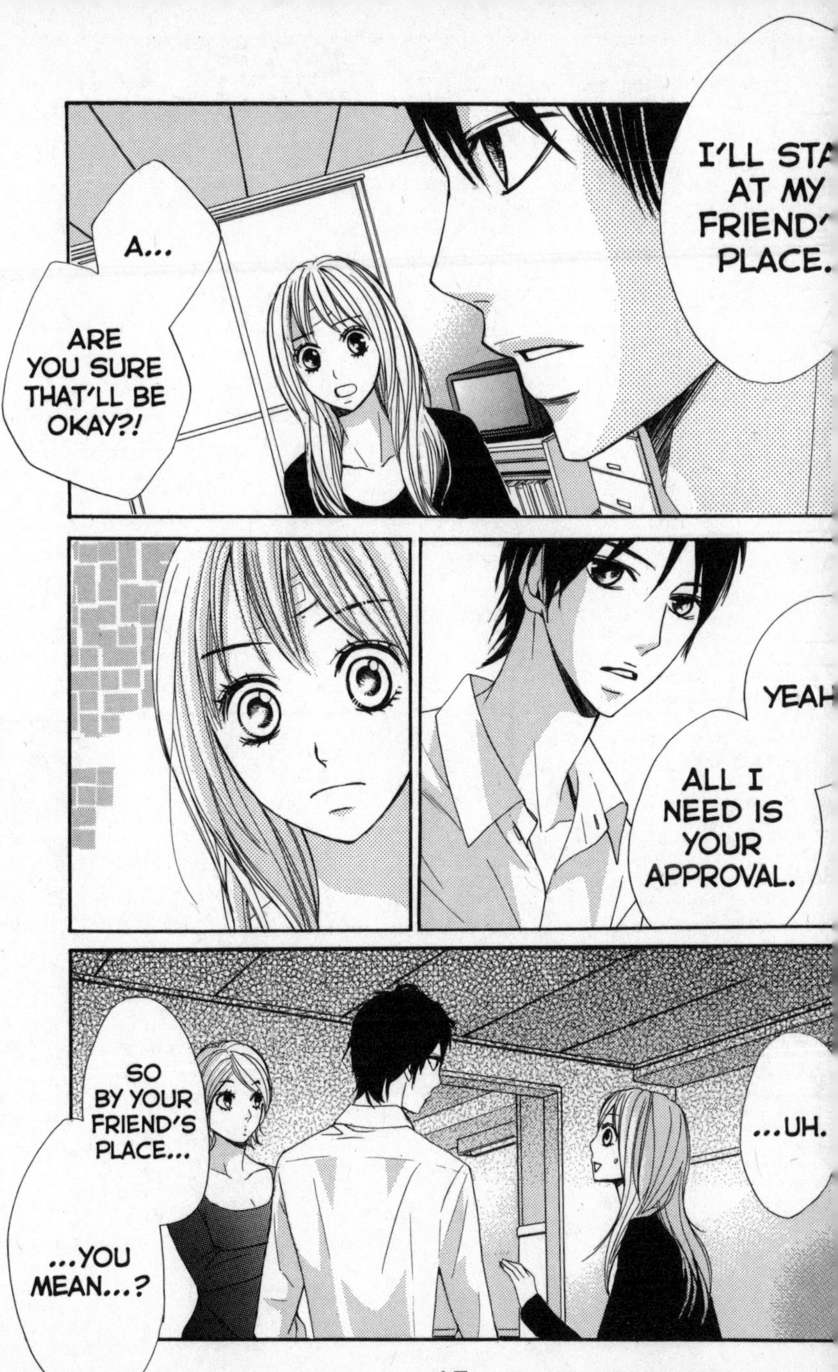
I'LL STA
AT MY
FRIEND'
PLACE.
A...
ARE YOU SURE THAT'LL BE OKAY?!
YEAH
ALL I NEED IS YOUR APPROVAL.
...UH.
SO BY YOUR FRIEND'S PLACE...
...YOU MEAN...?

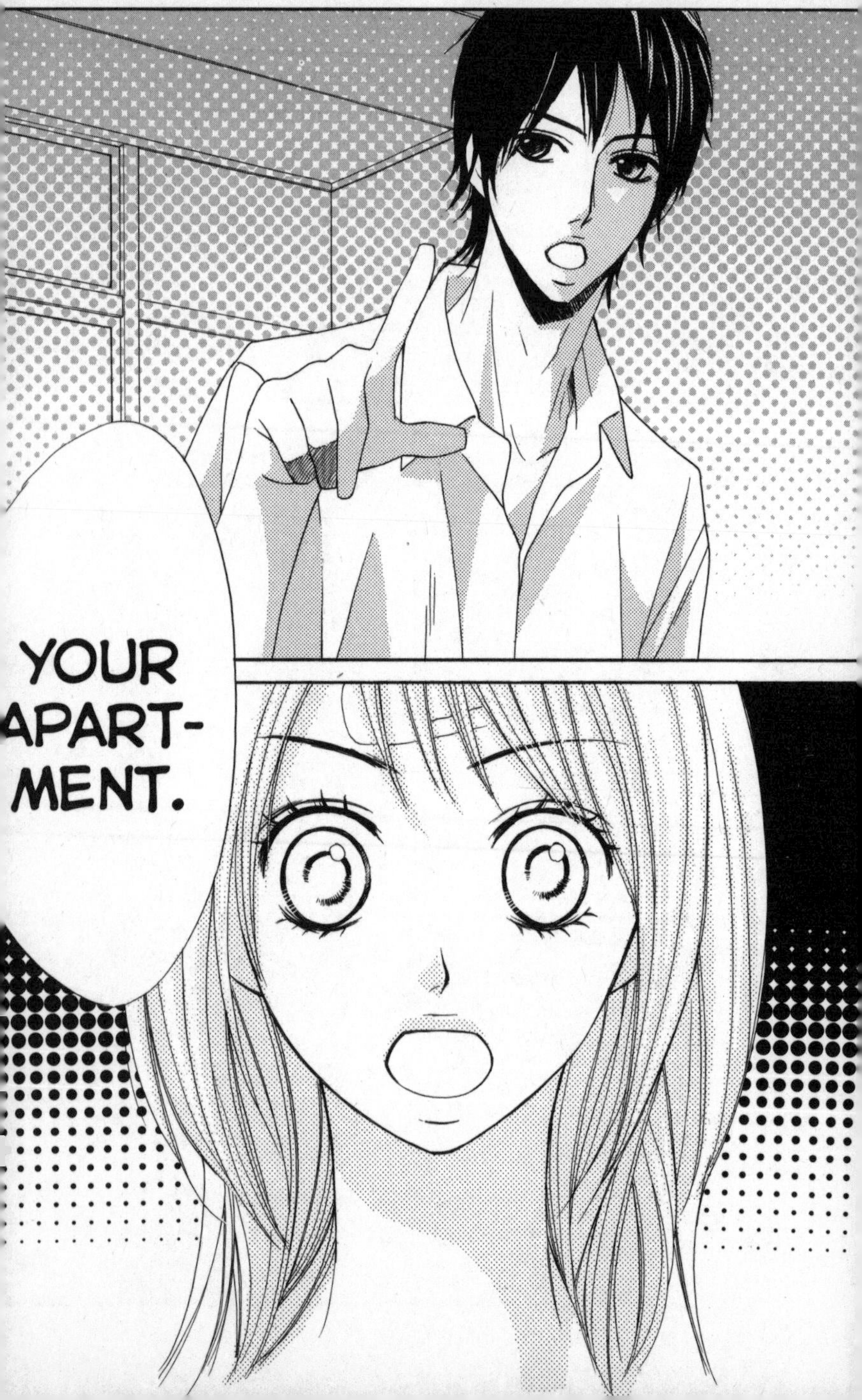
YOUR APART- MENT.

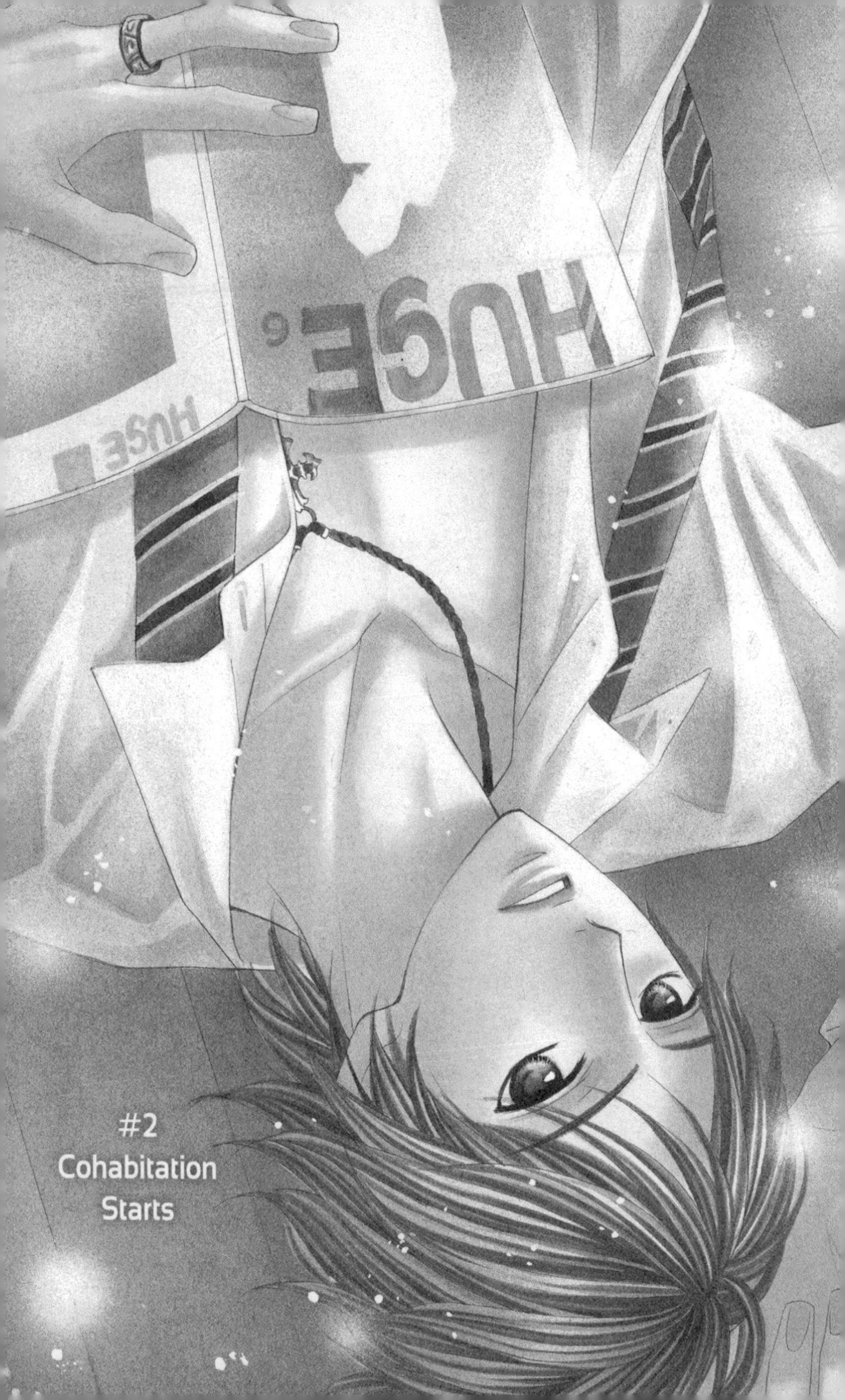
#2
Cohabitation
Starts

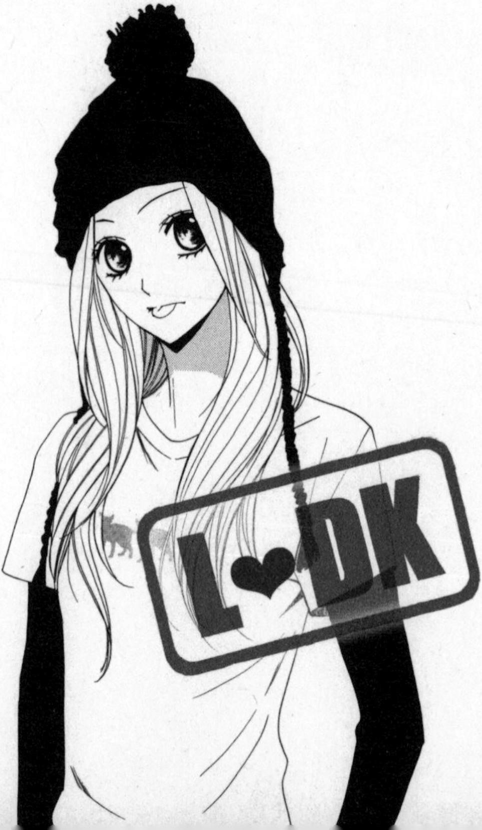
L♥DK

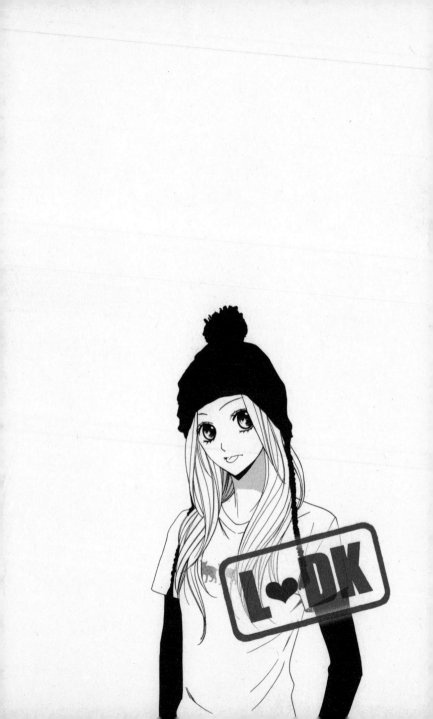

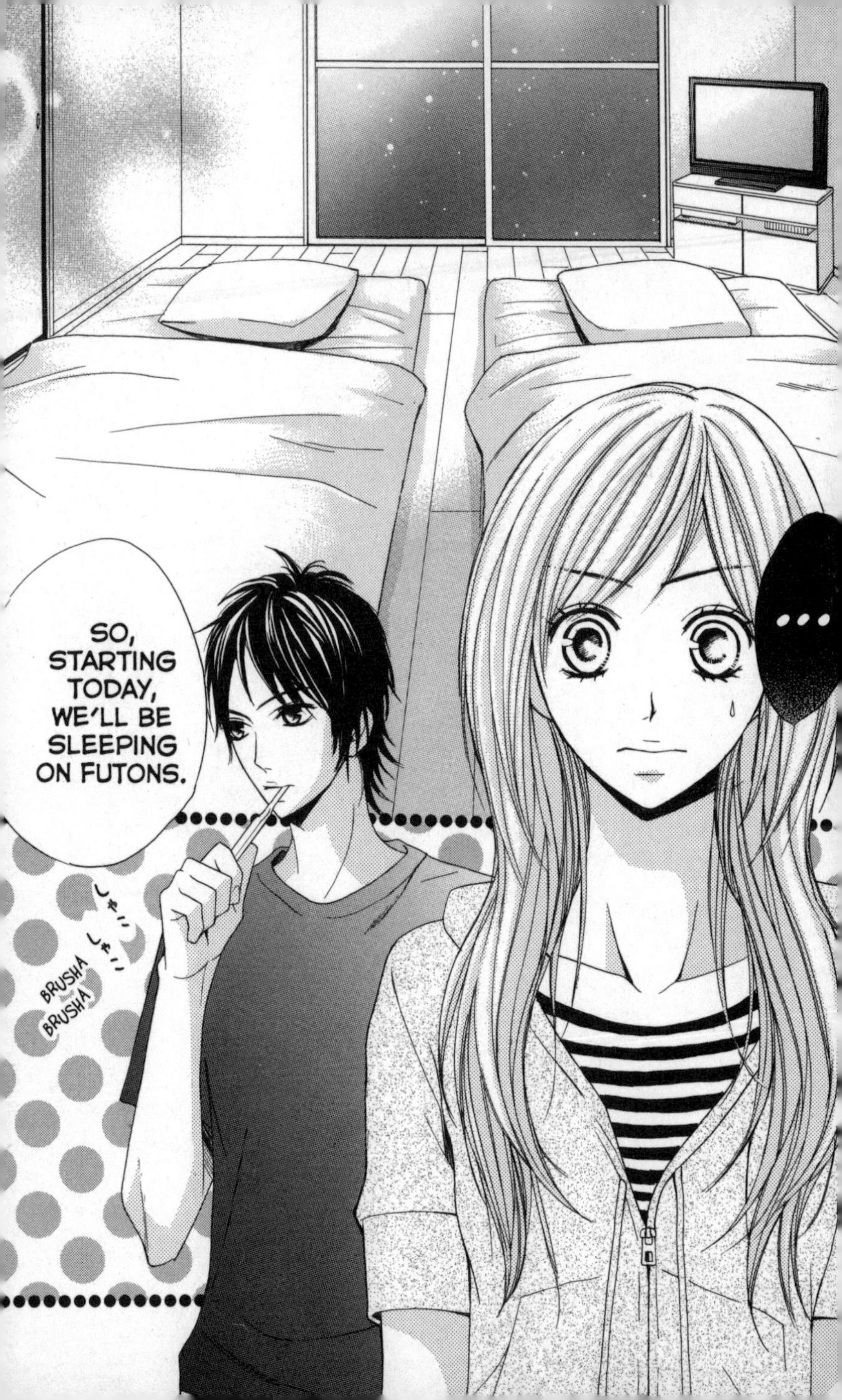
...
SO, STARTING TODAY, WE'LL BE SLEEPING ON FUTONS.
BRUSHA BRUSHA

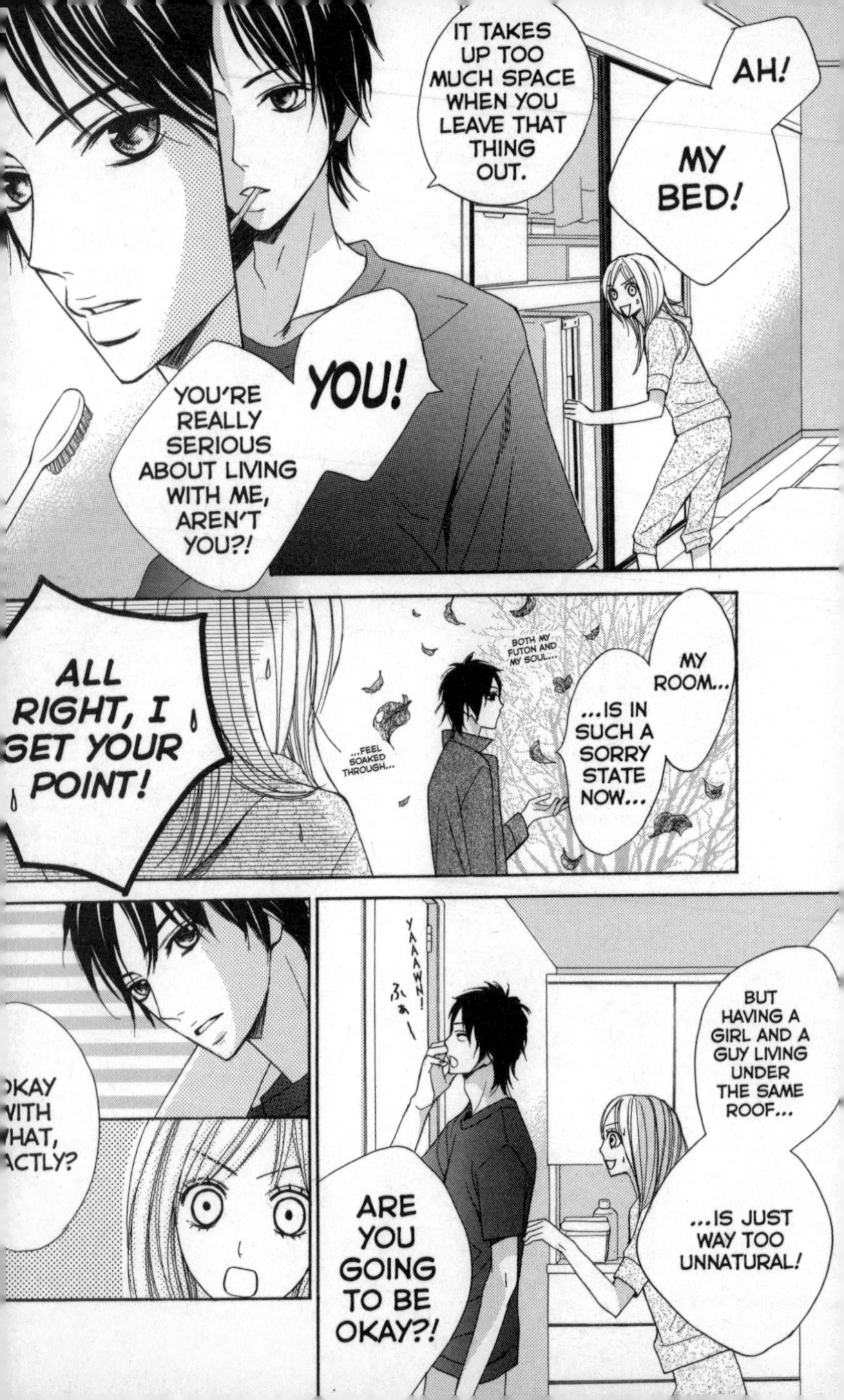
AH! MY BED!
IT TAKES UP TOO MUCH SPACE WHEN YOU LEAVE THAT THING OUT.
YOU!
YOU'RE REALLY SERIOUS ABOUT LIVING WITH ME, AREN'T YOU?!
MY ROOM...
...IS IN SUCH A SORRY STATE NOW...
BOTH MY FUTON AND MY SOUL...
...FEEL SOAKED THROUGH...
ALL RIGHT, I GET YOUR POINT!
BUT HAVING A GIRL AND A GUY LIVING UNDER THE SAME ROOF...
...IS JUST WAY TOO UNNATURAL!
YAAAWN!
ふぁ～
ARE YOU GOING TO BE OKAY?!
OKAY WITH HAT, ACTLY?

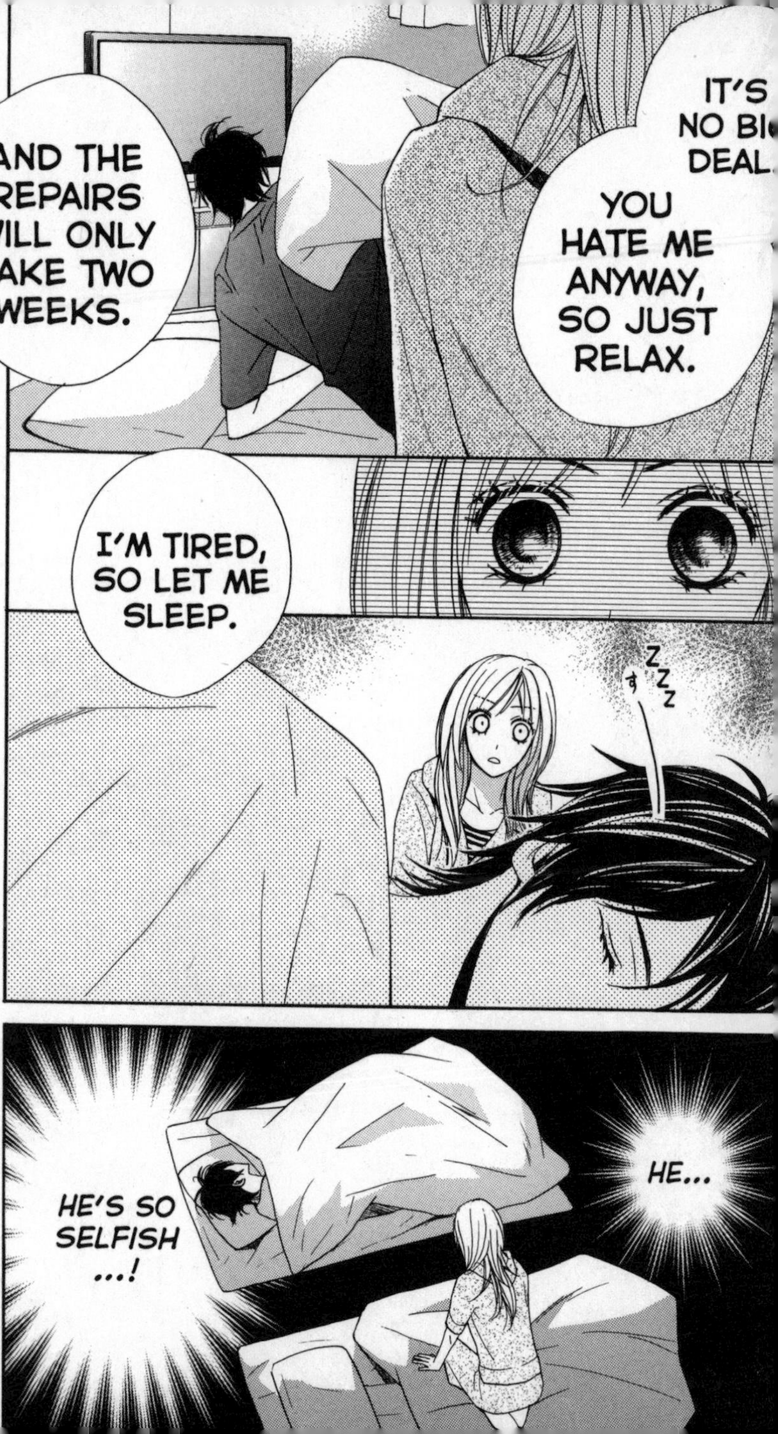
IT'S NO BI DEAL.
YOU HATE ME ANYWAY, SO JUST RELAX.
AND THE REPAIRS WILL ONLY TAKE TWO WEEKS.
I'M TIRED, SO LET ME SLEEP.
す
ZZZ
HE...
HE'S SO SELFISH ...!

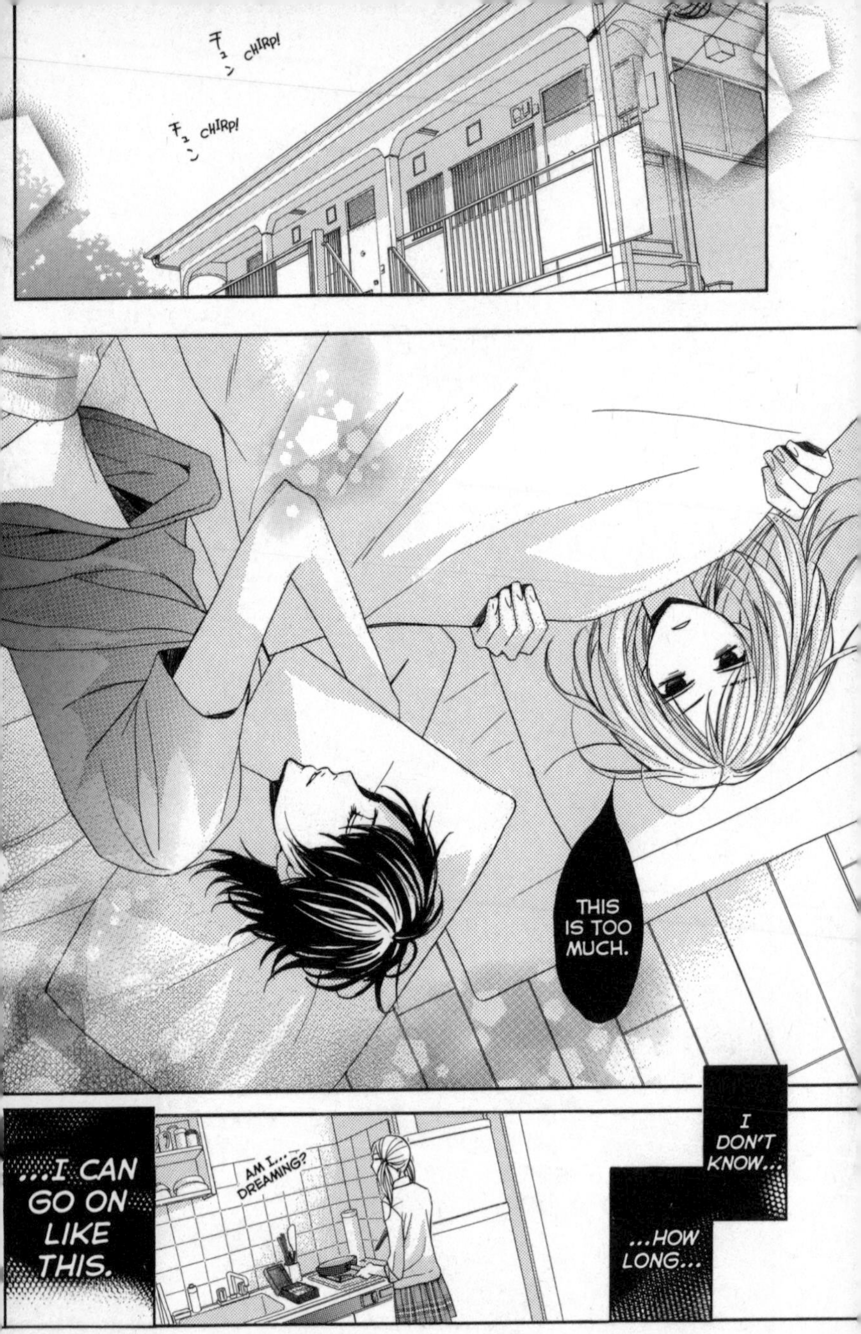
チュン CHIRP!
チュン CHIRP!
THIS IS TOO MUCH.
I DON'T KNOW...
...HOW LONG...
AM I... DREAMING?
...I CAN GO ON LIKE THIS.

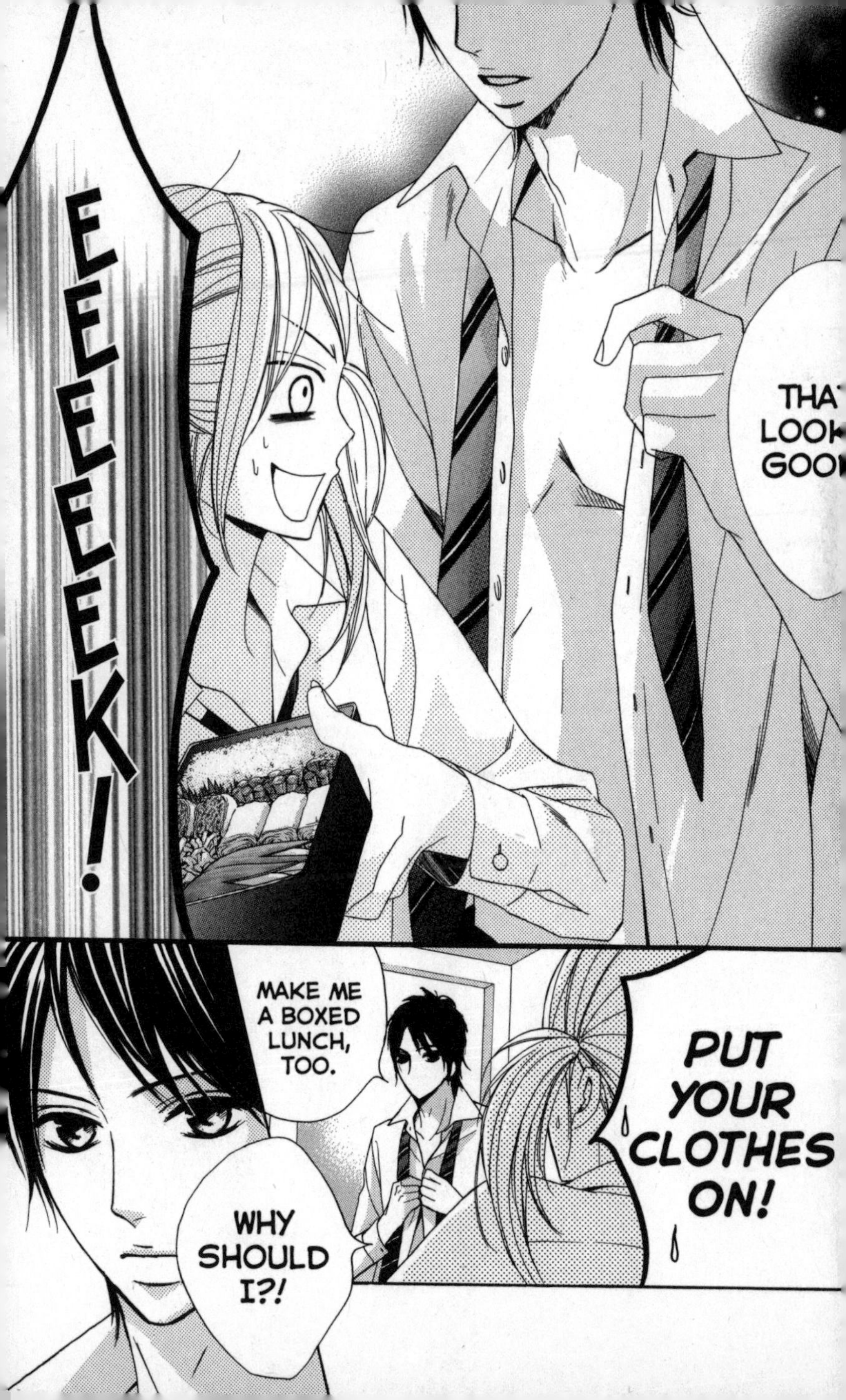
THA LOOK GOO
EEEEEK!
PUT YOUR CLOTHES ON!
MAKE ME A BOXED LUNCH, TOO.
WHY SHOULD I?!

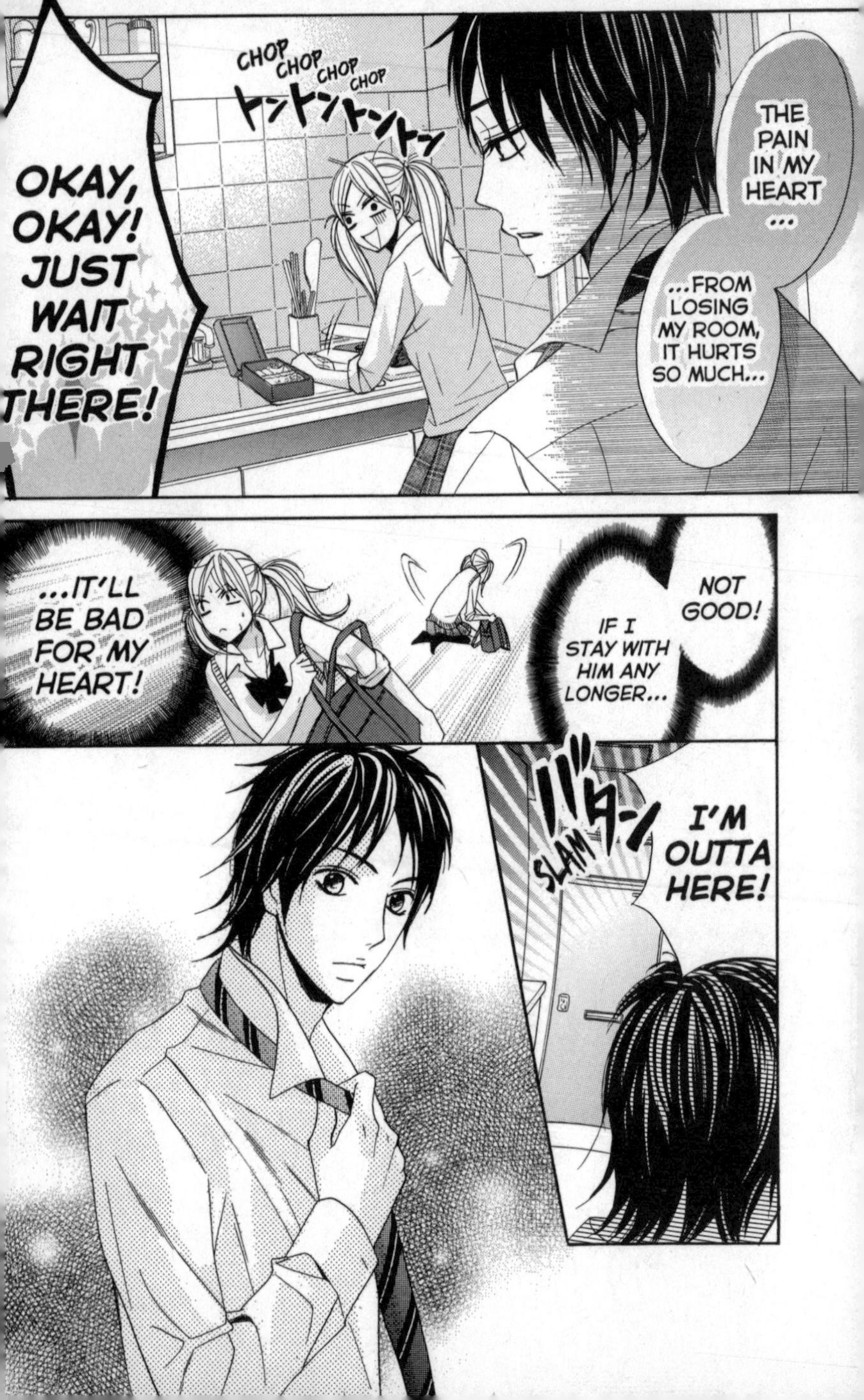
THE PAIN IN MY HEART...
...FROM LOSING MY ROOM, IT HURTS SO MUCH...
CHOP CHOP CHOP CHOP
OKAY, OKAY! JUST WAIT RIGHT THERE!
NOT GOOD!
IF I STAY WITH HIM ANY LONGER...
...IT'LL BE BAD FOR MY HEART!
I'M OUTTA HERE!
SLAM

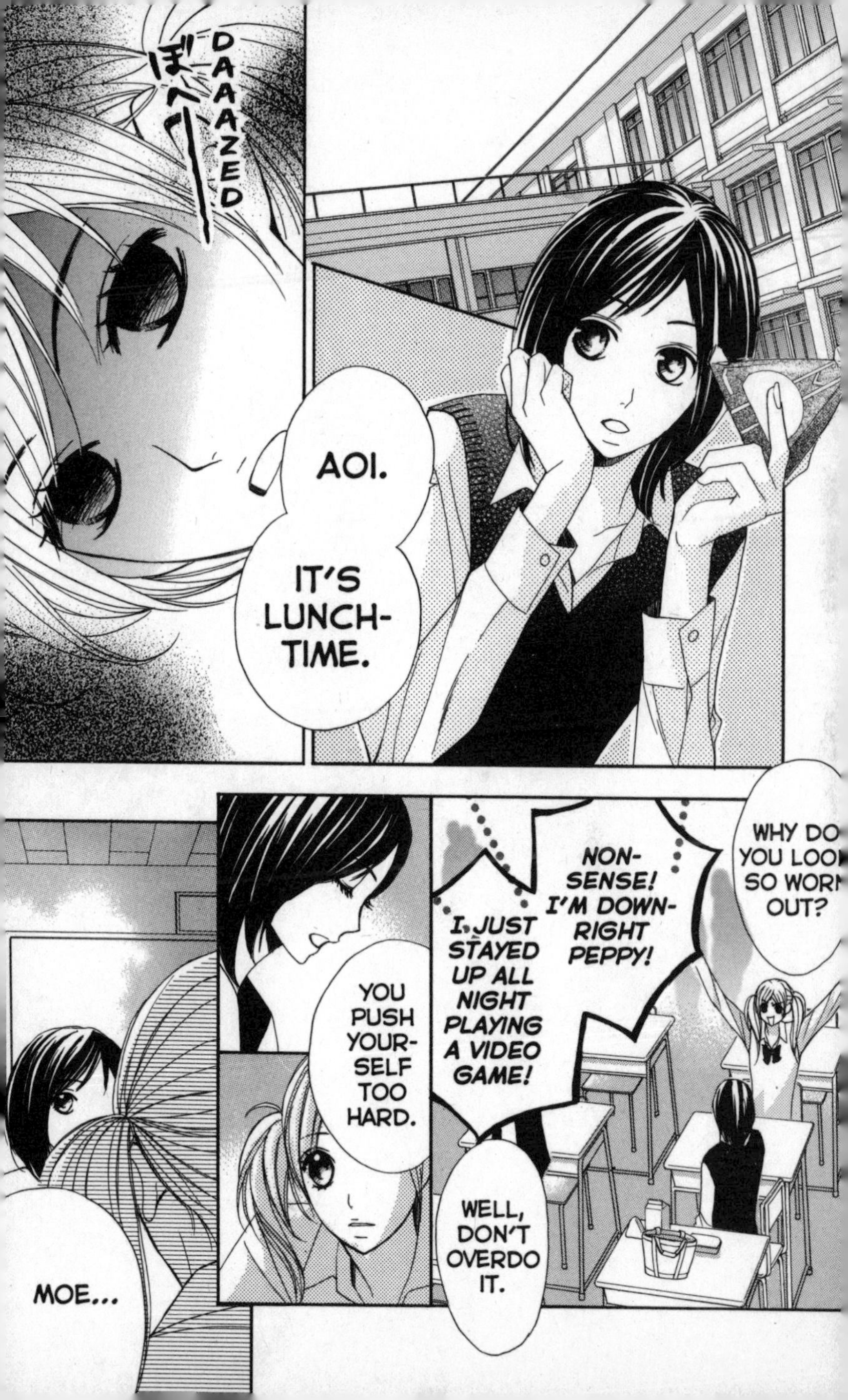
AOI.
IT'S LUNCH-TIME.
DAAAZED
ぼへー
WHY DO YOU LOOK SO WORN OUT?
NON-SENSE! I'M DOWN-RIGHT PEPPY!
I JUST STAYED UP ALL NIGHT PLAYING A VIDEO GAME!
WELL, DON'T OVERDO IT.
YOU PUSH YOUR-SELF TOO HARD.
MOE...

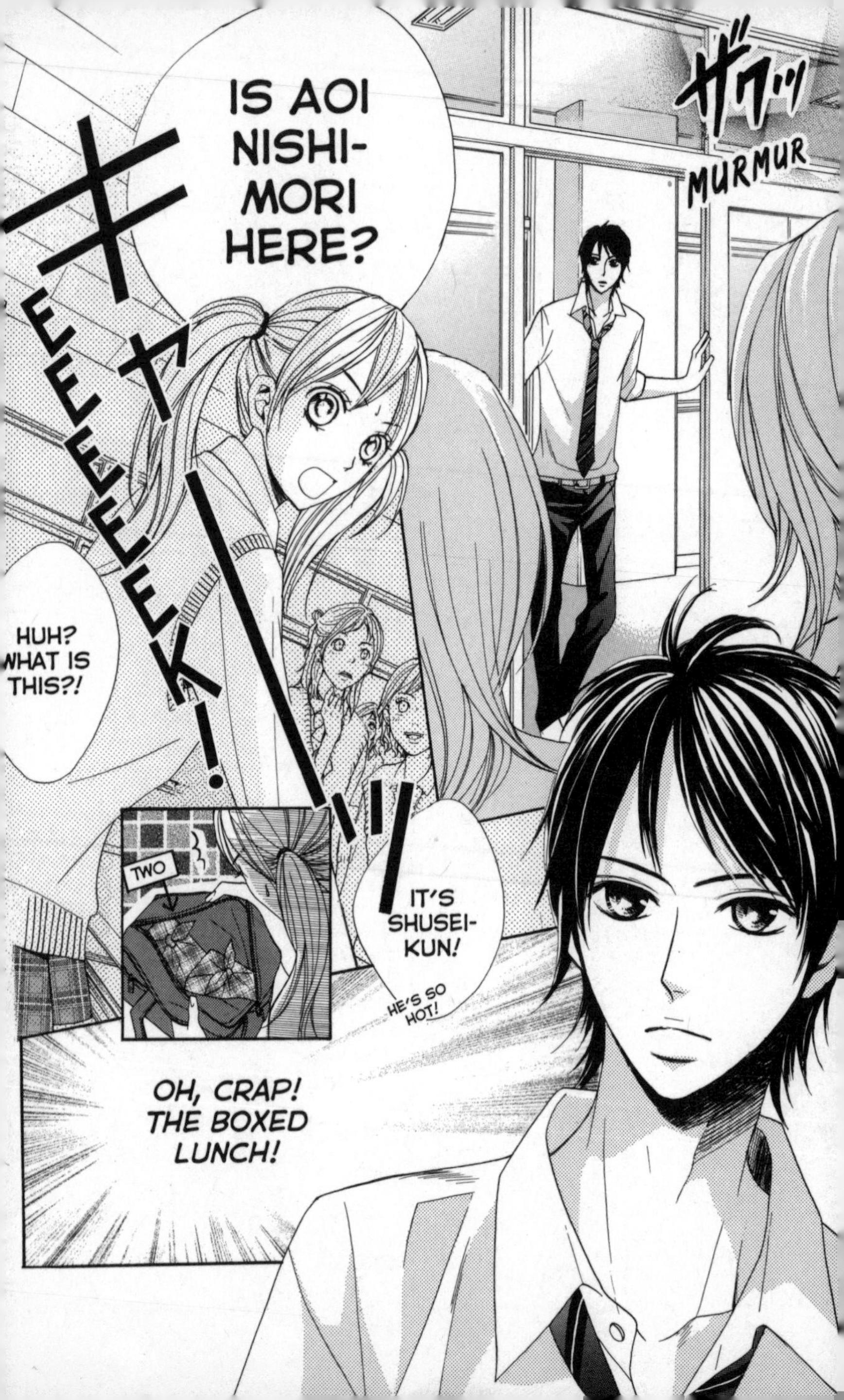

ザワッ
MURMUR
IS AOI NISHI-MORI HERE?
キャー
EEEEEEK!
IT'S SHUSEI-KUN!
HE'S SO HOT!
HUH? WHAT IS THIS?!
TWO
OH, CRAP! THE BOXED LUNCH!

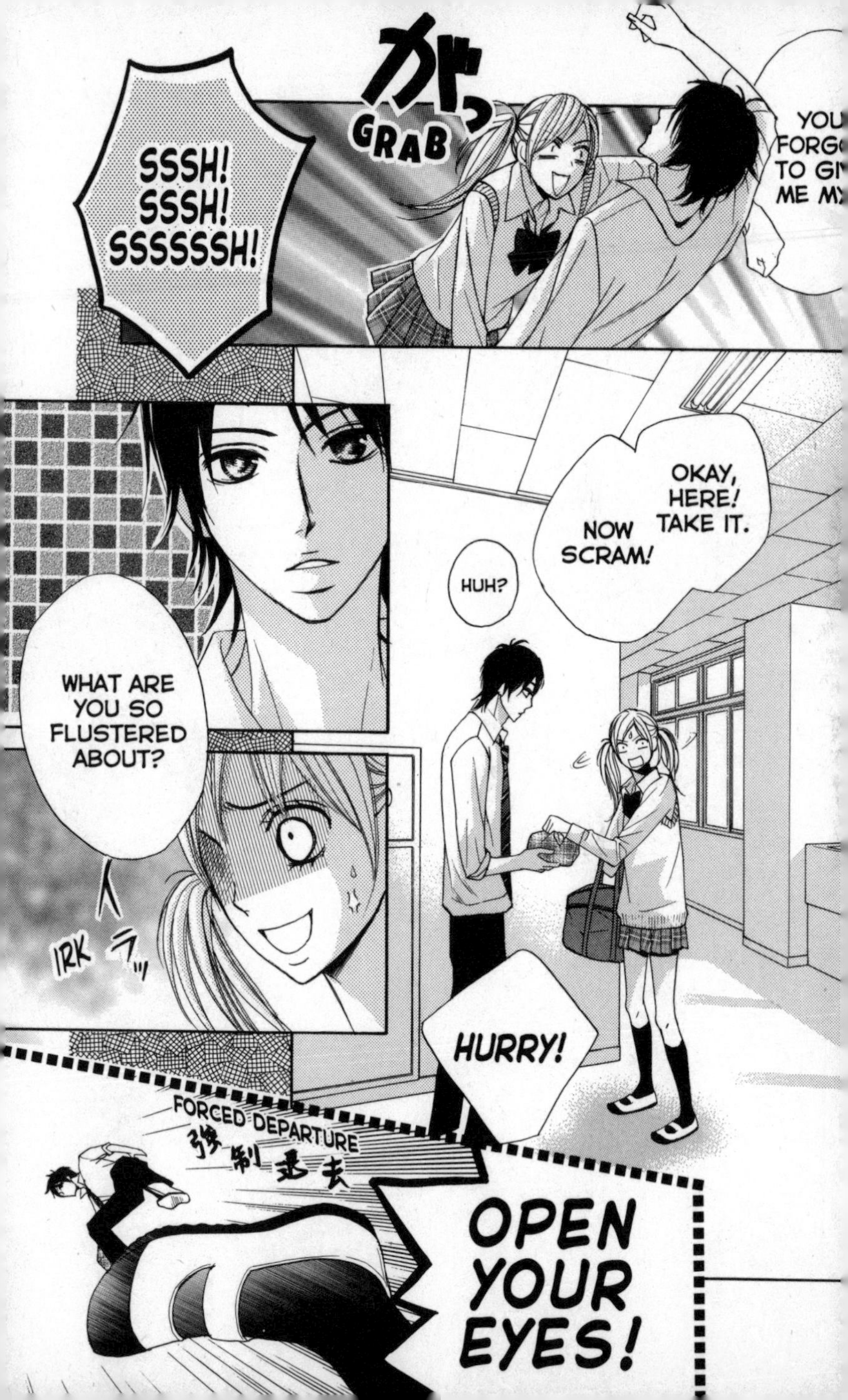
YOU FORGO TO GI ME M
がっ
GRAB
SSSH! SSSH! SSSSSSH!
OKAY, HERE! TAKE IT.
NOW SCRAM!
HUH?
HURRY!
WHAT ARE YOU SO FLUSTERED ABOUT?
IRK
ラッ
FORCED DEPARTURE
強制退去
OPEN YOUR EYES!

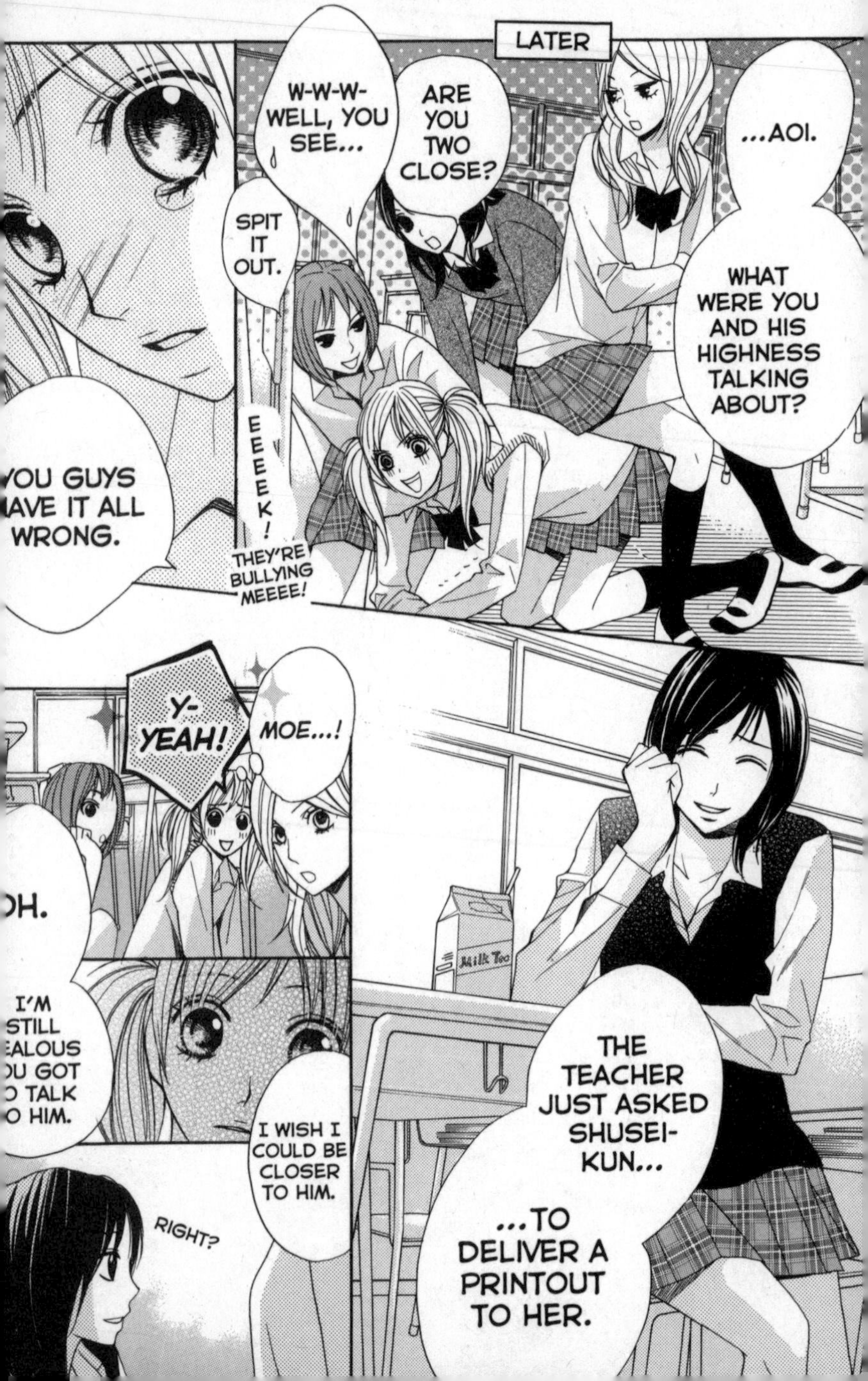

LATER
...AOI.
WHAT WERE YOU AND HIS HIGHNESS TALKING ABOUT?
ARE YOU TWO CLOSE?
W-W-W-WELL, YOU SEE...
SPIT IT OUT.
EEEEK!
THEY'RE BULLYING MEEEE!
OU GUYS AVE IT ALL WRONG.
THE TEACHER JUST ASKED SHUSEI-KUN...
...TO DELIVER A PRINTOUT TO HER.
MOE...!
Y-YEAH!
H.
I WISH I COULD BE CLOSER TO HIM.
I'M STILL EALOUS U GOT TALK O HIM.
RIGHT?

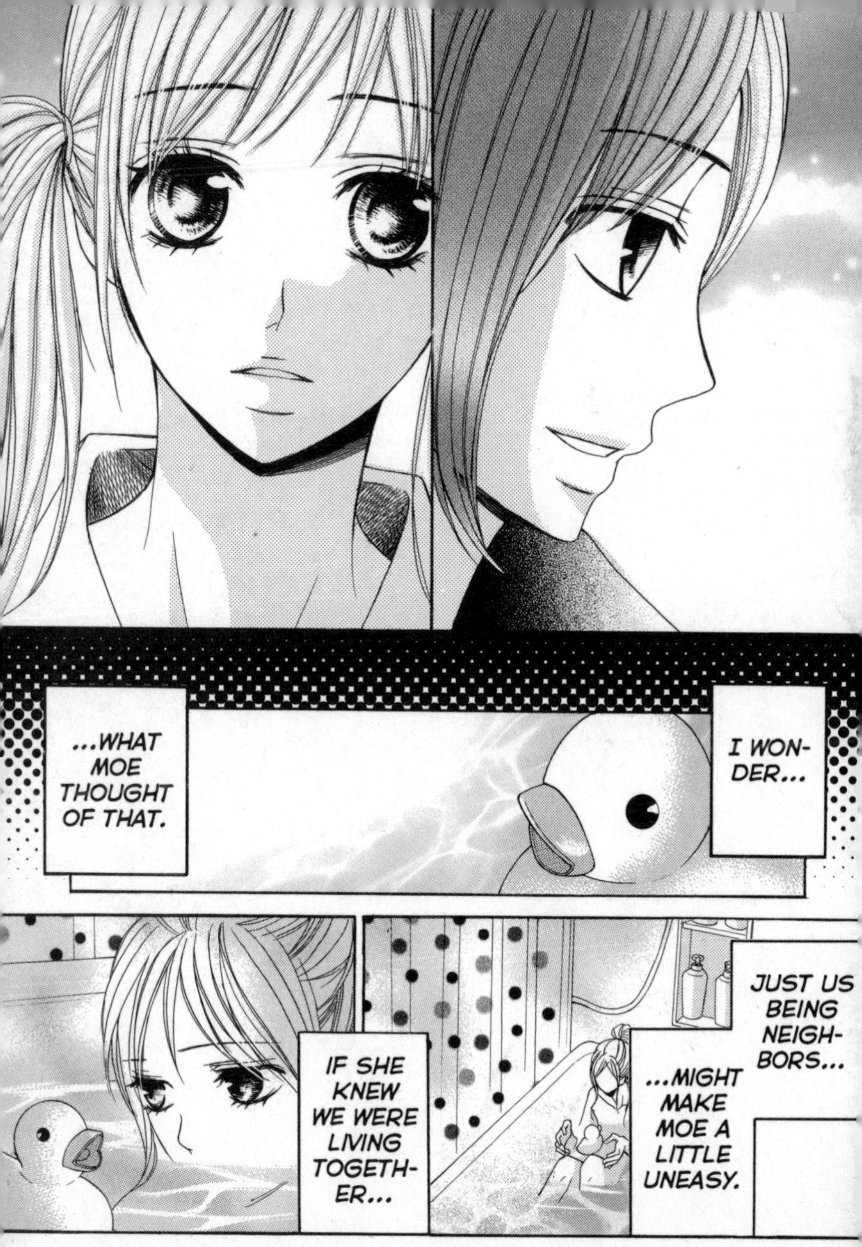
I WON-DER...
...WHAT MOE THOUGHT OF THAT.
JUST US BEING NEIGH-BORS...
...MIGHT MAKE MOE A LITTLE UNEASY.
IF SHE KNEW WE WERE LIVING TOGETH-ER...

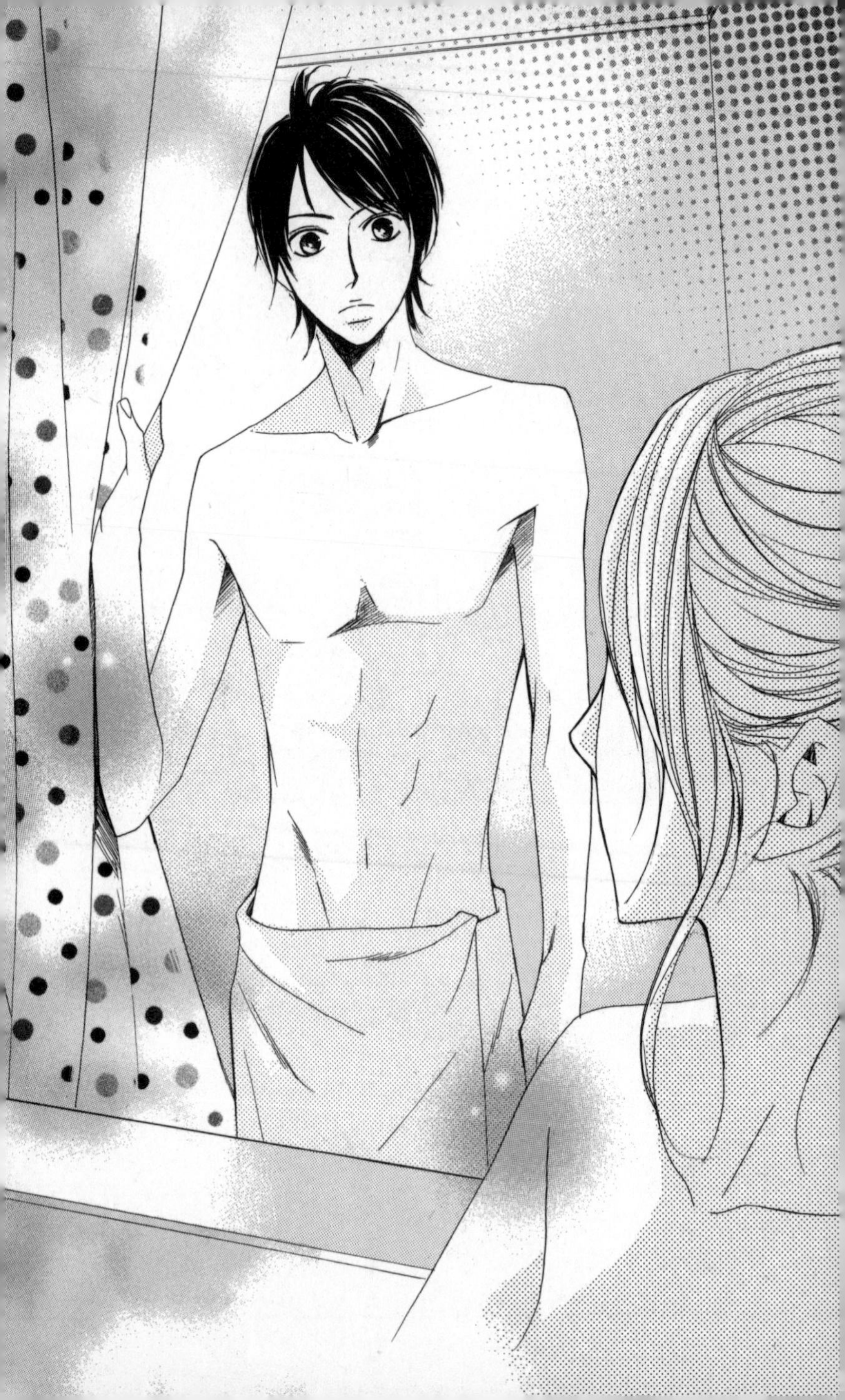

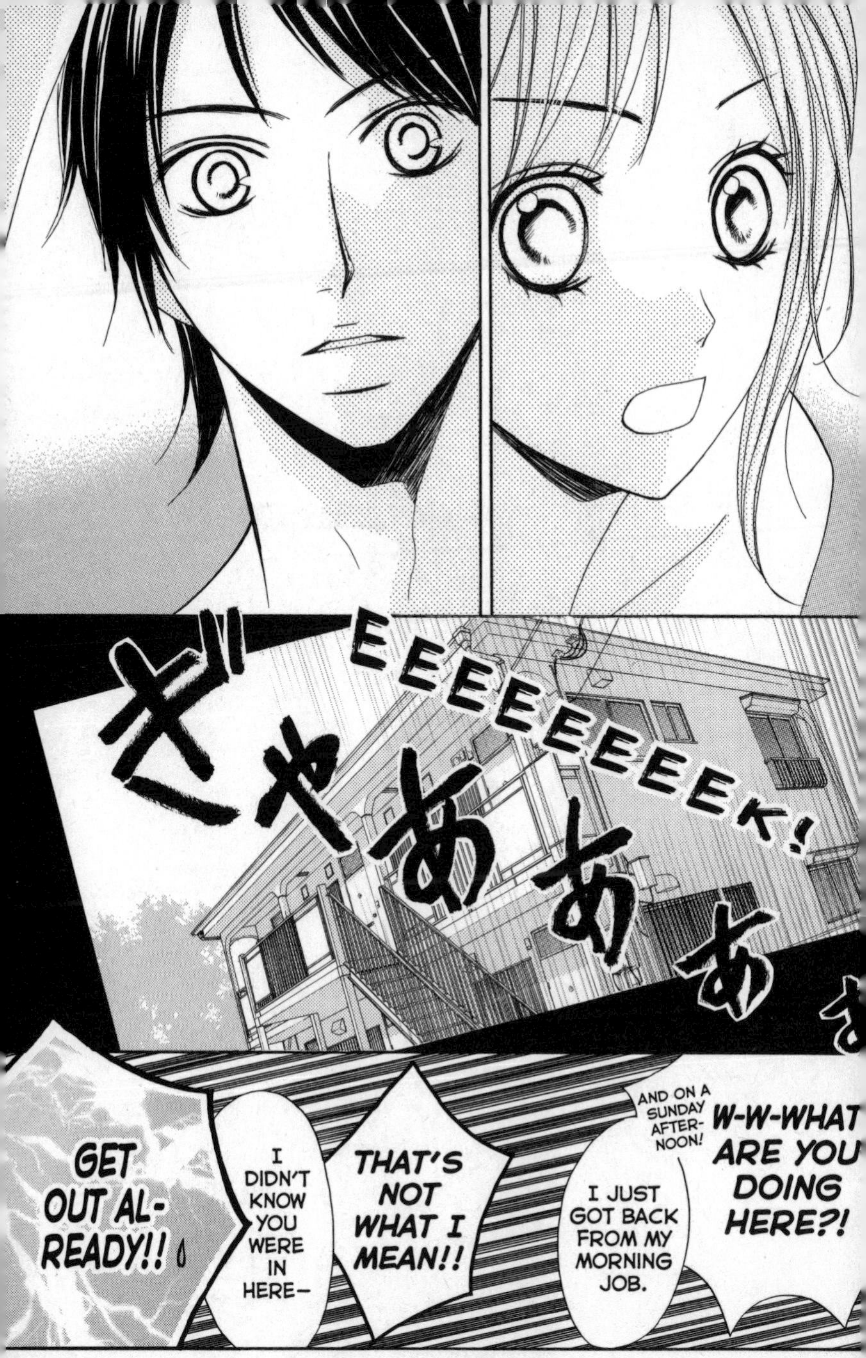
ぎゃあああ
EEEEEEEEEK!
W-W-WHAT ARE YOU DOING HERE?!
AND ON A SUNDAY AFTERNOON!
I JUST GOT BACK FROM MY MORNING JOB.
THAT'S NOT WHAT I MEAN!!
I DIDN'T KNOW YOU WERE IN HERE—
GET OUT ALREADY!!

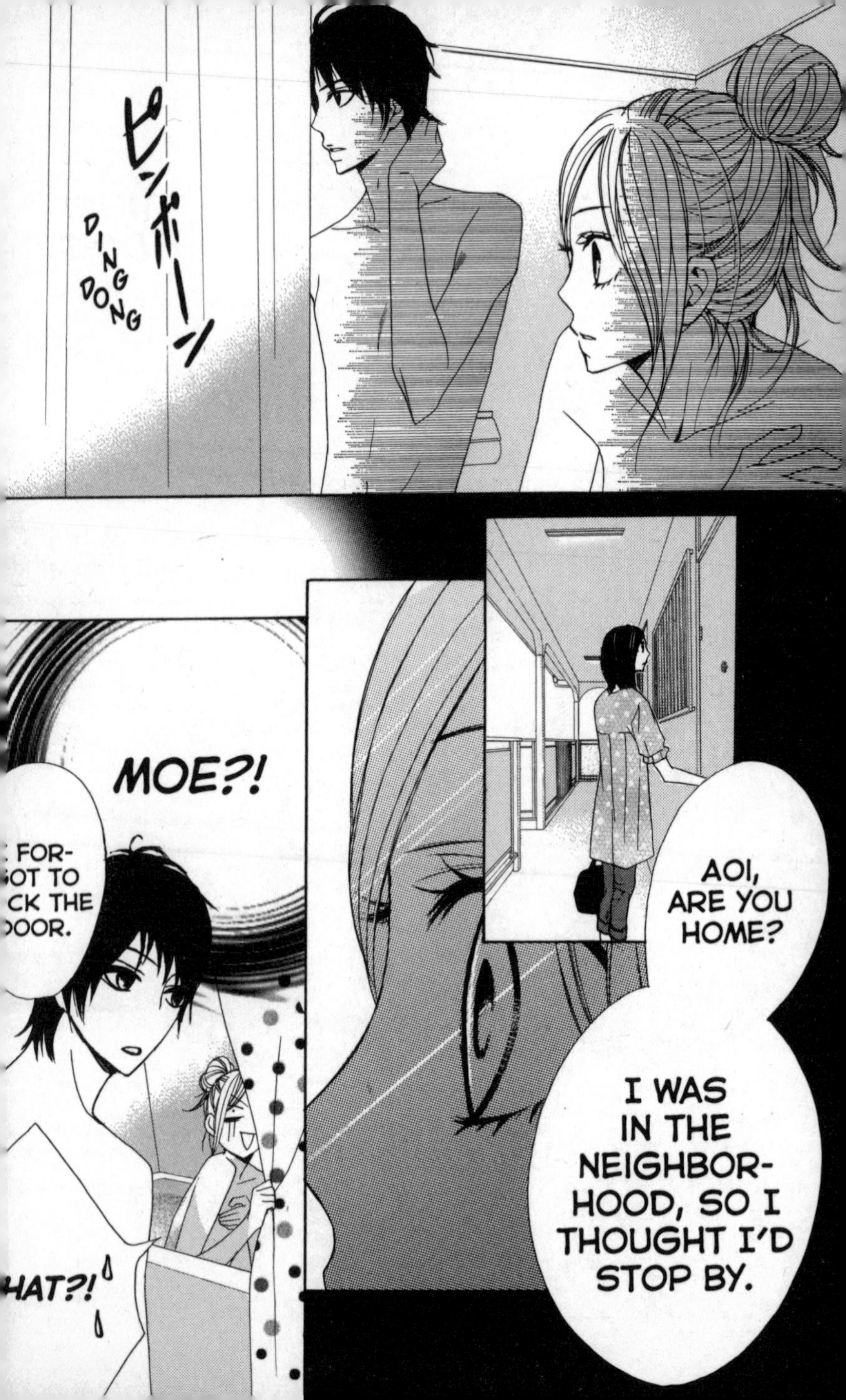
ピンポーン
DING DONG
AOI, ARE YOU HOME?
I WAS IN THE NEIGHBOR-HOOD, SO I THOUGHT I'D STOP BY.
MOE?!
FOR- OT TO CK THE DOOR.
HAT?!

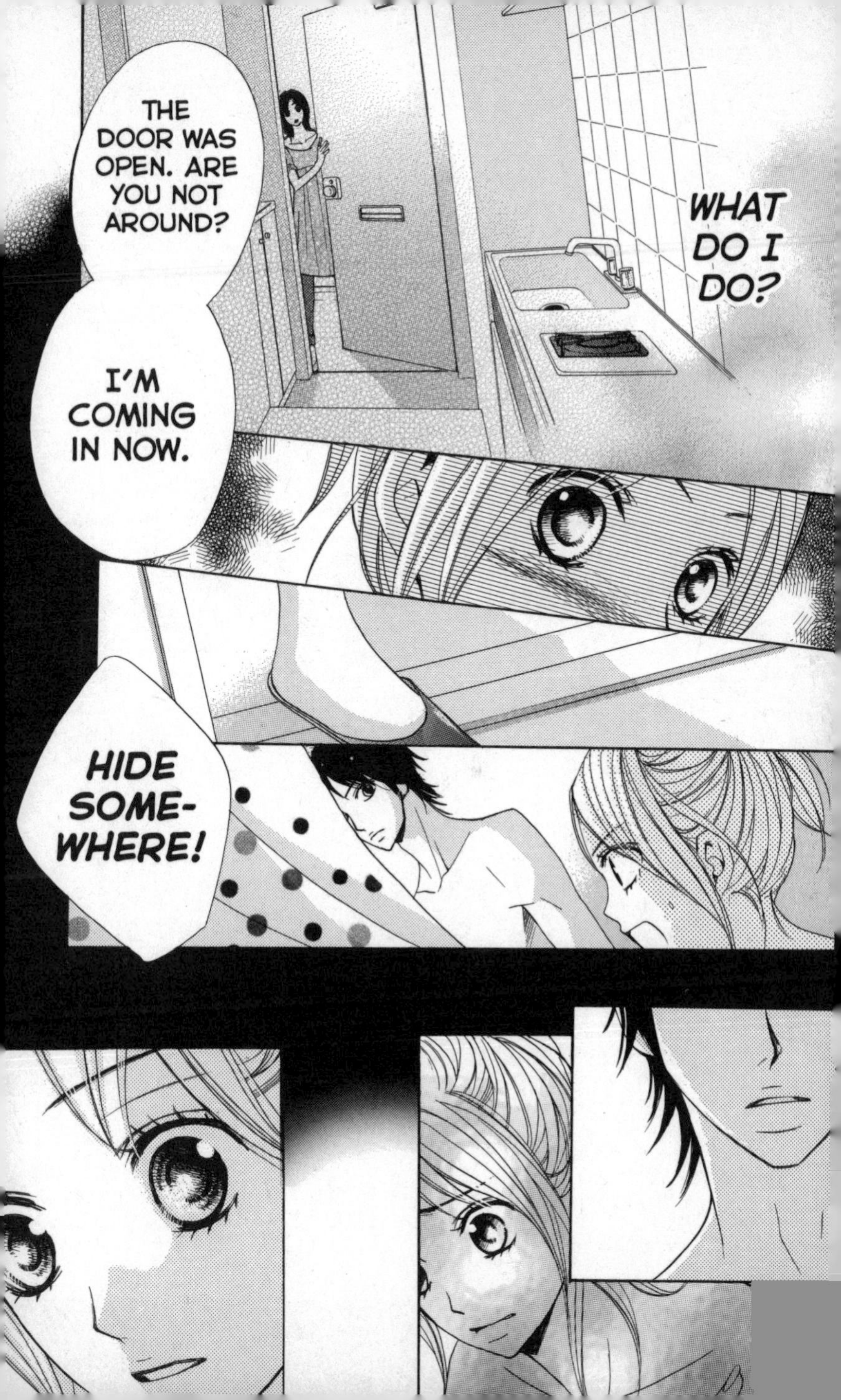
THE DOOR WAS OPEN. ARE YOU NOT AROUND?
I'M COMING IN NOW.
WHAT DO I DO?
HIDE SOMEWHERE!

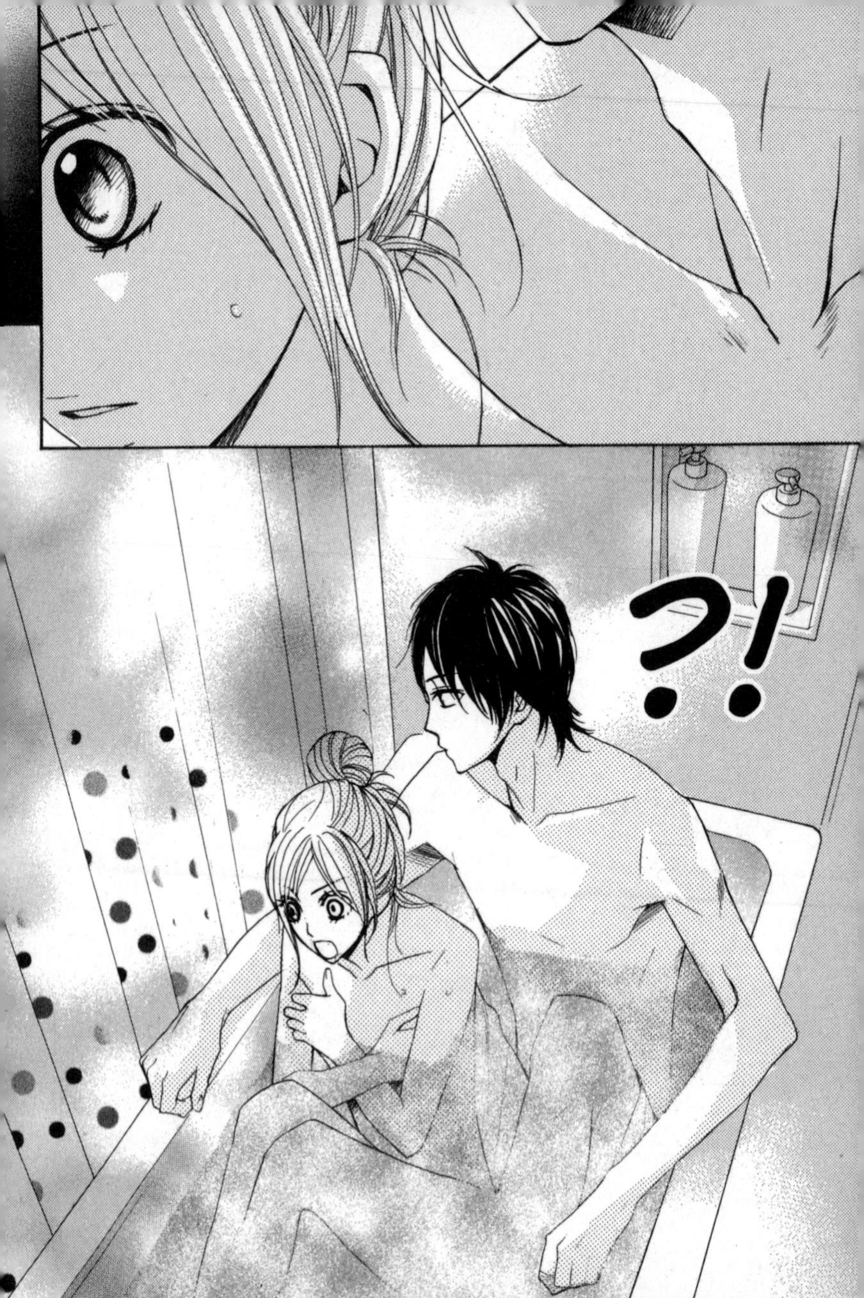
?!

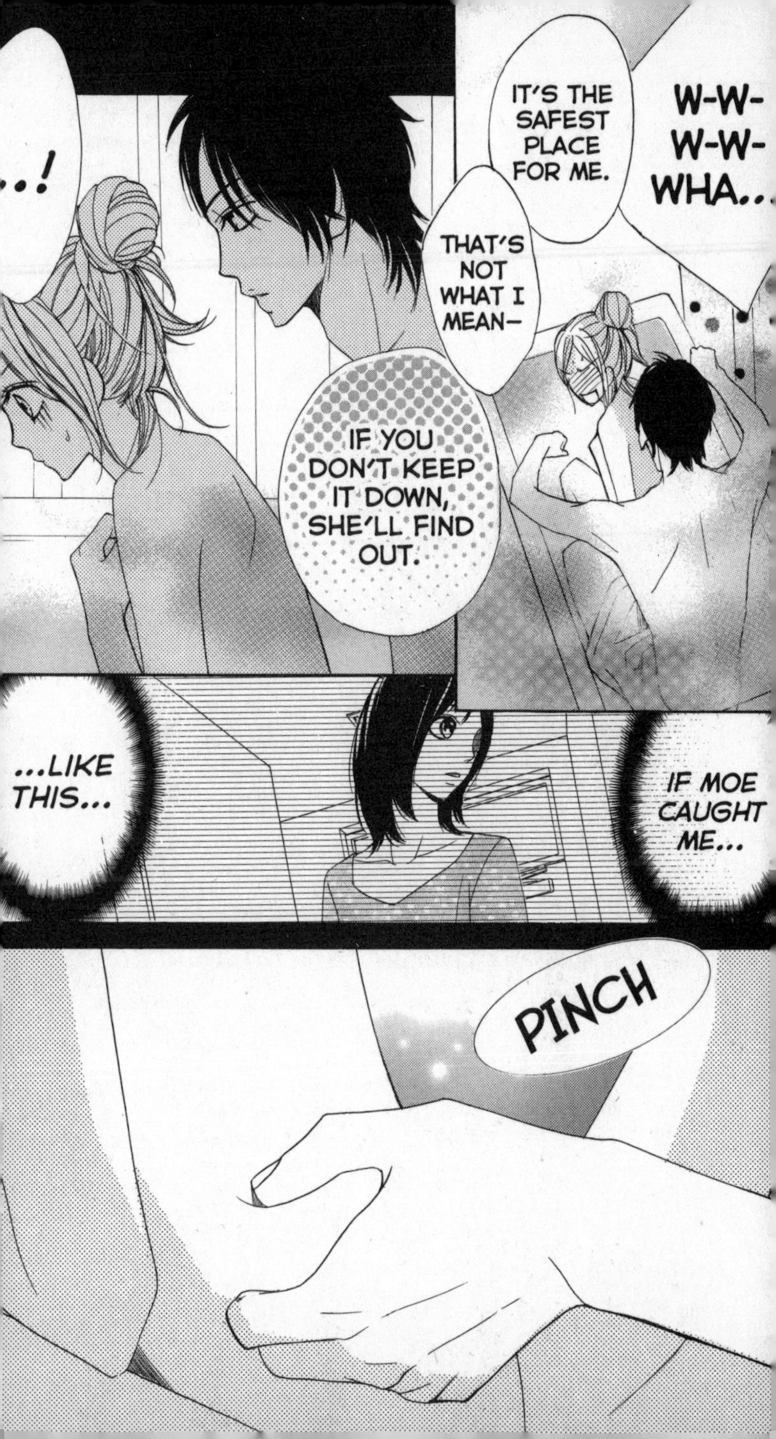
W-W-W-W-WHA...
IT'S THE SAFEST PLACE FOR ME.
THAT'S NOT WHAT I MEAN—
..!
IF YOU DON'T KEEP IT DOWN, SHE'LL FIND OUT.
IF MOE CAUGHT ME...
...LIKE THIS...
PINCH

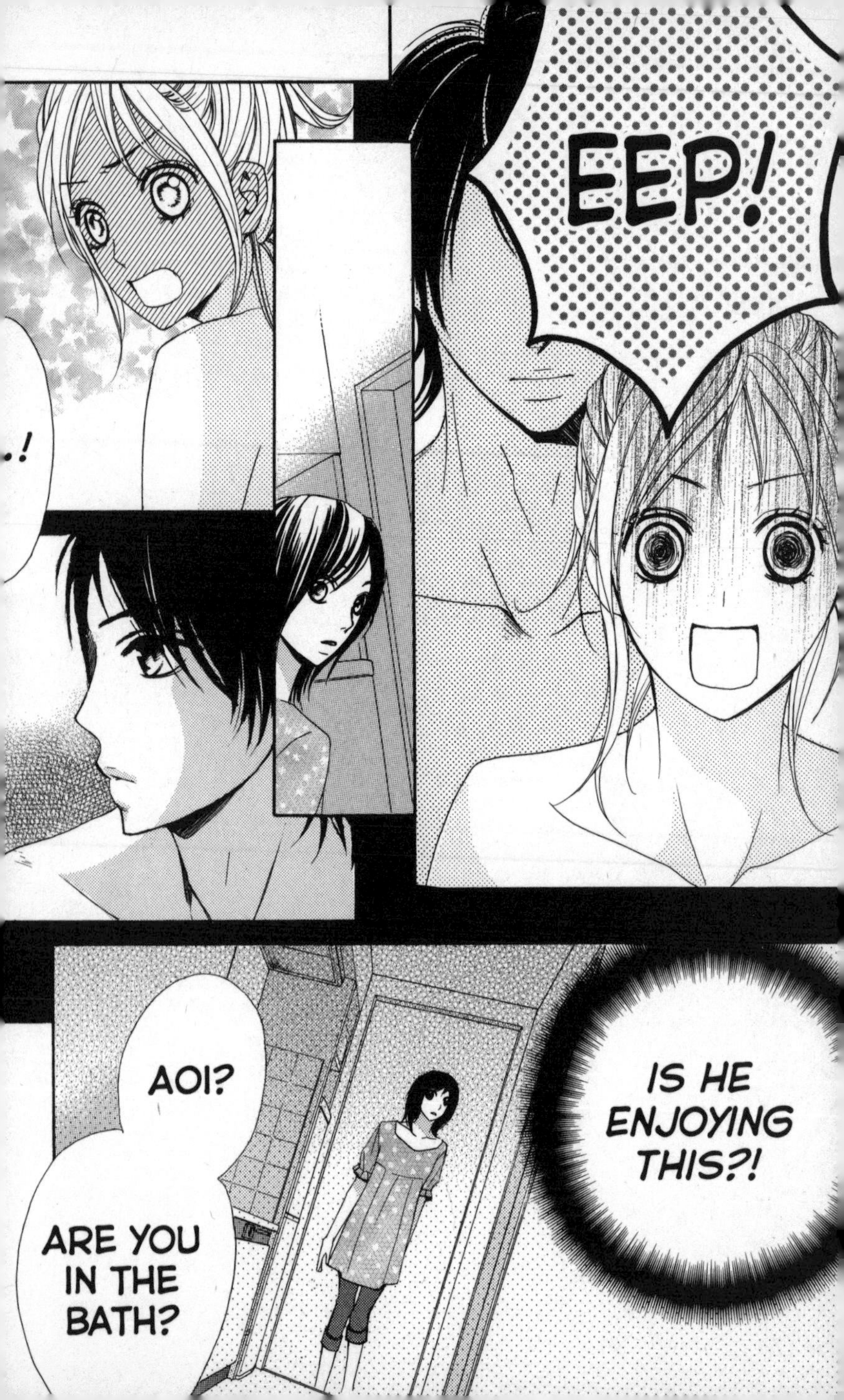
EEP!
IS HE ENJOYING THIS?!
AOI?
ARE YOU IN THE BATH?

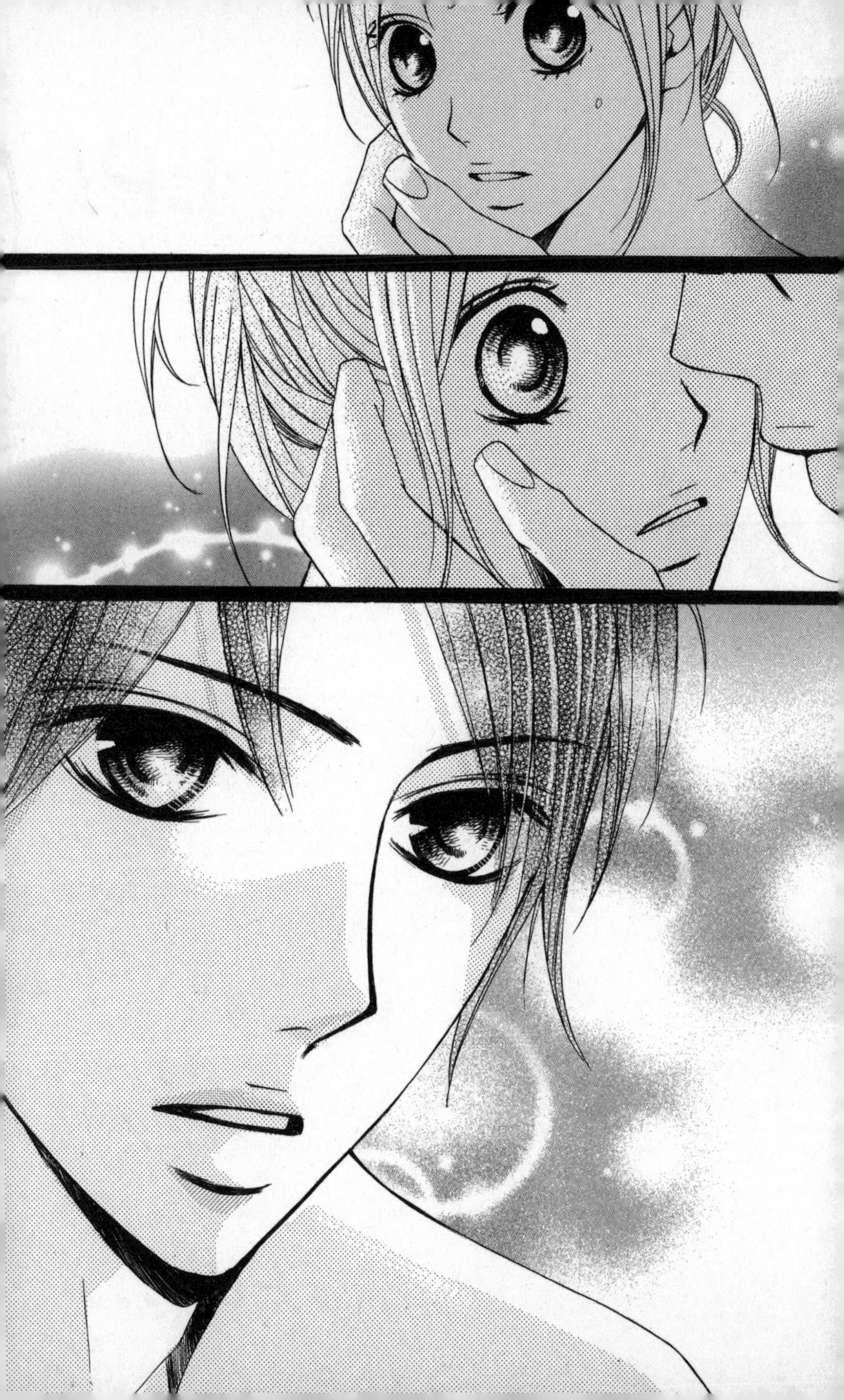

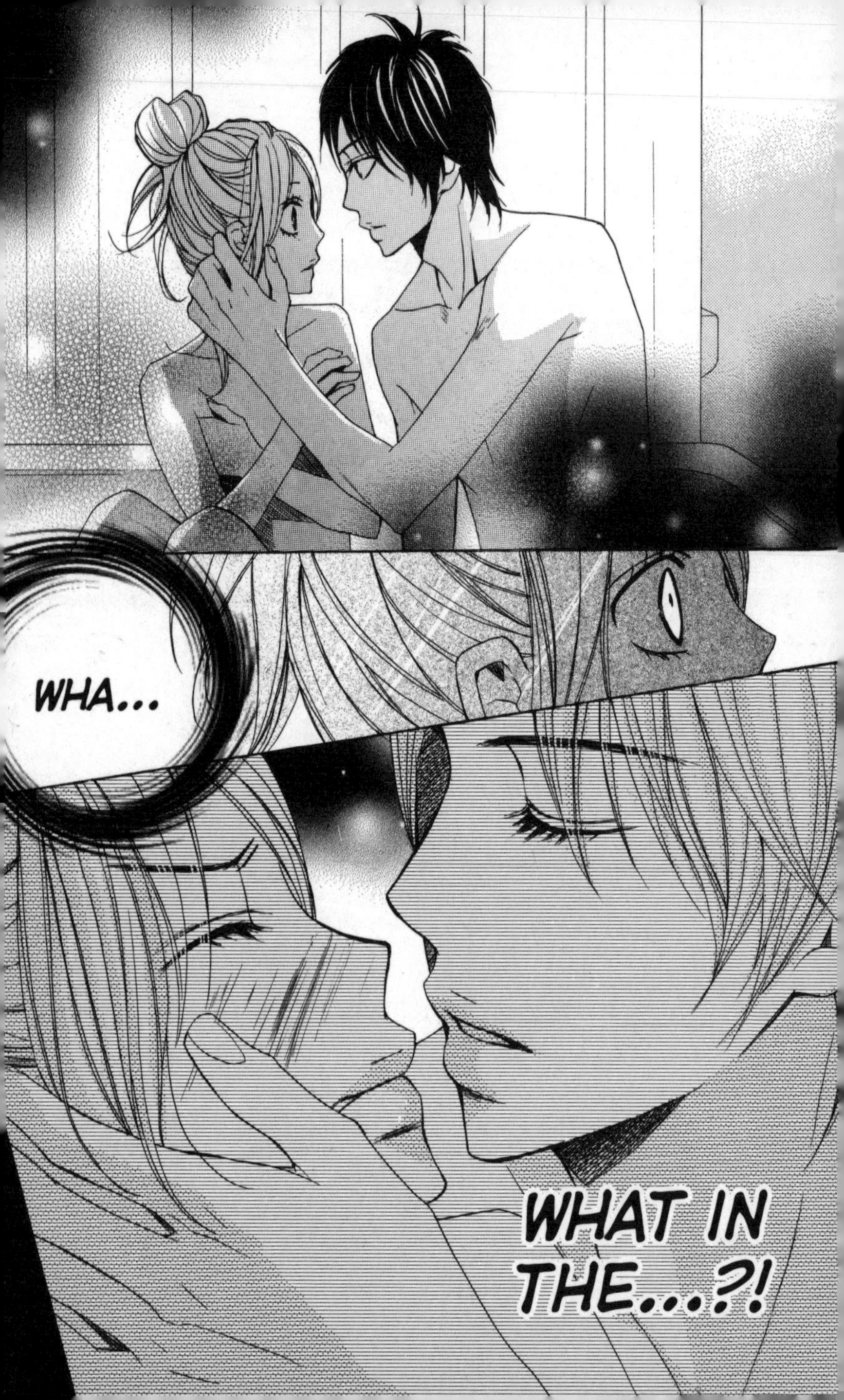
WHA...
WHAT IN THE...?!

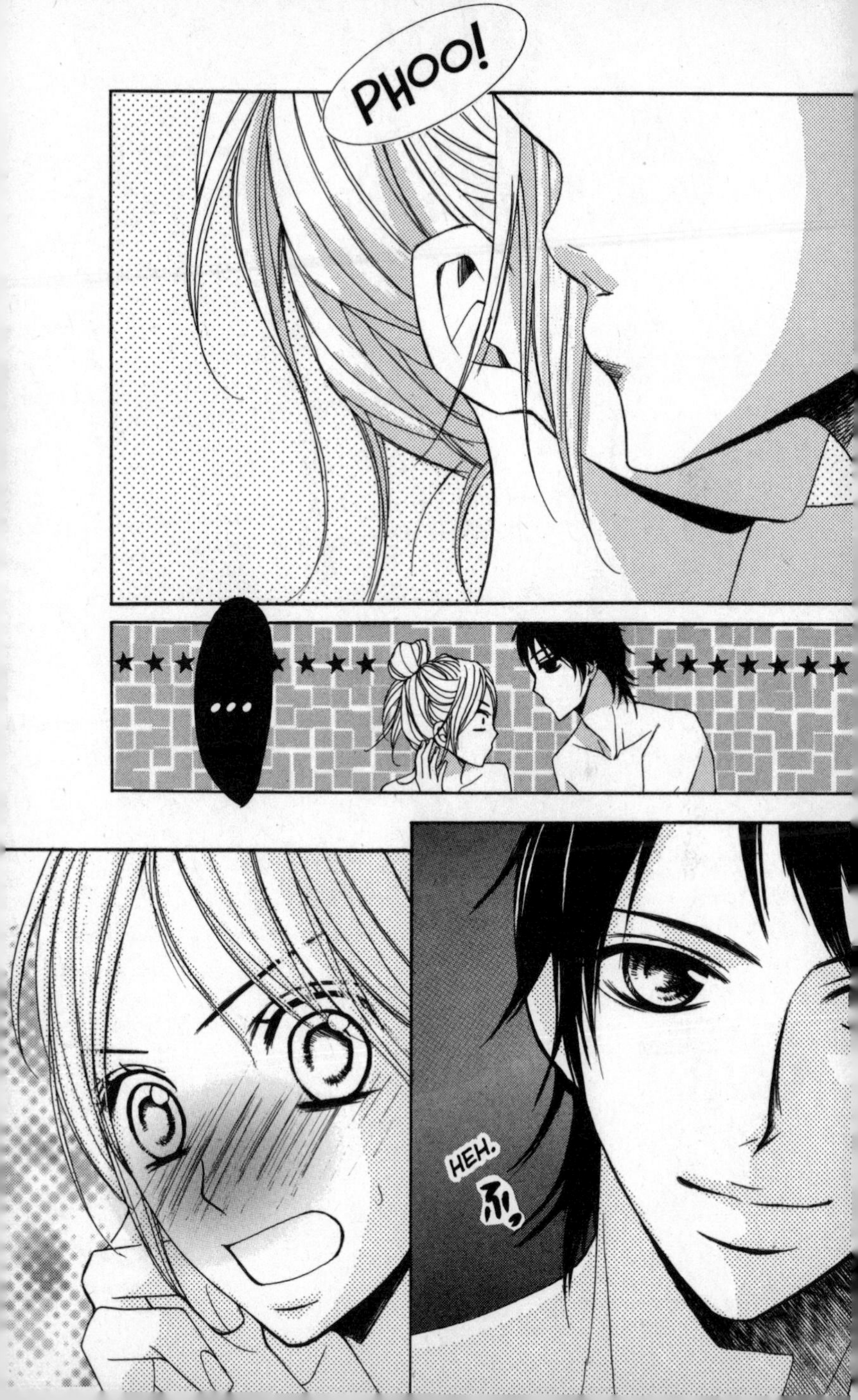
PHOO!
...
HEH.
ふっ

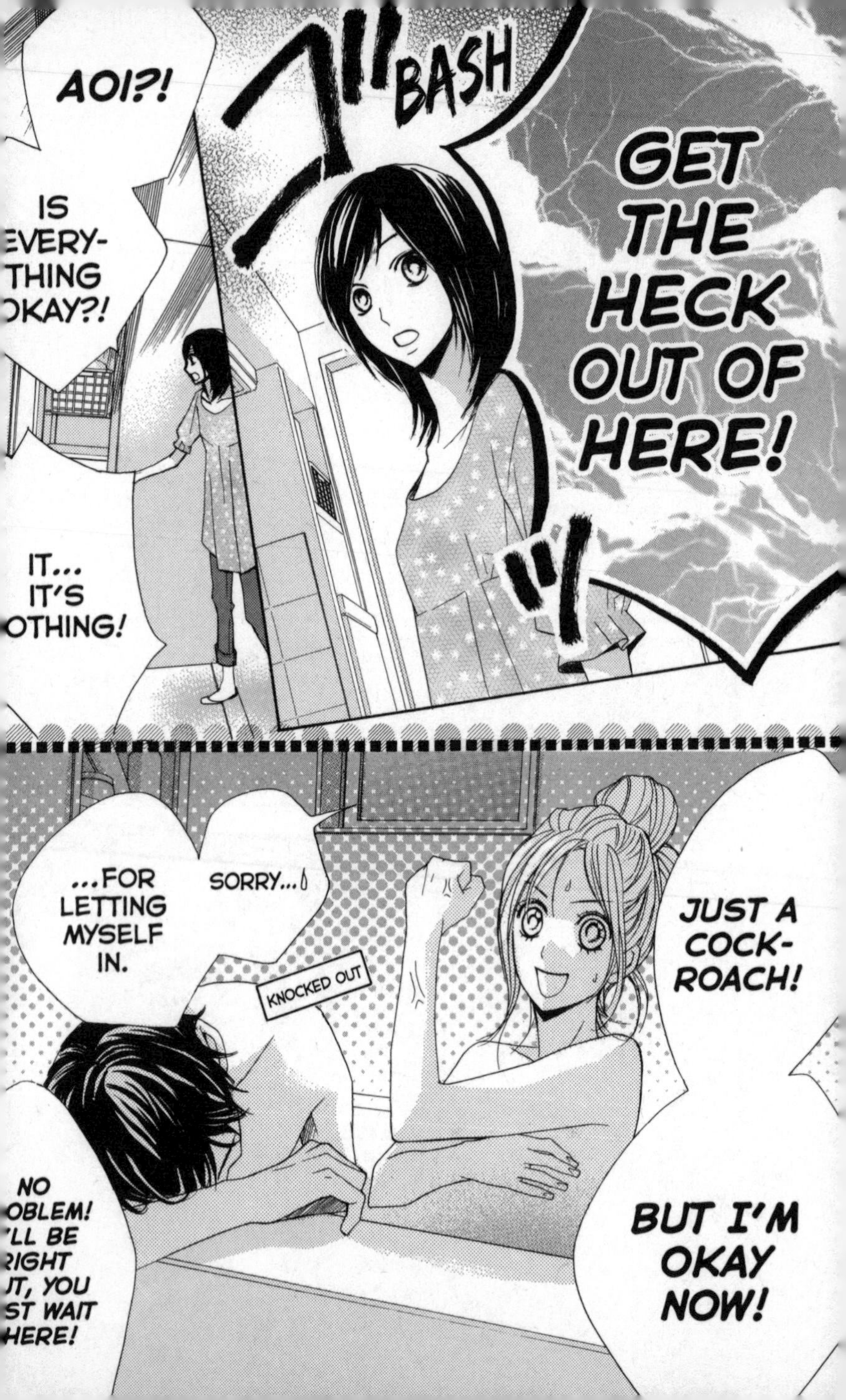
BASH
GET THE HECK OUT OF HERE!
AOI?!
IS EVERY-THING OKAY?!
IT... IT'S OTHING!
JUST A COCK-ROACH!
BUT I'M OKAY NOW!
SORRY...
...FOR LETTING MYSELF IN.
KNOCKED OUT
NO OBLEM! 'LL BE RIGHT IT, YOU ST WAIT HERE!

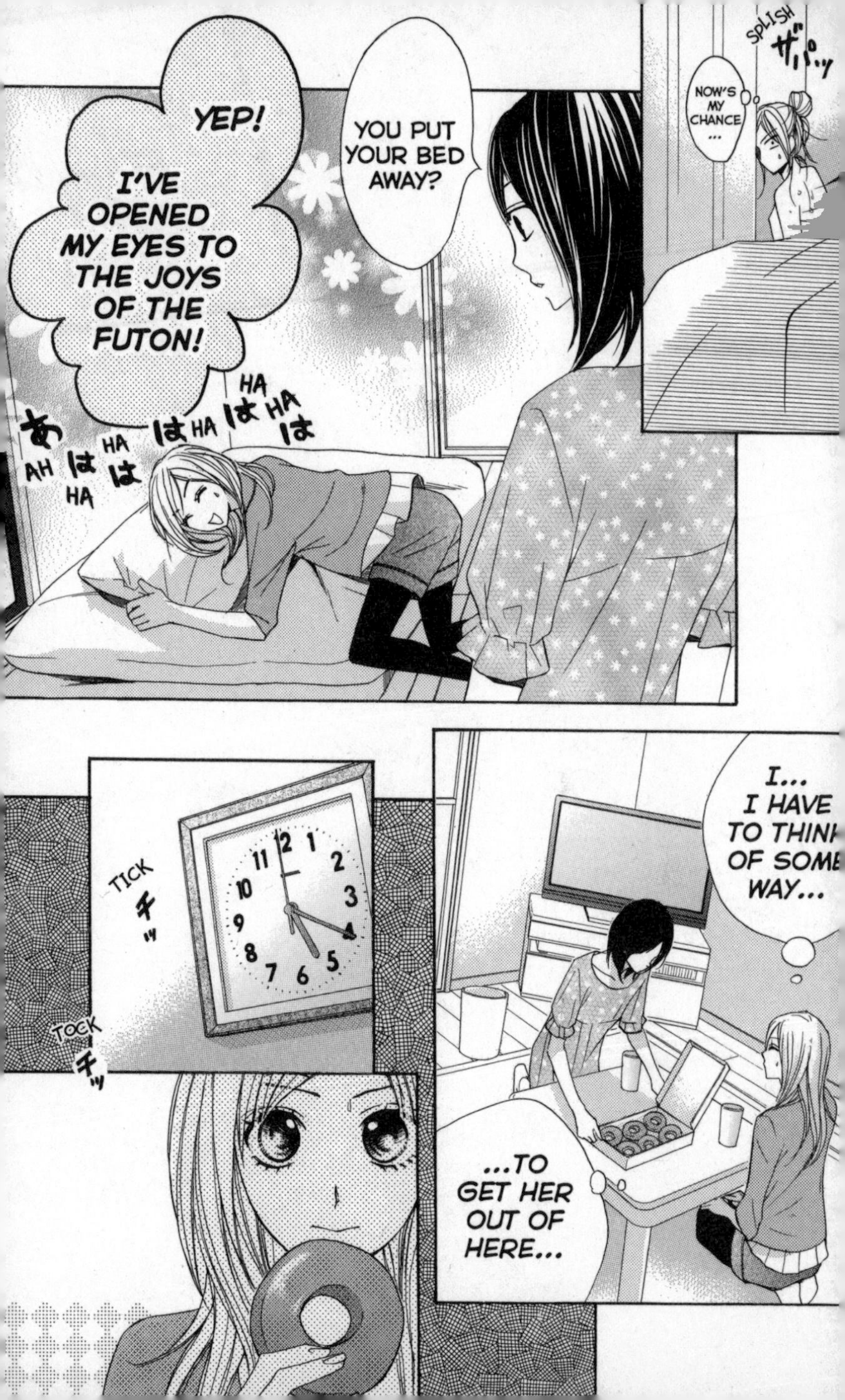
SPLISH
ザパッ
NOW'S MY CHANCE...
YOU PUT YOUR BED AWAY?
YEP!
I'VE OPENED MY EYES TO THE JOYS OF THE FUTON!
HA は HA は
HA は
HA は
AH あ HA は
I... I HAVE TO THINK OF SOME WAY...
...TO GET HER OUT OF HERE...
TICK チッ
TOCK チッ

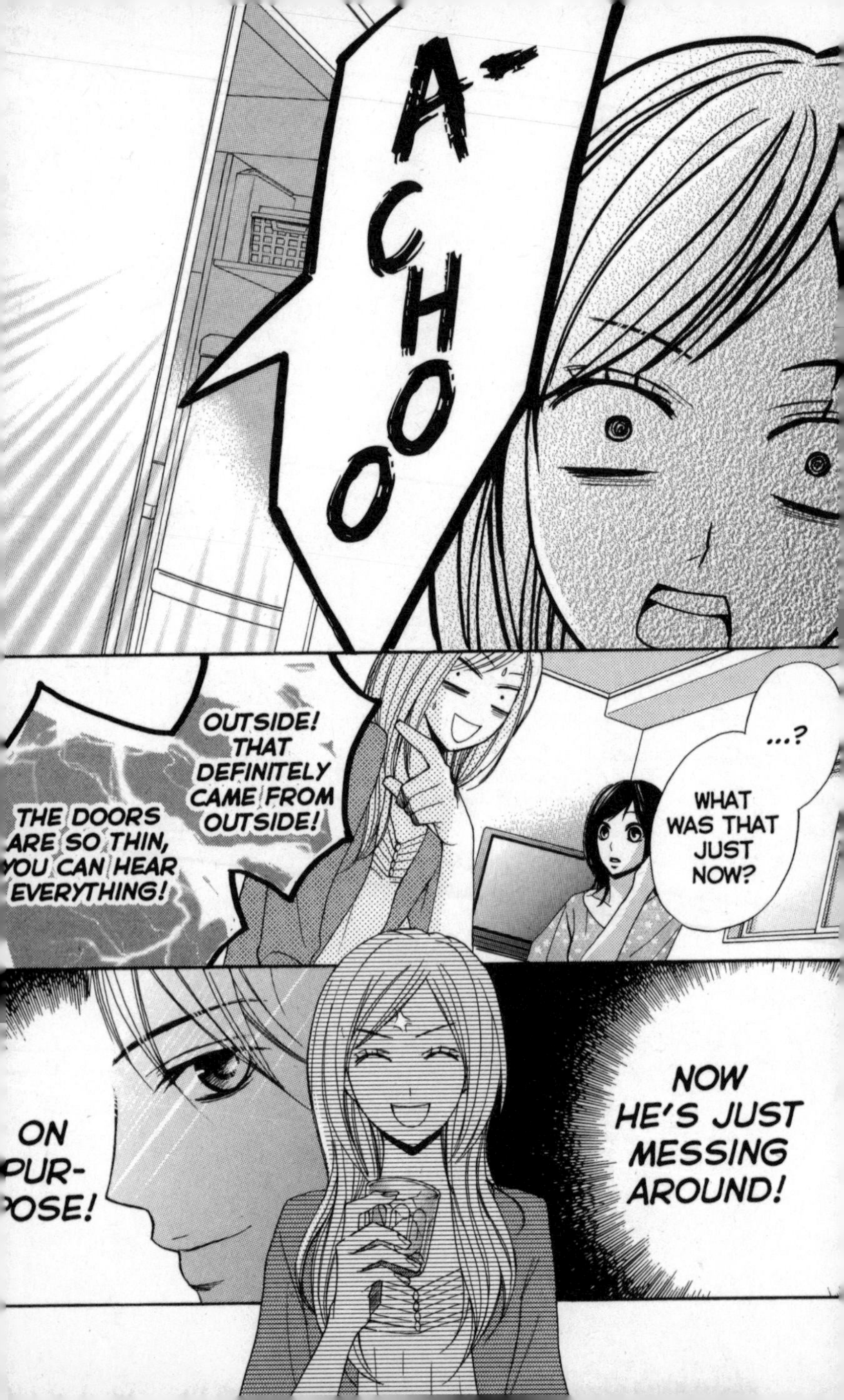
A-CHOO
...?
WHAT WAS THAT JUST NOW?
OUTSIDE! THAT DEFINITELY CAME FROM OUTSIDE!
THE DOORS ARE SO THIN, YOU CAN HEAR EVERYTHING!
NOW HE'S JUST MESSING AROUND!
ON PUR-POSE!

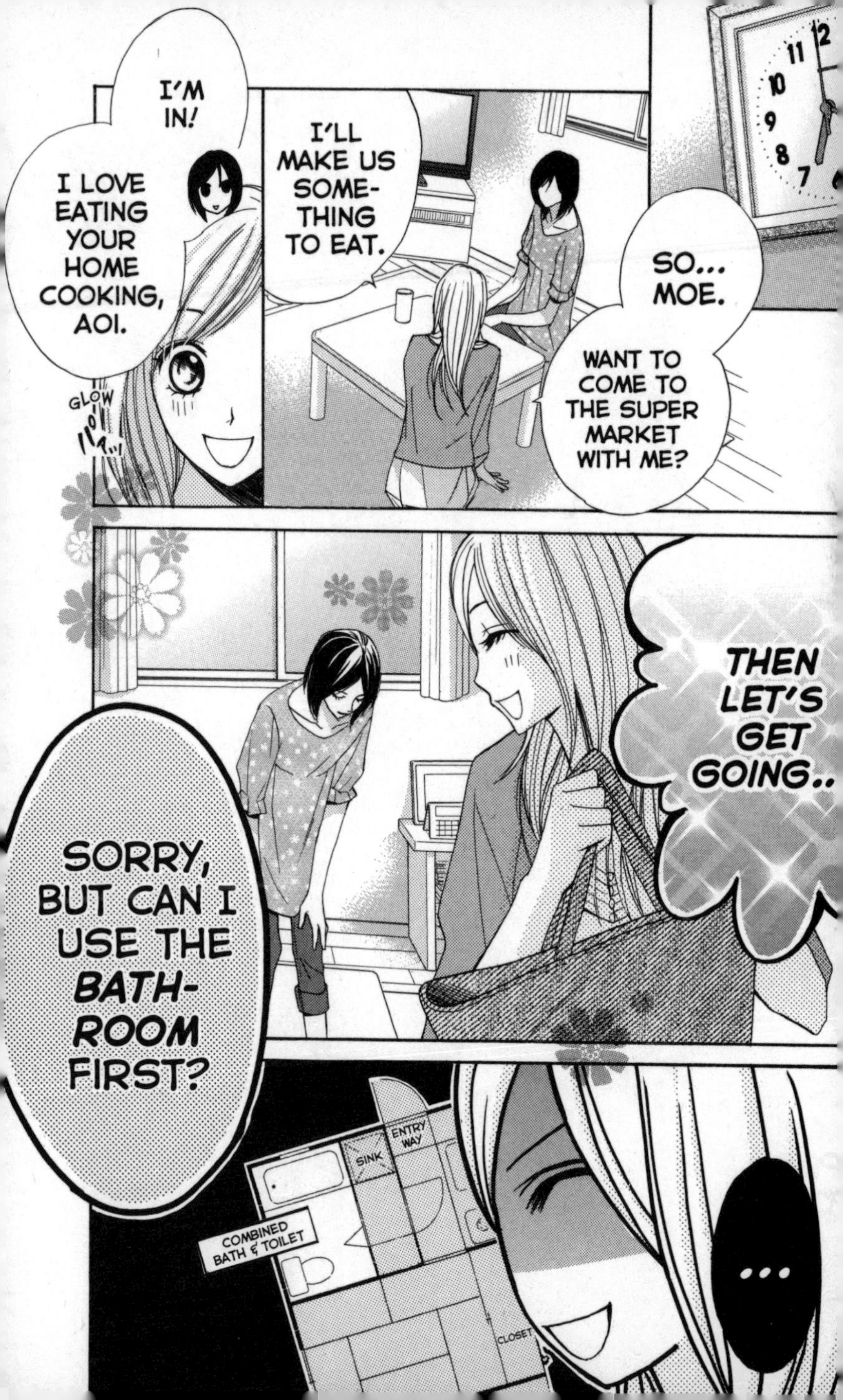
SO... MOE.
WANT TO COME TO THE SUPER MARKET WITH ME?
I'LL MAKE US SOME-THING TO EAT.
I'M IN!
I LOVE EATING YOUR HOME COOKING, AOI.
GLOW
THEN LET'S GET GOING..
SORRY, BUT CAN I USE THE *BATH-ROOM* FIRST?
ENTRY WAY
SINK
COMBINED BATH & TOILET
CLOSET
...

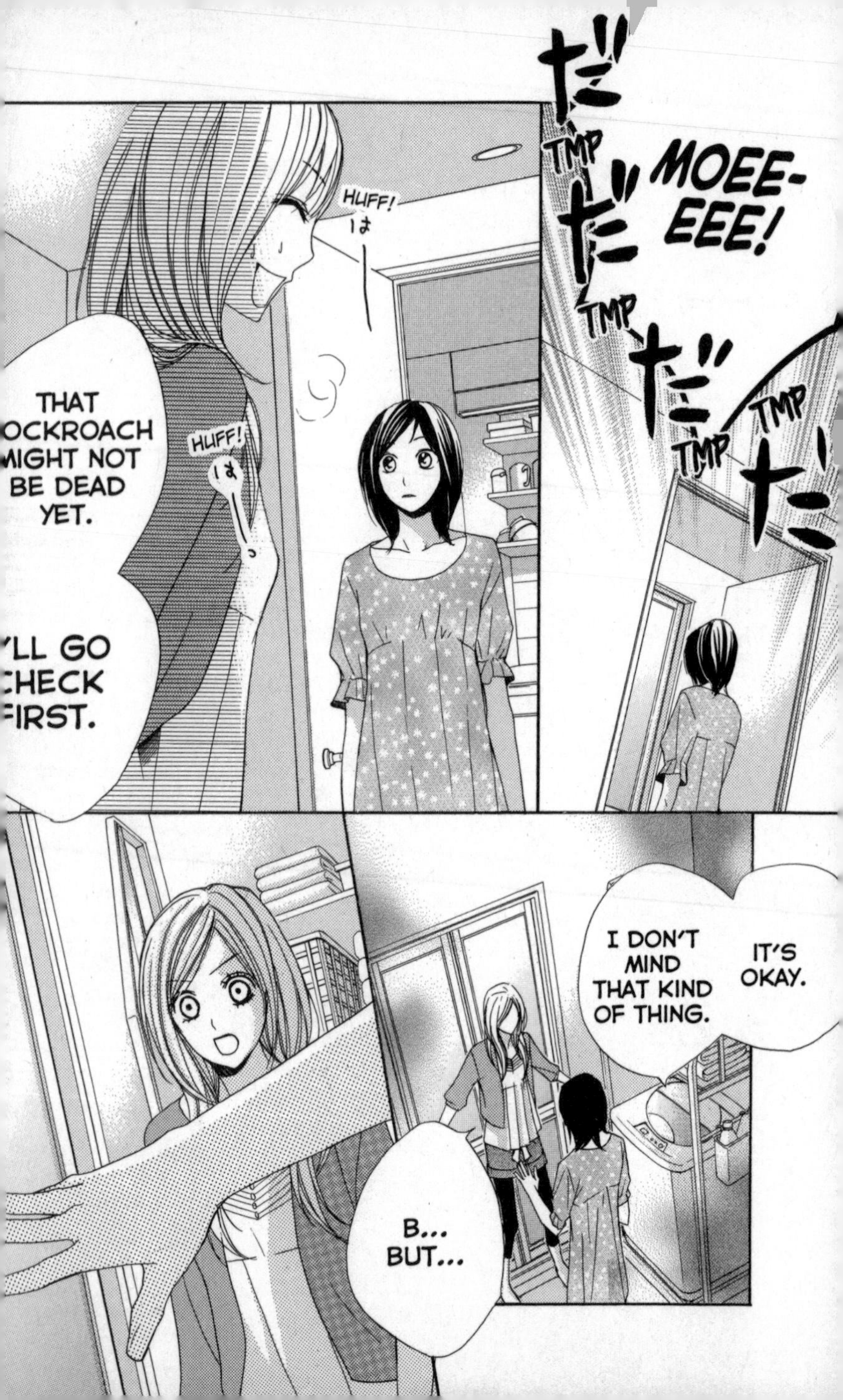
だ
TMP
だ
MOEEE-EEE!
TMP
だ
TMP
TMP
だ
HUFF!
は
THAT OCKROACH MIGHT NOT BE DEAD YET.
HUFF!
は
'LL GO HECK IRST.
IT'S OKAY.
I DON'T MIND THAT KIND OF THING.
B... BUT...

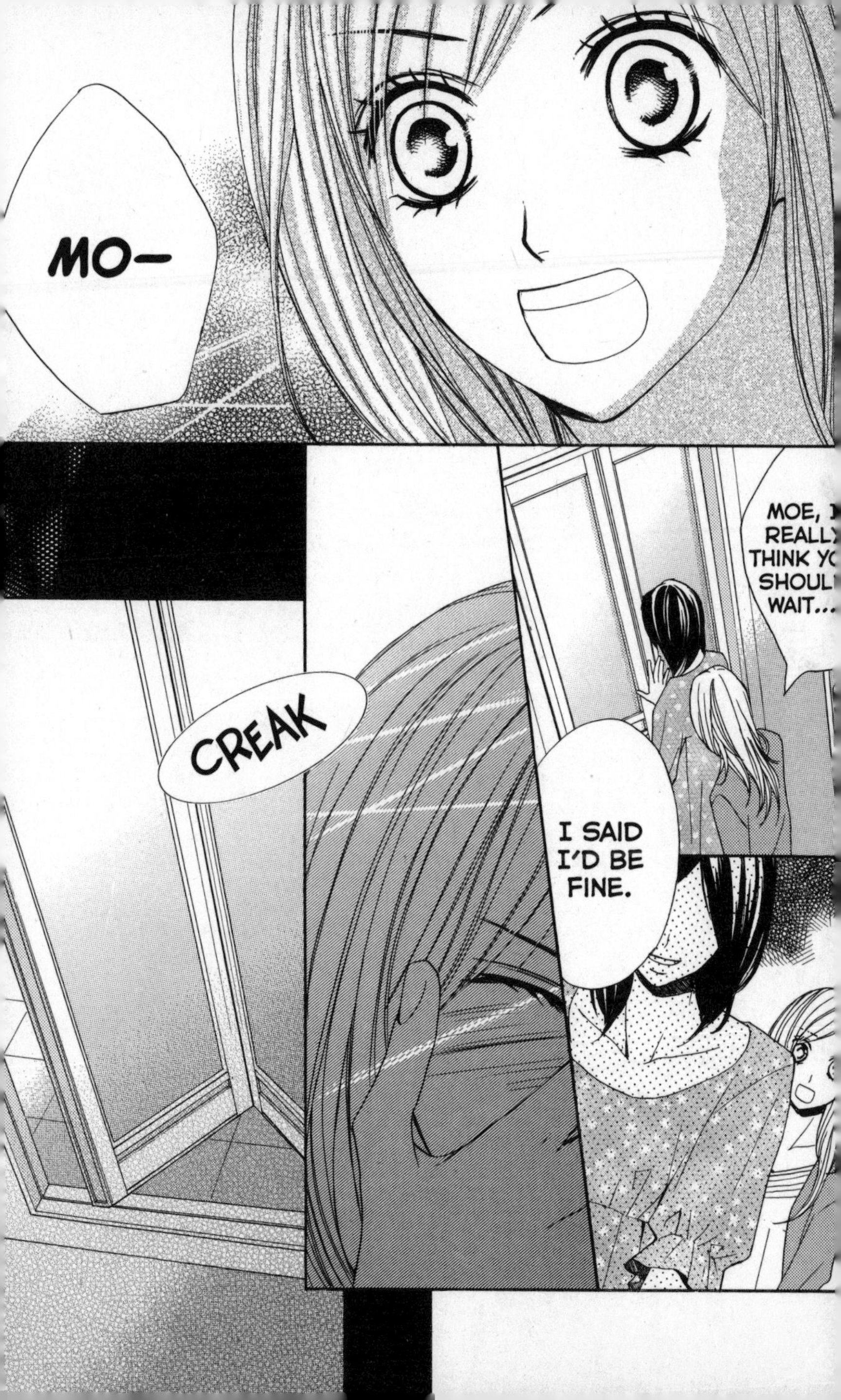
MO-
MOE, I REALLY THINK YO SHOUL WAIT...
I SAID I'D BE FINE.
CREAK

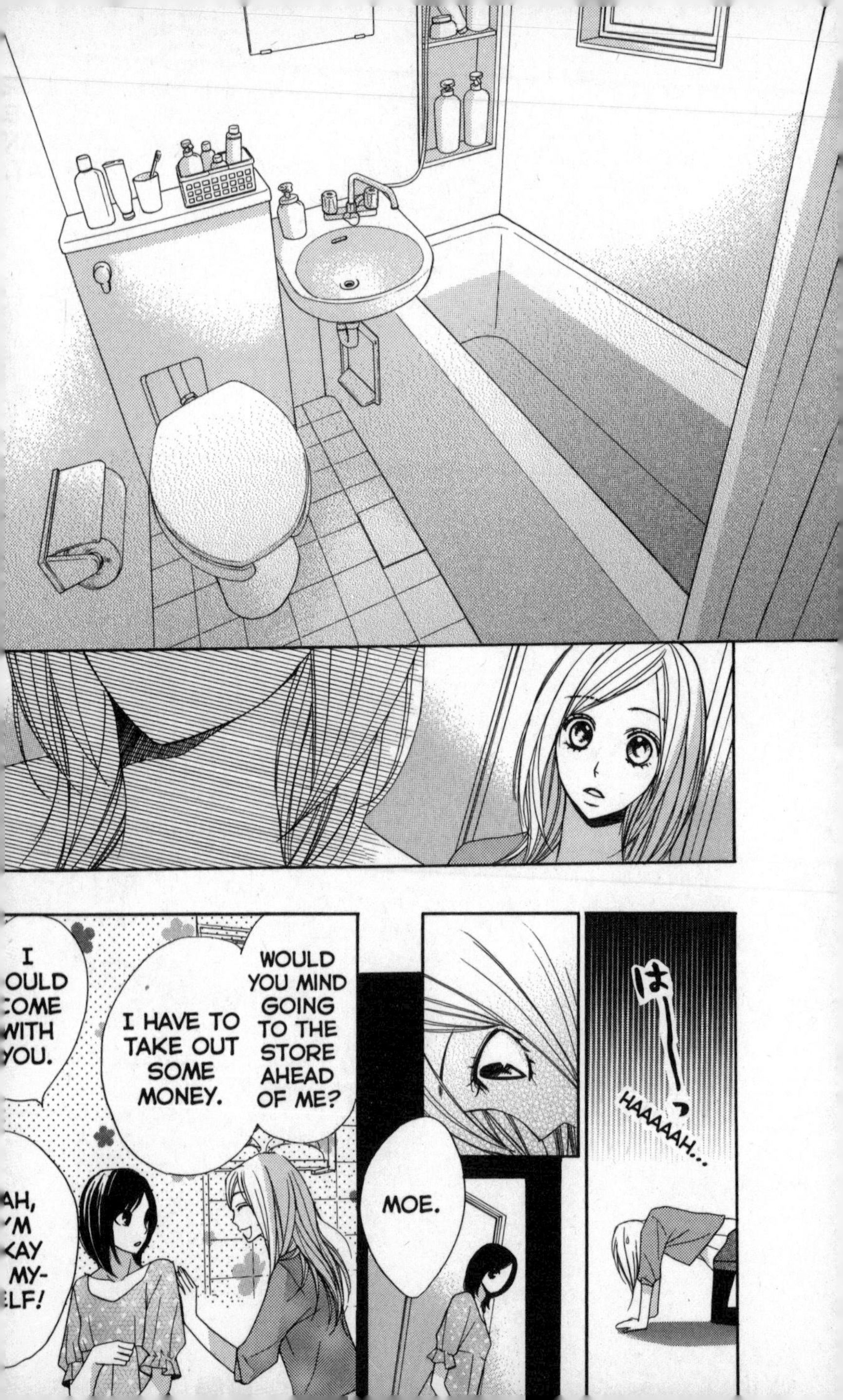
はーっ
HAAAAAH...
MOE.
WOULD YOU MIND GOING TO THE STORE AHEAD OF ME?
I HAVE TO TAKE OUT SOME MONEY.
I OULD COME WITH YOU.
AH, 'M KAY MY-ELF!

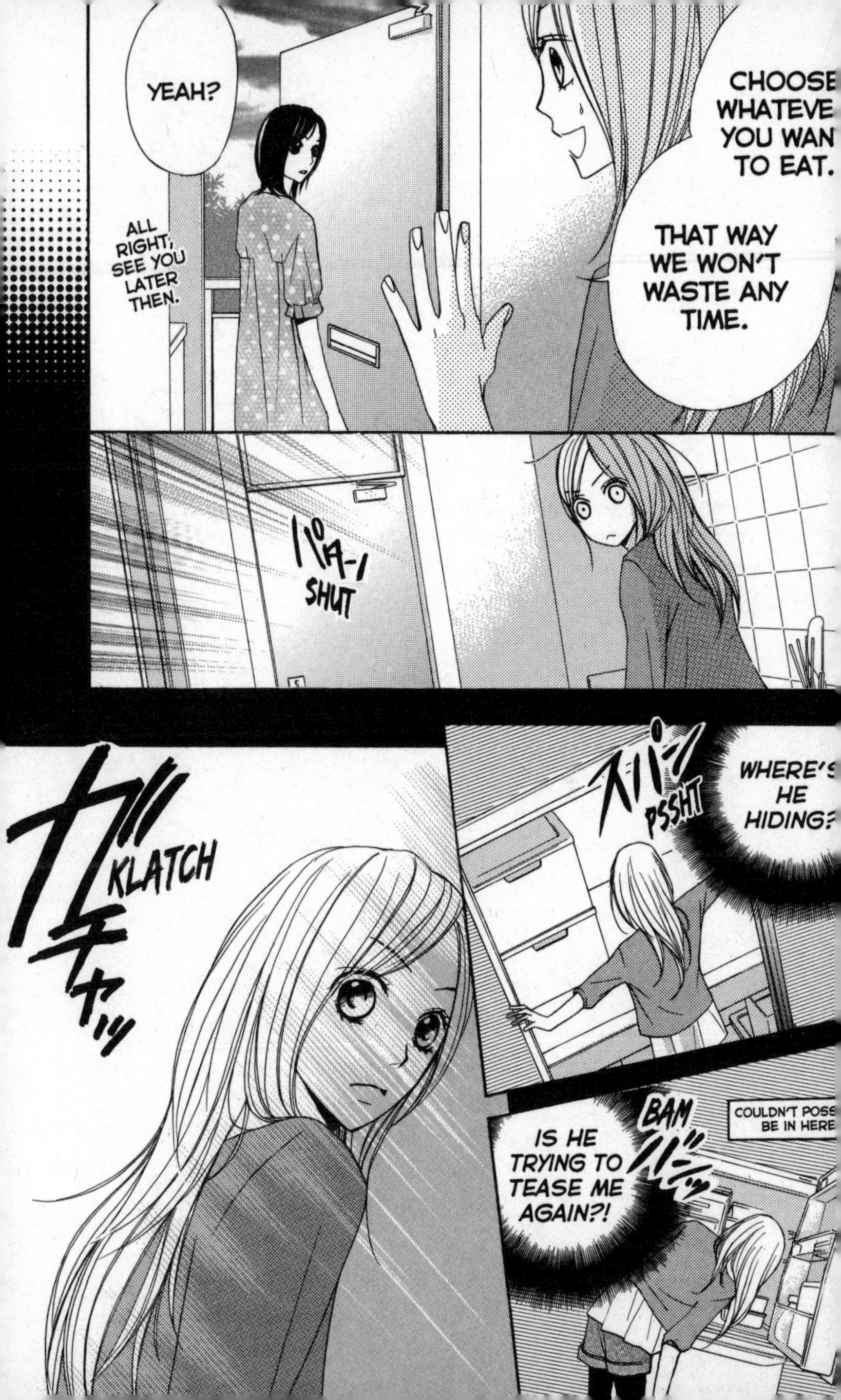
CHOOSE WHATEVE YOU WAN TO EAT.
THAT WAY WE WON'T WASTE ANY TIME.
YEAH?
ALL RIGHT, SEE YOU LATER THEN.
パタン
SHUT
スパーン
PSSHT
WHERE'S HE HIDING?
COULDN'T POSS BE IN HERE
BAM
バーン
IS HE TRYING TO TEASE ME AGAIN?!
ガチャッ
KLATCH

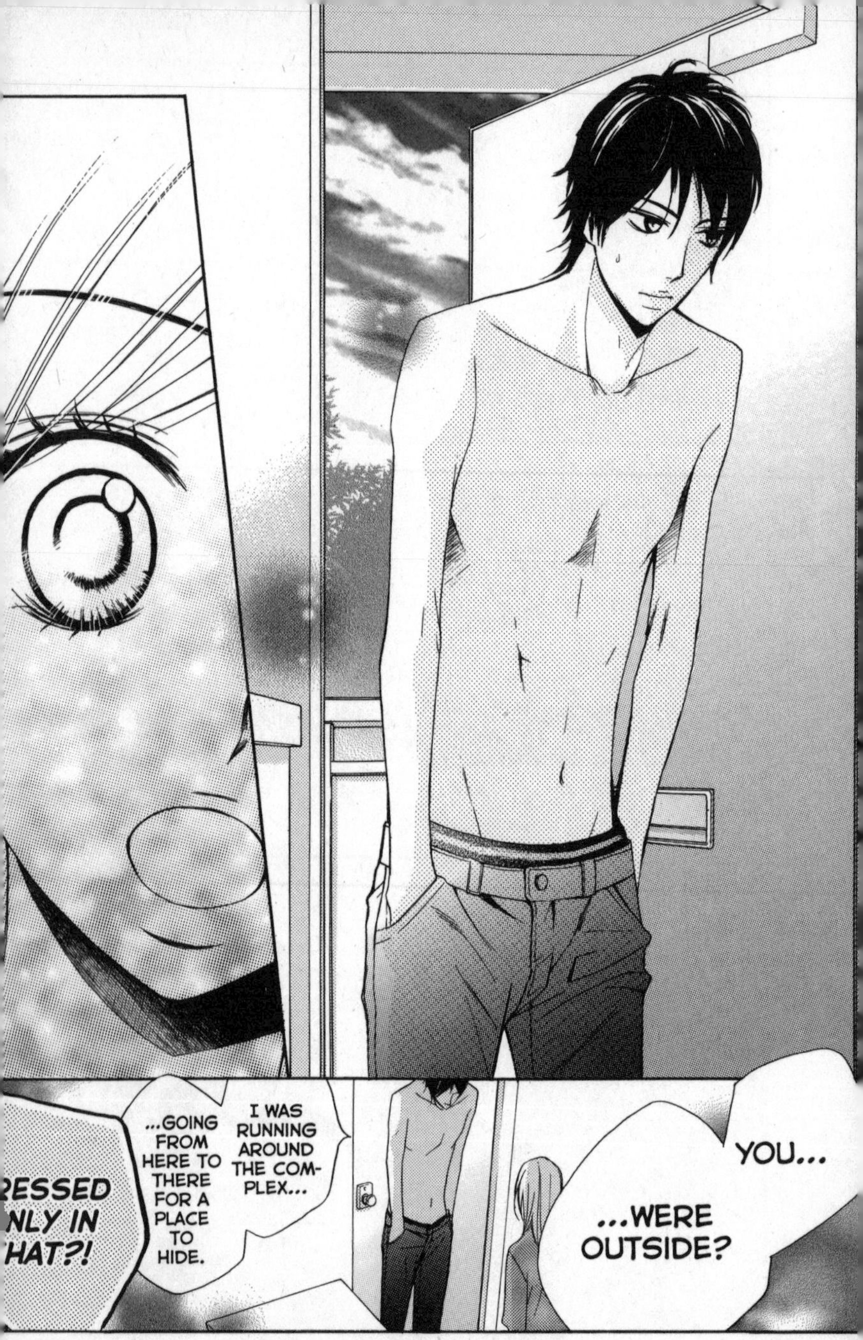
YOU...
...WERE OUTSIDE?
I WAS RUNNING AROUND THE COMPLEX...
...GOING FROM HERE TO THERE FOR A PLACE TO HIDE.
RESSED NLY IN HAT?!

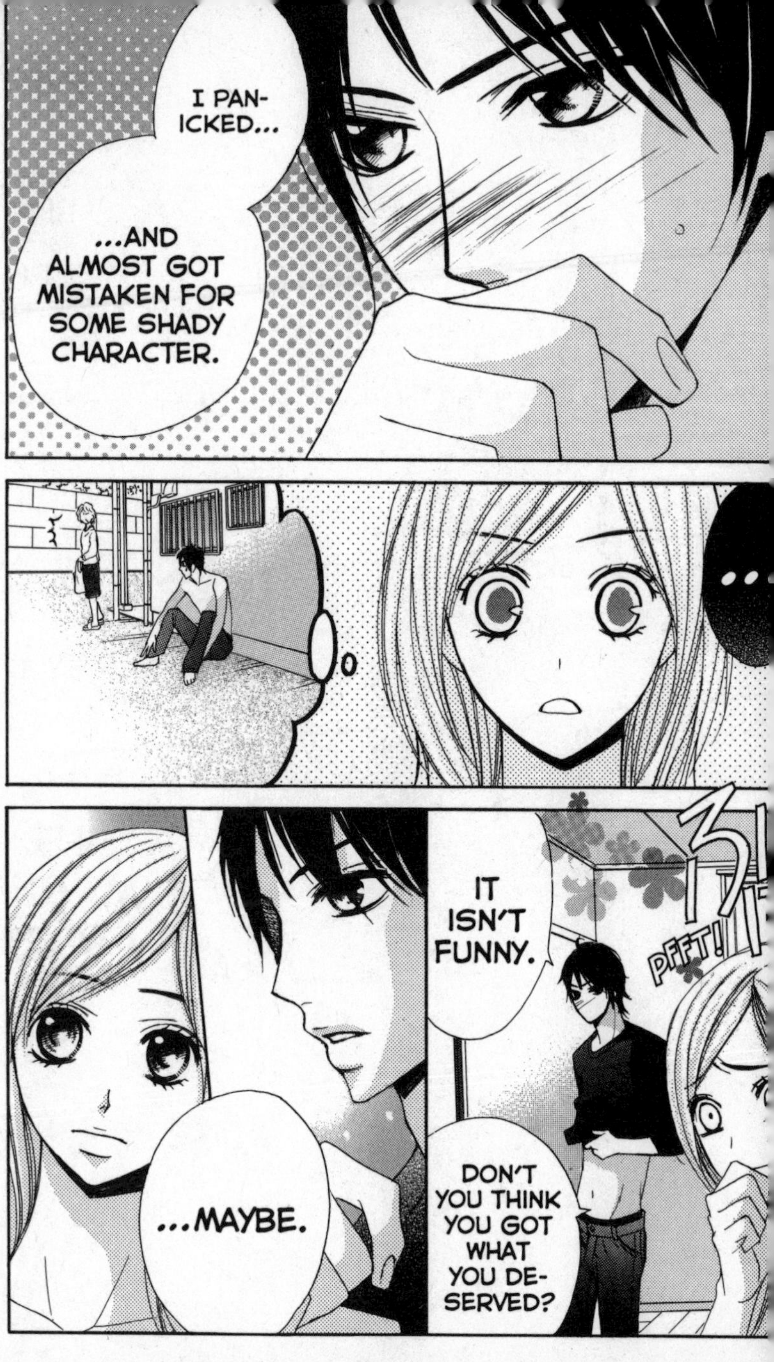
I PAN-
ICKED...
...AND
ALMOST GOT
MISTAKEN FOR
SOME SHADY
CHARACTER.
...
PFFT!
IT
ISN'T
FUNNY.
DON'T
YOU THINK
YOU GOT
WHAT
YOU DE-
SERVED?
...MAYBE.

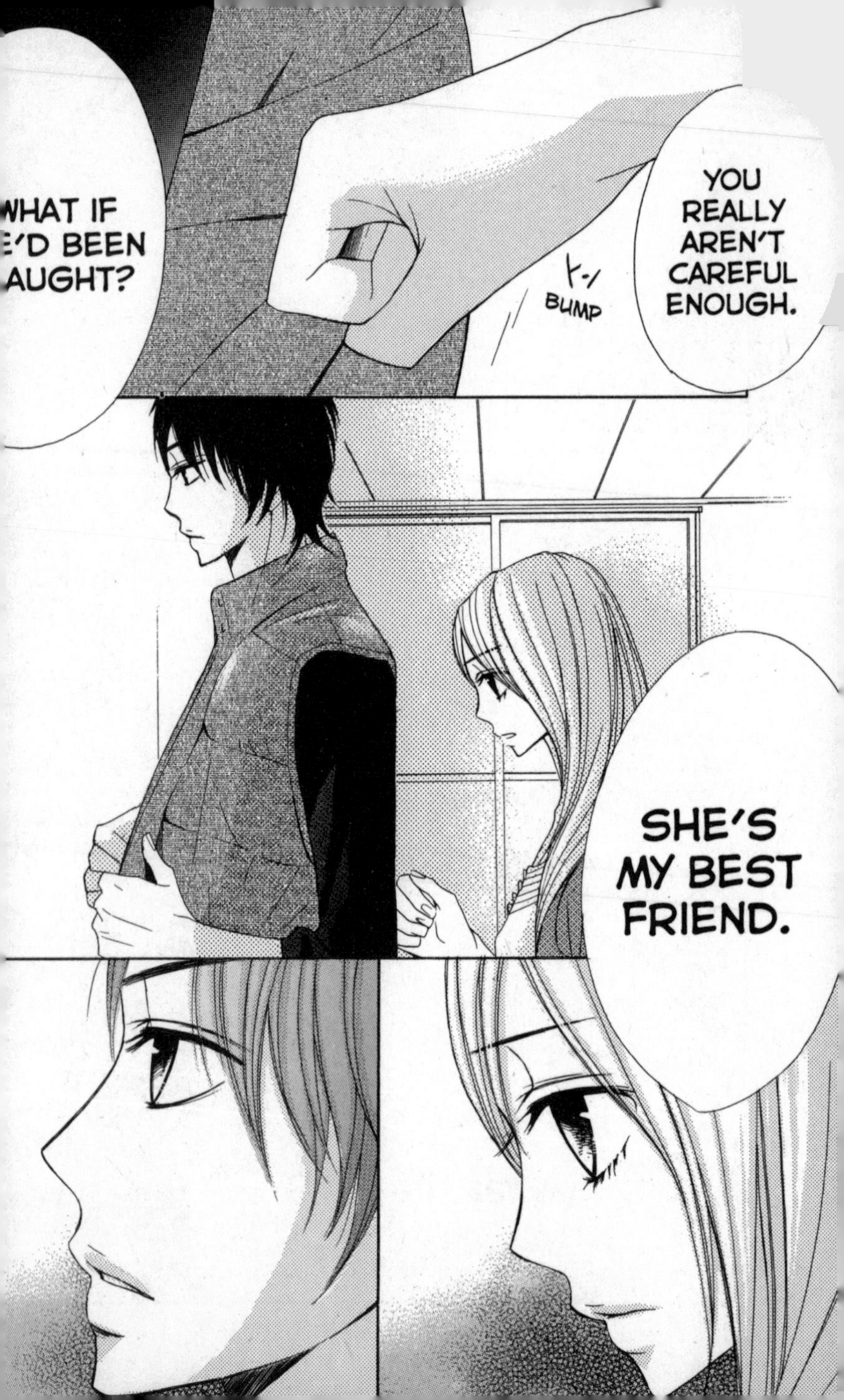
YOU REALLY AREN'T CAREFUL ENOUGH.
BUMP
WHAT IF E'D BEEN AUGHT?
SHE'S MY BEST FRIEND.

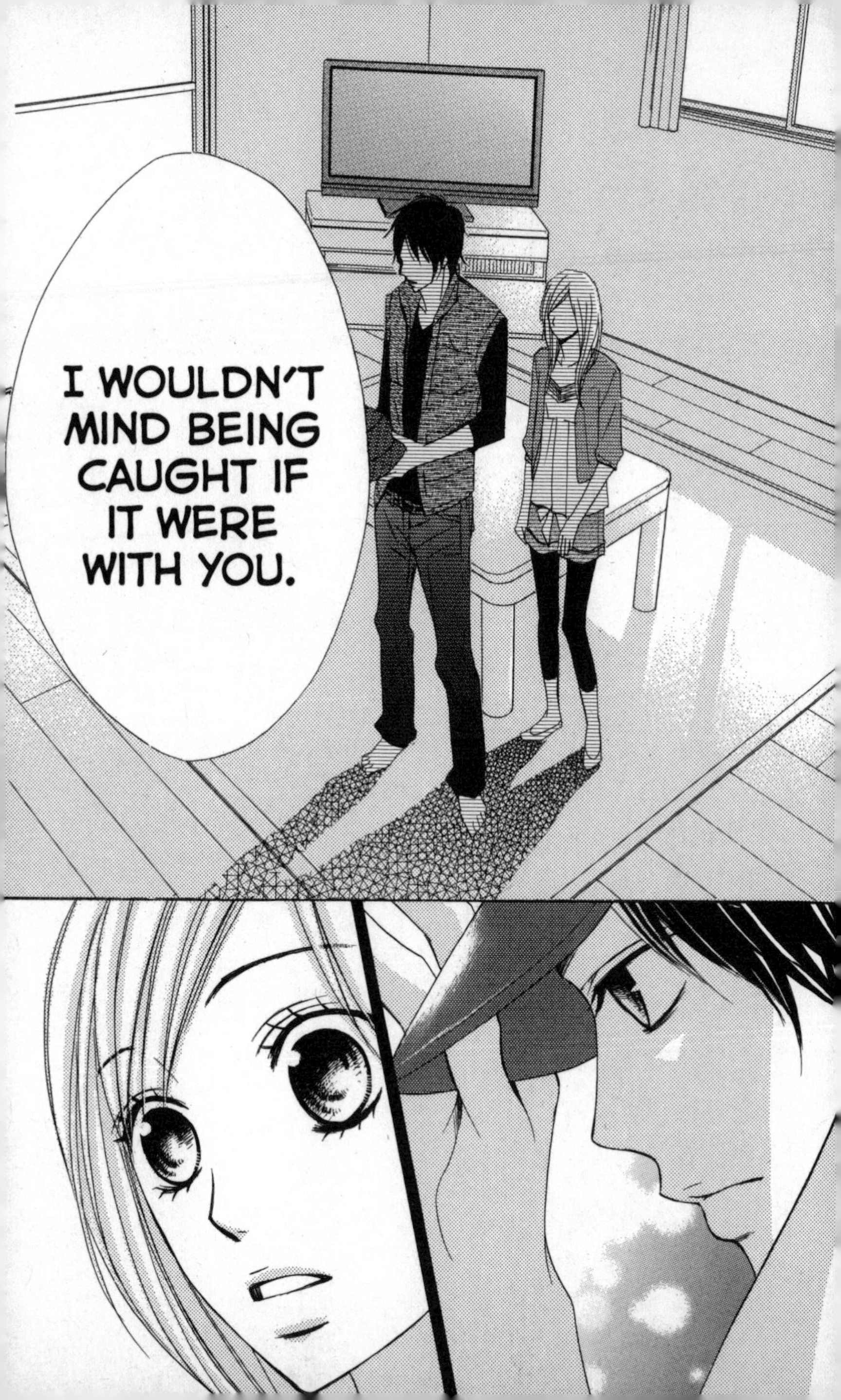
I WOULDN'T MIND BEING CAUGHT IF IT WERE WITH YOU.

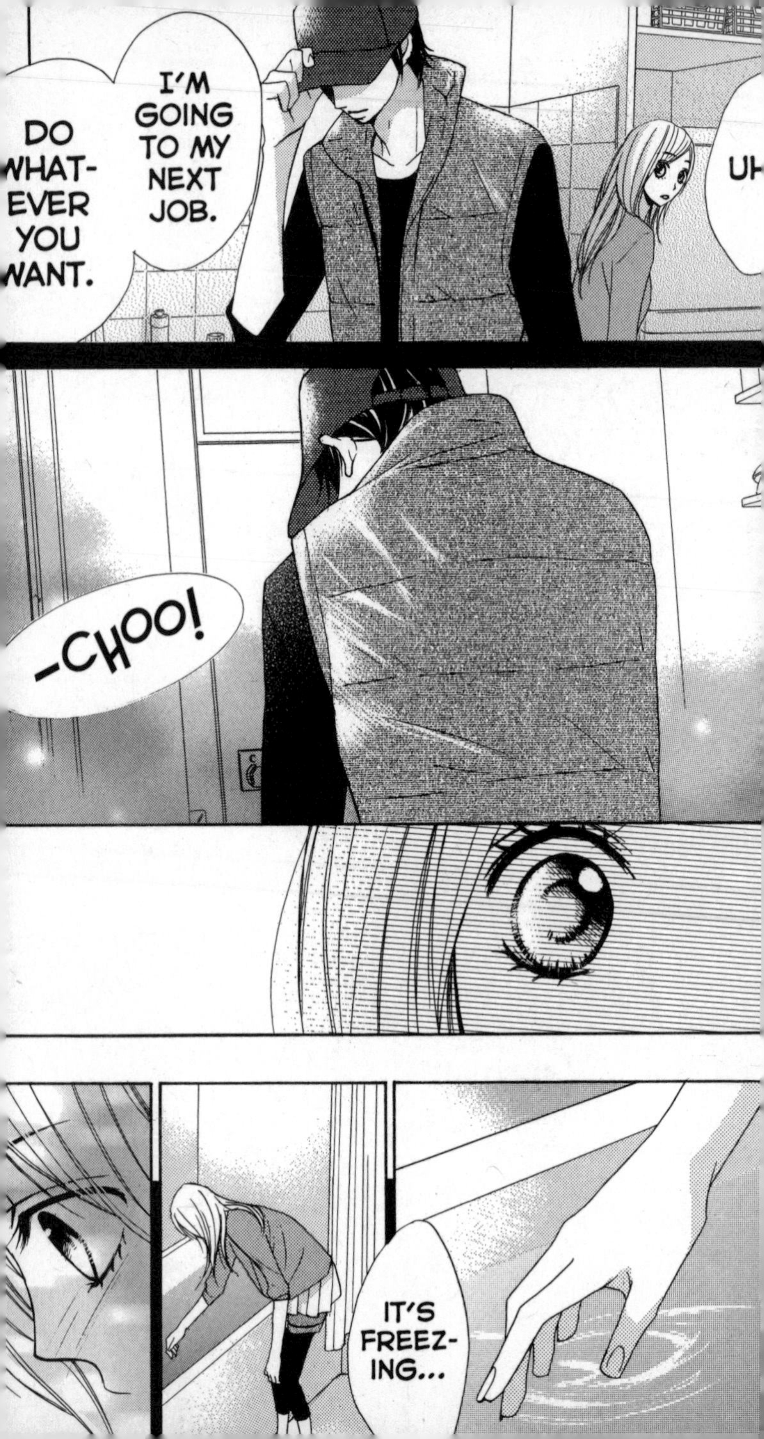
UH
I'M GOING TO MY NEXT JOB.
DO WHATEVER YOU WANT.
-CHOO!
IT'S FREEZING...

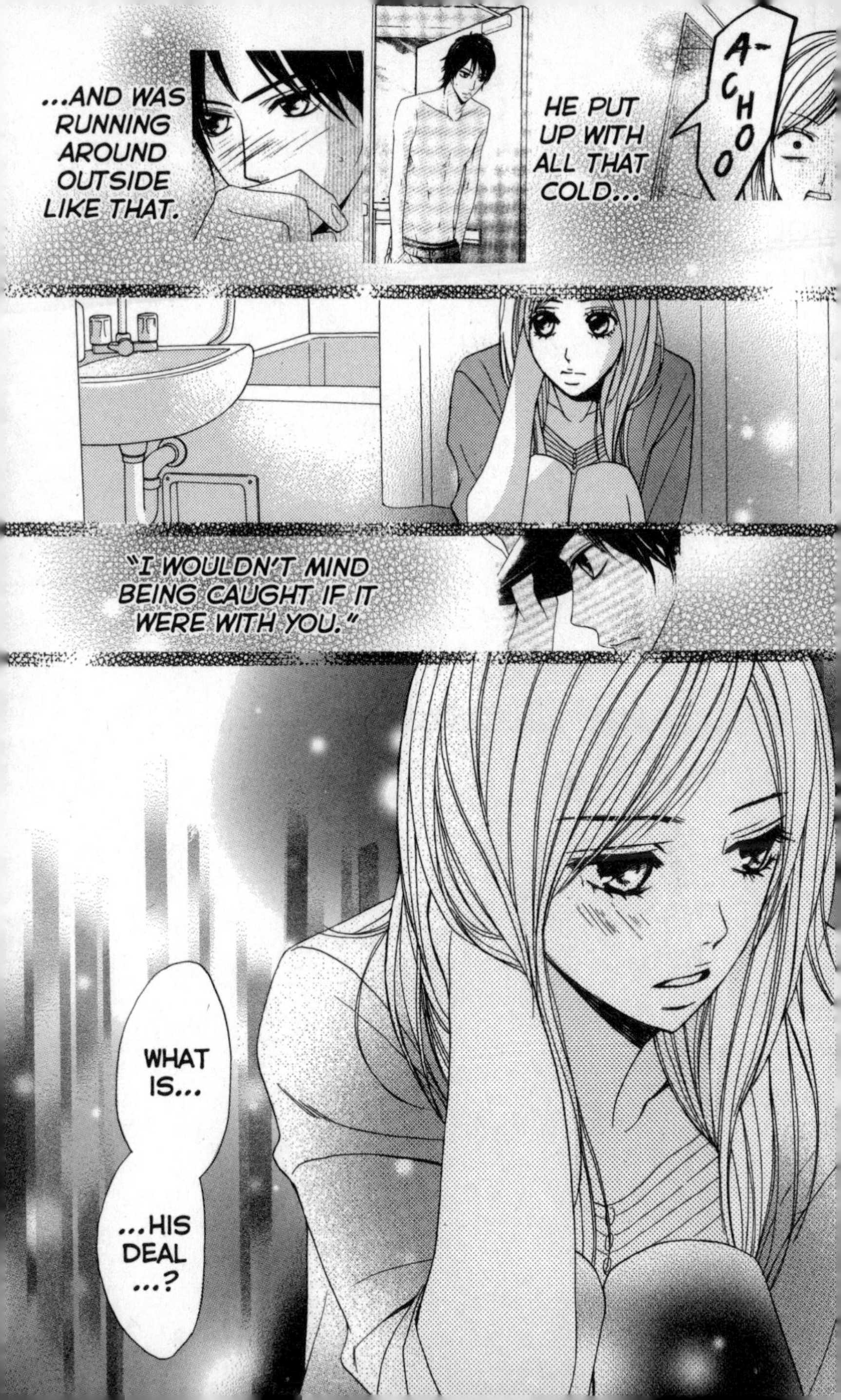
A-CHOO
HE PUT UP WITH ALL THAT COLD...
...AND WAS RUNNING AROUND OUTSIDE LIKE THAT.
"I WOULDN'T MIND BEING CAUGHT IF IT WERE WITH YOU."
WHAT IS...
...HIS DEAL...?

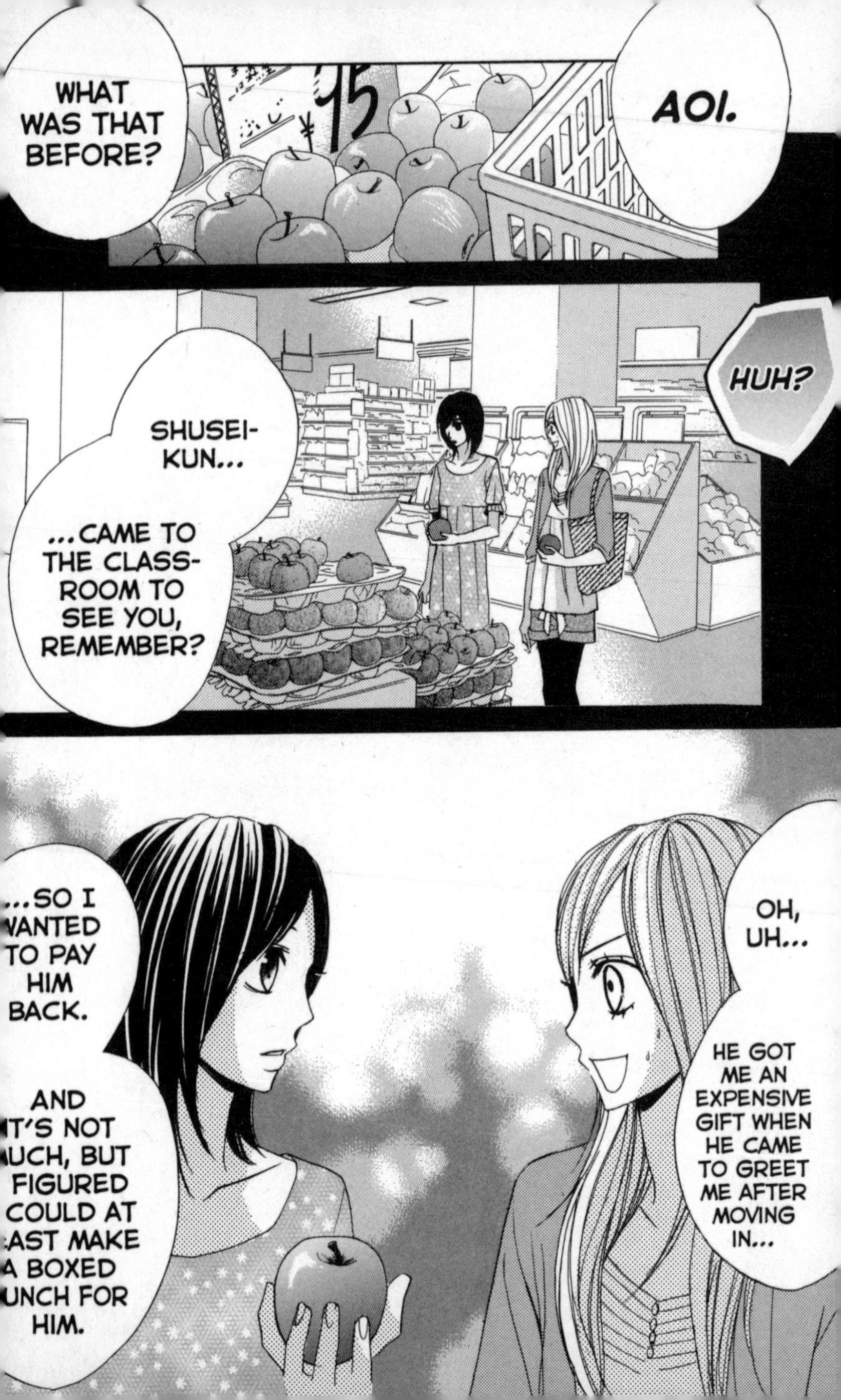
AOI.
WHAT WAS THAT BEFORE?
HUH?
SHUSEI-KUN...
...CAME TO THE CLASS-ROOM TO SEE YOU, REMEMBER?
OH, UH...
HE GOT ME AN EXPENSIVE GIFT WHEN HE CAME TO GREET ME AFTER MOVING IN...
...SO I VANTED TO PAY HIM BACK.
AND 'T'S NOT UCH, BUT FIGURED COULD AT AST MAKE A BOXED UNCH FOR HIM.

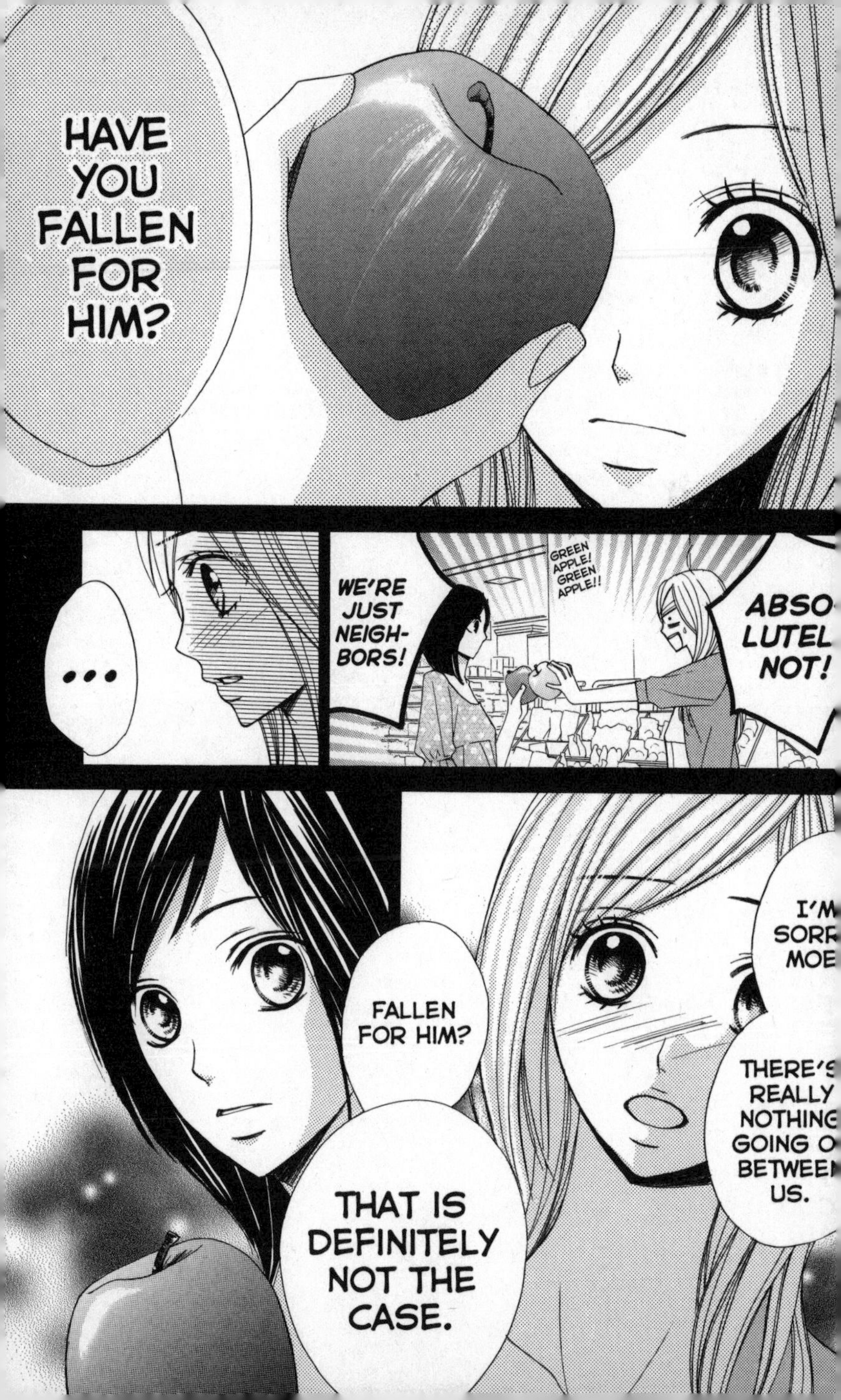
HAVE YOU FALLEN FOR HIM?
ABSO LUTEL NOT!
GREEN APPLE! GREEN APPLE!!
WE'RE JUST NEIGH-BORS!
...
I'M SORR MOE
THERE'S REALLY NOTHING GOING O BETWEE US.
FALLEN FOR HIM?
THAT IS DEFINITELY NOT THE CASE.

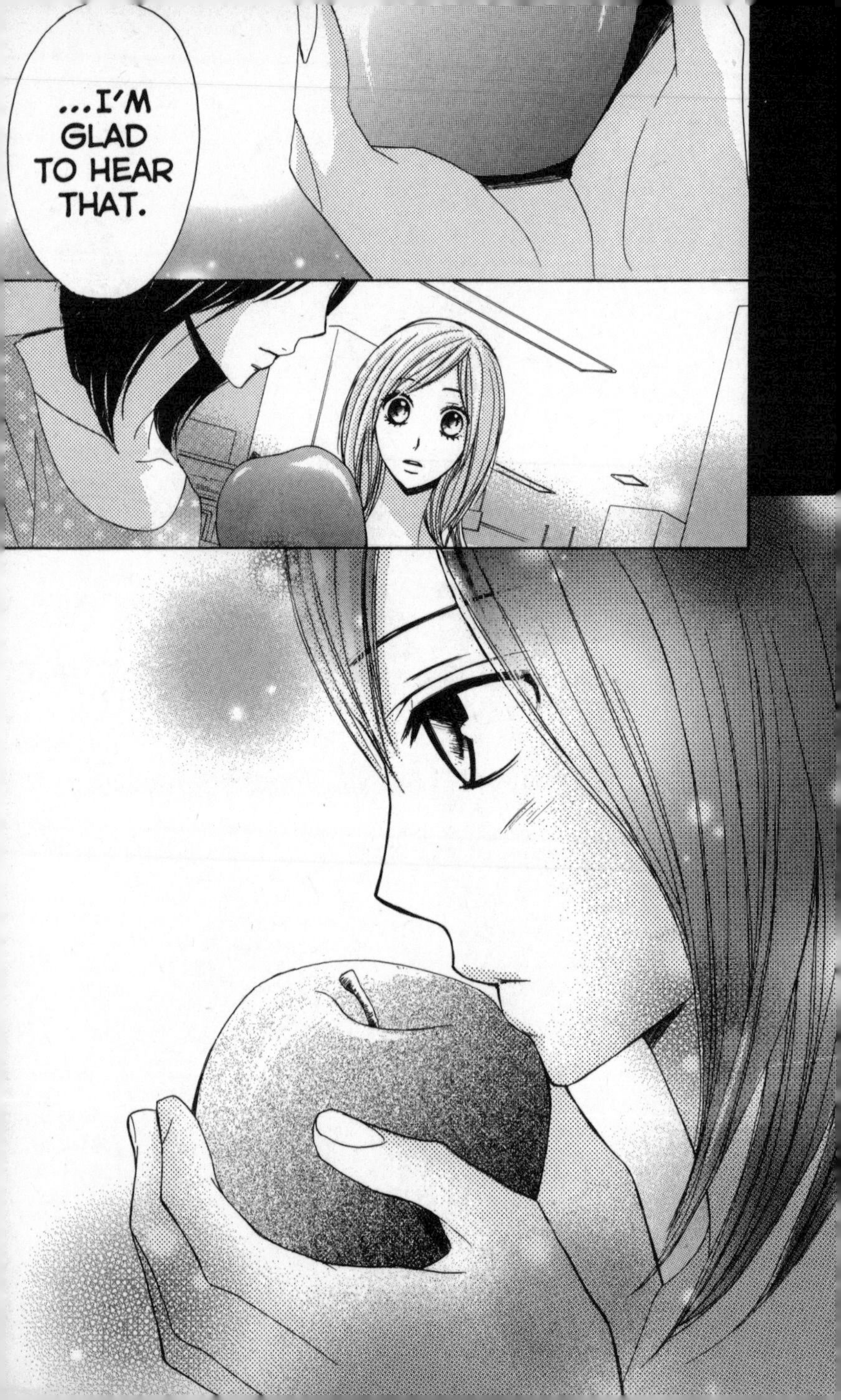
...I'M GLAD TO HEAR THAT.

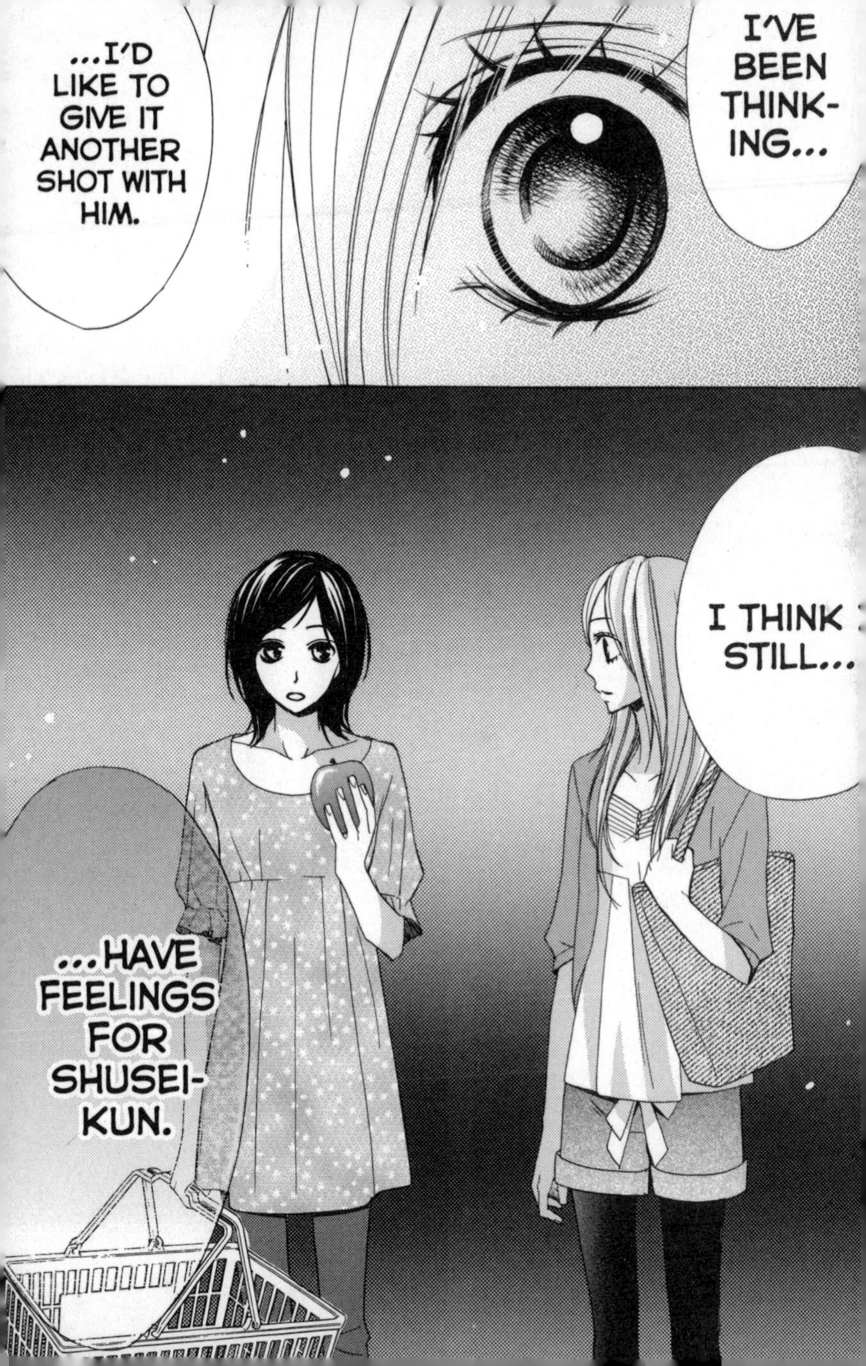
I'VE BEEN THINKING...
...I'D LIKE TO GIVE IT ANOTHER SHOT WITH HIM.
I THINK STILL...
...HAVE FEELINGS FOR SHUSEI-KUN.

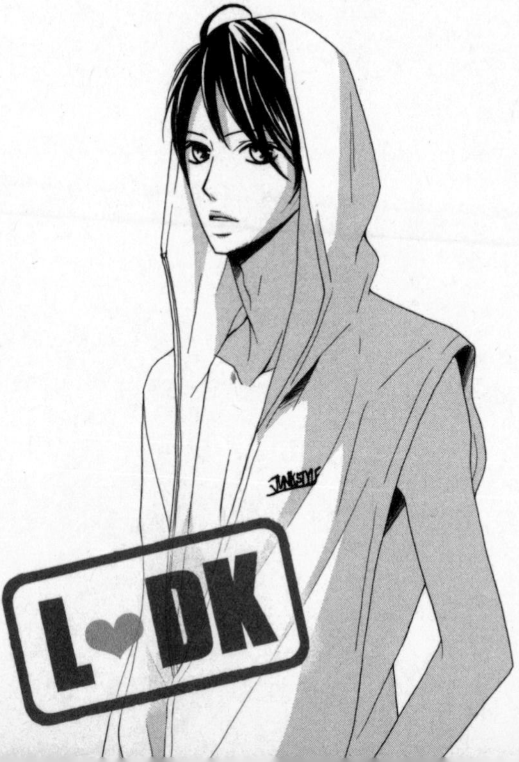
L♥DK

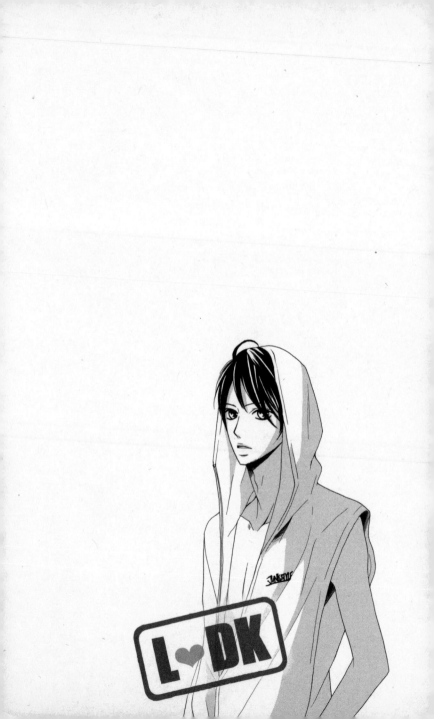

#3
True Feelings

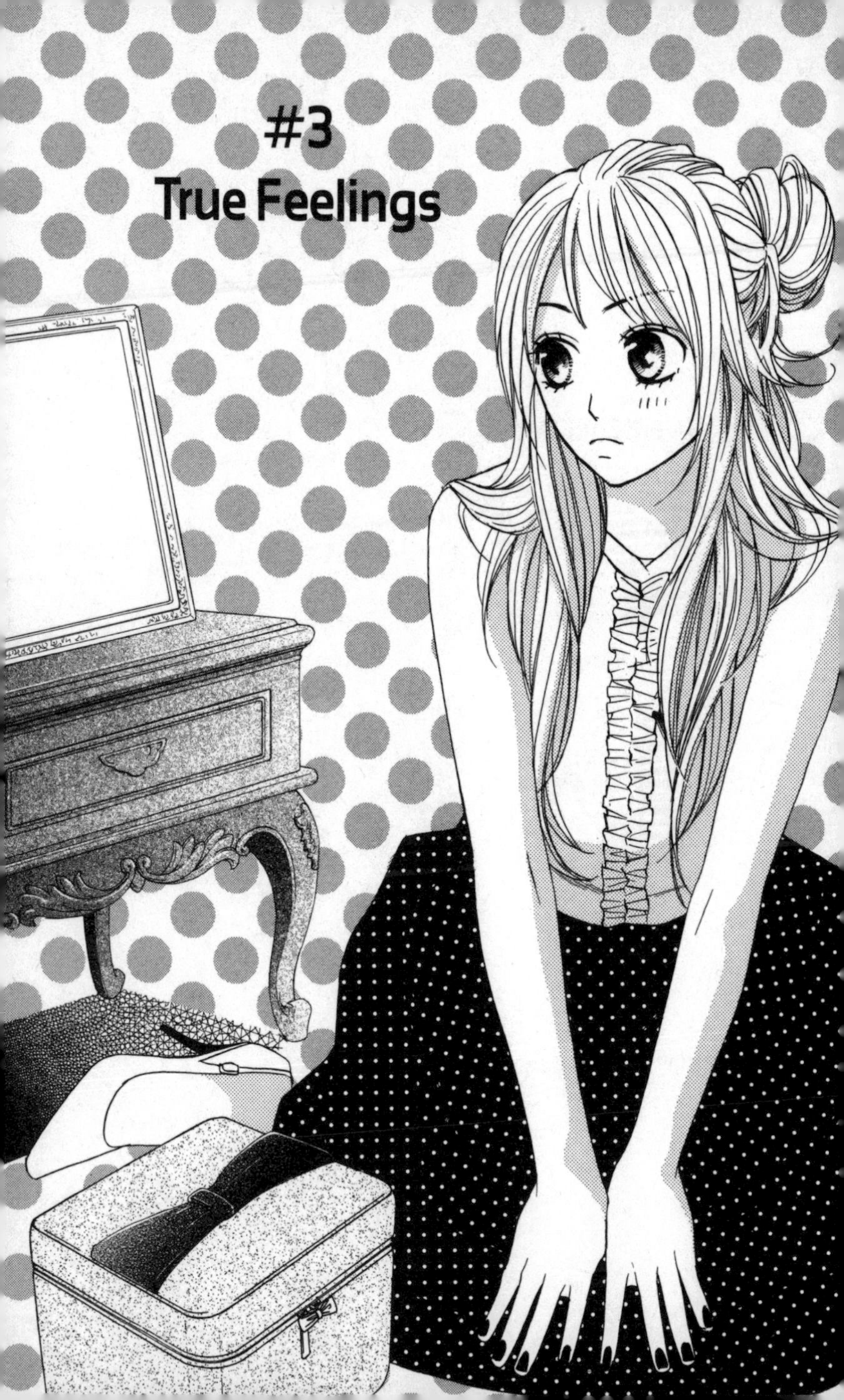

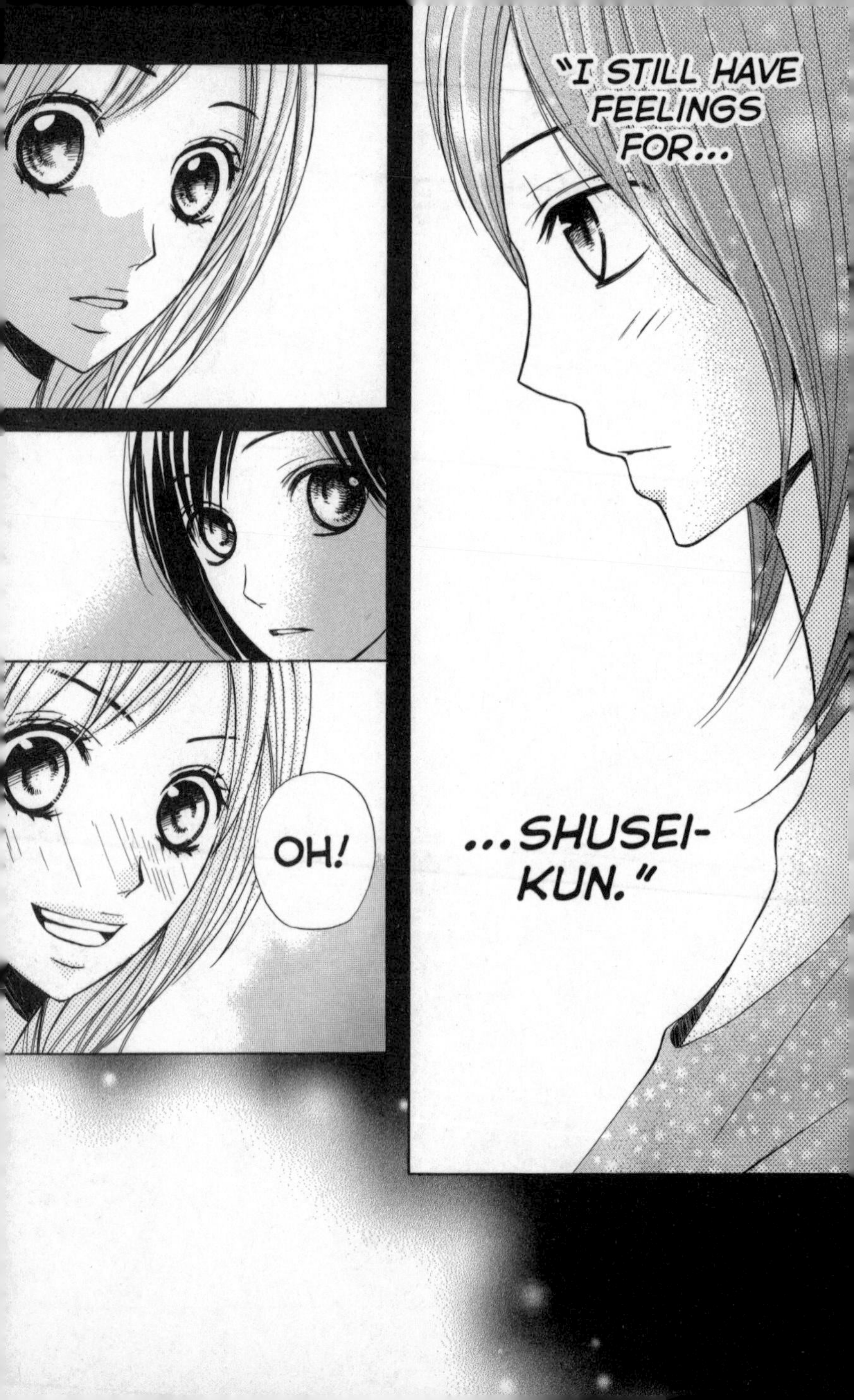
"I STILL HAVE FEELINGS FOR...
...SHUSEI-KUN."
OH!

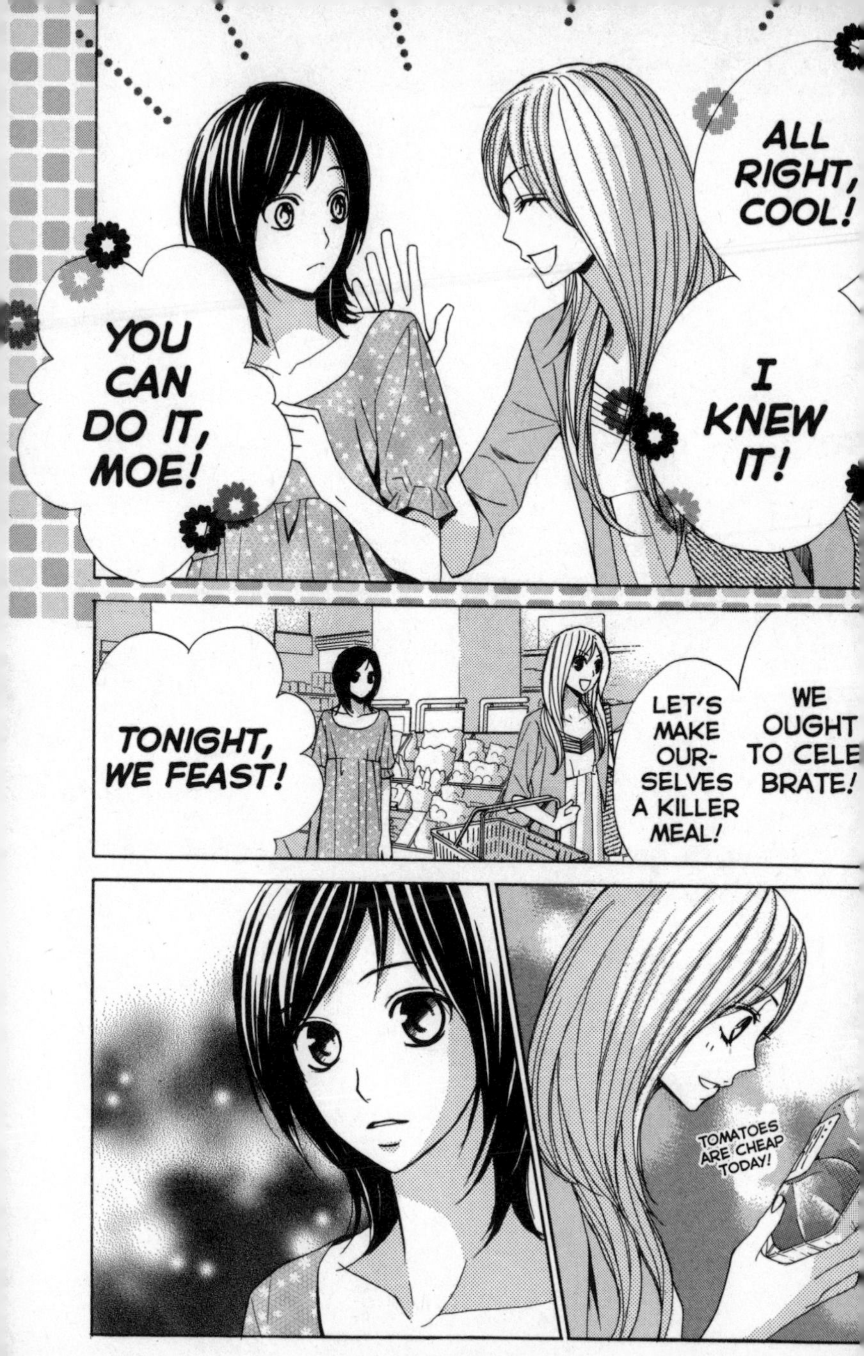
ALL RIGHT, COOL!
I KNEW IT!
YOU CAN DO IT, MOE!
WE OUGHT TO CELE BRATE!
LET'S MAKE OUR-SELVES A KILLER MEAL!
TONIGHT, WE FEAST!
TOMATOES ARE CHEAP TODAY!

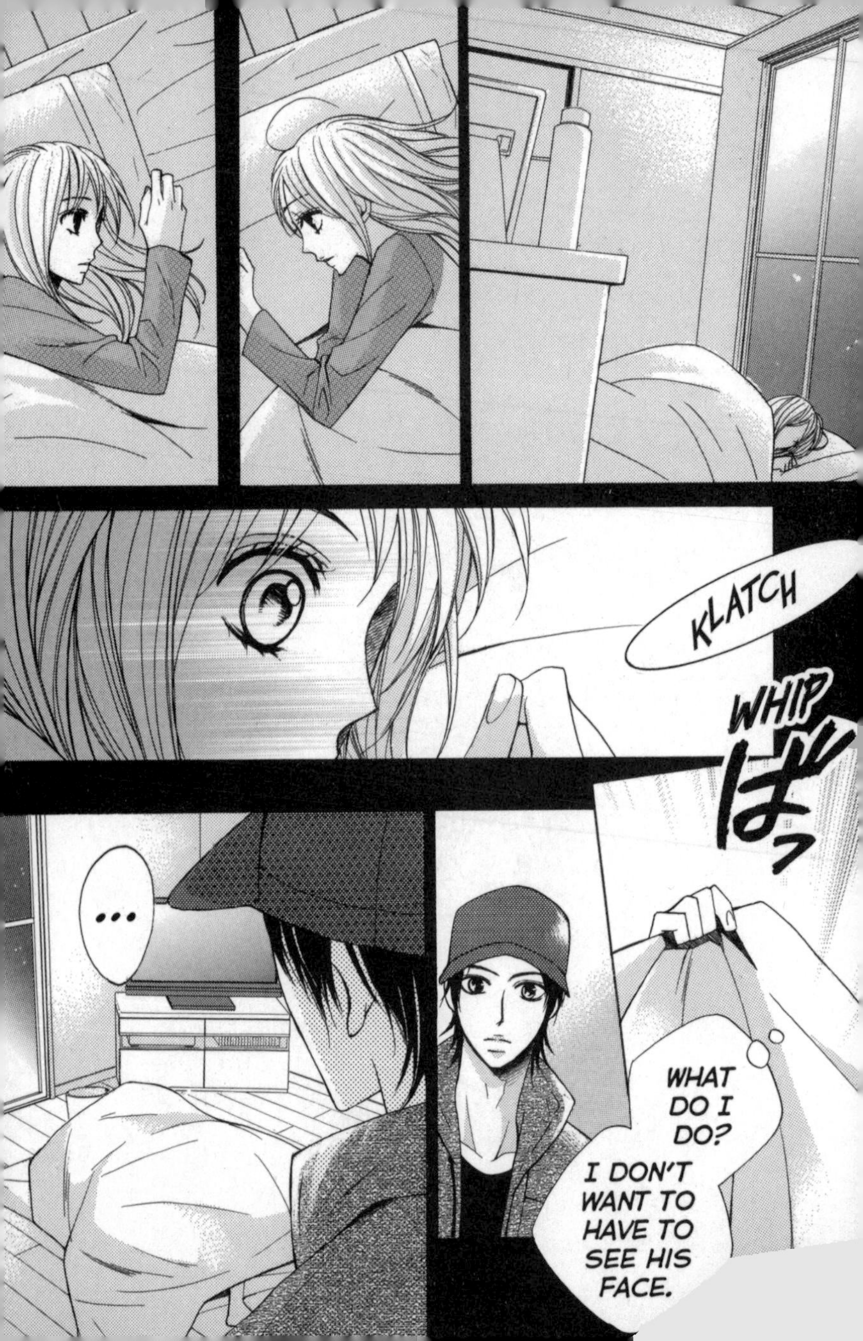
KLATCH
WHIP
ばっ
WHAT DO I DO?
I DON'T WANT TO HAVE TO SEE HIS FACE.
...

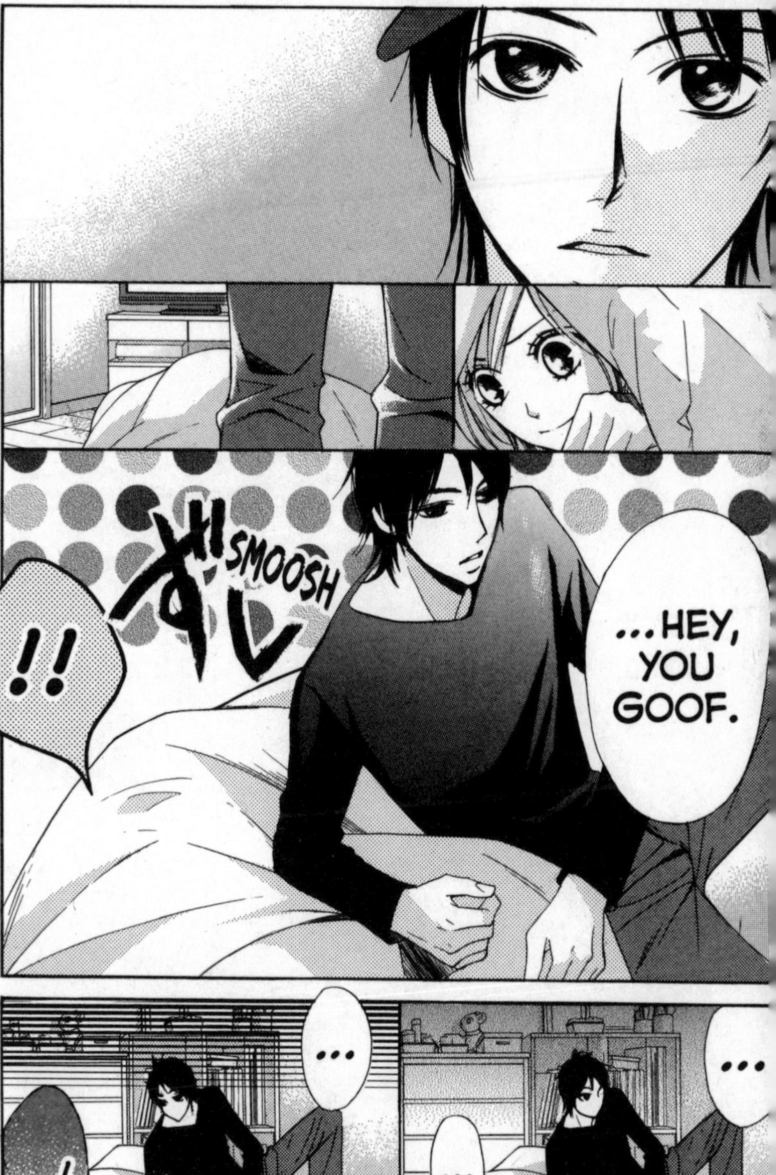
...HEY, YOU GOOF.
SMOOSH
!!
...
...
...
...!

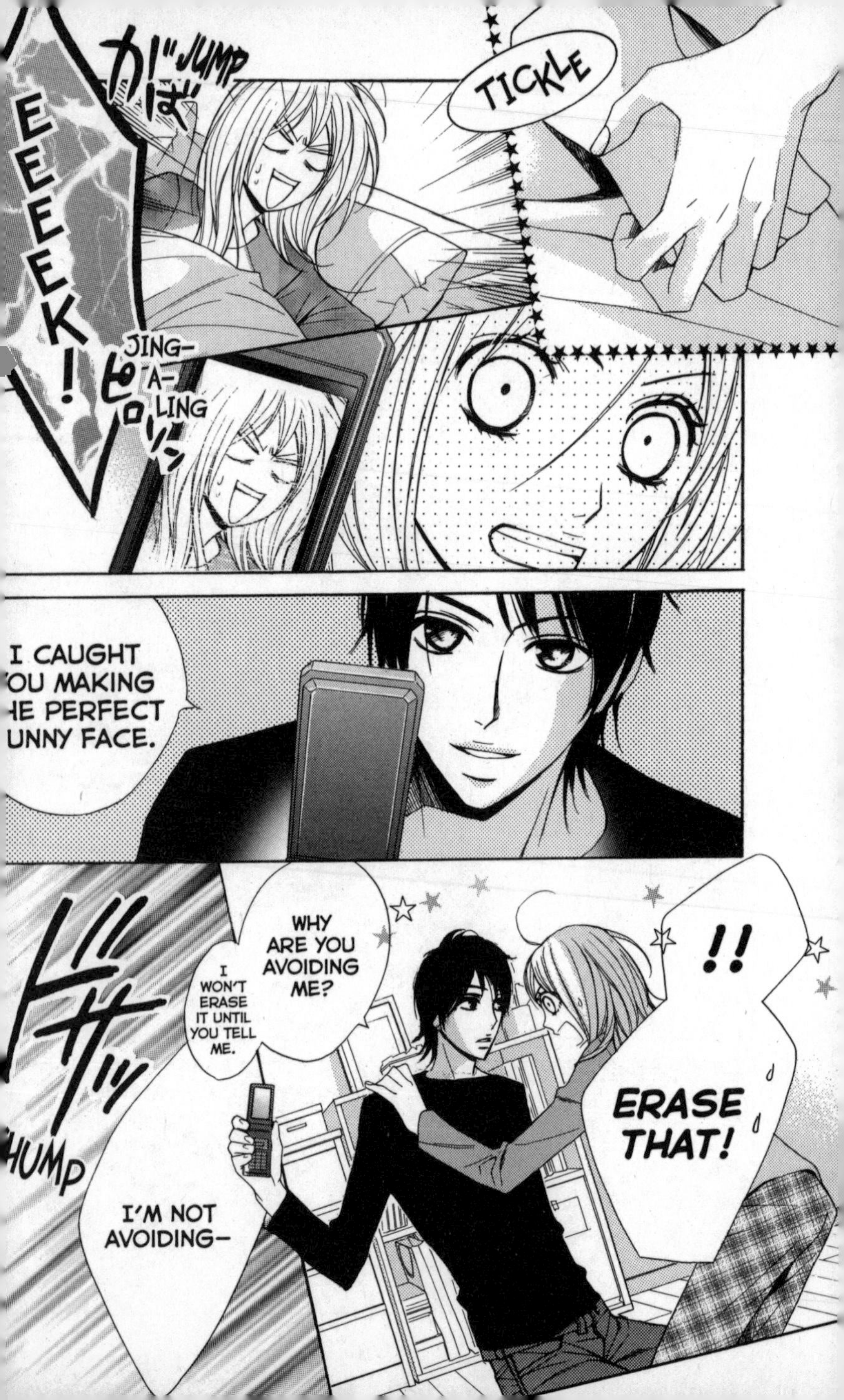
TICKLE
JUMP
EEEEEK!
JING-A-LING
I CAUGHT
OU MAKING
HE PERFECT
UNNY FACE.
!!
ERASE THAT!
WHY ARE YOU AVOIDING ME?
I WON'T ERASE IT UNTIL YOU TELL ME.
I'M NOT AVOIDING–
HUMP

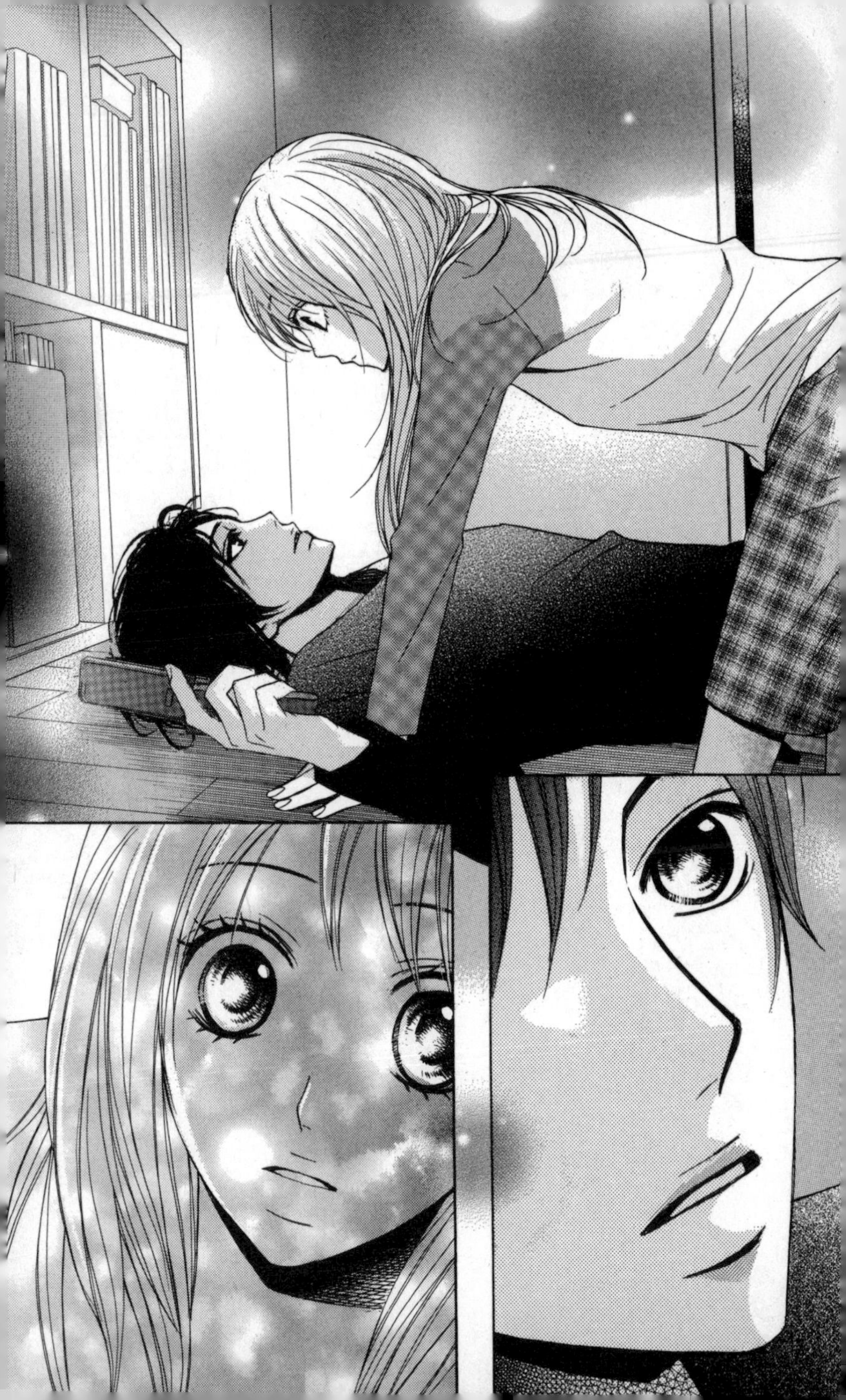

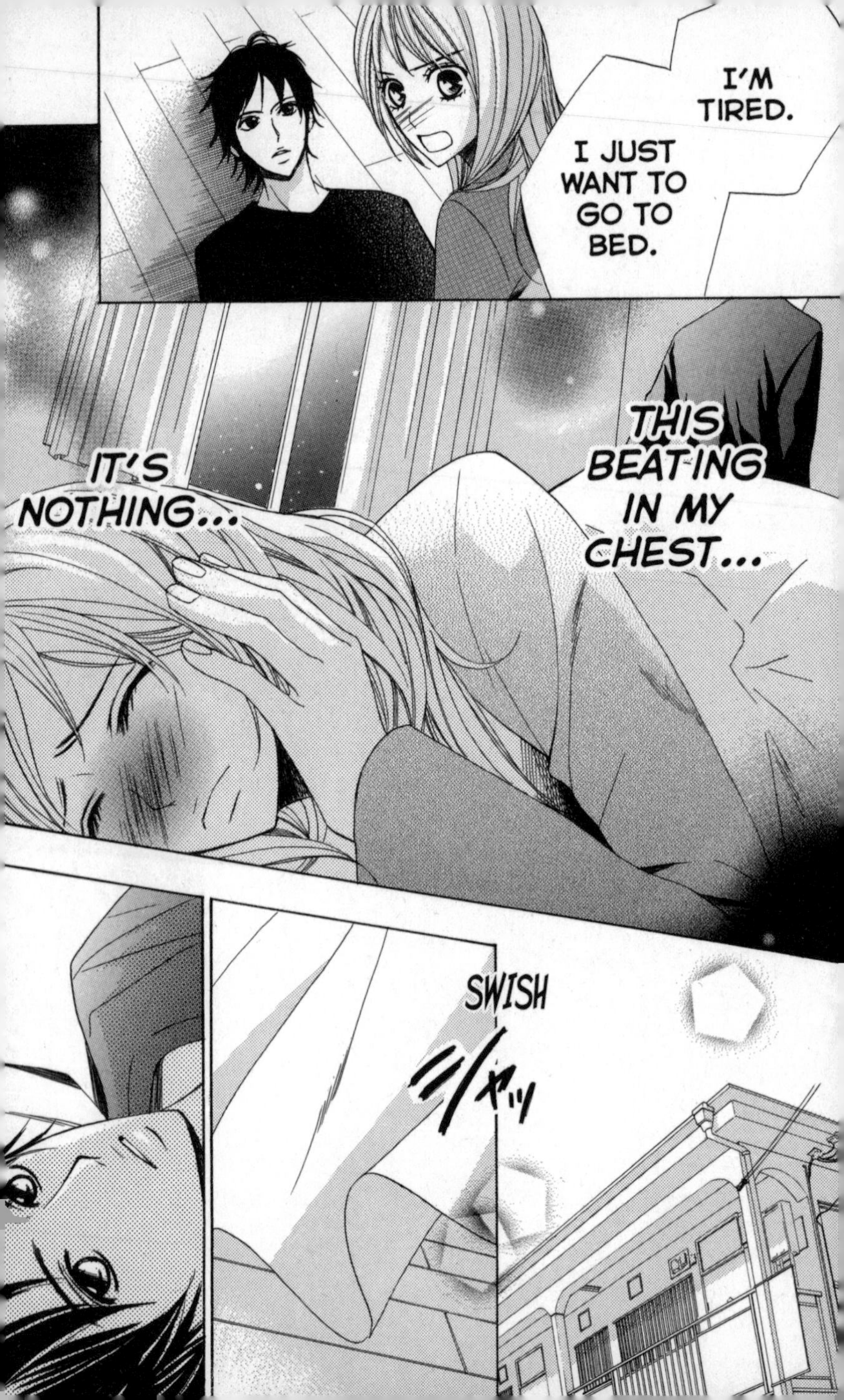
I'M TIRED.
I JUST WANT TO GO TO BED.
THIS BEATING IN MY CHEST...
IT'S NOTHING...
SWISH
シャッ

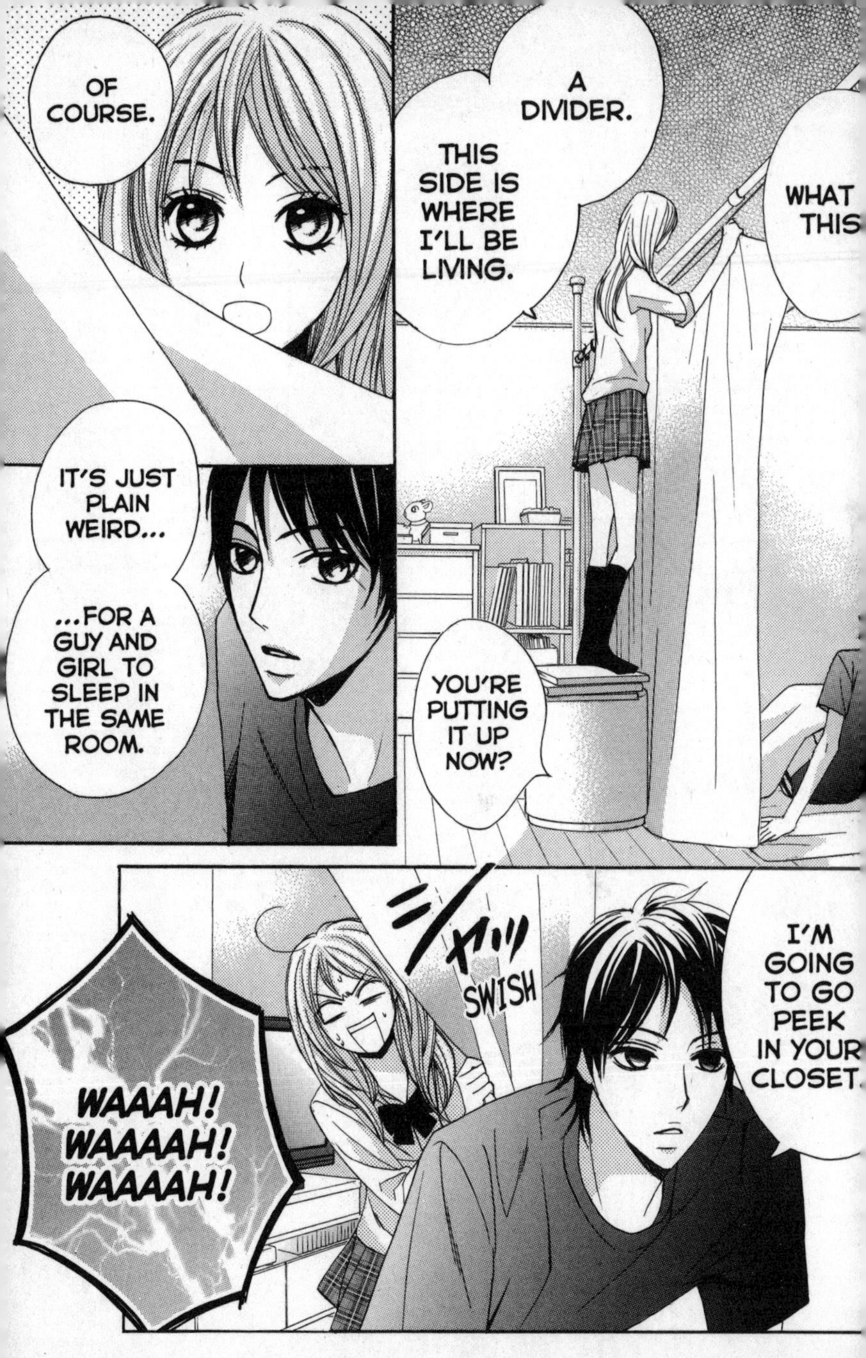
WHAT THIS
A DIVIDER.
THIS SIDE IS WHERE I'LL BE LIVING.
YOU'RE PUTTING IT UP NOW?
OF COURSE.
IT'S JUST PLAIN WEIRD...
...FOR A GUY AND GIRL TO SLEEP IN THE SAME ROOM.
I'M GOING TO GO PEEK IN YOUR CLOSET.
シャッ
SWISH
WAAAH! WAAAAH! WAAAAH!

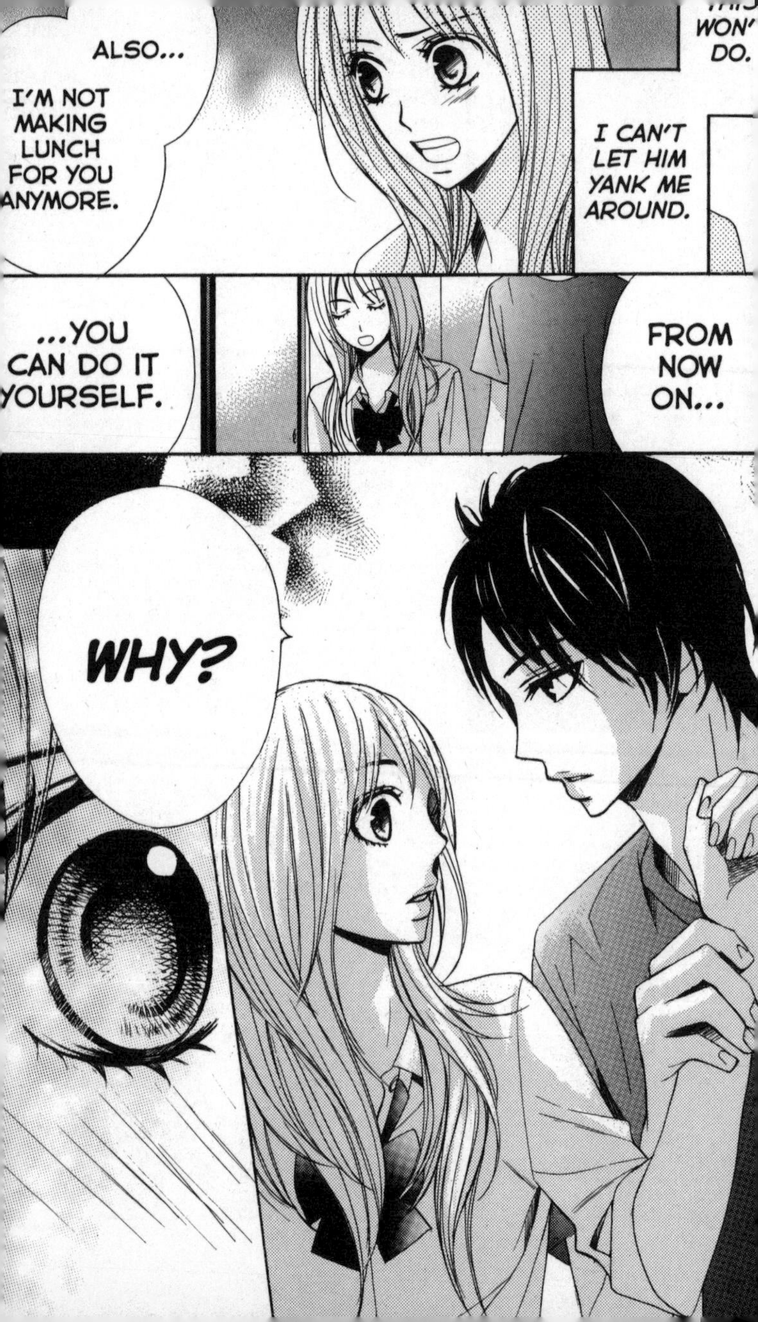
WON'
DO.
I CAN'T LET HIM YANK ME AROUND.
ALSO...
I'M NOT MAKING LUNCH FOR YOU ANYMORE.
FROM NOW ON...
...YOU CAN DO IT YOURSELF.
WHY?

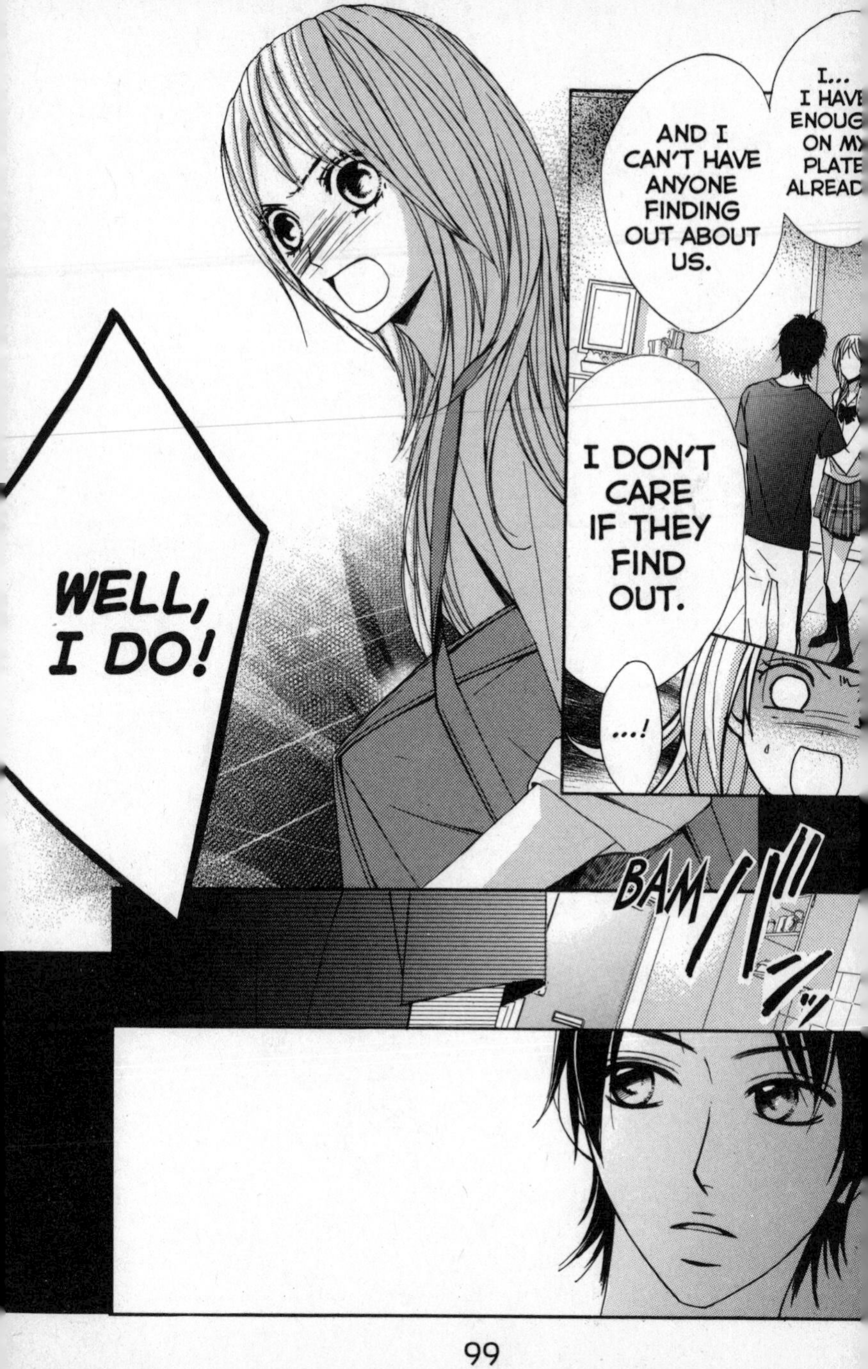
I... I HAVE ENOUG ON M PLATE ALREAD
AND I CAN'T HAVE ANYONE FINDING OUT ABOUT US.
I DON'T CARE IF THEY FIND OUT.
...!
WELL, I DO!
BAM

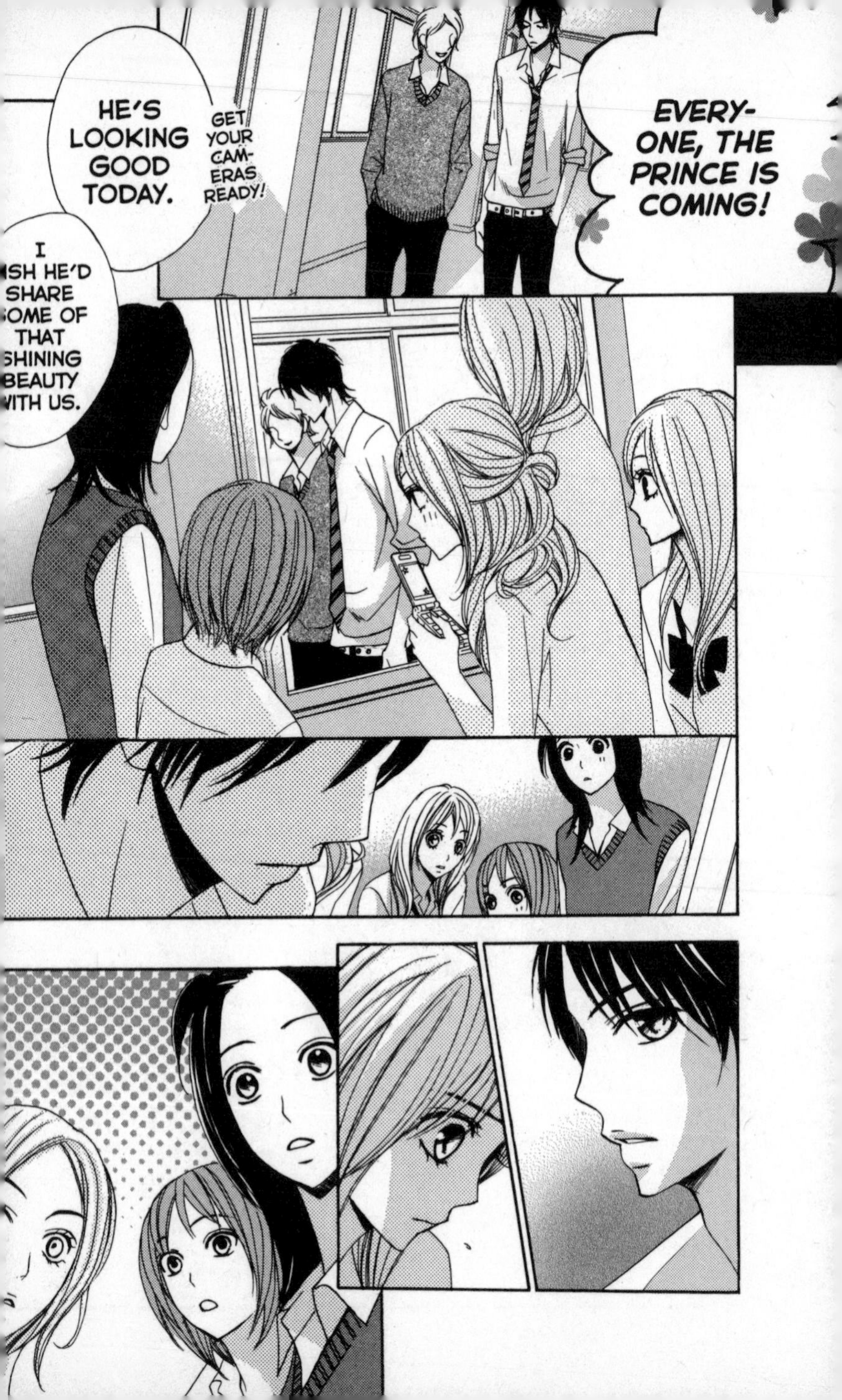
EVERY-ONE, THE PRINCE IS COMING!
GET YOUR CAM-ERAS READY!
HE'S LOOKING GOOD TODAY.
I SH HE'D SHARE OME OF THAT HINING BEAUTY ITH US.

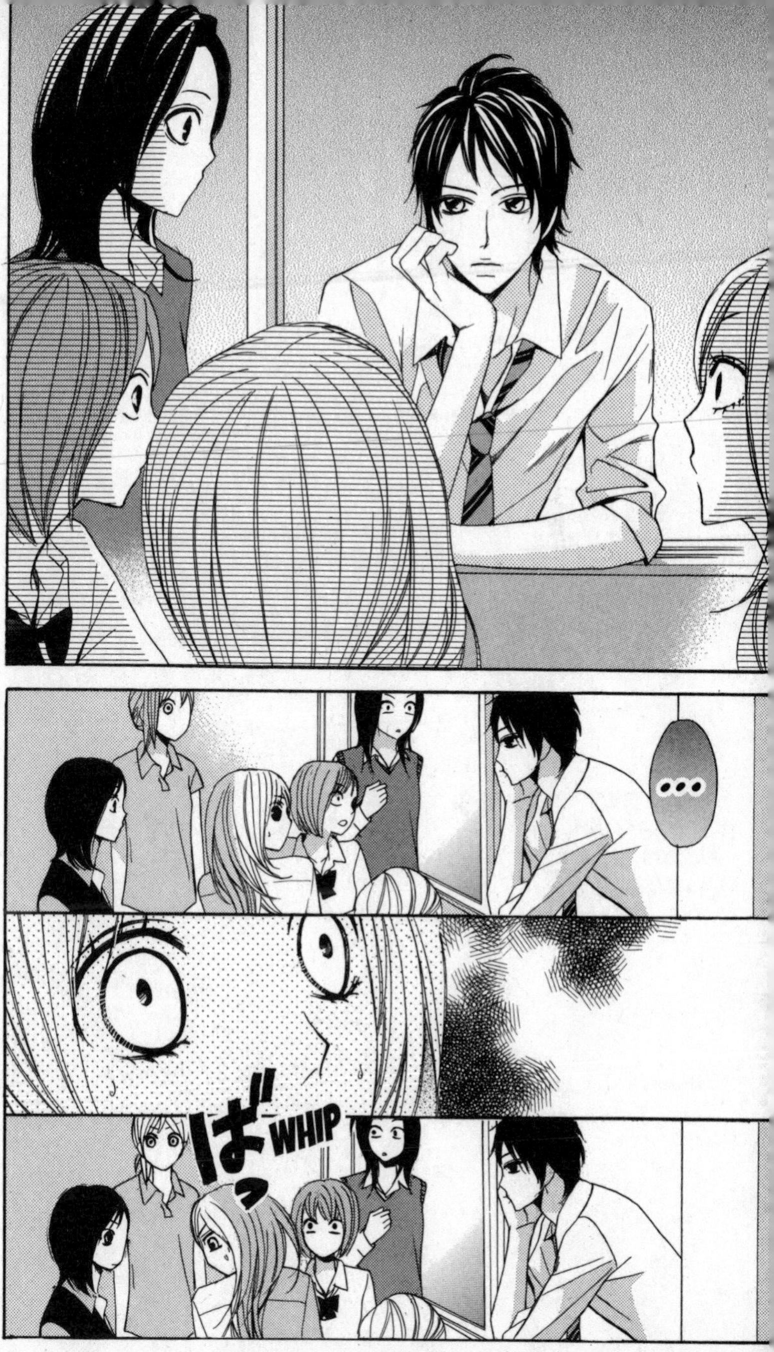
...
ばっ
WHIP

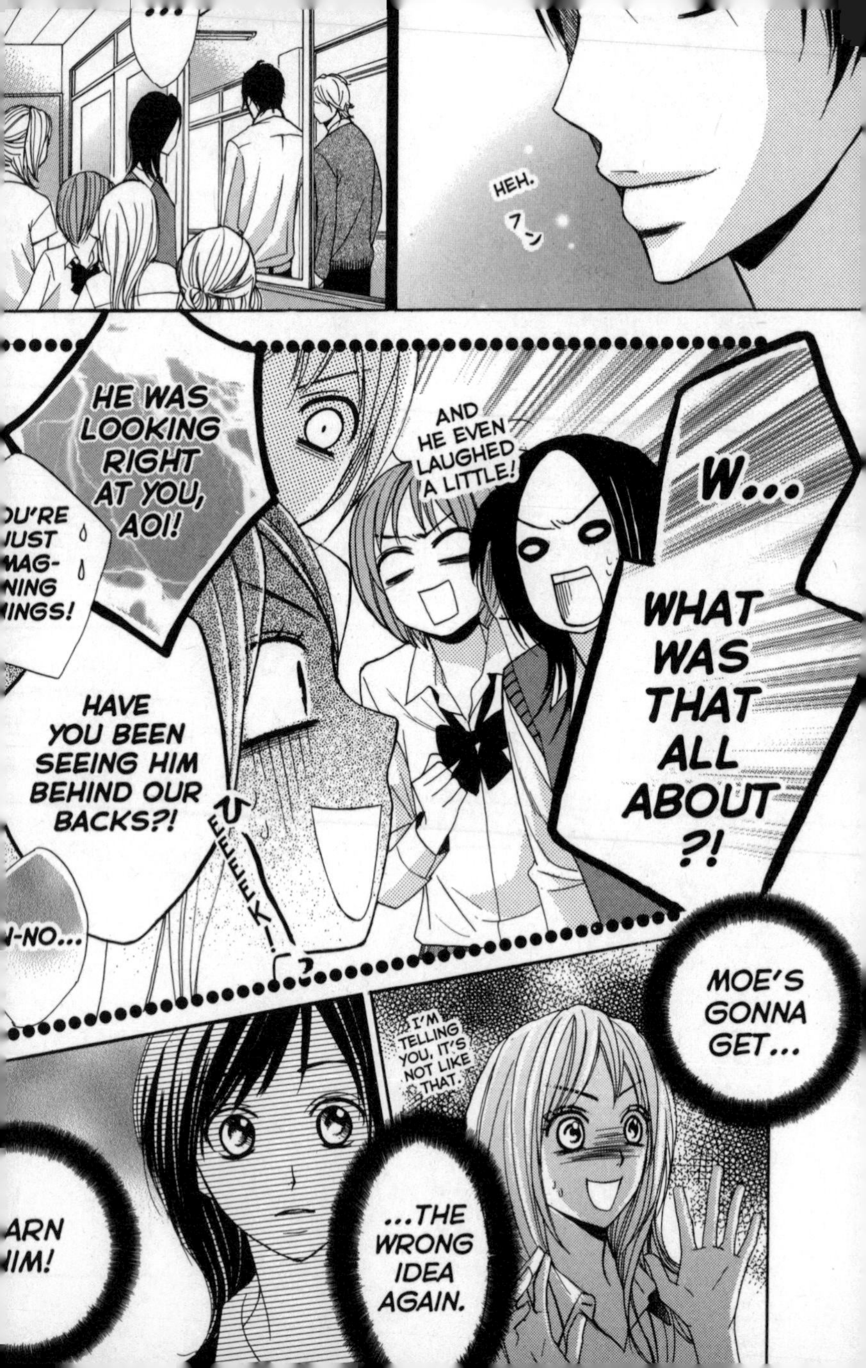
HEH.
フン
...
W...
WHAT WAS THAT ALL ABOUT?!
AND HE EVEN LAUGHED A LITTLE!
HE WAS LOOKING RIGHT AT YOU, AOI!
HAVE YOU BEEN SEEING HIM BEHIND OUR BACKS?!
OU'RE JUST MAG- NING INGS!
-NO...
MOE'S GONNA GET...
I'M TELLING YOU, IT'S NOT LIKE THAT.
...THE WRONG IDEA AGAIN.
ARN IM!

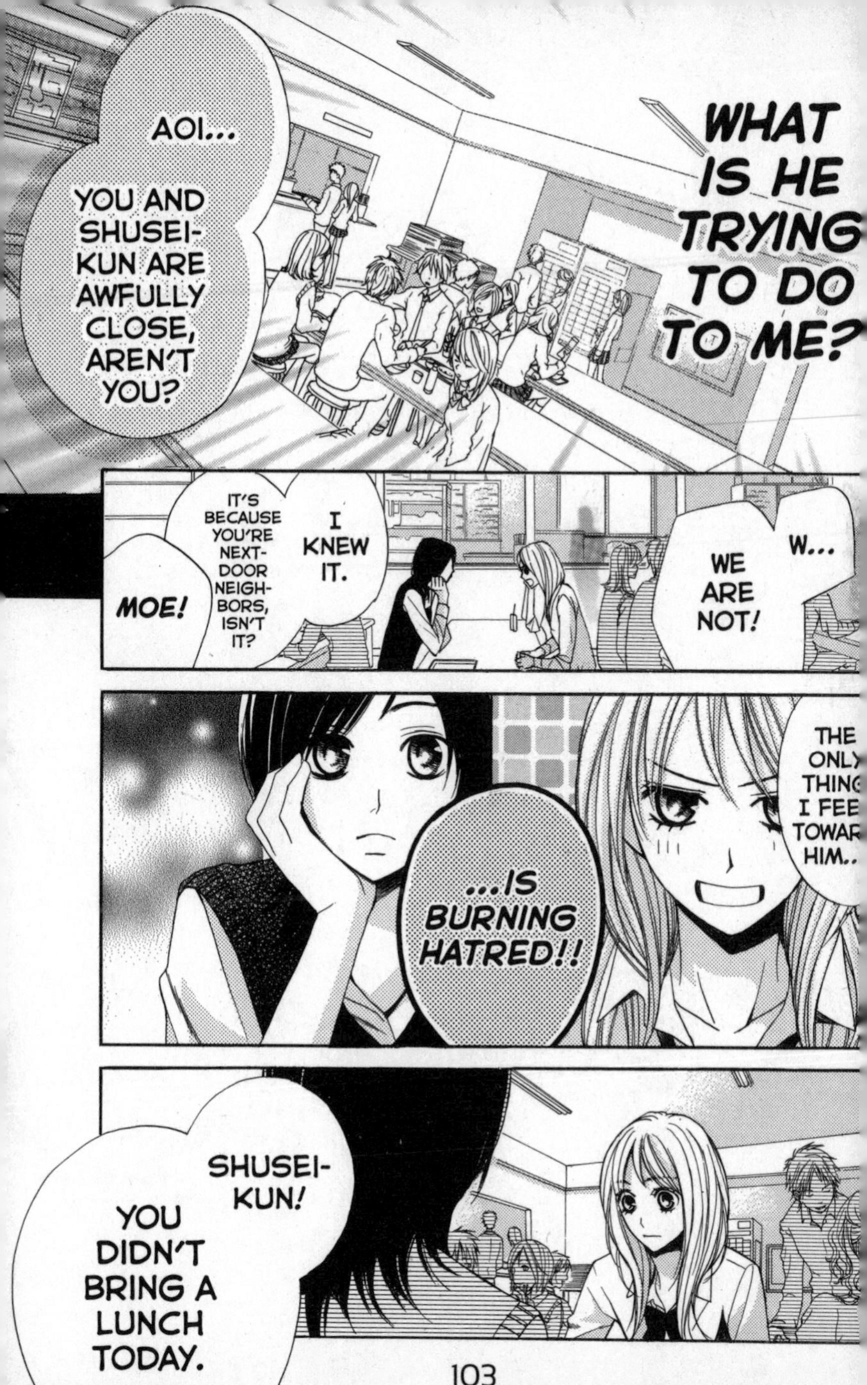
WHAT IS HE TRYING TO DO TO ME?
AOI... YOU AND SHUSEI-KUN ARE AWFULLY CLOSE, AREN'T YOU?
W... WE ARE NOT!
I KNEW IT.
IT'S BECAUSE YOU'RE NEXT-DOOR NEIGHBORS, ISN'T IT?
MOE!
THE ONLY THING I FEE TOWAR HIM..
...IS BURNING HATRED!!
SHUSEI-KUN!
YOU DIDN'T BRING A LUNCH TODAY.

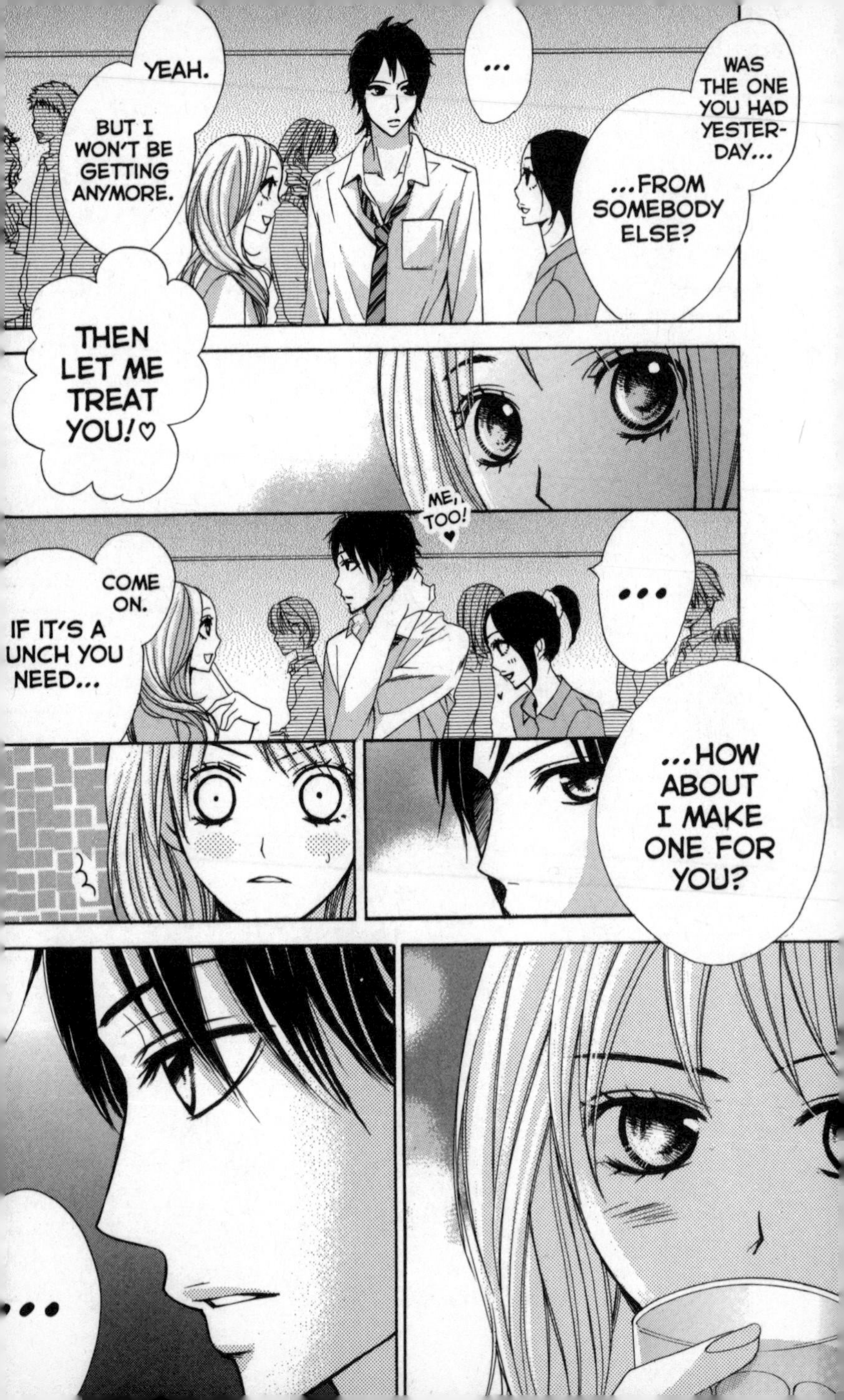
WAS THE ONE YOU HAD YESTER-DAY... ...FROM SOMEBODY ELSE?
...
YEAH. BUT I WON'T BE GETTING ANYMORE.
THEN LET ME TREAT YOU!♡
...
ME, TOO!♥
COME ON. IF IT'S A UNCH YOU NEED...
...HOW ABOUT I MAKE ONE FOR YOU?
...

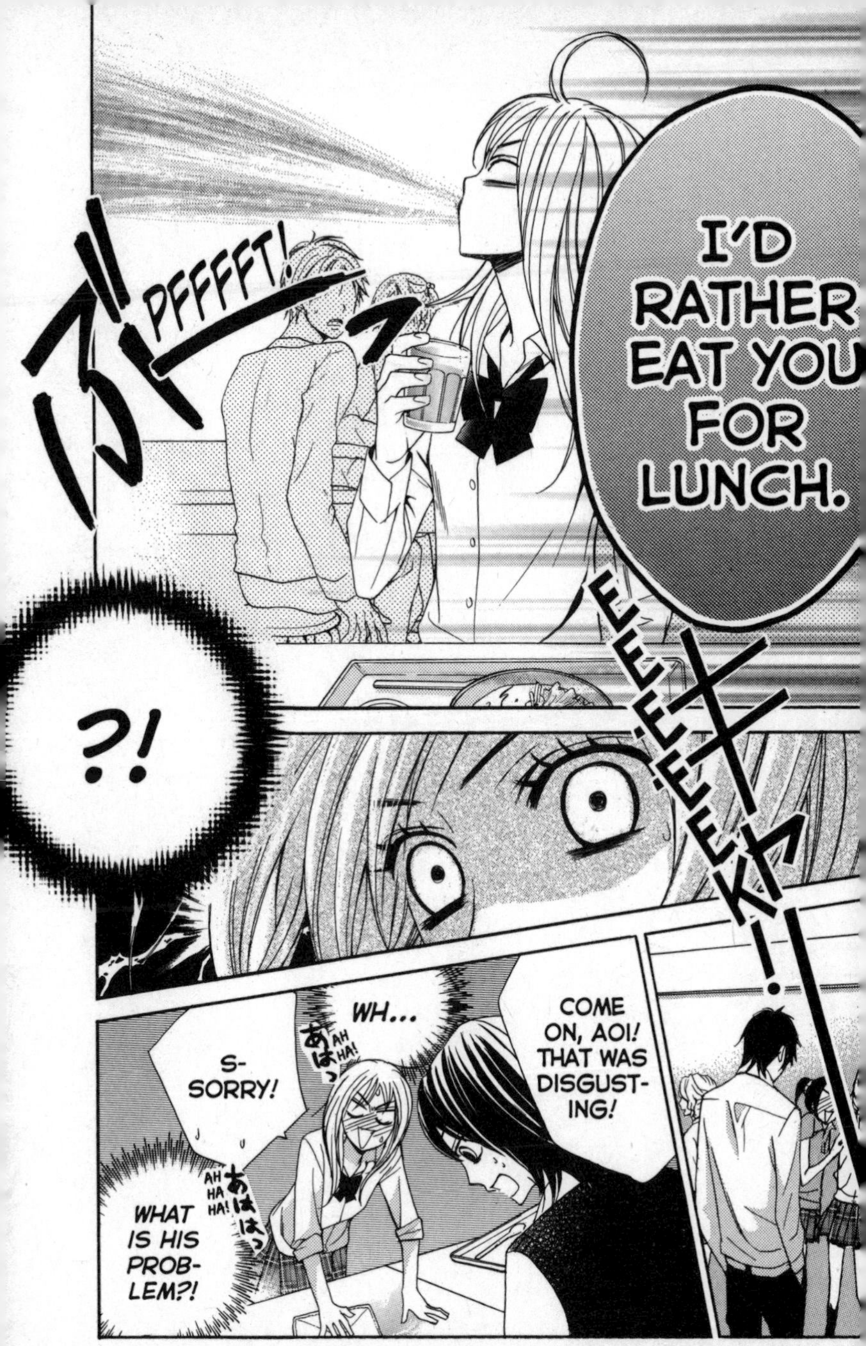
I'D RATHER EAT YOU FOR LUNCH.
ぶーっ
PFFFFT!
EEEEEEK!
?!
COME ON, AOI! THAT WAS DISGUST-ING!
WH...
S-SORRY!
あはっ
AH HA!
あははっ
AH HA HA!
WHAT IS HIS PROB-LEM?!

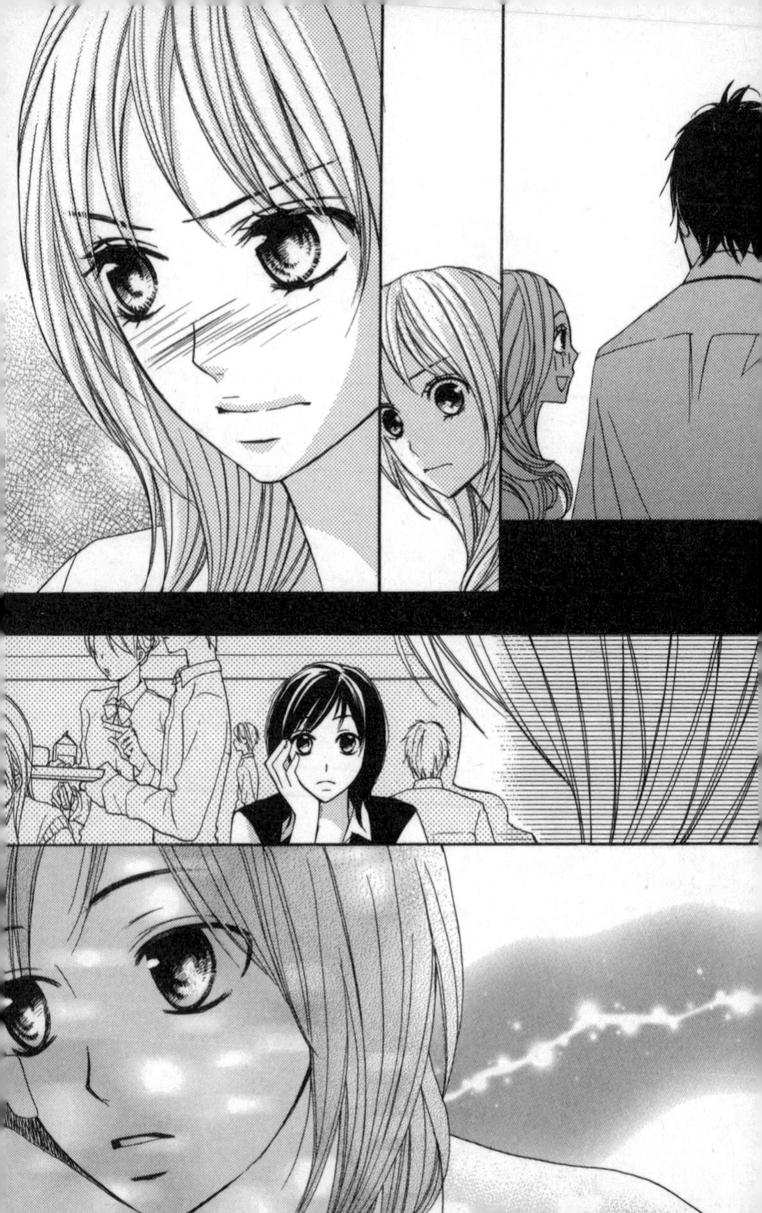

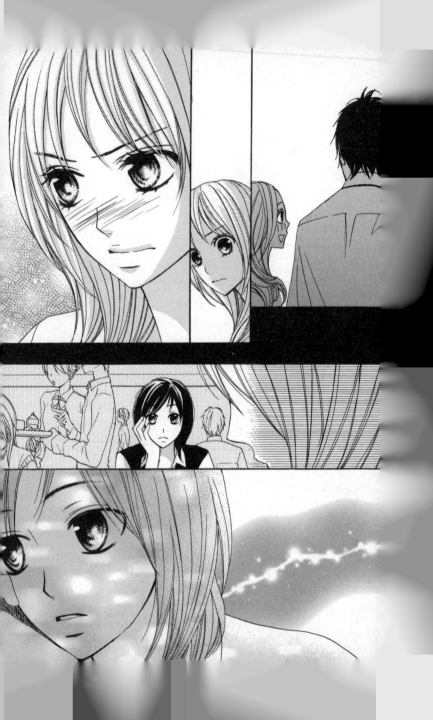

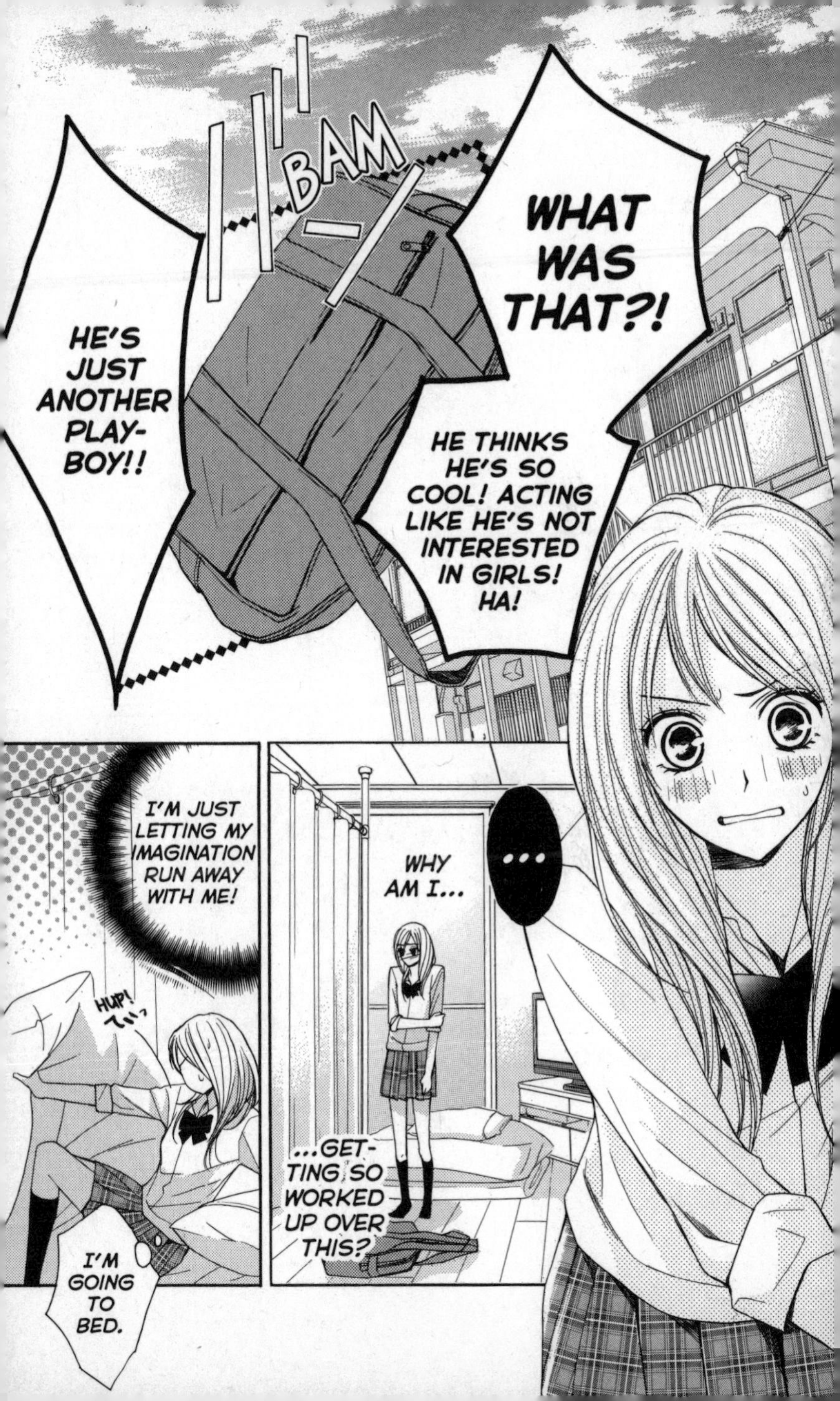
WHAT WAS THAT?!
HE THINKS HE'S SO COOL! ACTING LIKE HE'S NOT INTERESTED IN GIRLS! HA!
BAM
HE'S JUST ANOTHER PLAY-BOY!!
...
WHY AM I...
...GET-TING SO WORKED UP OVER THIS?
I'M JUST LETTING MY IMAGINATION RUN AWAY WITH ME!
HUP!
I'M GOING TO BED.

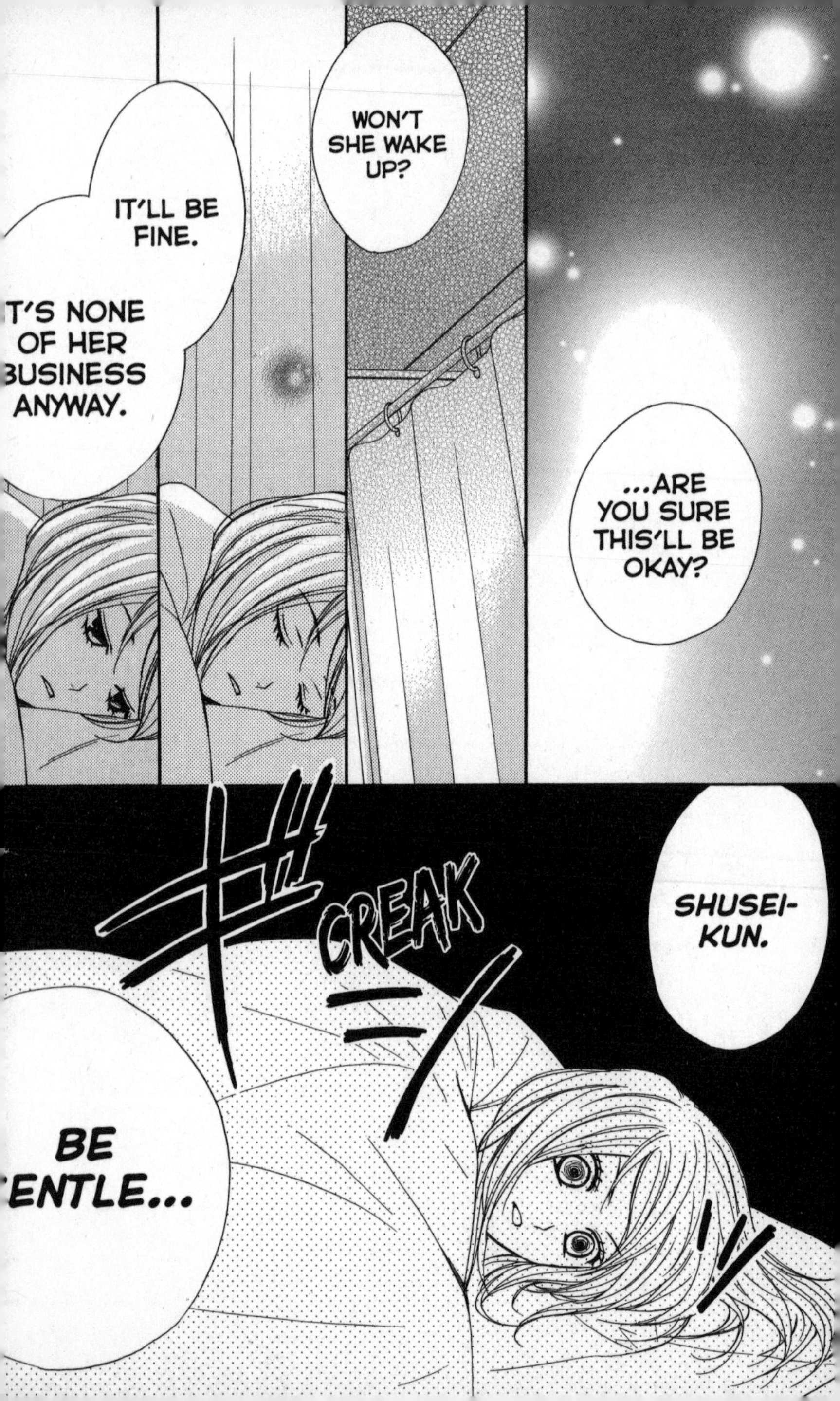
...ARE YOU SURE THIS'LL BE OKAY?
WON'T SHE WAKE UP?
IT'LL BE FINE.
T'S NONE OF HER BUSINESS ANYWAY.
SHUSEI-KUN.
CREAK
BE ENTLE...

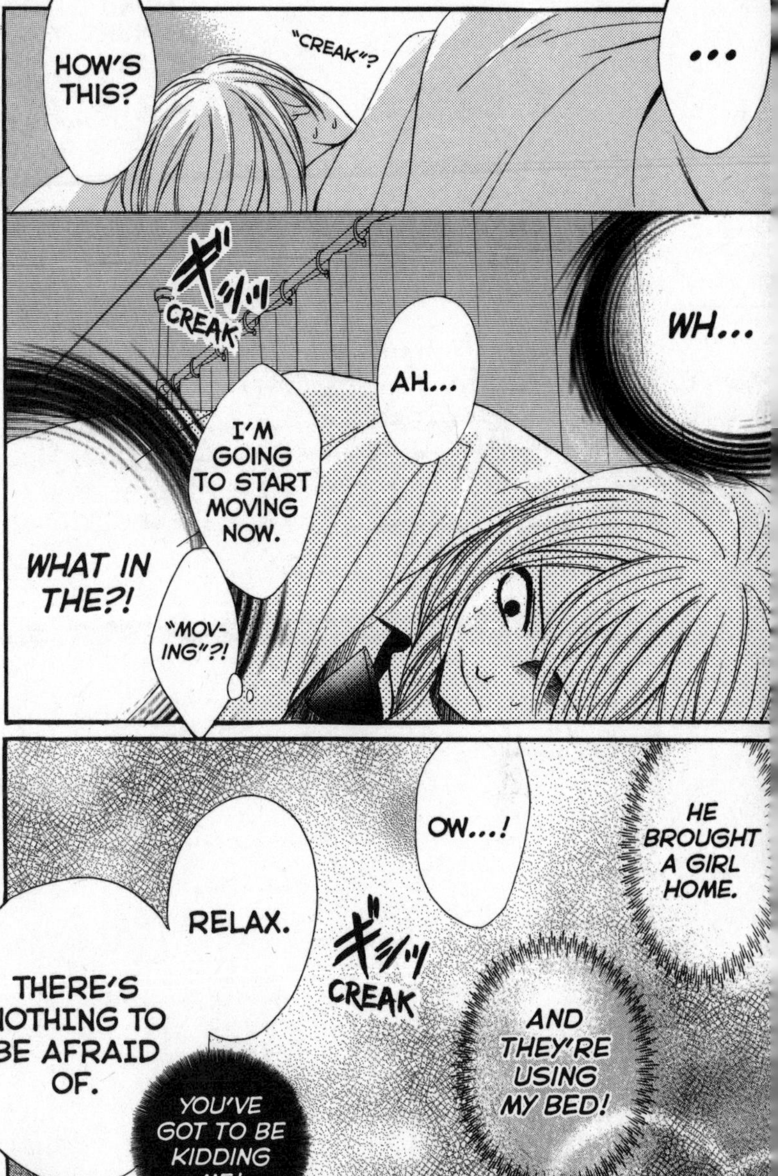

...
"CREAK"?
HOW'S THIS?
WH...
AH...
I'M GOING TO START MOVING NOW.
CREAK
WHAT IN THE?!
"MOV-ING"?!
HE BROUGHT A GIRL HOME.
OW...!
AND THEY'RE USING MY BED!
CREAK
RELAX.
THERE'S NOTHING TO BE AFRAID OF.
YOU'VE GOT TO BE KIDDING ME!

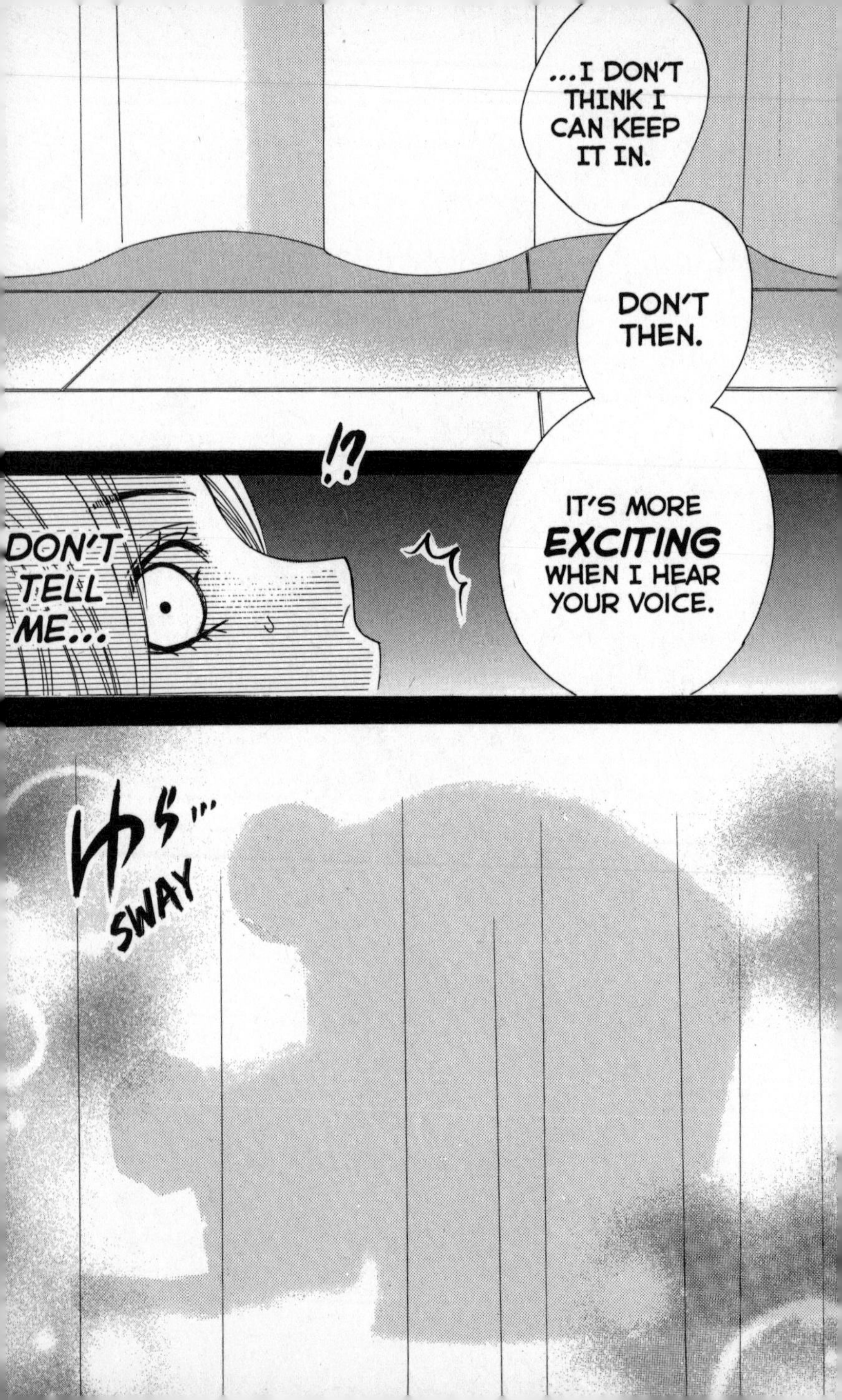
...I DON'T THINK I CAN KEEP IT IN.
DON'T THEN.
IT'S MORE EXCITING WHEN I HEAR YOUR VOICE.
!?
DON'T TELL ME...
ゆら... SWAY

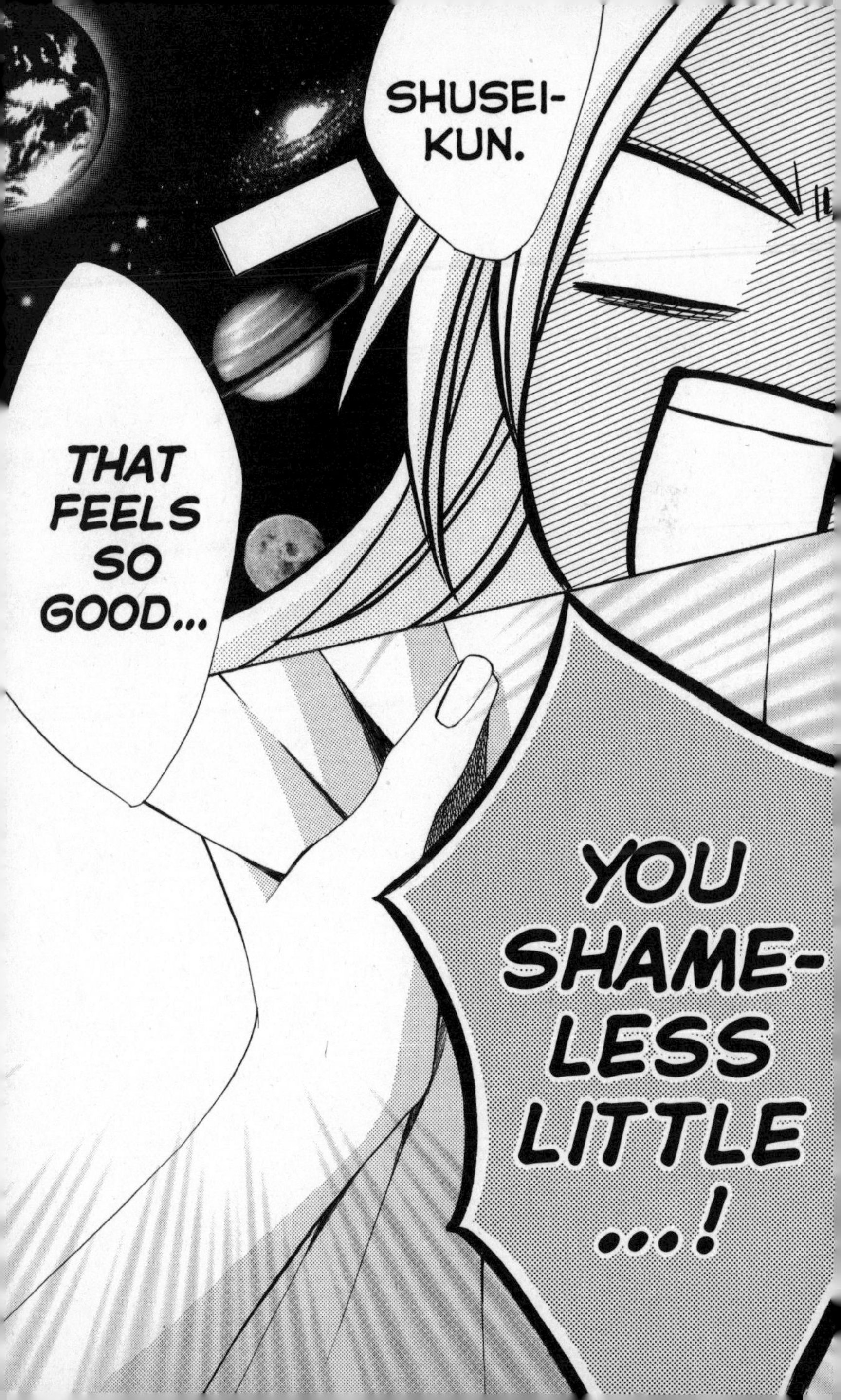
SHUSEI-KUN.
THAT FEELS SO GOOD...
YOU SHAME-LESS LITTLE ...!

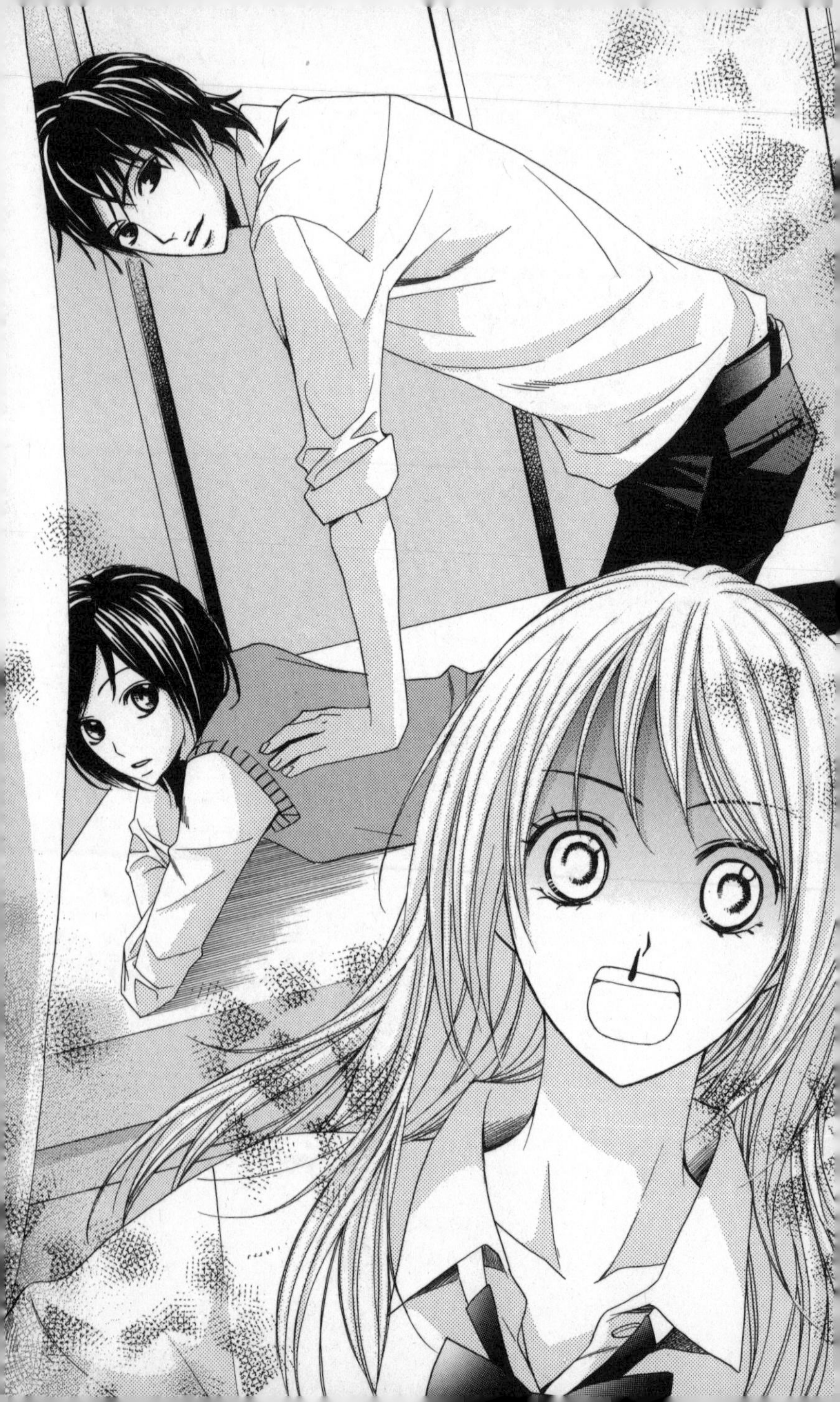

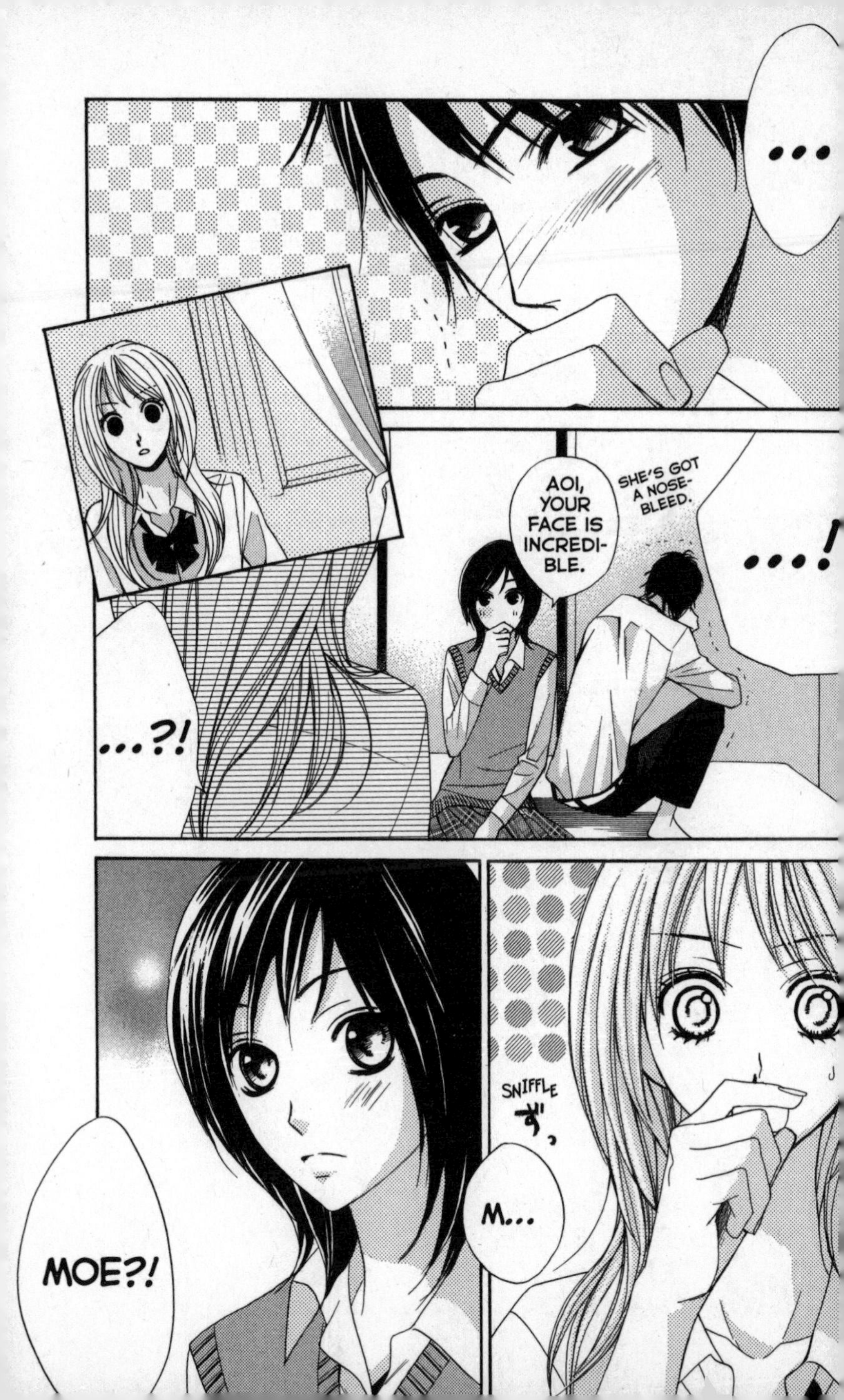
...
...!
AOI, YOUR FACE IS INCREDIBLE.
SHE'S GOT A NOSE-BLEED.
...?!
SNIFFLE
M...
MOE?!

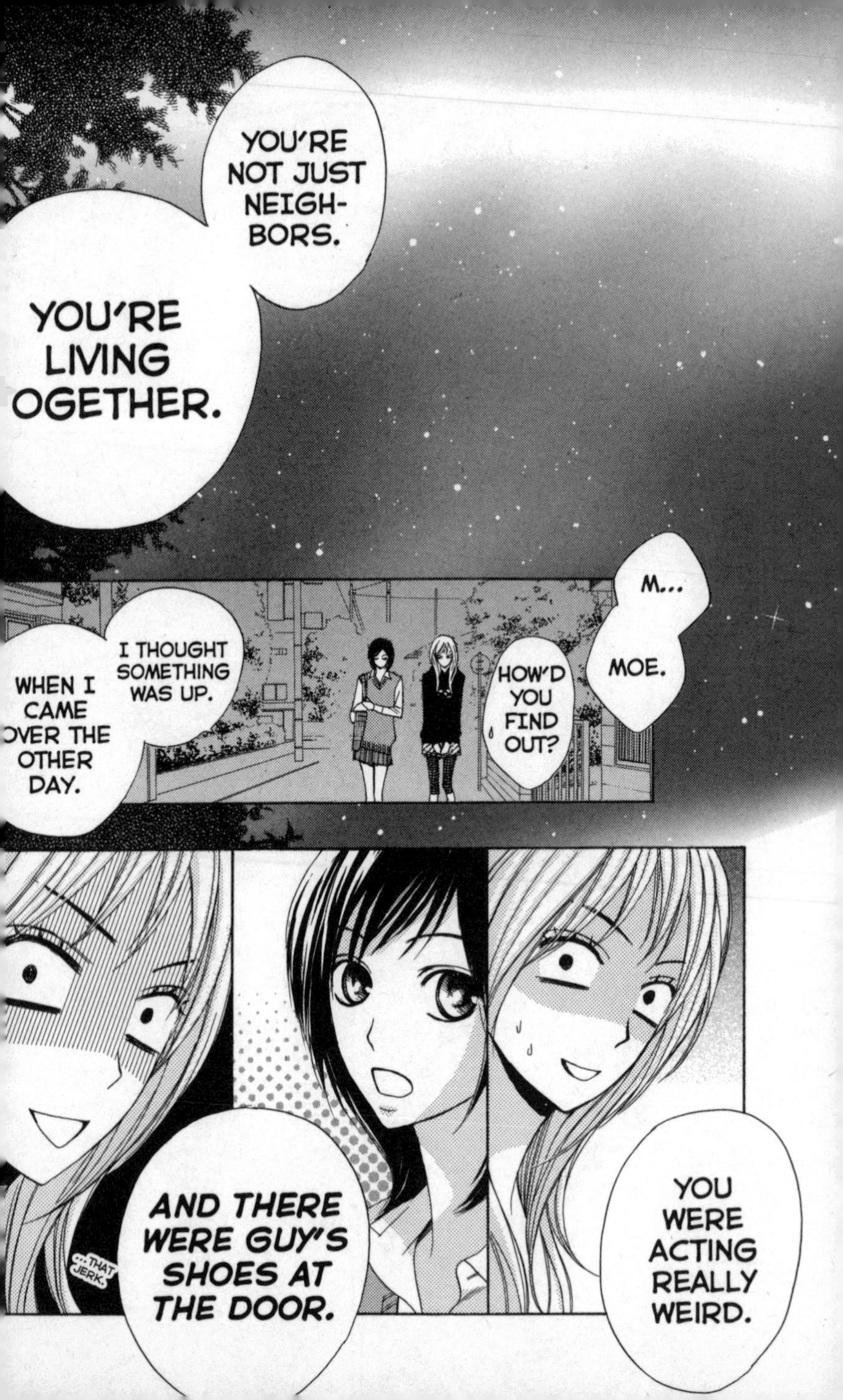
YOU'RE NOT JUST NEIGH-BORS.
YOU'RE LIVING OGETHER.
M...
MOE.
HOW'D YOU FIND OUT?
I THOUGHT SOMETHING WAS UP.
WHEN I CAME VER THE OTHER DAY.
YOU WERE ACTING REALLY WEIRD.
AND THERE WERE GUY'S SHOES AT THE DOOR.
...THAT JERK.

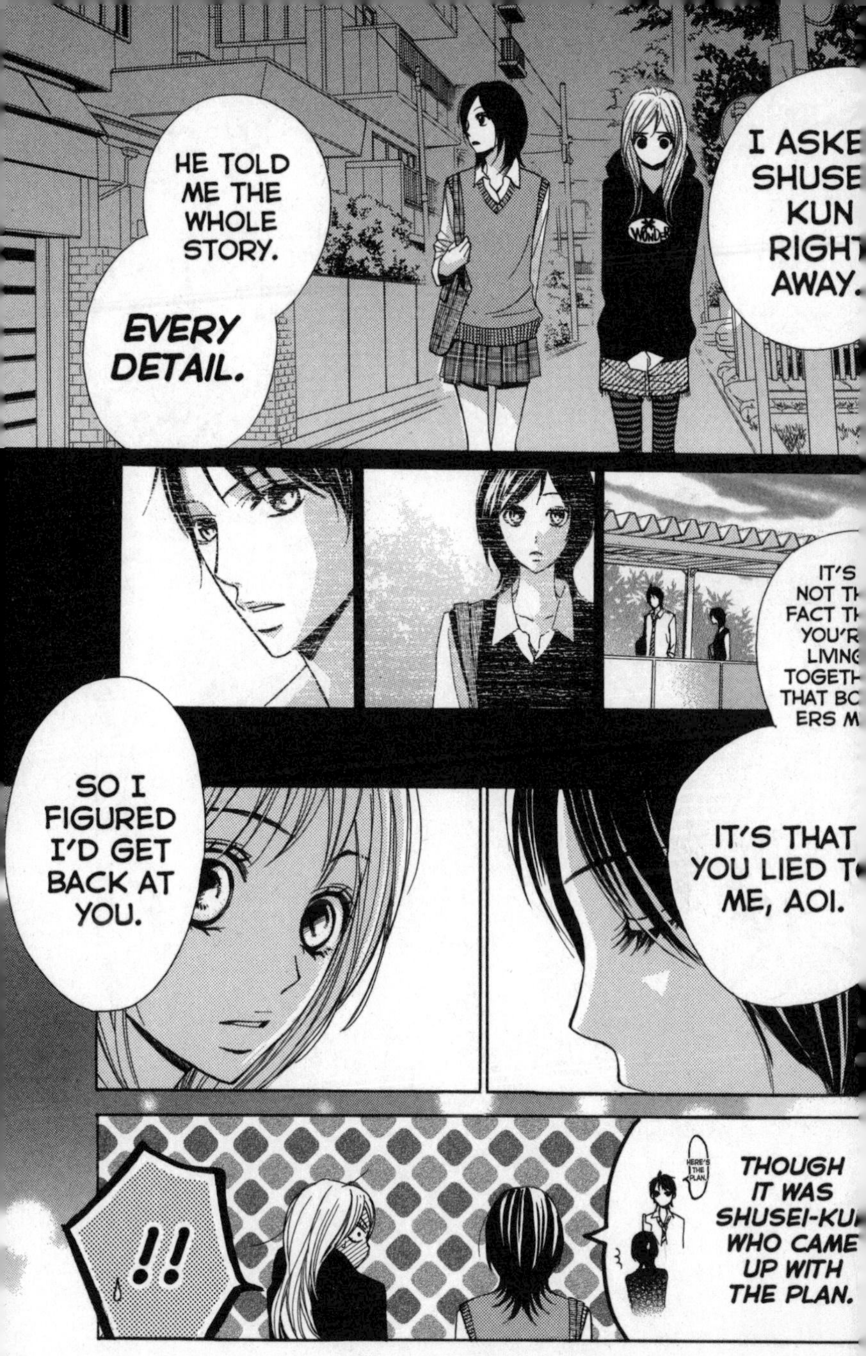

I ASKE SHUSE KUN RIGHT AWAY.
HE TOLD ME THE WHOLE STORY.
EVERY DETAIL.
IT'S NOT TH FACT TH YOU'R LIVING TOGETH THAT BO ERS M
IT'S THAT YOU LIED T ME, AOI.
SO I FIGURED I'D GET BACK AT YOU.
HERE'S THE PLAN.
THOUGH IT WAS SHUSEI-KU WHO CAME UP WITH THE PLAN.
!!

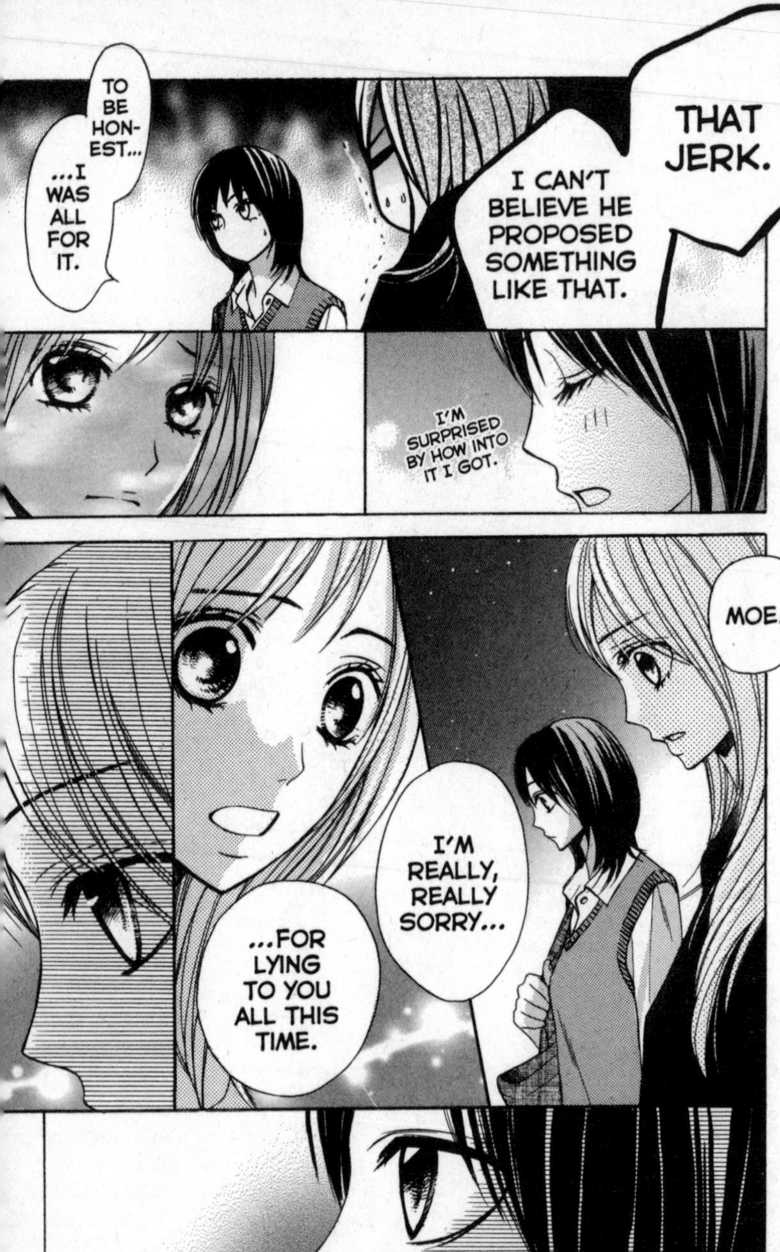
THAT JERK.
I CAN'T BELIEVE HE PROPOSED SOMETHING LIKE THAT.
TO BE HON-EST...
...I WAS ALL FOR IT.
I'M SURPRISED BY HOW INTO IT I GOT.
MOE.
I'M REALLY, REALLY SORRY...
...FOR LYING TO YOU ALL THIS TIME.

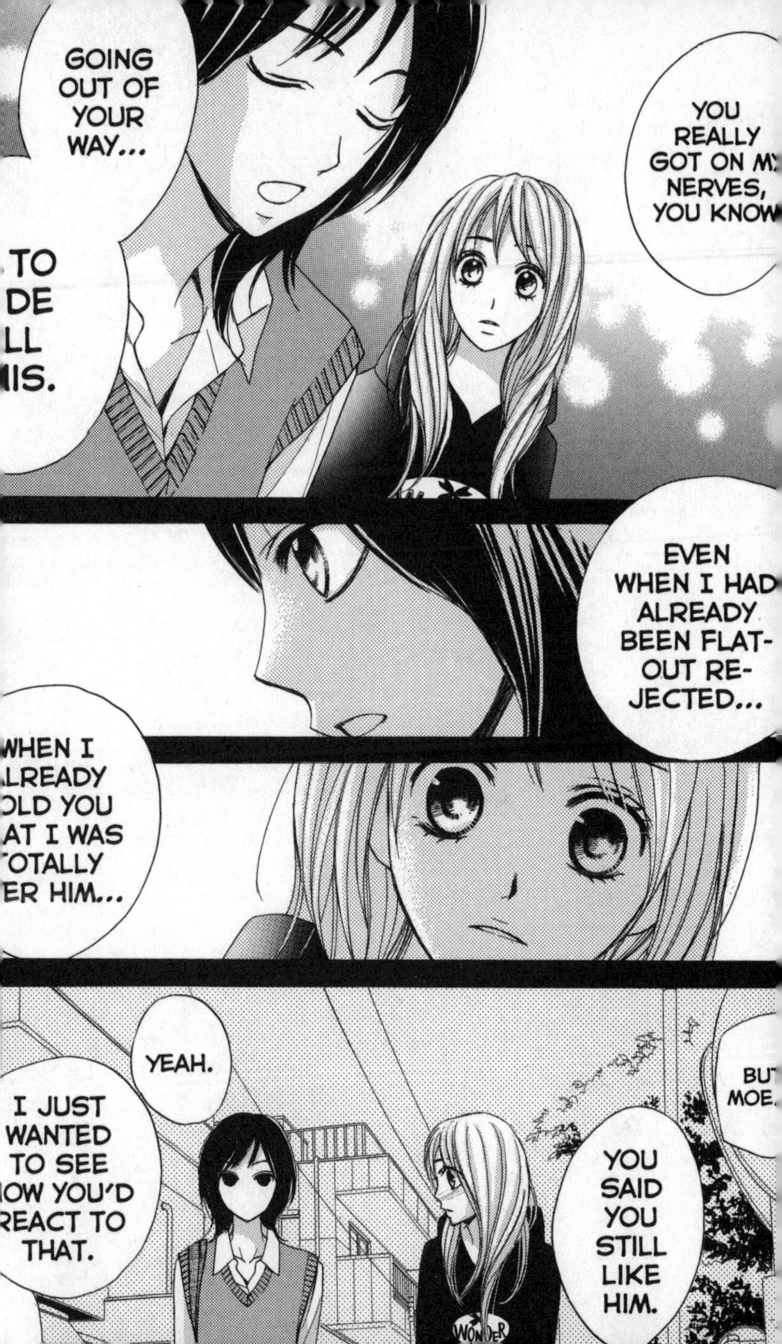
YOU REALLY GOT ON M NERVES, YOU KNOW
GOING OUT OF YOUR WAY...
TO DE LL IS.
EVEN WHEN I HAD ALREADY BEEN FLAT-OUT RE-JECTED...
WHEN I LREADY OLD YOU AT I WAS OTALLY ER HIM...
BU MOE.
YOU SAID YOU STILL LIKE HIM.
YEAH.
I JUST WANTED TO SEE OW YOU'D REACT TO THAT.
WONDER

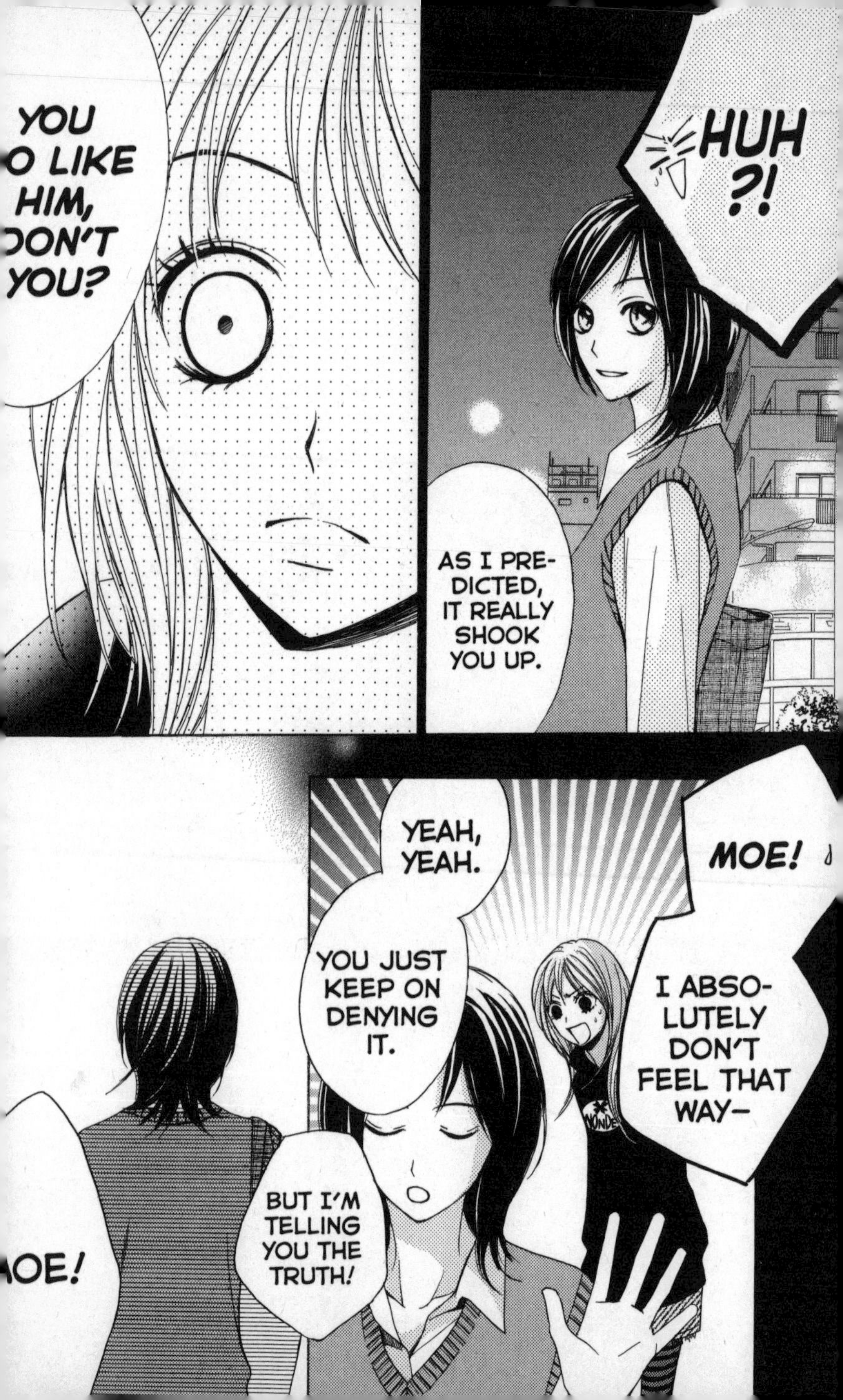
HUH ?!
AS I PREDICTED, IT REALLY SHOOK YOU UP.
YOU O LIKE HIM, DON'T YOU?
MOE!
I ABSOLUTELY DON'T FEEL THAT WAY–
YEAH, YEAH.
YOU JUST KEEP ON DENYING IT.
BUT I'M TELLING YOU THE TRUTH!
OE!

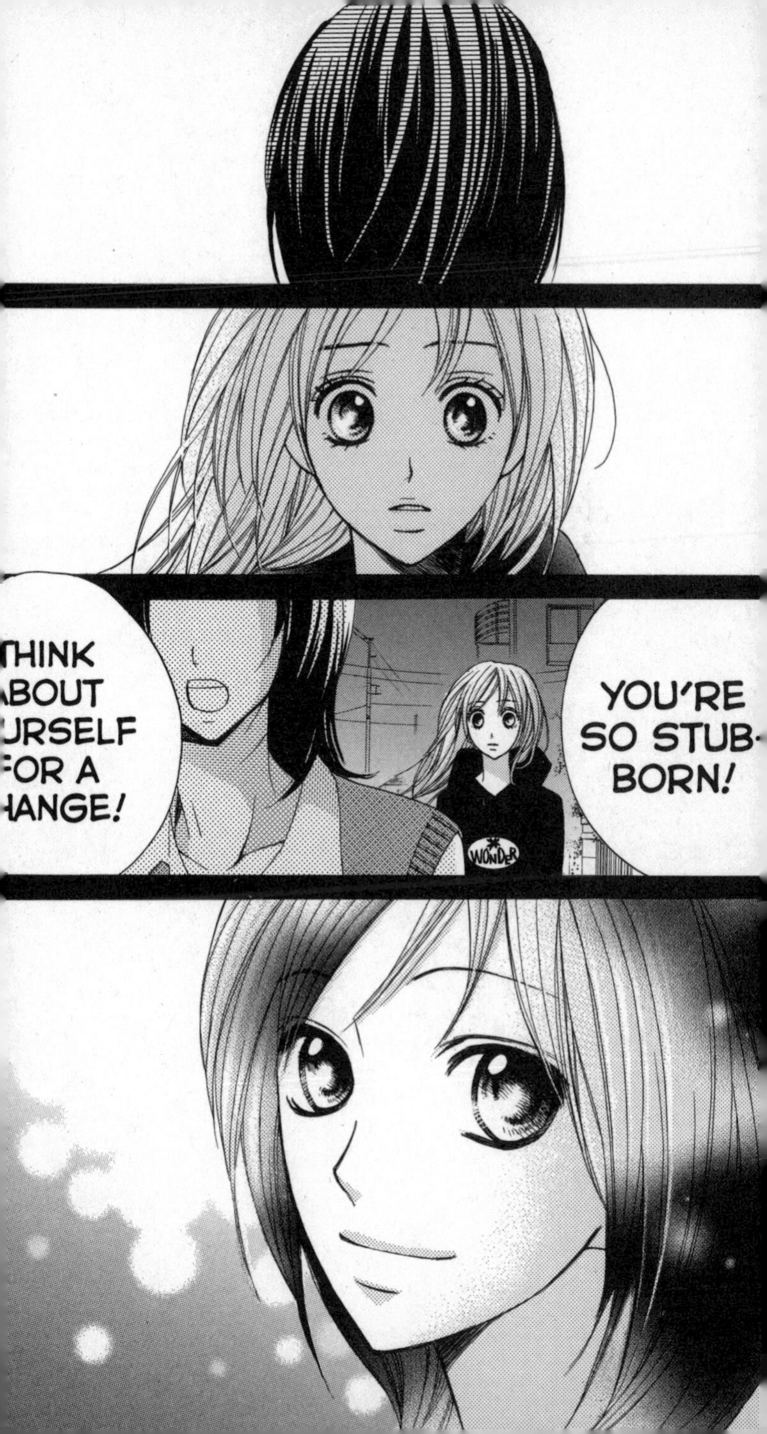
YOU'RE SO STUB-BORN!
THINK ABOUT URSELF FOR A HANGE!
WONDER

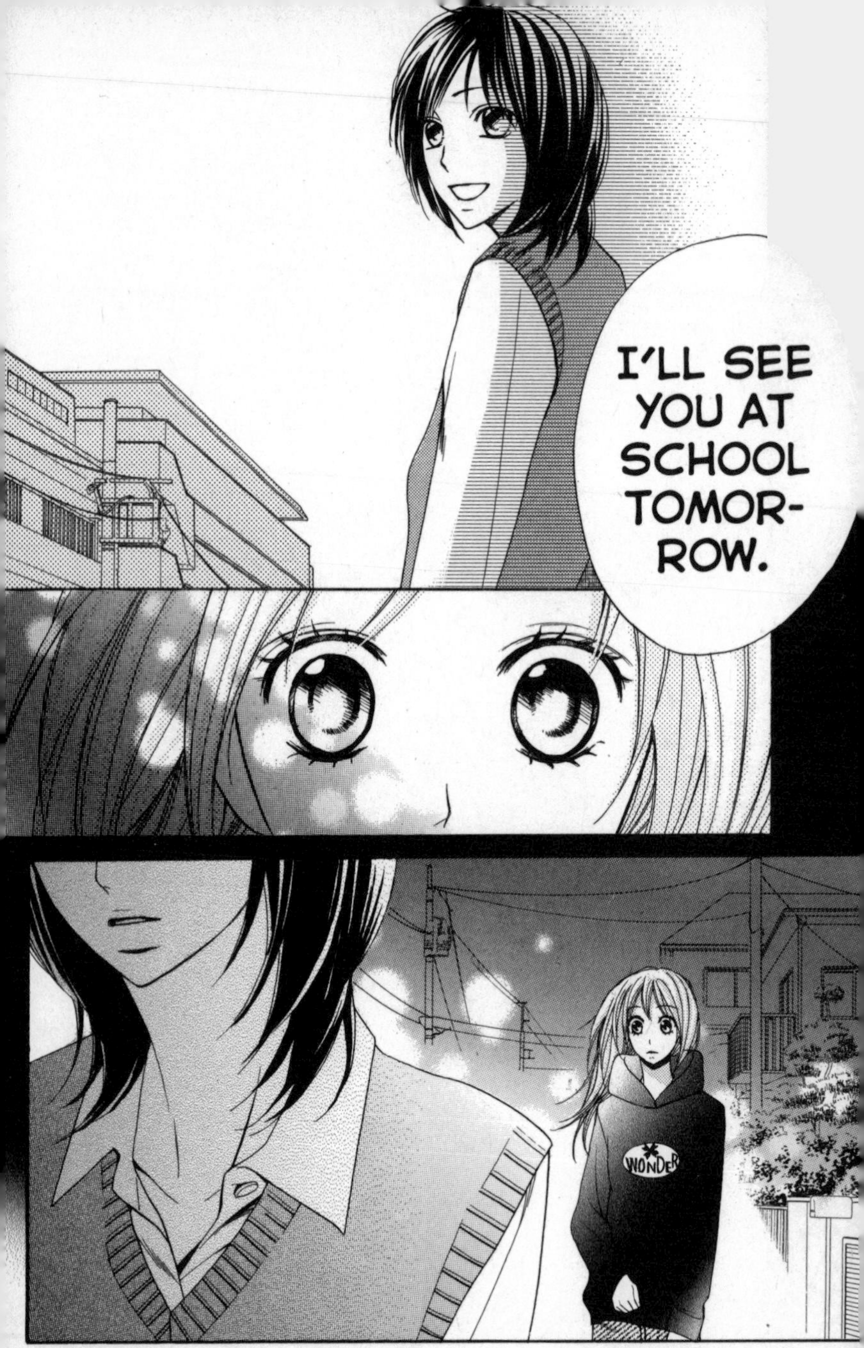
I'LL SEE YOU AT SCHOOL TOMOR- ROW.
WONDER

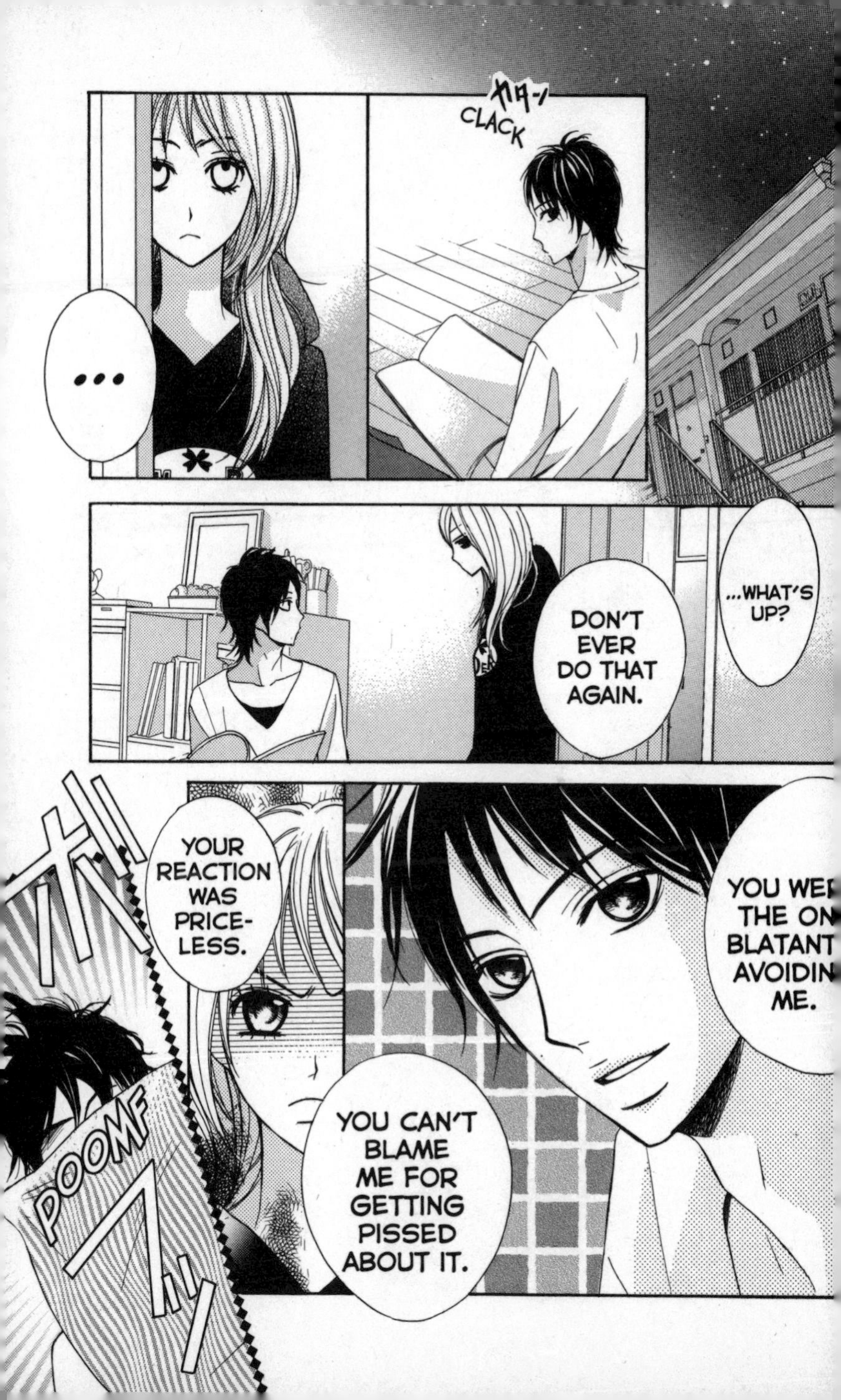
CLACK
...
...WHAT'S UP?
DON'T EVER DO THAT AGAIN.
YOU WER THE ON BLATANT AVOIDIN ME.
YOU CAN'T BLAME ME FOR GETTING PISSED ABOUT IT.
YOUR REACTION WAS PRICE-LESS.
POOMF

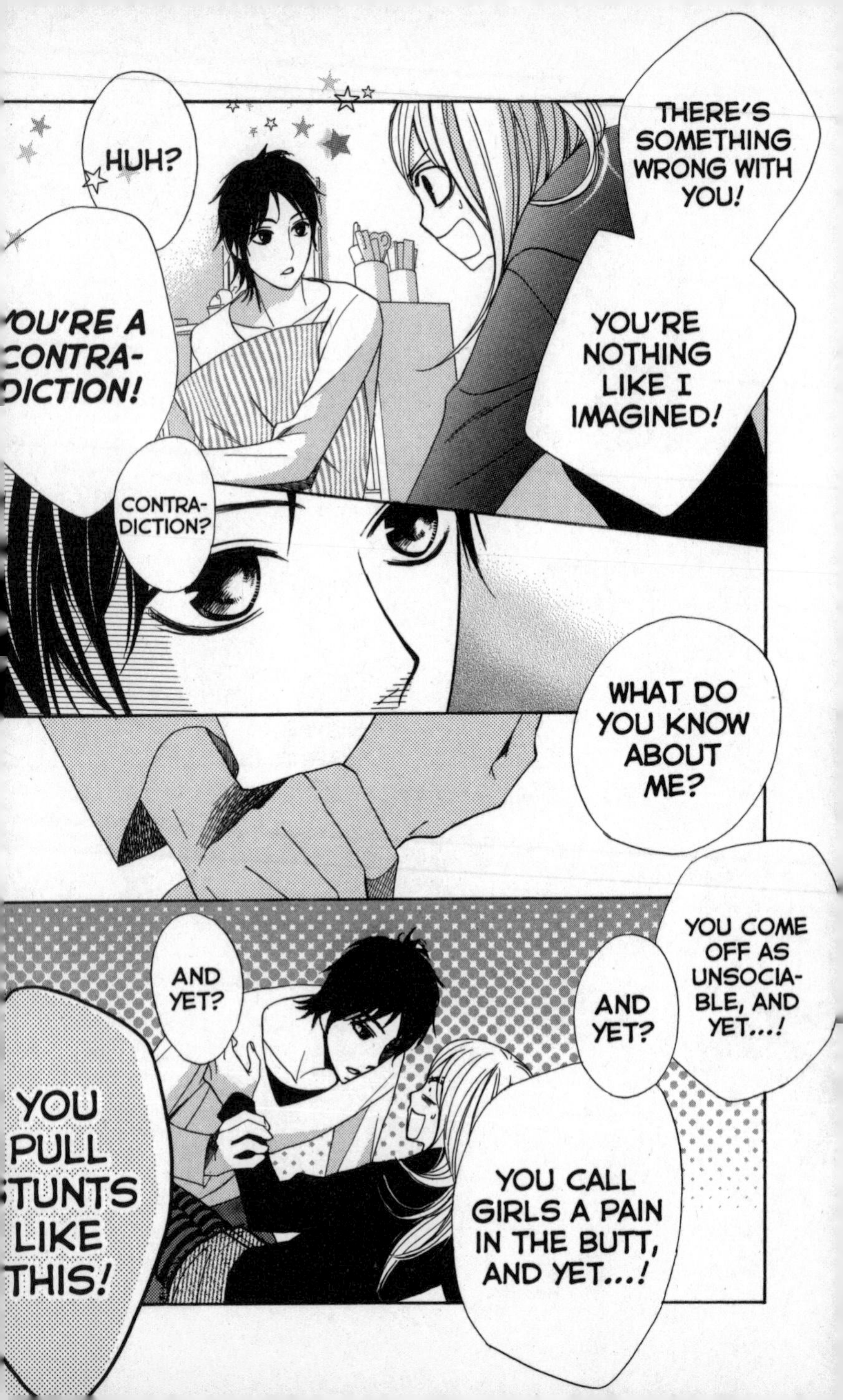
THERE'S SOMETHING WRONG WITH YOU!
YOU'RE NOTHING LIKE I IMAGINED!
HUH?
OU'RE A CONTRA-DICTION!
CONTRA-DICTION?
WHAT DO YOU KNOW ABOUT ME?
YOU COME OFF AS UNSOCIA-BLE, AND YET...!
AND YET?
AND YET?
YOU CALL GIRLS A PAIN IN THE BUTT, AND YET...!
YOU PULL TUNTS LIKE THIS!

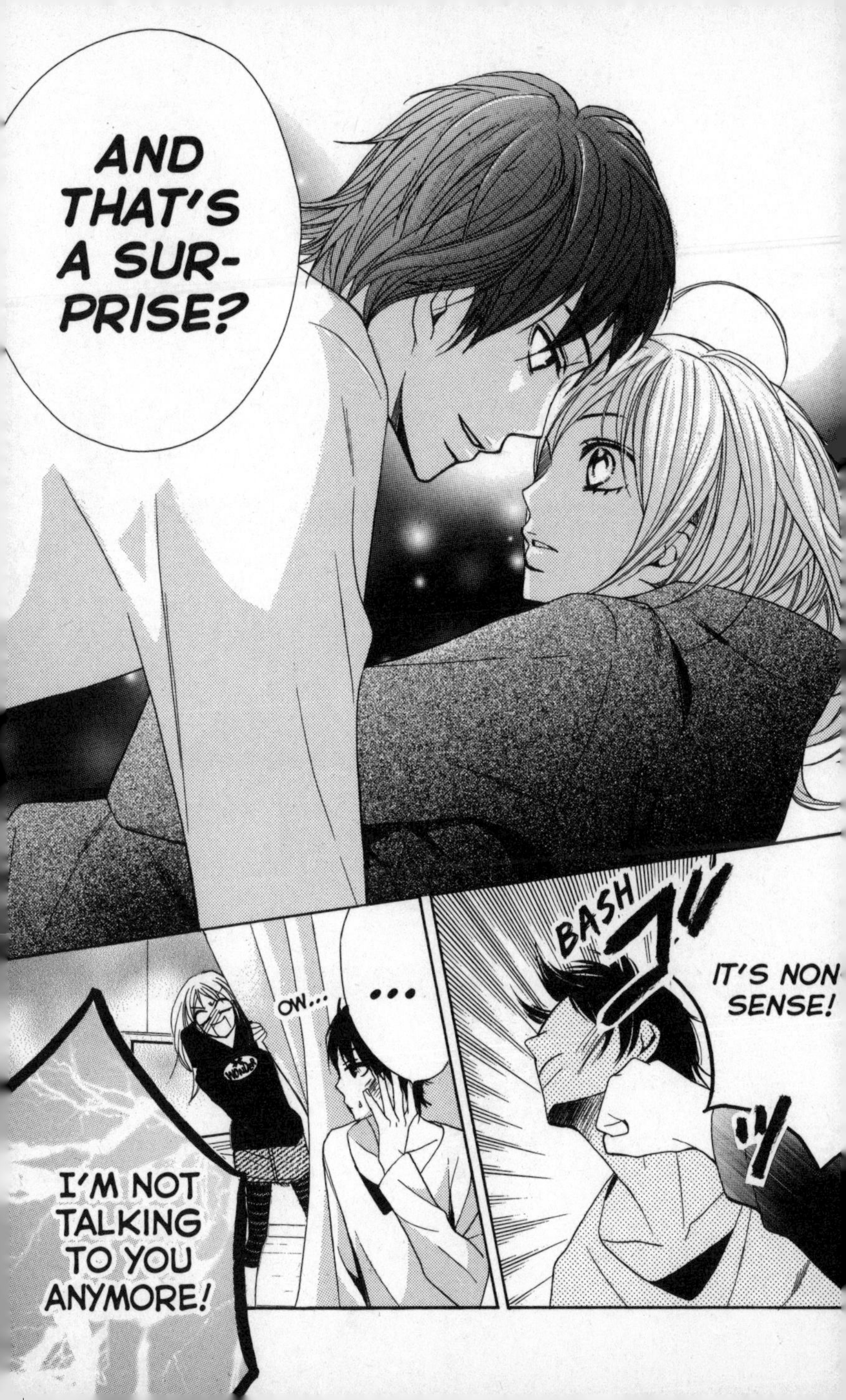
AND THAT'S A SUR-PRISE?
BASH
IT'S NON SENSE!
...
OW...
I'M NOT TALKING TO YOU ANYMORE!

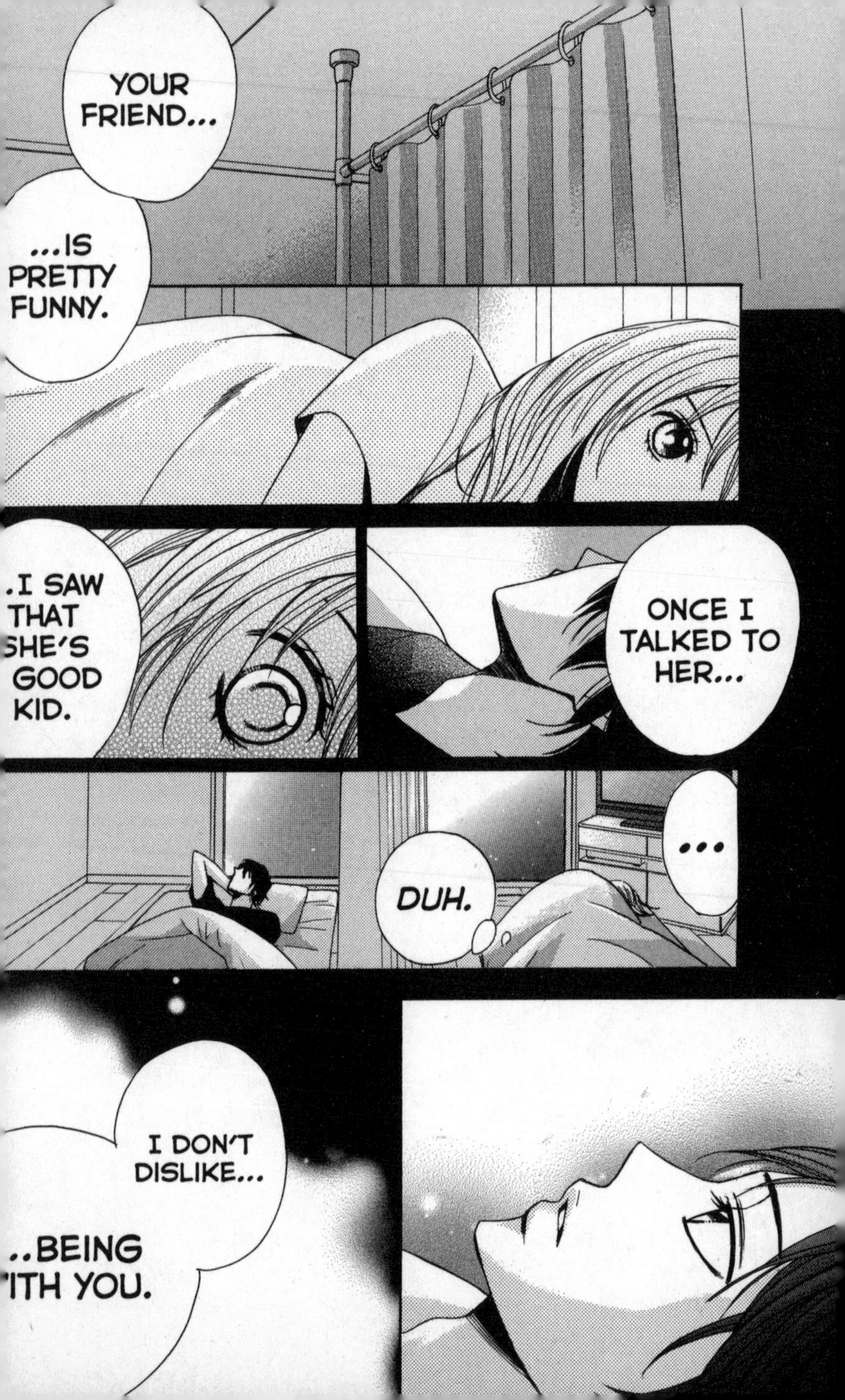
YOUR FRIEND...
...IS PRETTY FUNNY.
ONCE I TALKED TO HER...
.I SAW THAT HE'S GOOD KID.
...
DUH.
I DON'T DISLIKE...
..BEING ITH YOU.

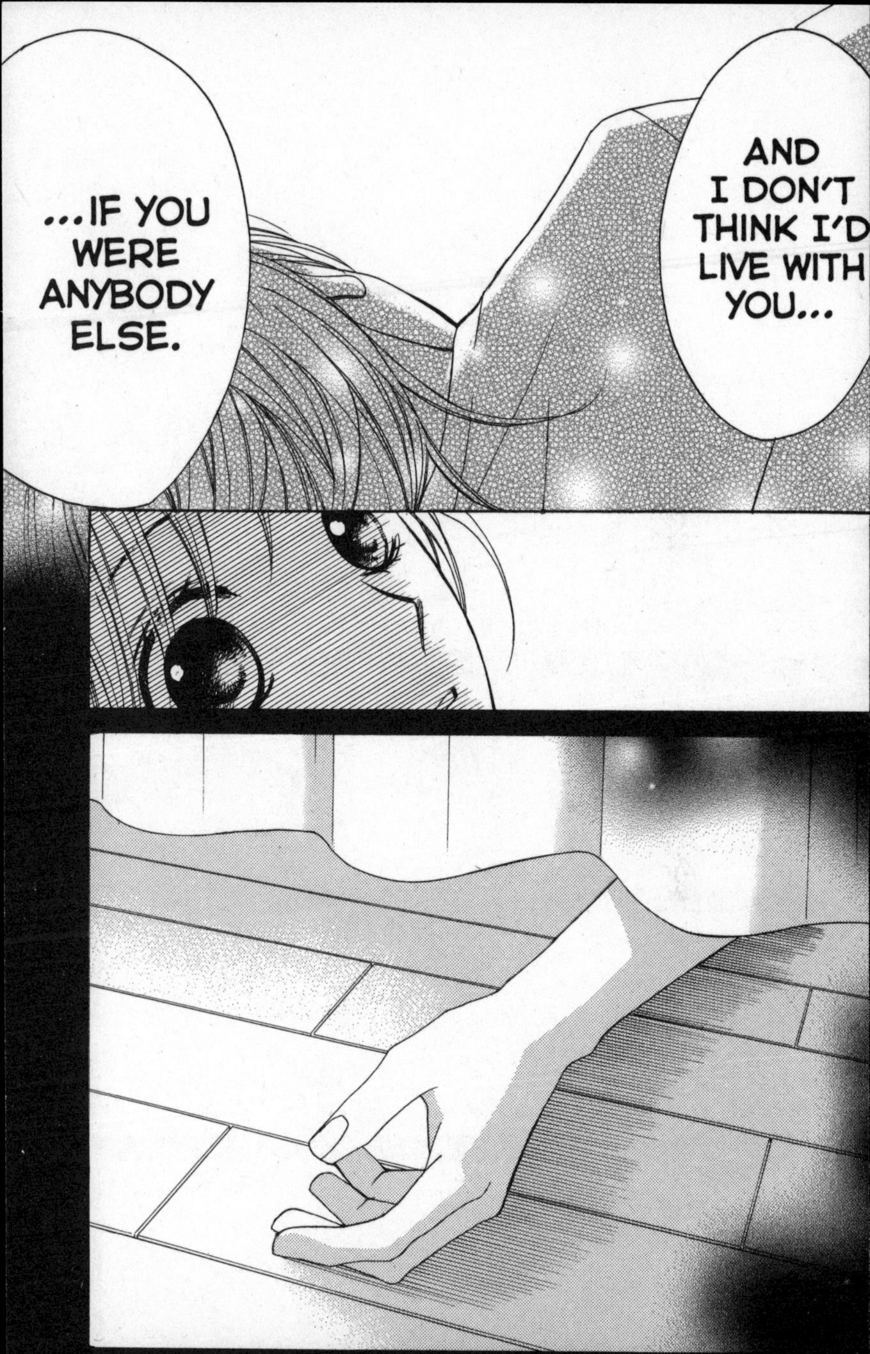
AND I DON'T THINK I'D LIVE WITH YOU...
...IF YOU WERE ANYBODY ELSE.

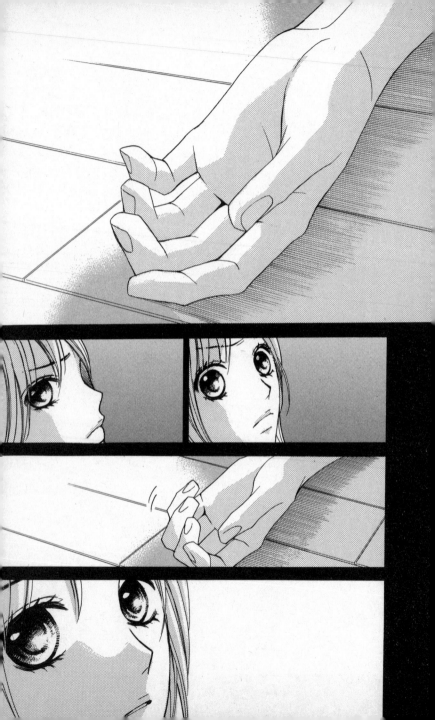

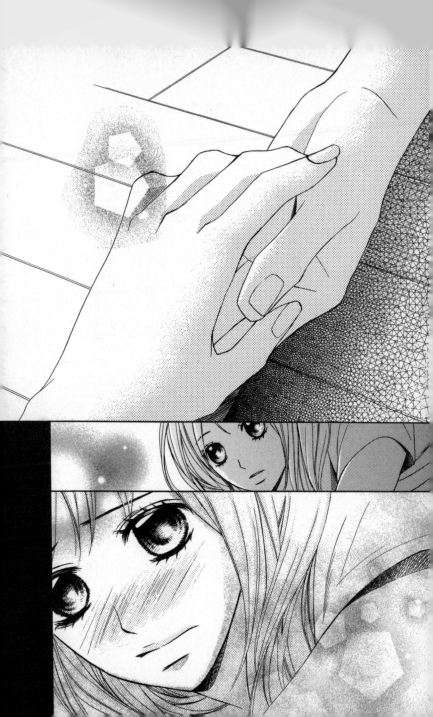

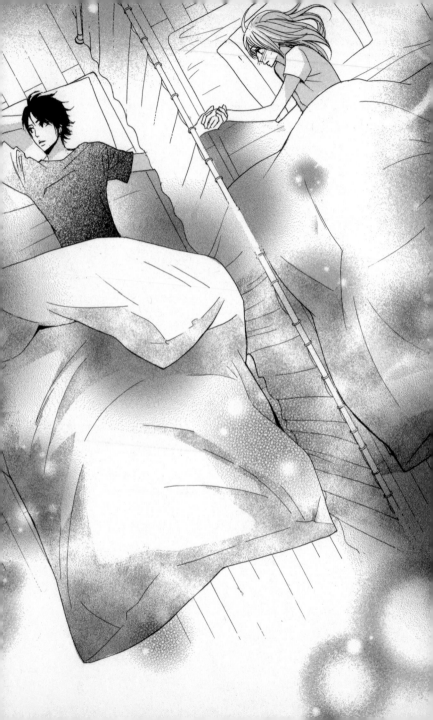

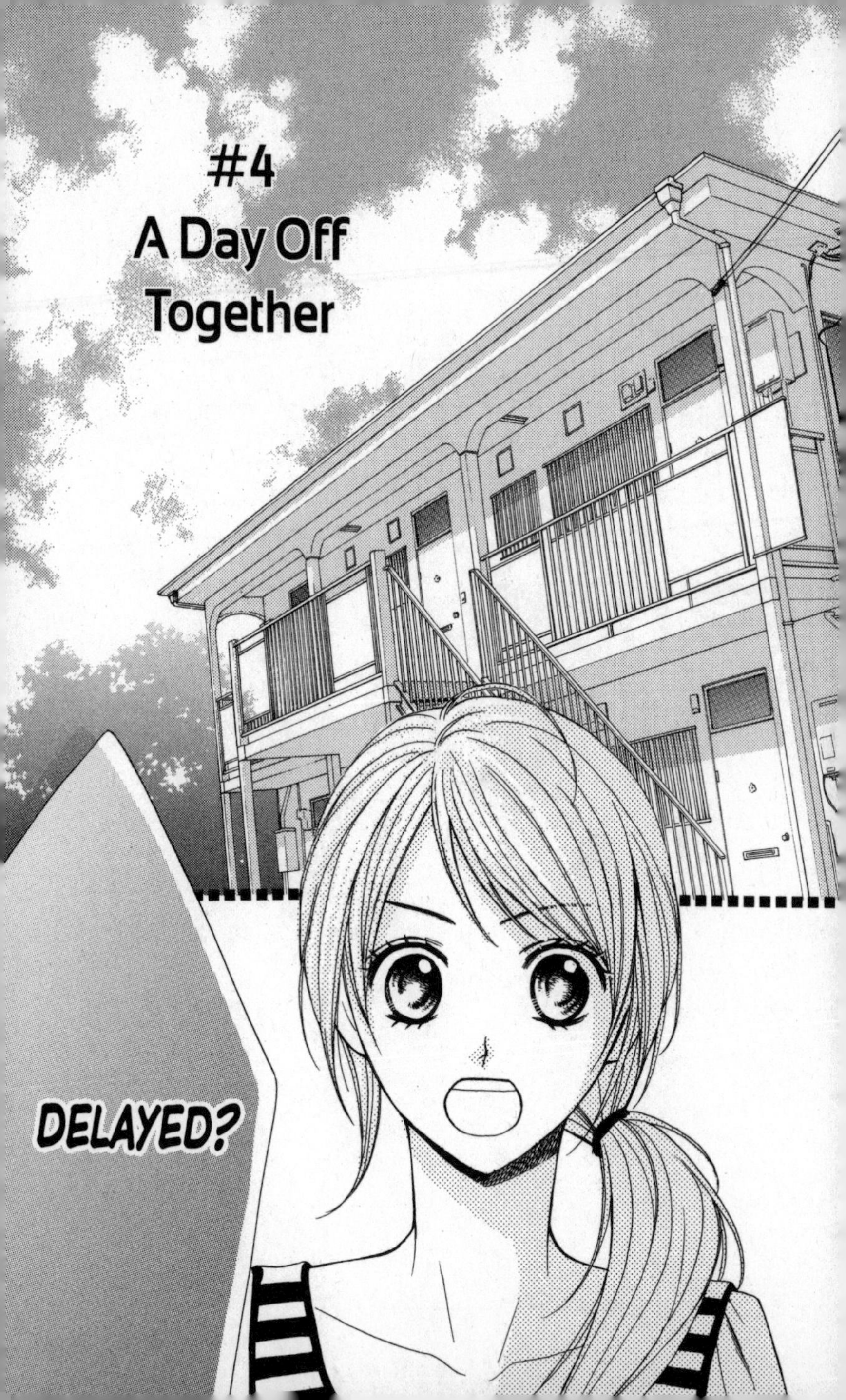
#4
A Day Off Together
DELAYED?

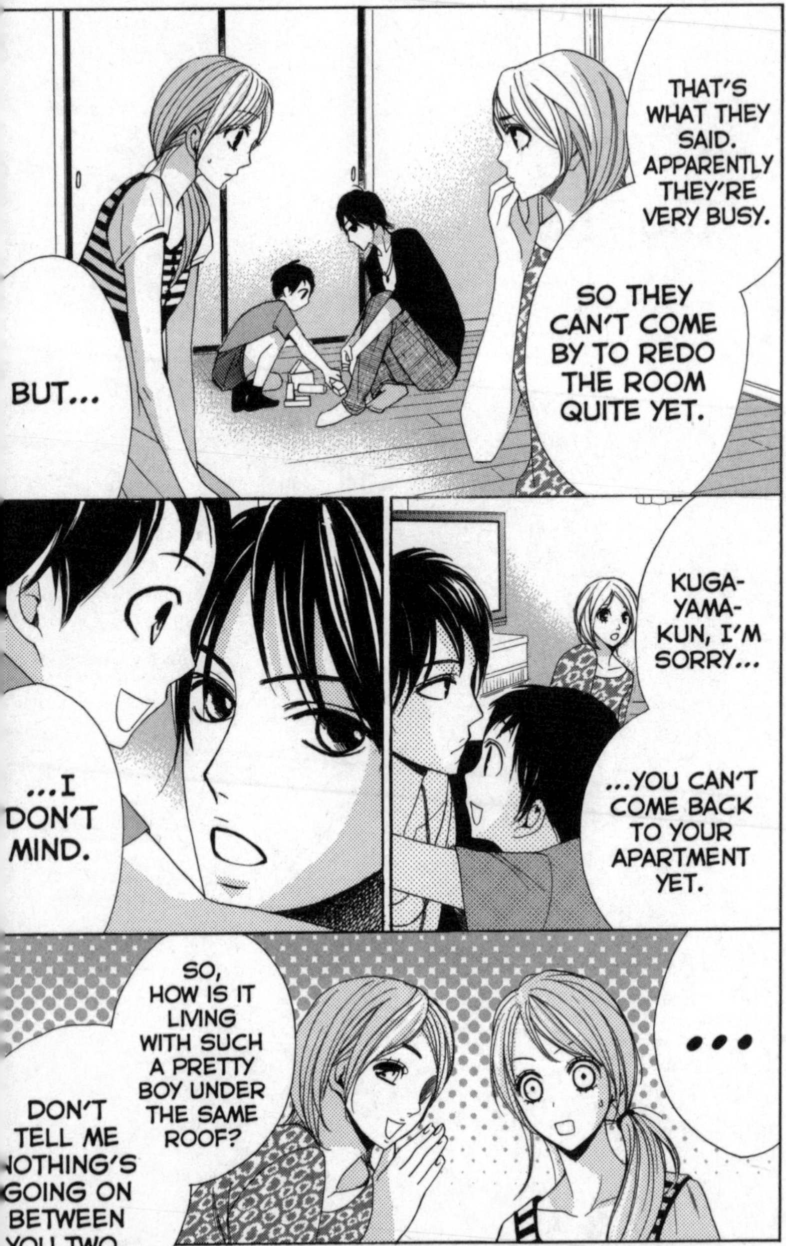
THAT'S WHAT THEY SAID. APPARENTLY THEY'RE VERY BUSY.
SO THEY CAN'T COME BY TO REDO THE ROOM QUITE YET.
BUT...
KUGA-YAMA-KUN, I'M SORRY...
...YOU CAN'T COME BACK TO YOUR APARTMENT YET.
...I DON'T MIND.
...
SO, HOW IS IT LIVING WITH SUCH A PRETTY BOY UNDER THE SAME ROOF?
DON'T TELL ME NOTHING'S GOING ON BETWEEN YOU TWO.

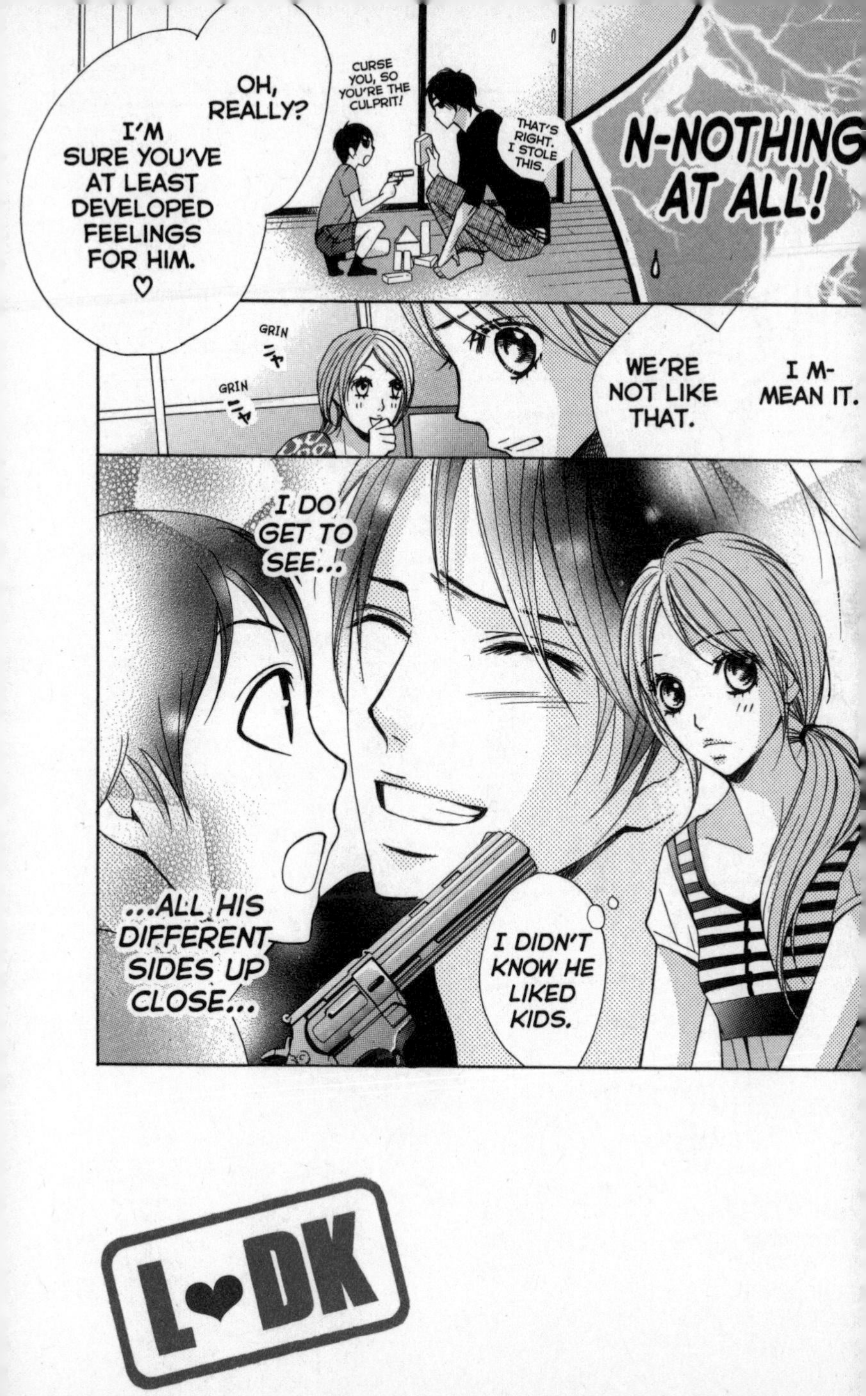
N-NOTHING AT ALL!
CURSE YOU, SO YOU'RE THE CULPRIT!
THAT'S RIGHT. I STOLE THIS.
OH, REALLY? I'M SURE YOU'VE AT LEAST DEVELOPED FEELINGS FOR HIM. ♡
WE'RE NOT LIKE THAT. I M- MEAN IT.
GRIN ニャ
GRIN ニャ
I DO GET TO SEE...
I DIDN'T KNOW HE LIKED KIDS.
...ALL HIS DIFFERENT SIDES UP CLOSE...

L♥DK

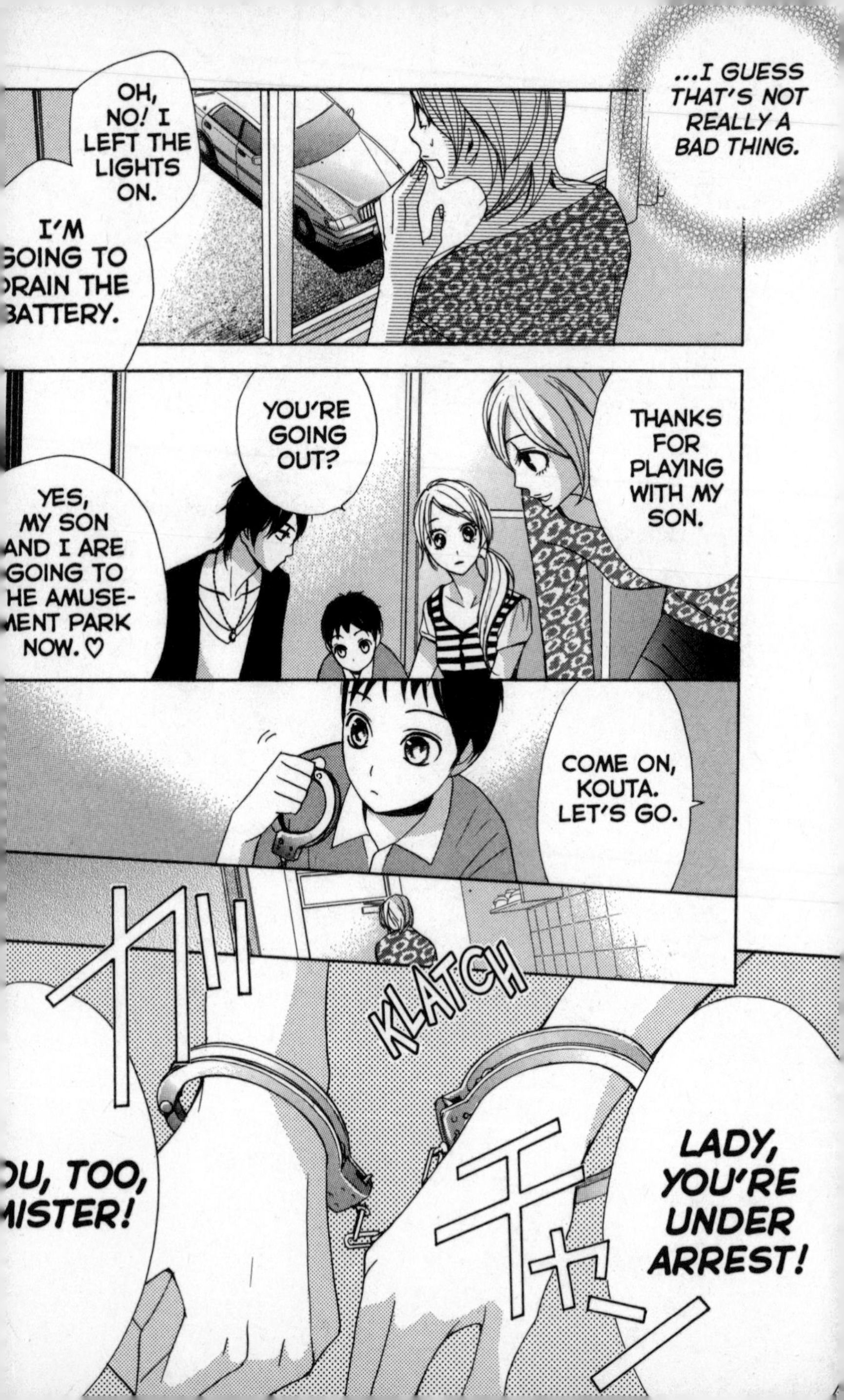
...I GUESS THAT'S NOT REALLY A BAD THING.
OH, NO! I LEFT THE LIGHTS ON.
I'M GOING TO DRAIN THE BATTERY.
THANKS FOR PLAYING WITH MY SON.
YOU'RE GOING OUT?
YES, MY SON AND I ARE GOING TO THE AMUSEMENT PARK NOW. ♡
COME ON, KOUTA. LET'S GO.
KLATCH
LADY, YOU'RE UNDER ARREST!
YOU, TOO, MISTER!

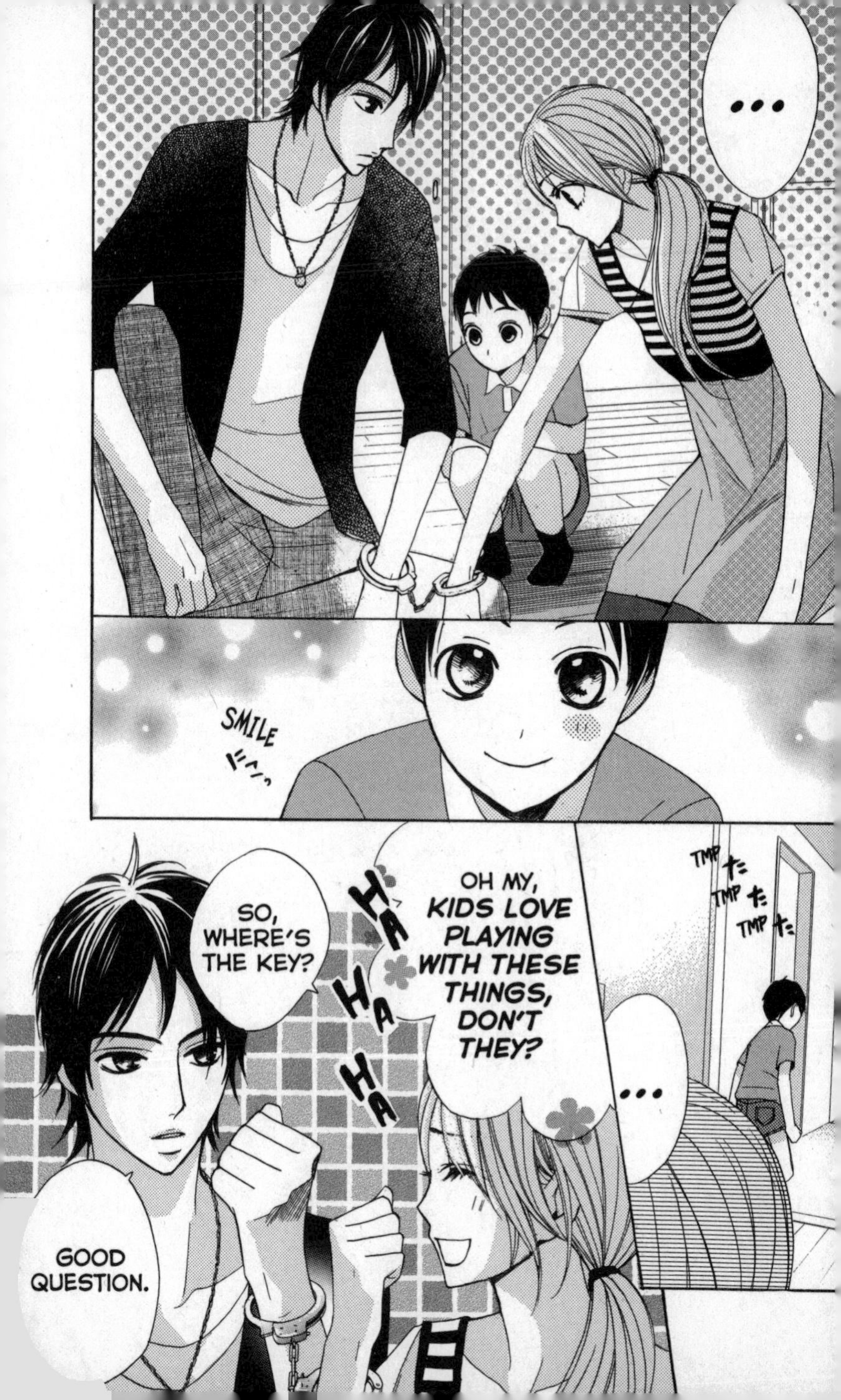
...
SMILE
TMP
TMP
TMP
OH MY, KIDS LOVE PLAYING WITH THESE THINGS, DON'T THEY?
HA HA HA
SO, WHERE'S THE KEY?
...
GOOD QUESTION.

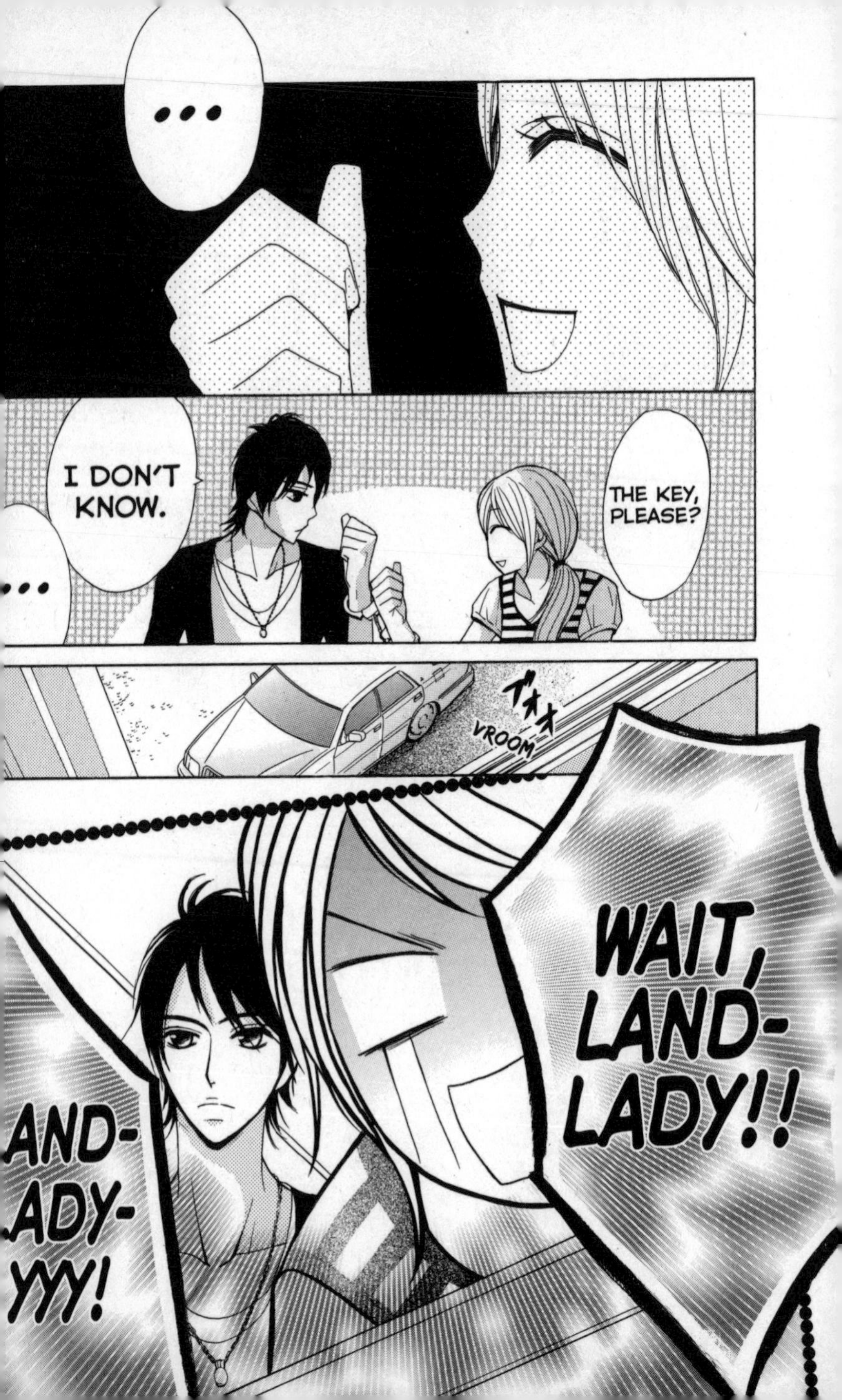
...
THE KEY, PLEASE?
I DON'T KNOW.
...
ブオオ
VROOM
WAIT, LAND-LADY!!
AND-ADY-YYY!

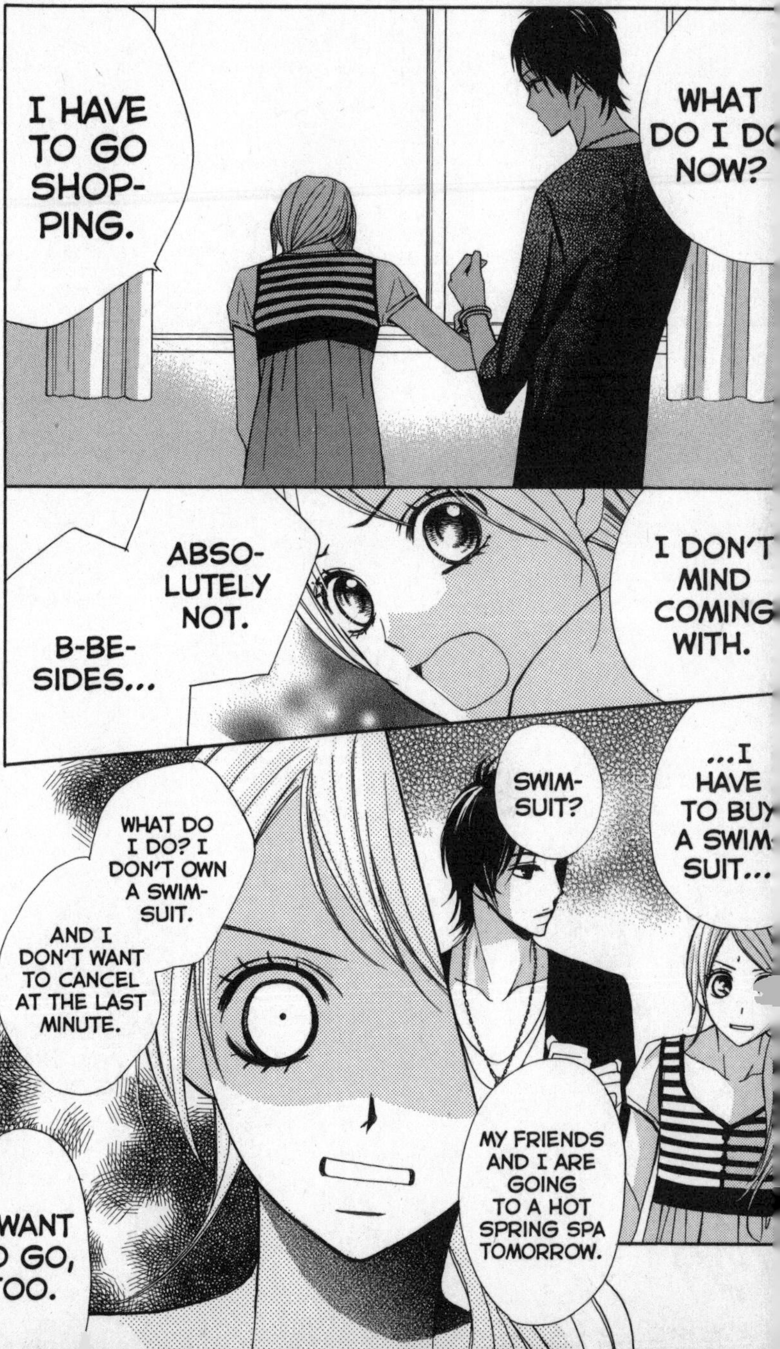
WHAT DO I DO NOW?
I HAVE TO GO SHOPPING.
I DON'T MIND COMING WITH.
ABSOLUTELY NOT.
B-BESIDES...
...I HAVE TO BUY A SWIMSUIT...
SWIMSUIT?
WHAT DO I DO? I DON'T OWN A SWIMSUIT.
AND I DON'T WANT TO CANCEL AT THE LAST MINUTE.
MY FRIENDS AND I ARE GOING TO A HOT SPRING SPA TOMORROW.
I WANT TO GO, TOO.

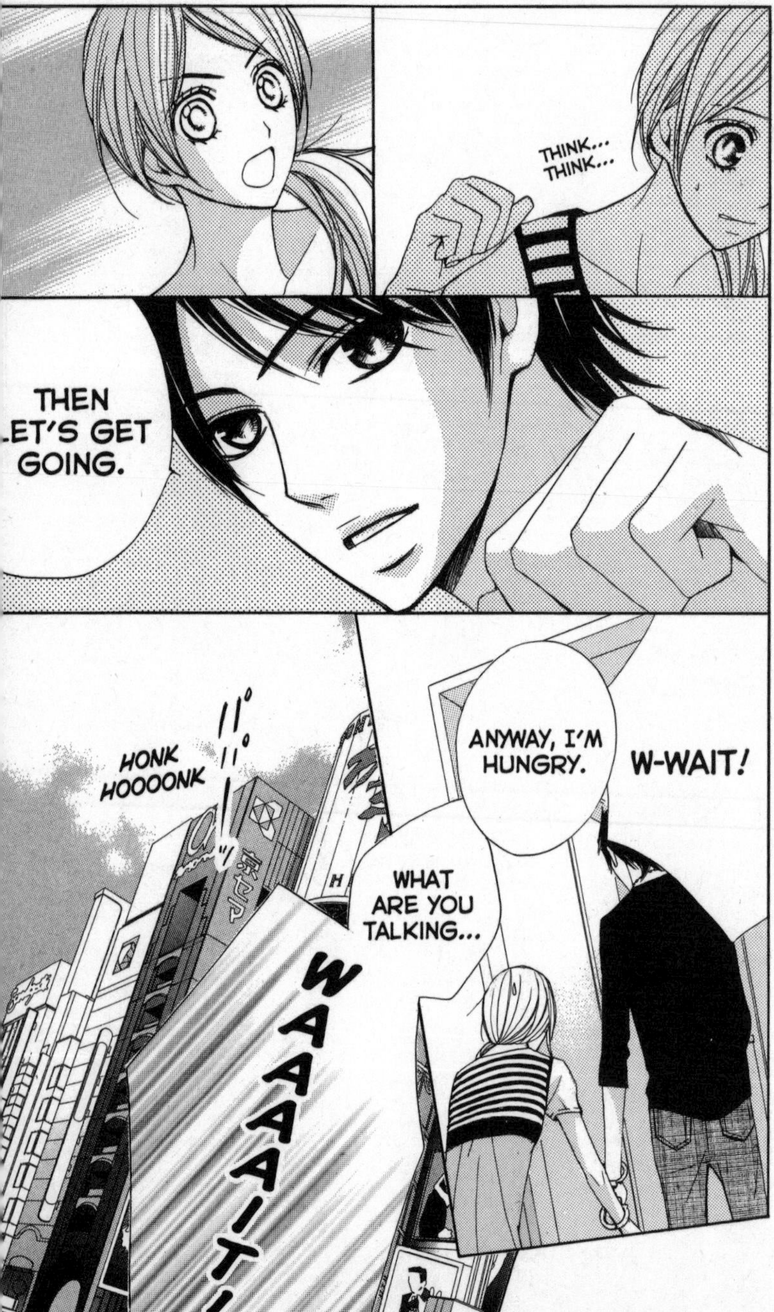
THINK... THINK...
THEN LET'S GET GOING.
W-WAIT!
ANYWAY, I'M HUNGRY.
WHAT ARE YOU TALKING...
HONK HOOOONK
WAAAAAIT!!

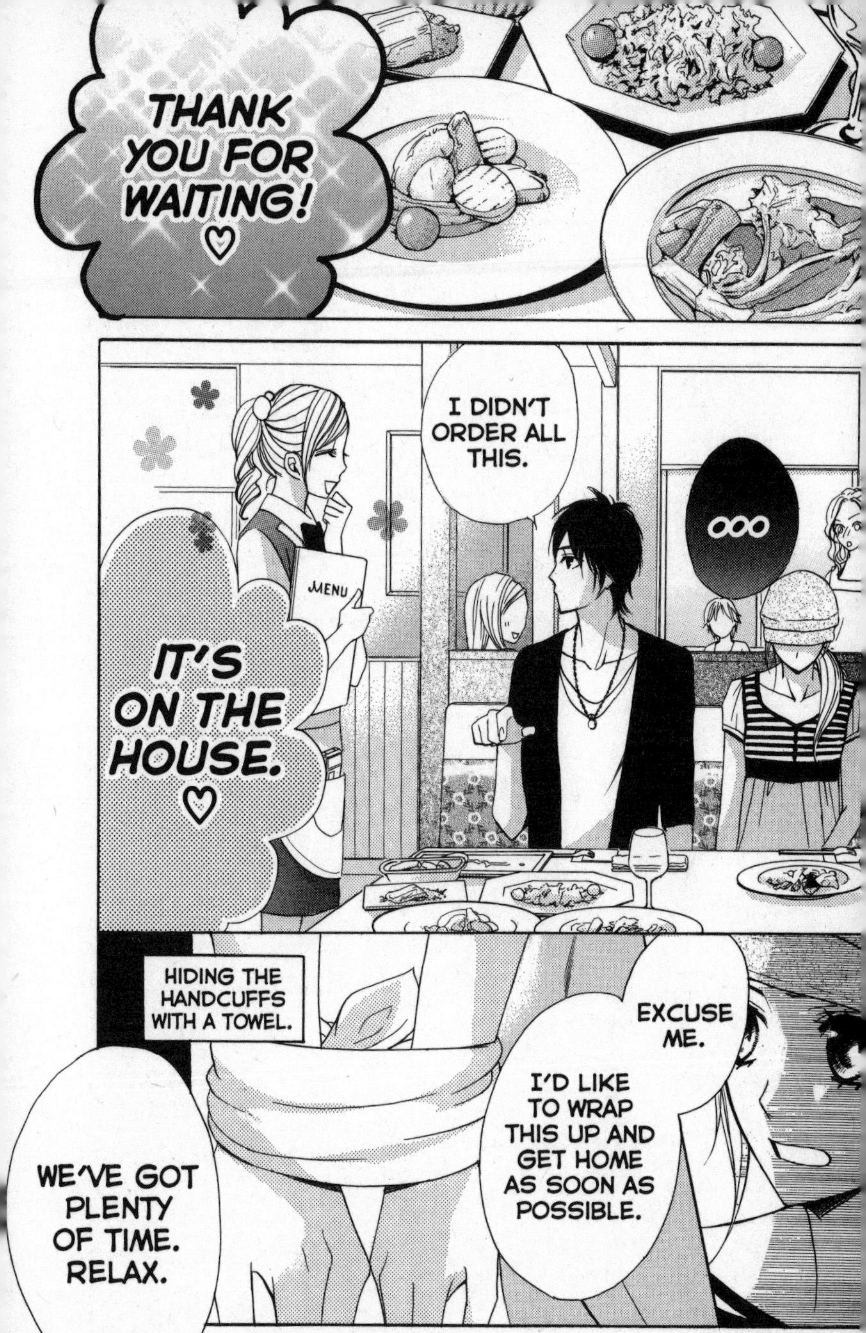
THANK YOU FOR WAITING! ♡
...
I DIDN'T ORDER ALL THIS.
MENU
IT'S ON THE HOUSE. ♡
EXCUSE ME.
I'D LIKE TO WRAP THIS UP AND GET HOME AS SOON AS POSSIBLE.
HIDING THE HANDCUFFS WITH A TOWEL.
WE'VE GOT PLENTY OF TIME. RELAX.

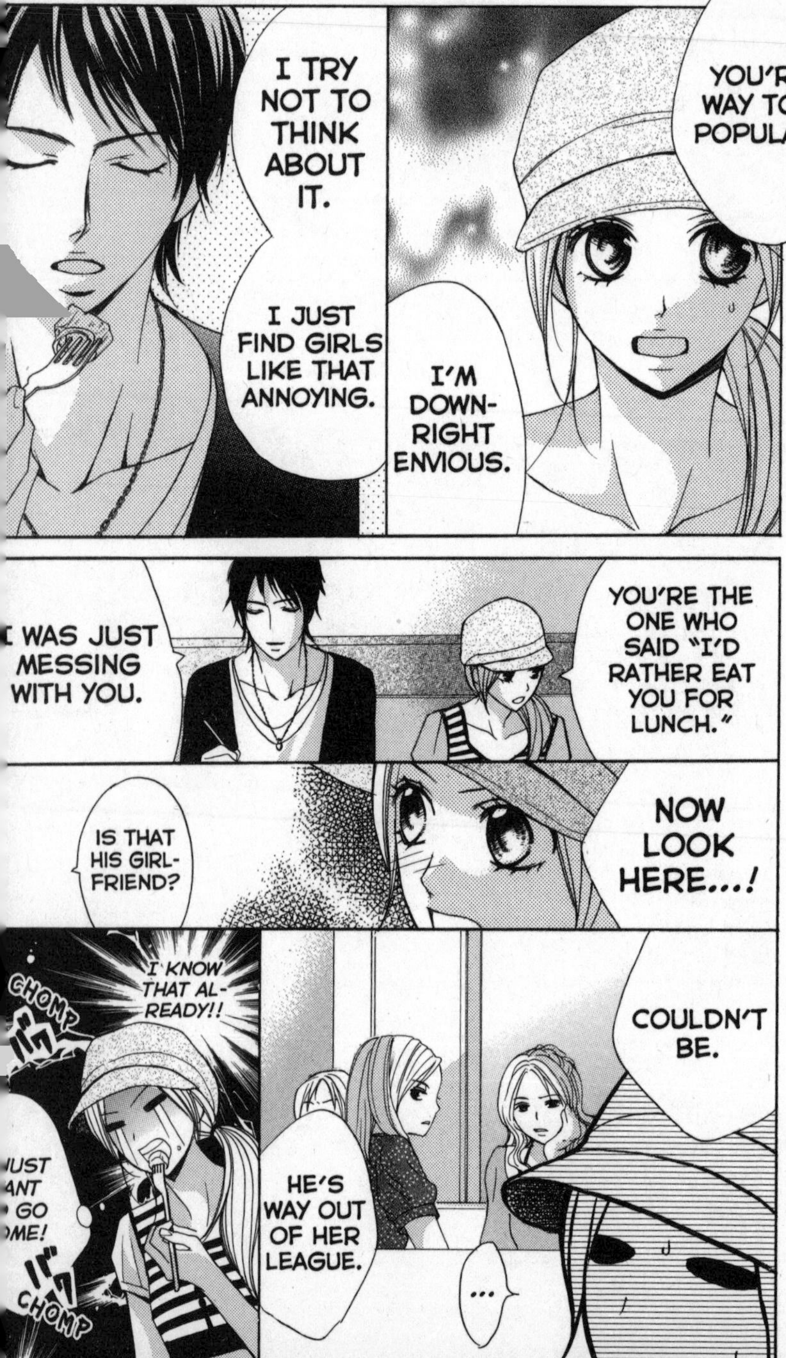
YOU'RE WAY TOO POPULAR.
I'M DOWN-RIGHT ENVIOUS.
I TRY NOT TO THINK ABOUT IT.
I JUST FIND GIRLS LIKE THAT ANNOYING.
YOU'RE THE ONE WHO SAID "I'D RATHER EAT YOU FOR LUNCH."
I WAS JUST MESSING WITH YOU.
NOW LOOK HERE...!
IS THAT HIS GIRL-FRIEND?
COULDN'T BE.
HE'S WAY OUT OF HER LEAGUE.
...
I KNOW THAT AL-READY!!
CHOMP
CHOMP

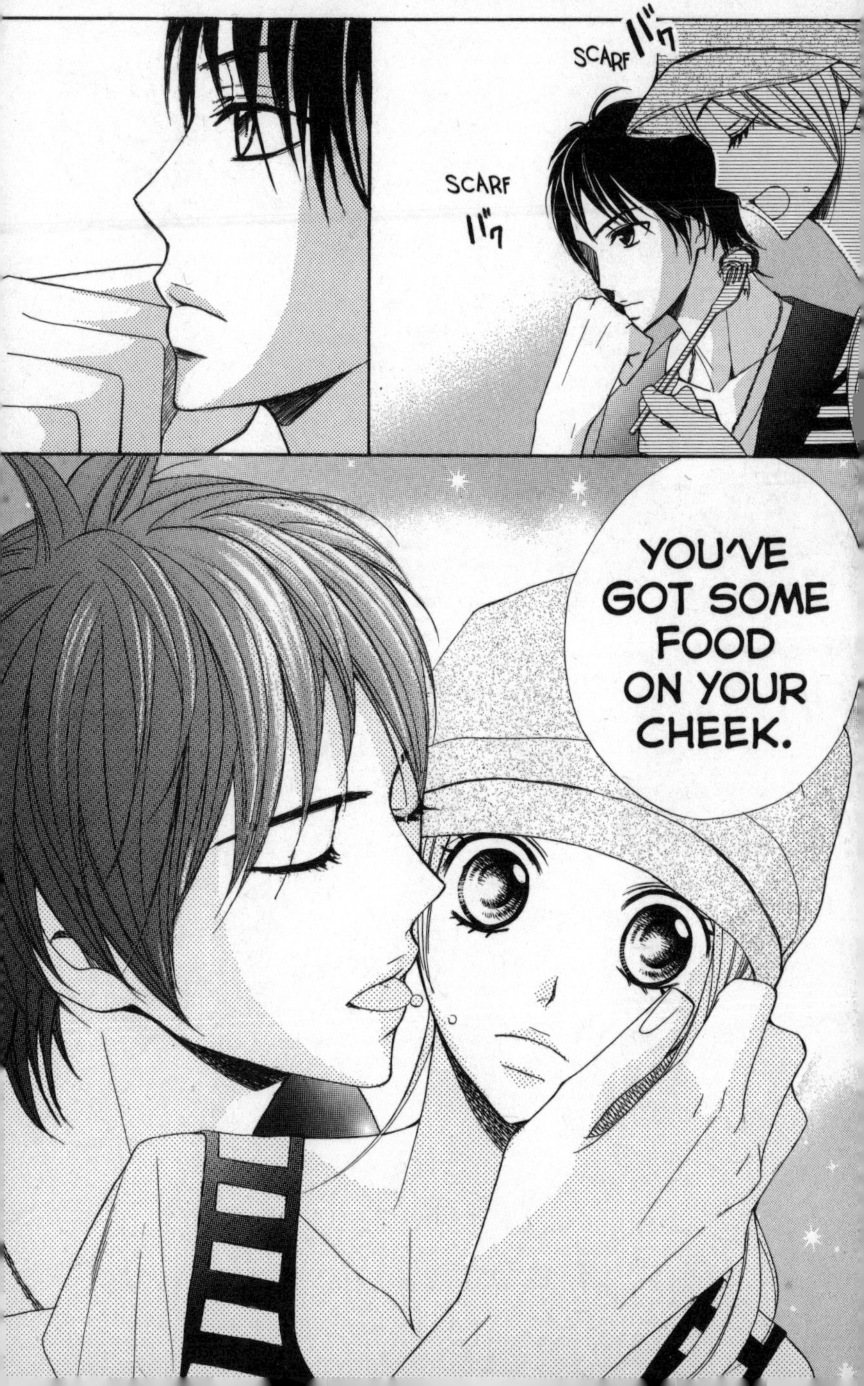
SCARF
バク
SCARF
バク
YOU'VE GOT SOME FOOD ON YOUR CHEEK.

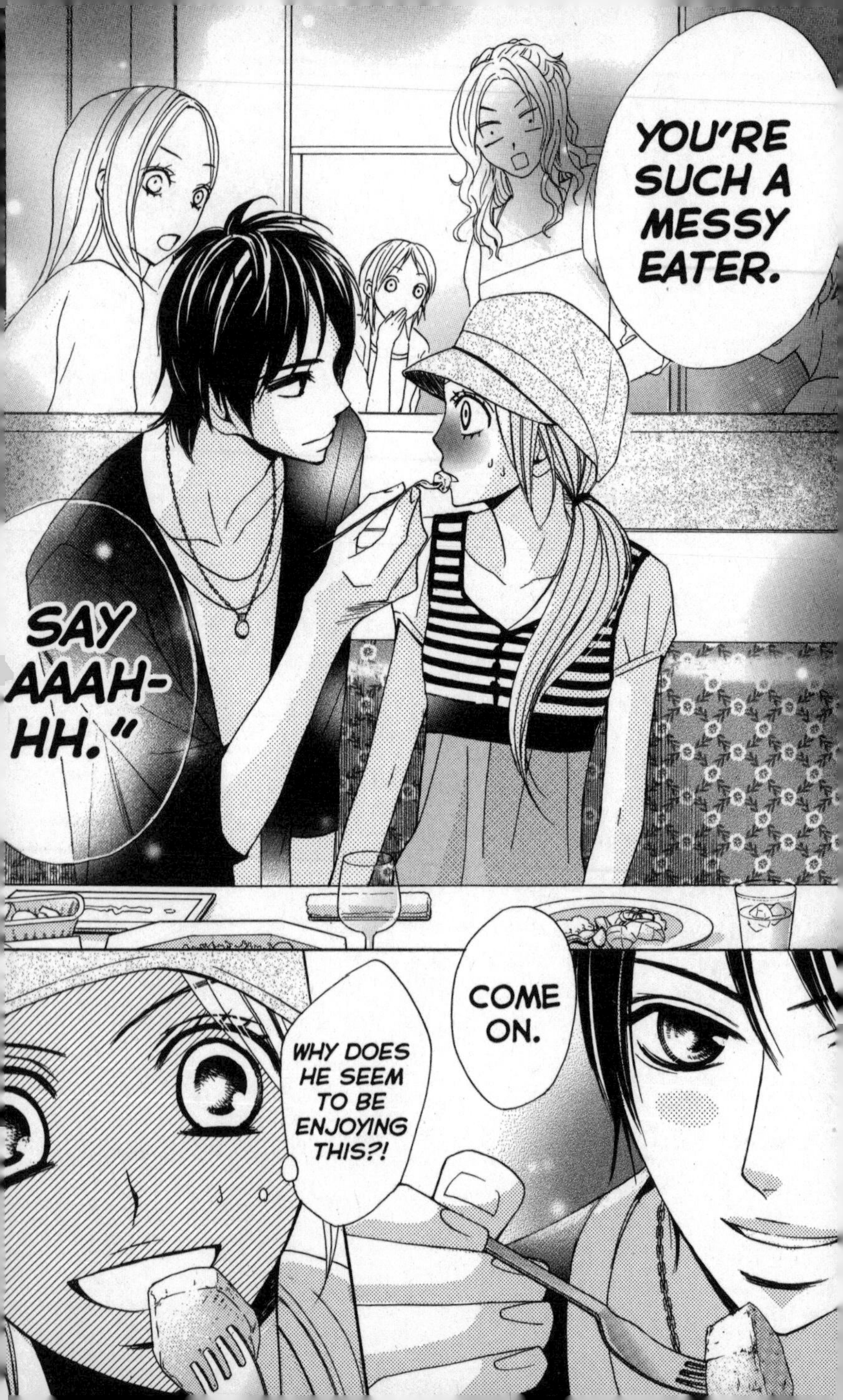
YOU'RE SUCH A MESSY EATER.
SAY AAAH-HH."
COME ON.
WHY DOES HE SEEM TO BE ENJOYING THIS?!

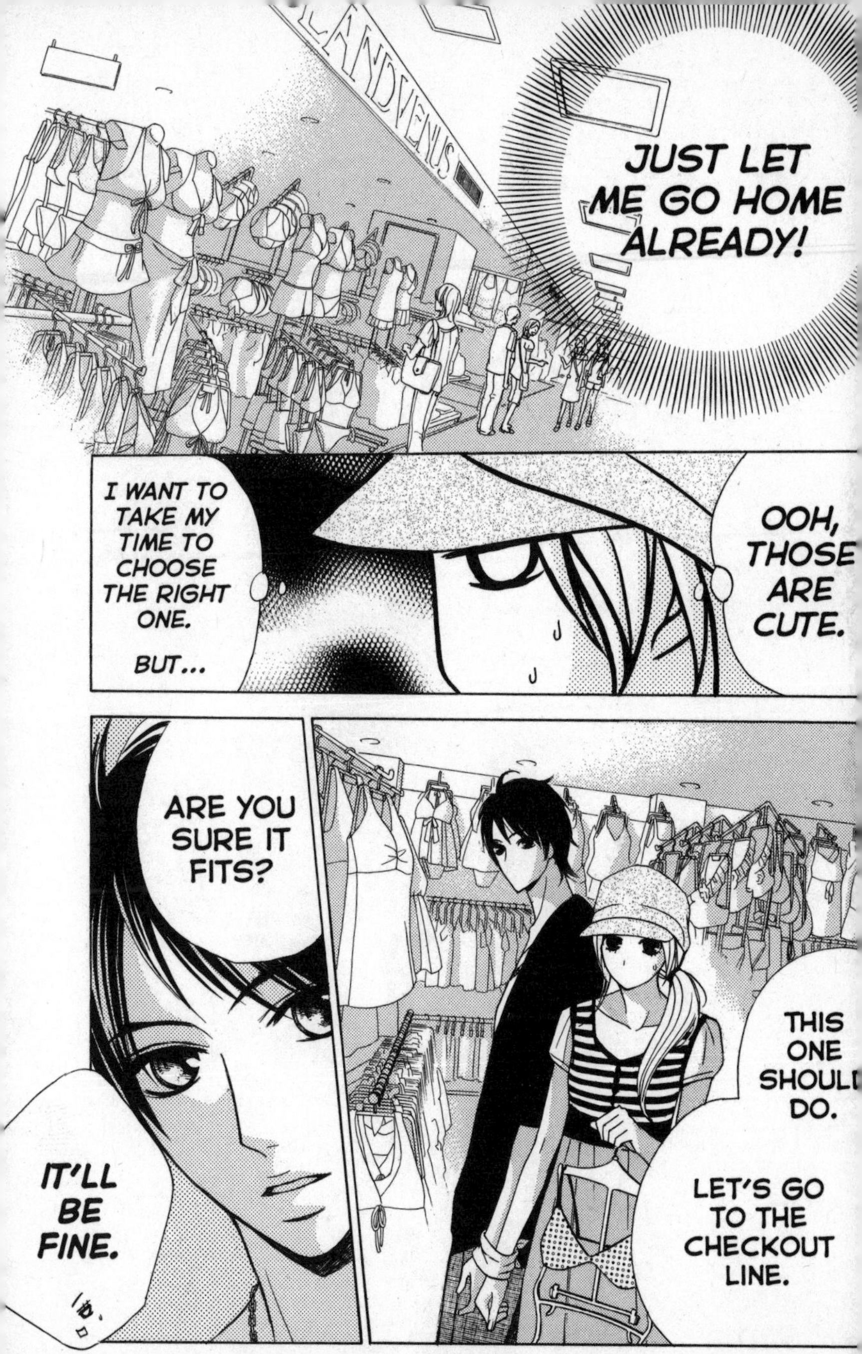
JUST LET ME GO HOME ALREADY!
OOH, THOSE ARE CUTE.
I WANT TO TAKE MY TIME TO CHOOSE THE RIGHT ONE.
BUT...
THIS ONE SHOULD DO.
LET'S GO TO THE CHECKOUT LINE.
ARE YOU SURE IT FITS?
IT'LL BE FINE.

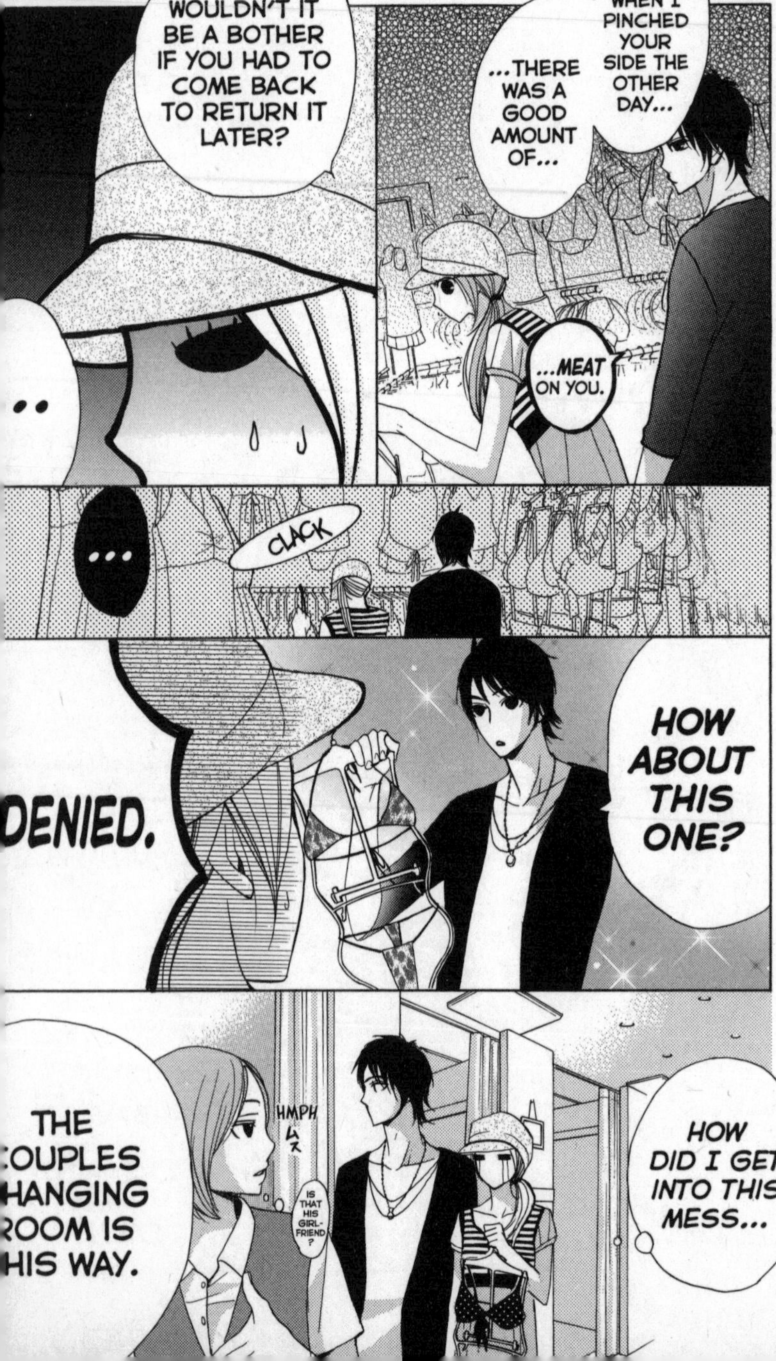
WHEN I PINCHED YOUR SIDE THE OTHER DAY...
...THERE WAS A GOOD AMOUNT OF...
...MEAT ON YOU.
WOULDN'T IT BE A BOTHER IF YOU HAD TO COME BACK TO RETURN IT LATER?
..
...
CLACK
HOW ABOUT THIS ONE?
DENIED.
HOW DID I GET INTO THIS MESS...
IS THAT HIS GIRLFRIEND?
HMPH
ムス
THE OUPLES HANGING OOM IS HIS WAY.

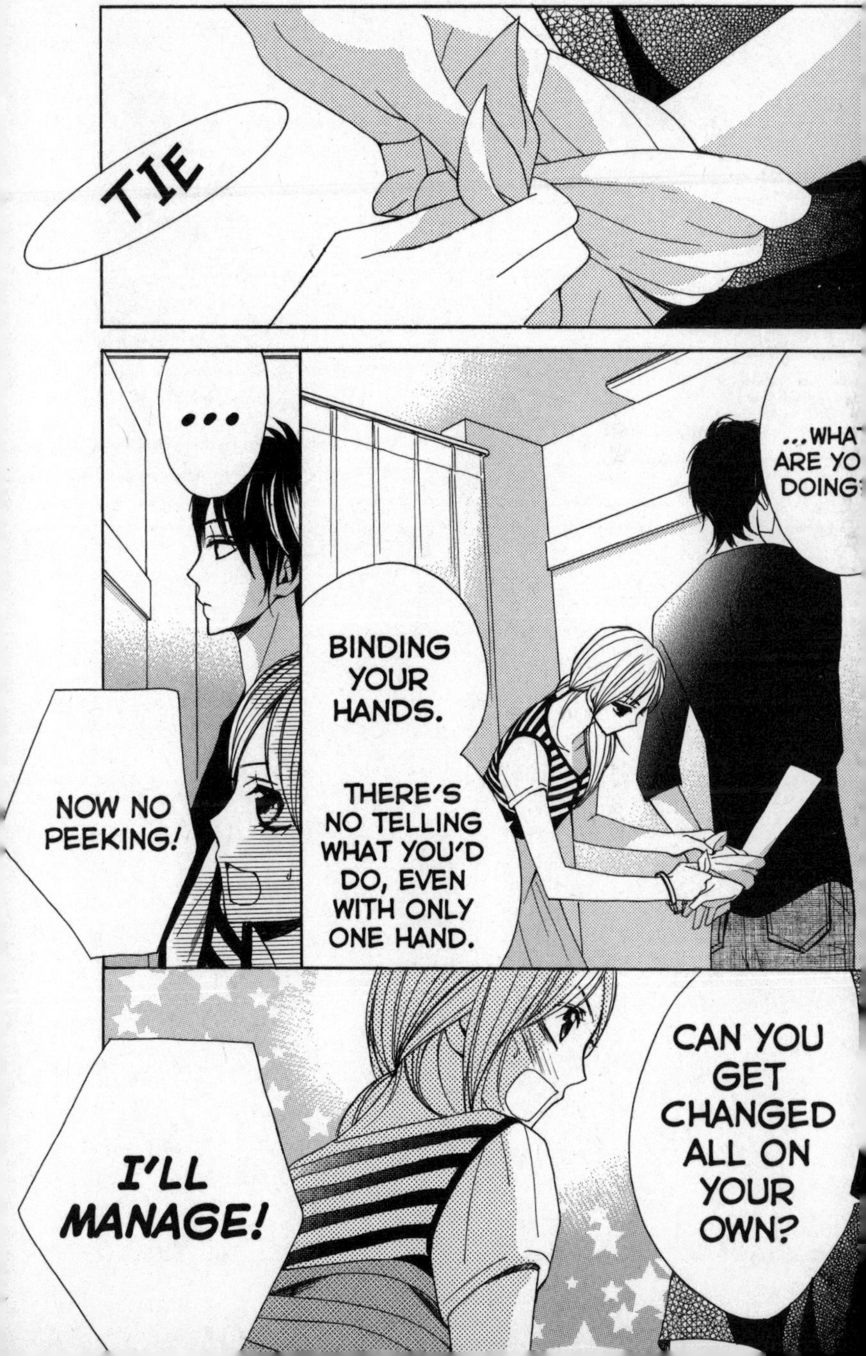
TIE
...WHAT ARE YO DOING
BINDING YOUR HANDS.
THERE'S NO TELLING WHAT YOU'D DO, EVEN WITH ONLY ONE HAND.
...
NOW NO PEEKING!
CAN YOU GET CHANGED ALL ON YOUR OWN?
I'LL MANAGE!

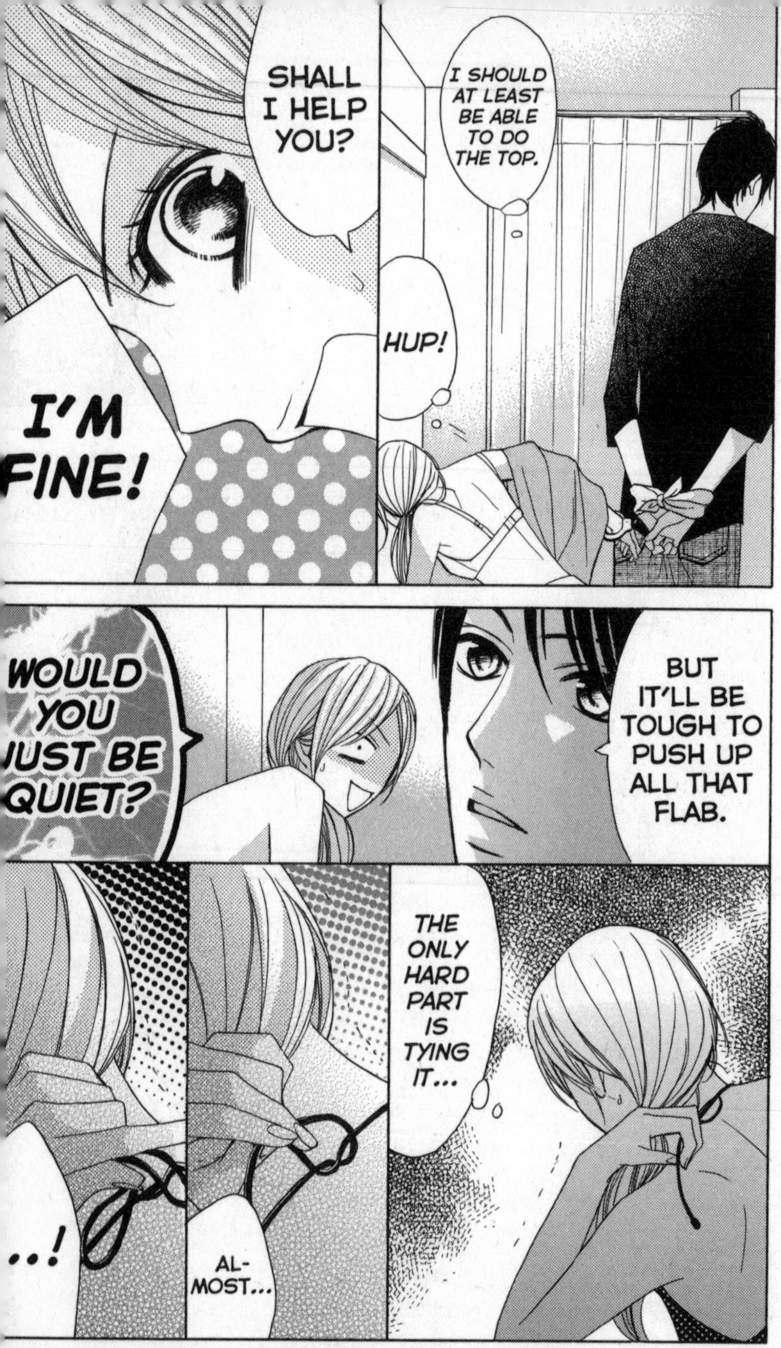
I SHOULD AT LEAST BE ABLE TO DO THE TOP.
HUP!
SHALL I HELP YOU?
I'M FINE!
BUT IT'LL BE TOUGH TO PUSH UP ALL THAT FLAB.
WOULD YOU JUST BE QUIET?
THE ONLY HARD PART IS TYING IT...
AL-MOST...
..!

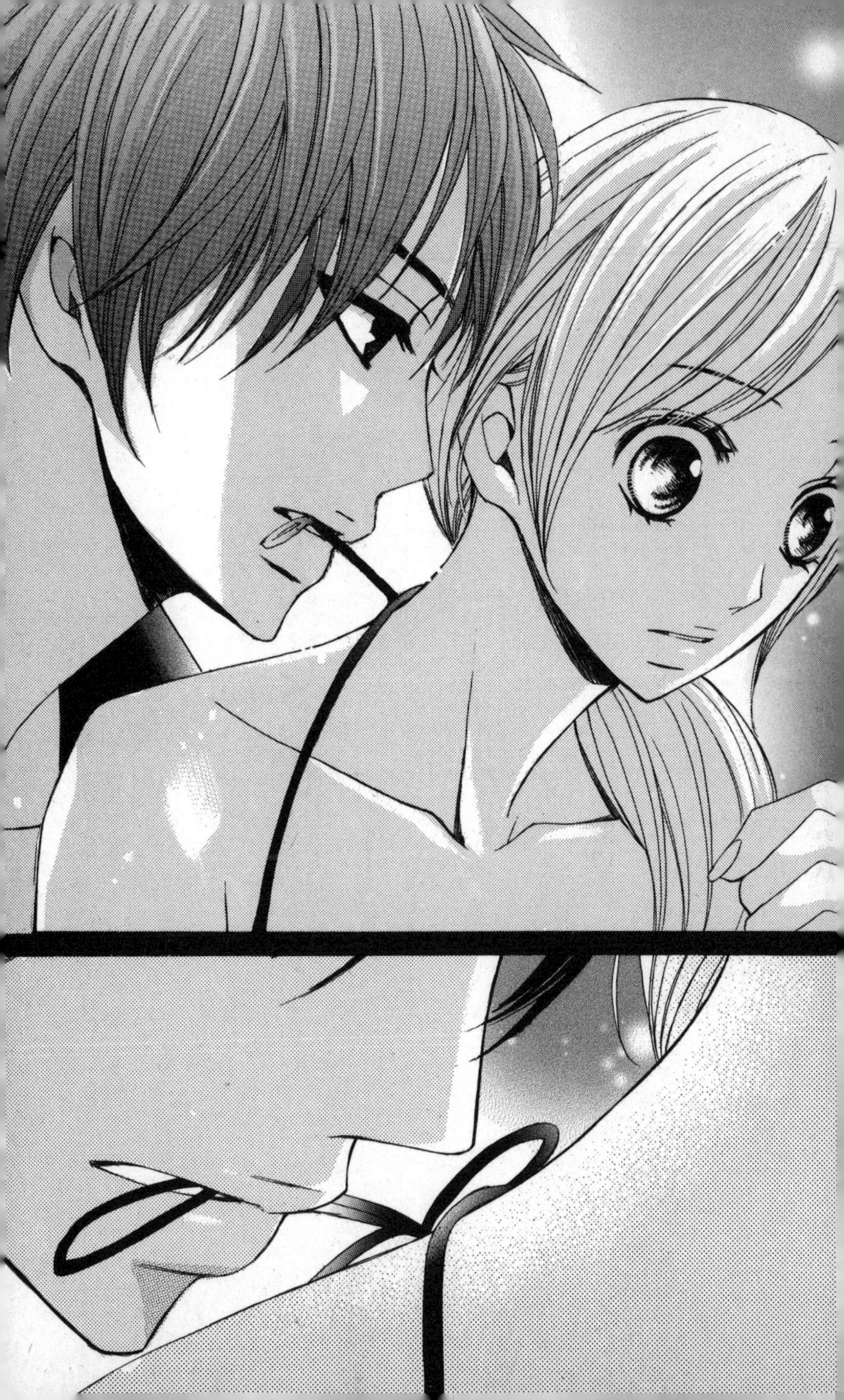

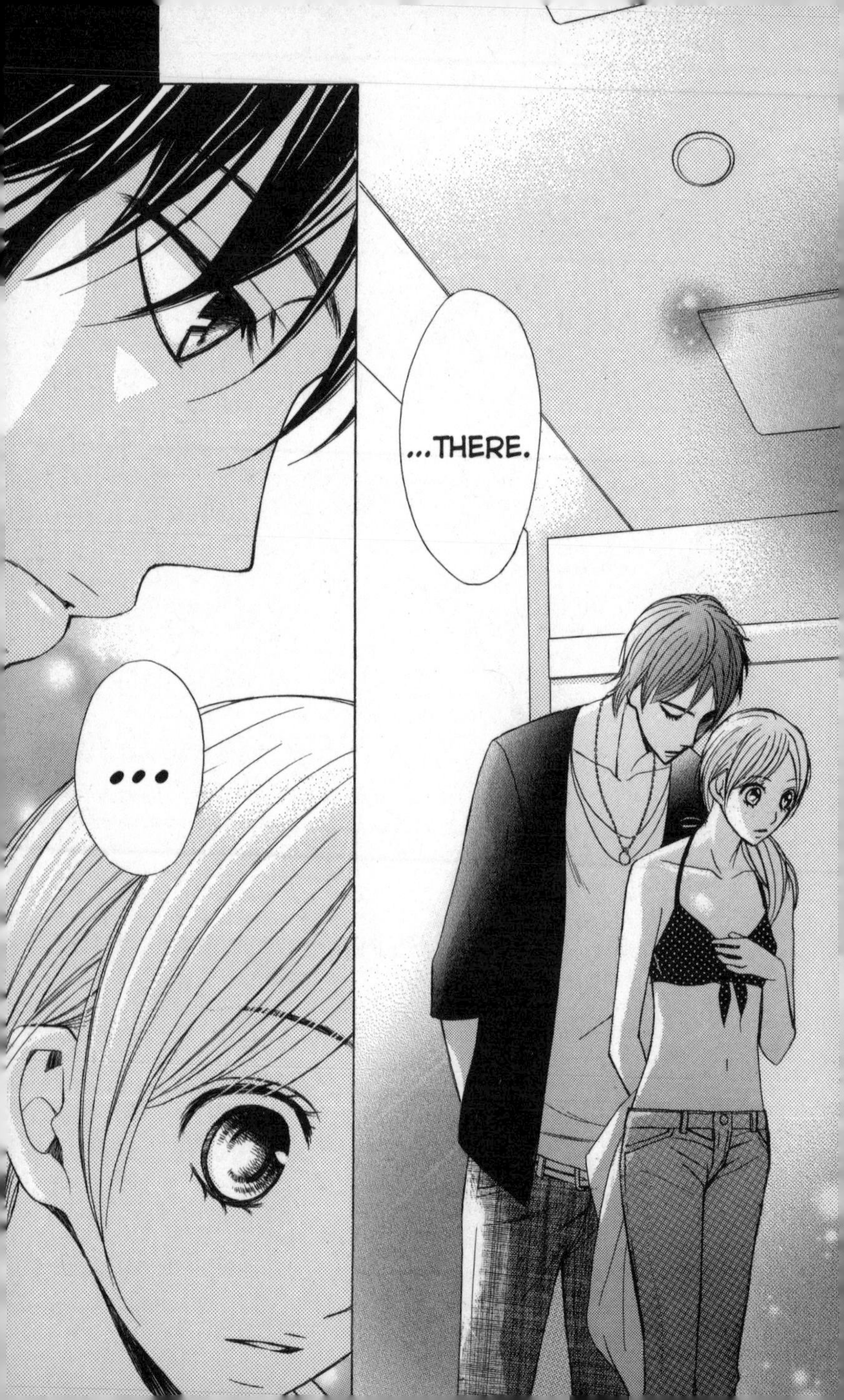
...THERE.
...

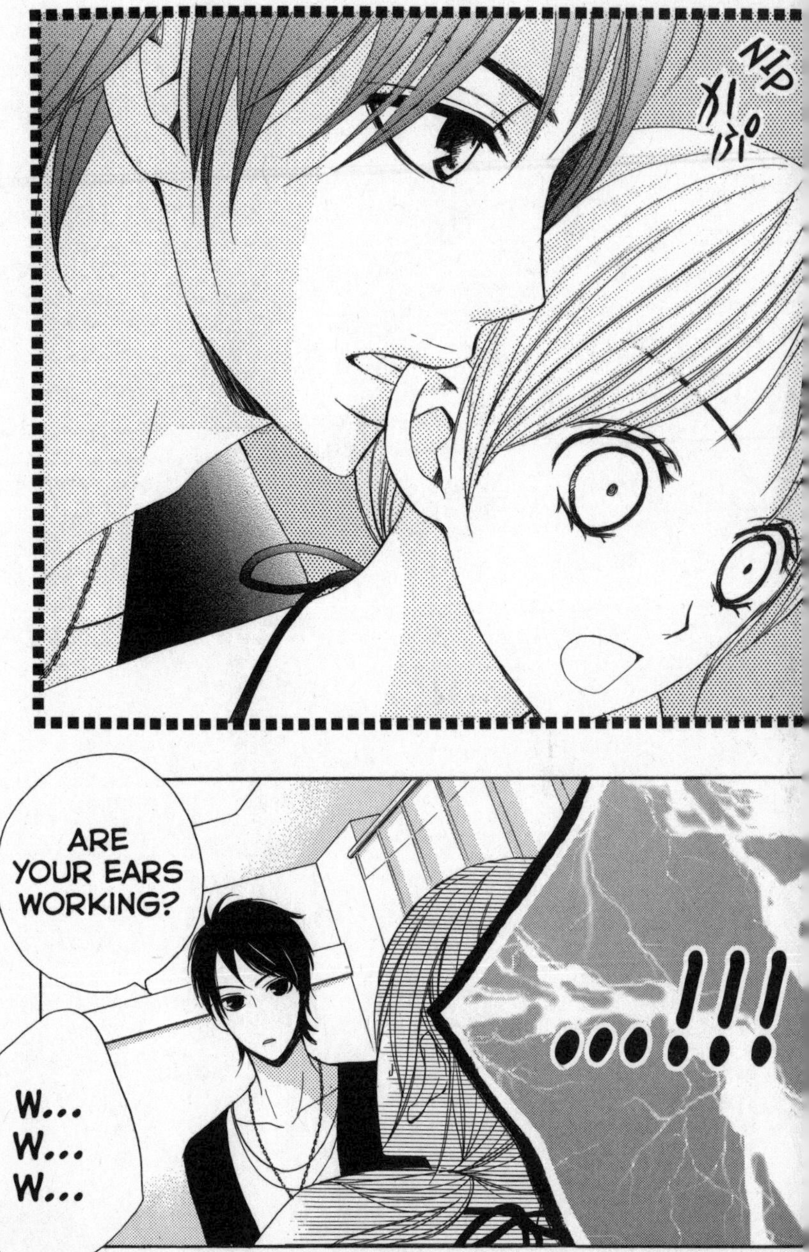
NIP
...!!!
ARE YOUR EARS WORKING?
W... W... W...

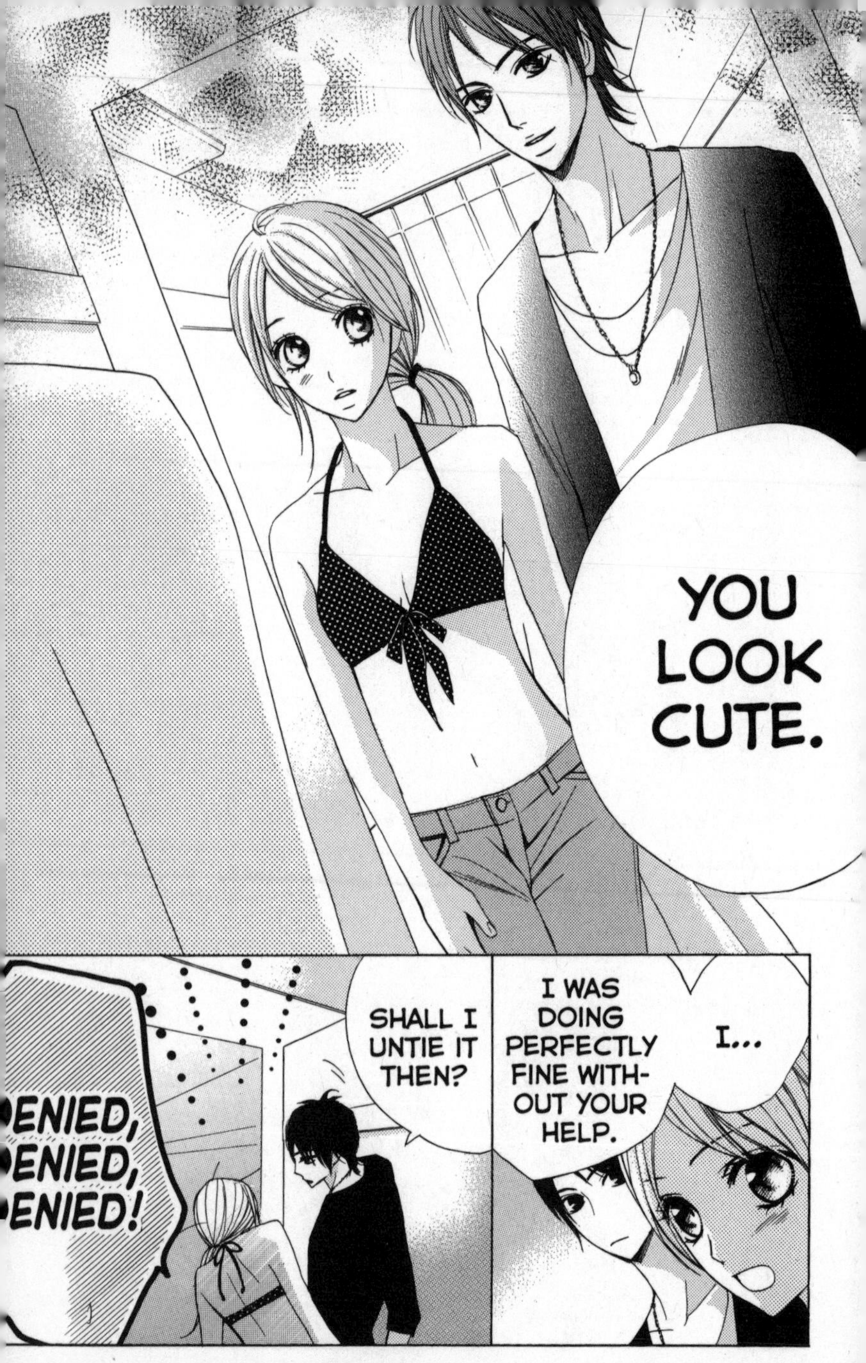
YOU LOOK CUTE.
I...
I WAS DOING PERFECTLY FINE WITH-OUT YOUR HELP.
SHALL I UNTIE IT THEN?
ENIED, ENIED, ENIED!

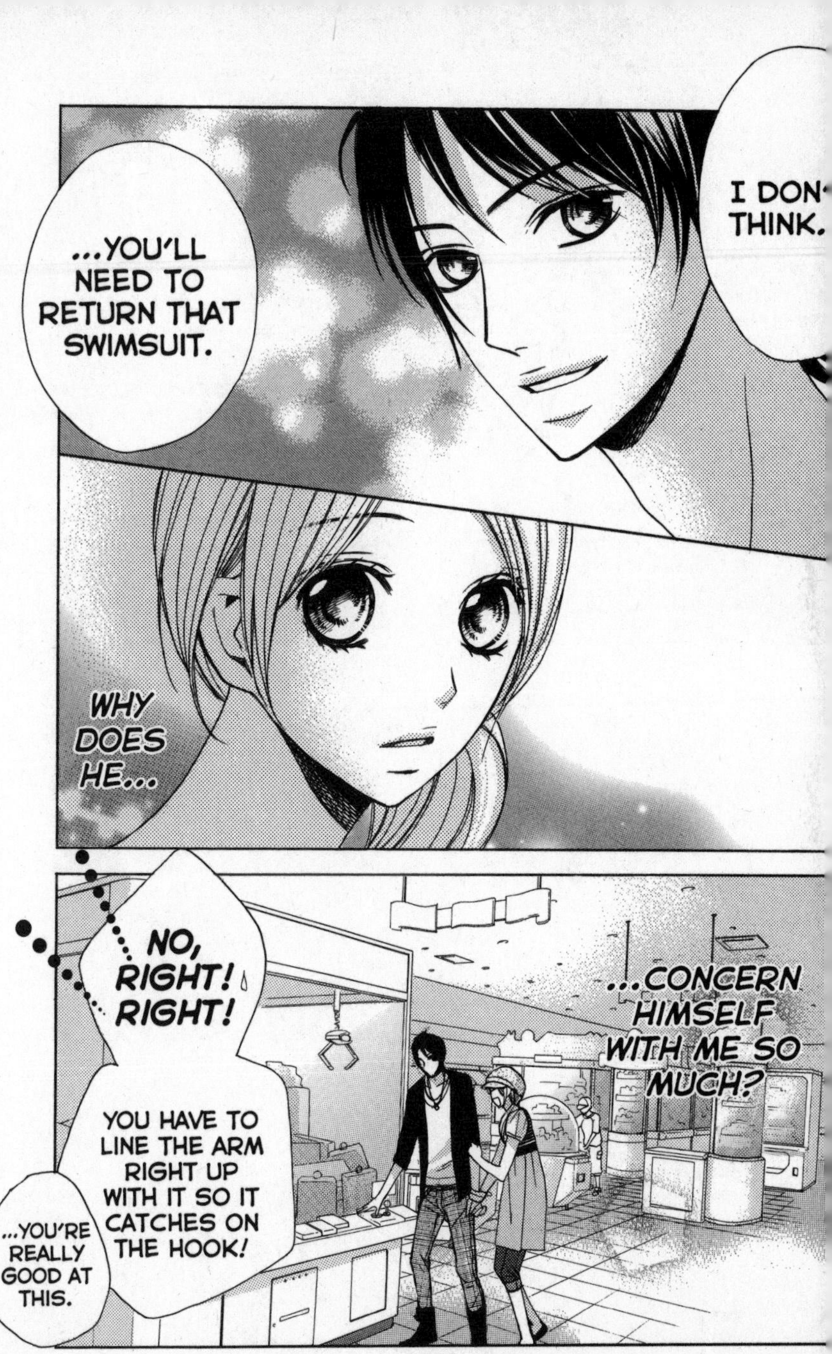
I DON'
THINK.
...YOU'LL NEED TO RETURN THAT SWIMSUIT.
WHY DOES HE...
...CONCERN HIMSELF WITH ME SO MUCH?
NO, RIGHT! RIGHT!
YOU HAVE TO LINE THE ARM RIGHT UP WITH IT SO IT CATCHES ON THE HOOK!
...YOU'RE REALLY GOOD AT THIS.

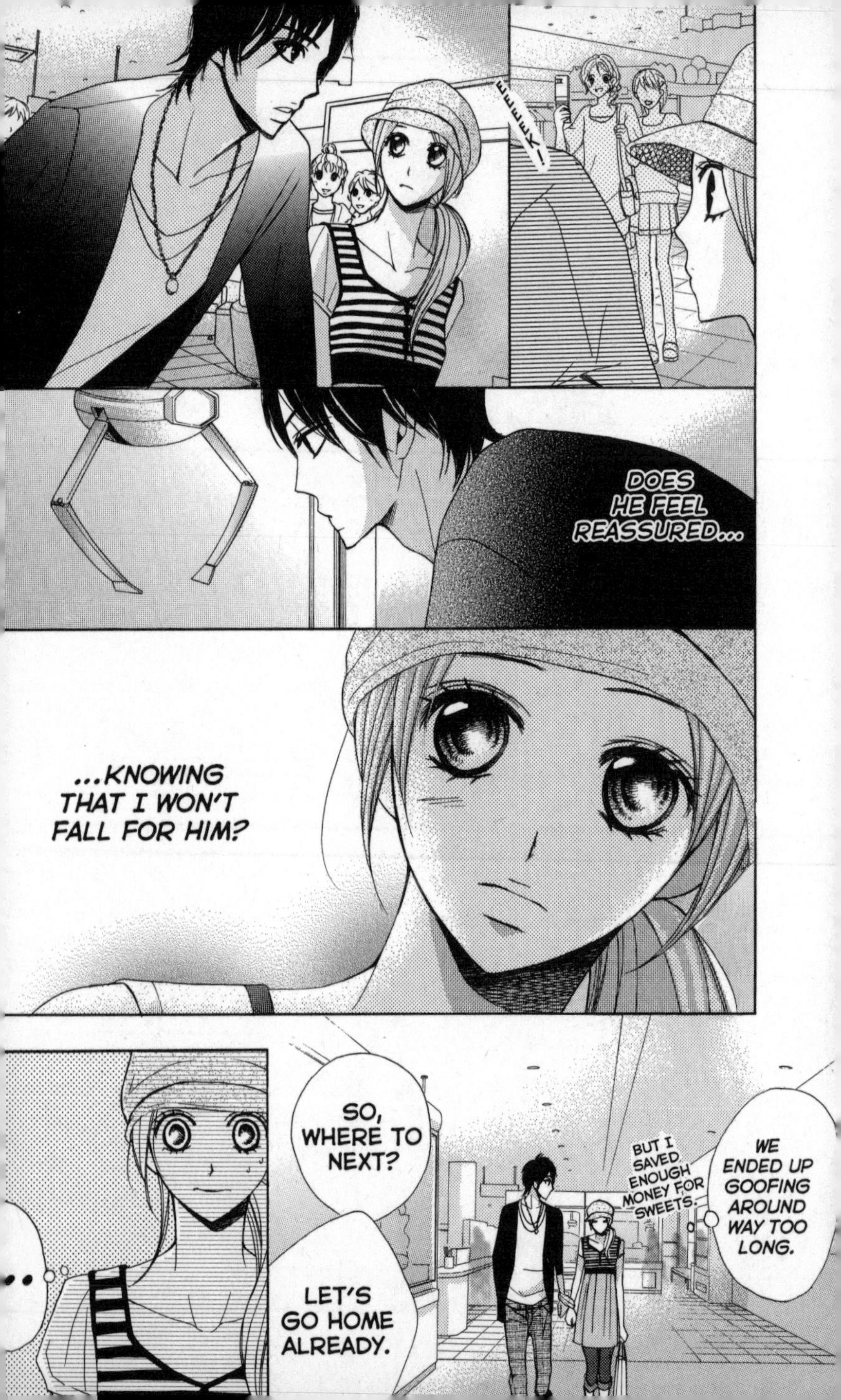
EEEEK!
DOES HE FEEL REASSURED...
...KNOWING THAT I WON'T FALL FOR HIM?
WE ENDED UP GOOFING AROUND WAY TOO LONG.
BUT I SAVED ENOUGH MONEY FOR SWEETS.
SO, WHERE TO NEXT?
LET'S GO HOME ALREADY.
..

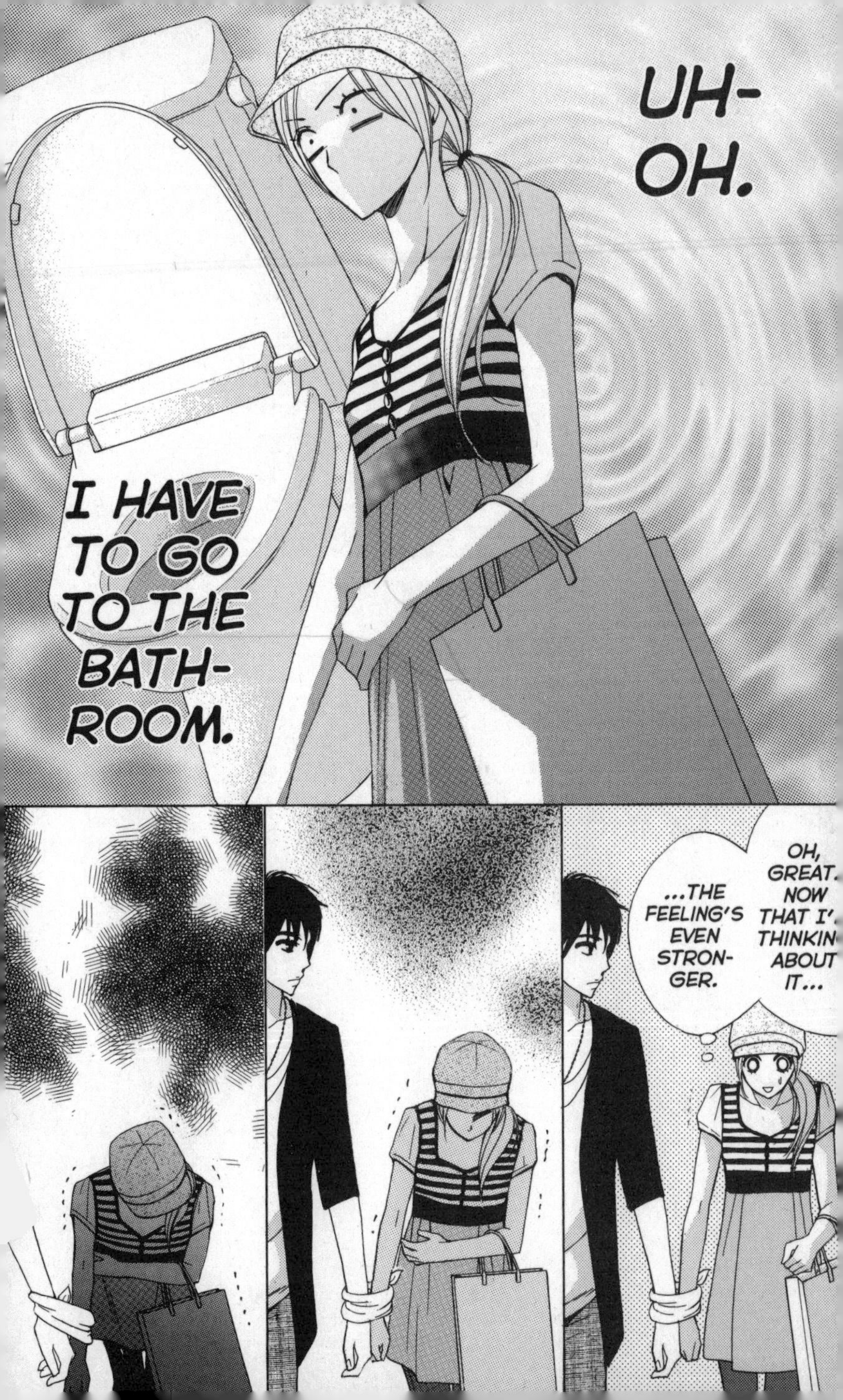

UH-OH.
I HAVE TO GO TO THE BATH-ROOM.
OH, GREAT. NOW THAT I' THINKIN ABOUT IT...
...THE FEELING'S EVEN STRON-GER.

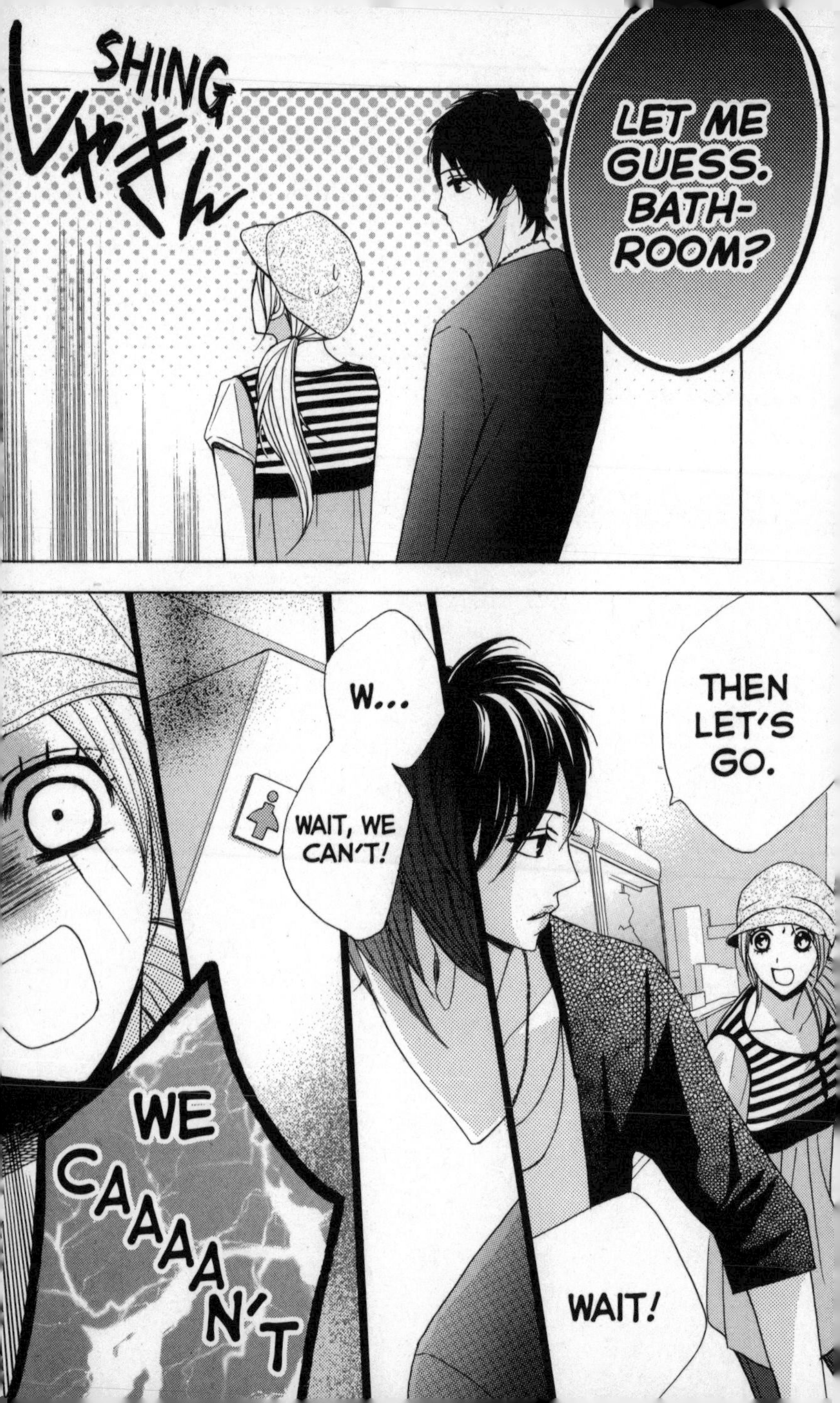
LET ME GUESS. BATH-ROOM?
SHING
しゃきん
THEN LET'S GO.
WAIT!
W...
WAIT, WE CAN'T!
WE CAAAAN'T

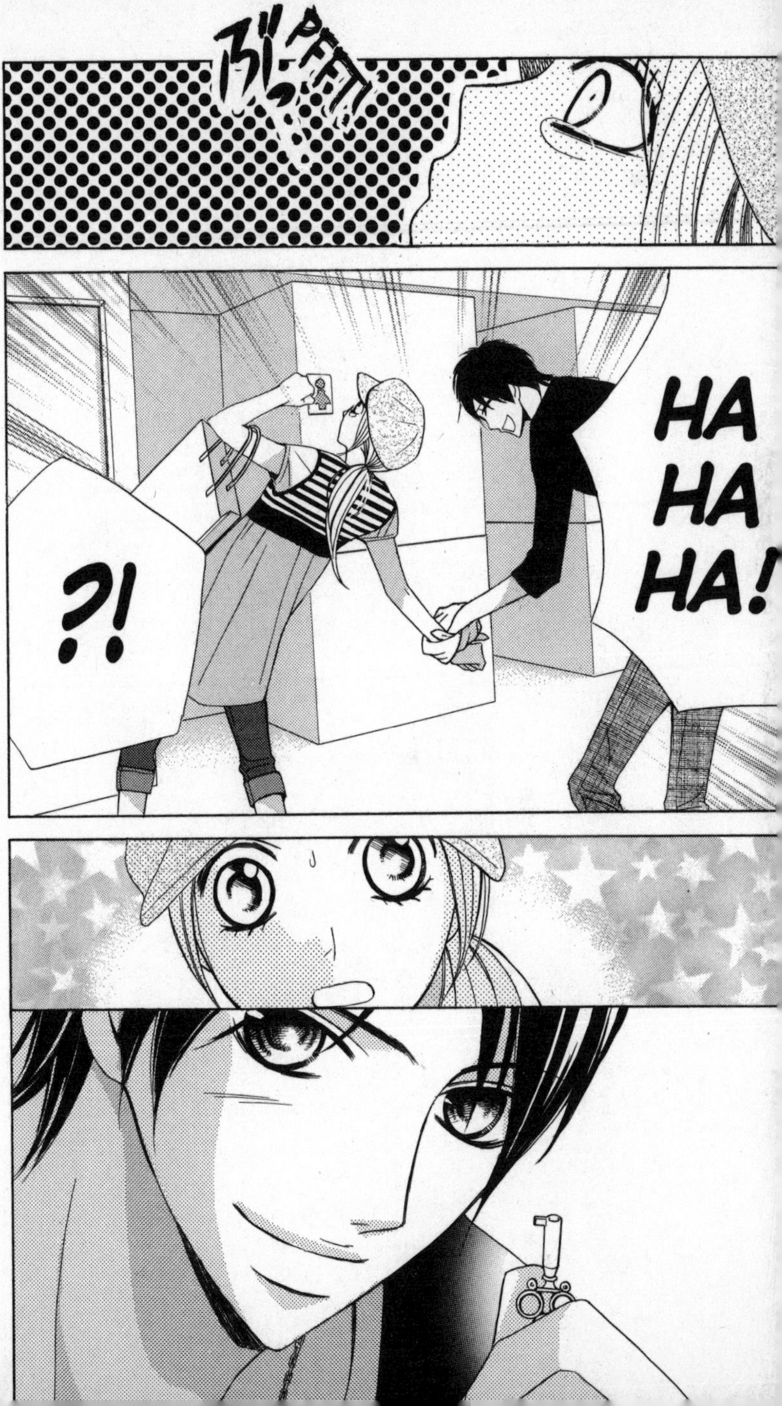
ぷーッ PFFT!
HA HA HA!
?!

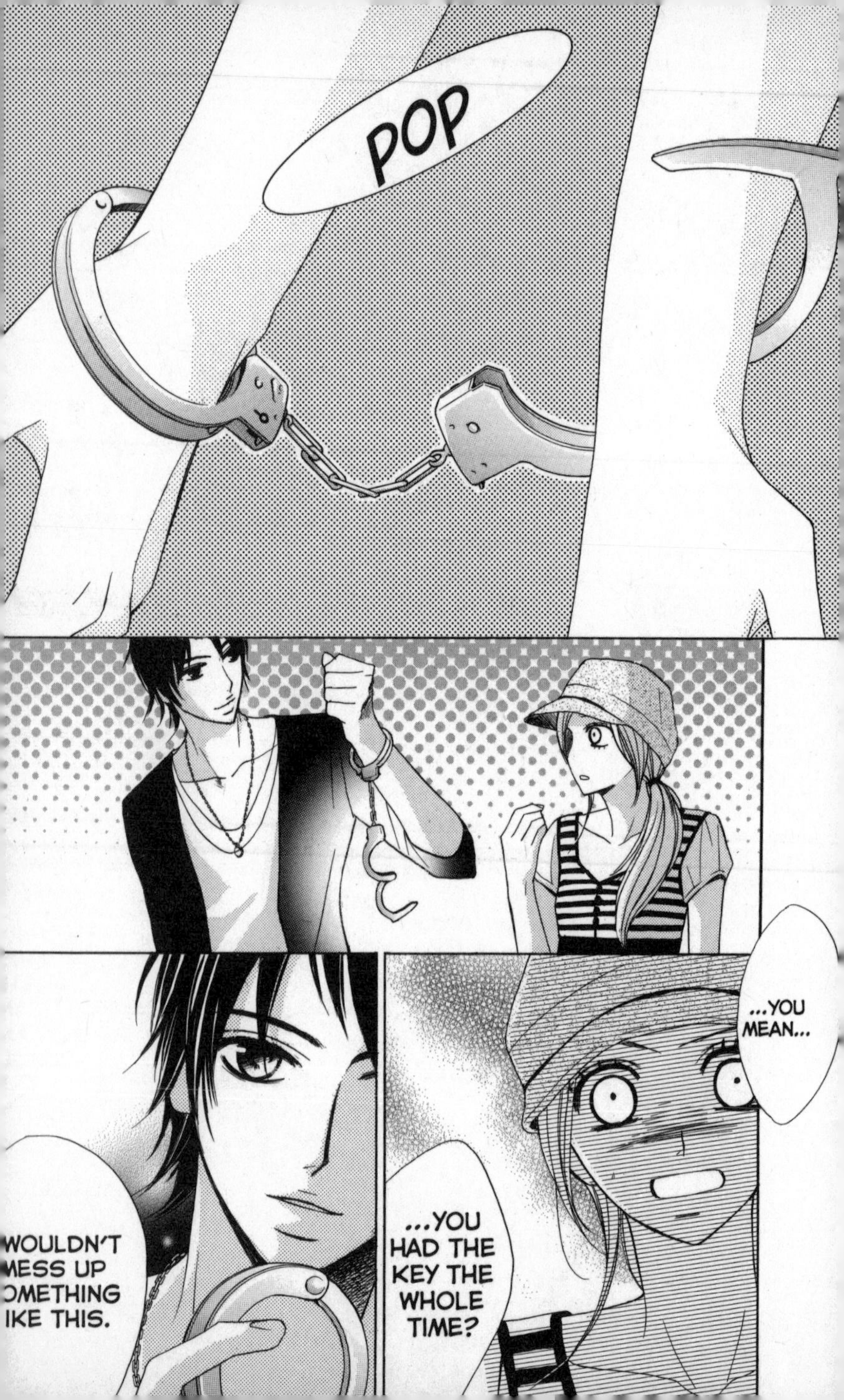
POP
...YOU MEAN...
...YOU HAD THE KEY THE WHOLE TIME?
WOULDN'T MESS UP OMETHING IKE THIS.

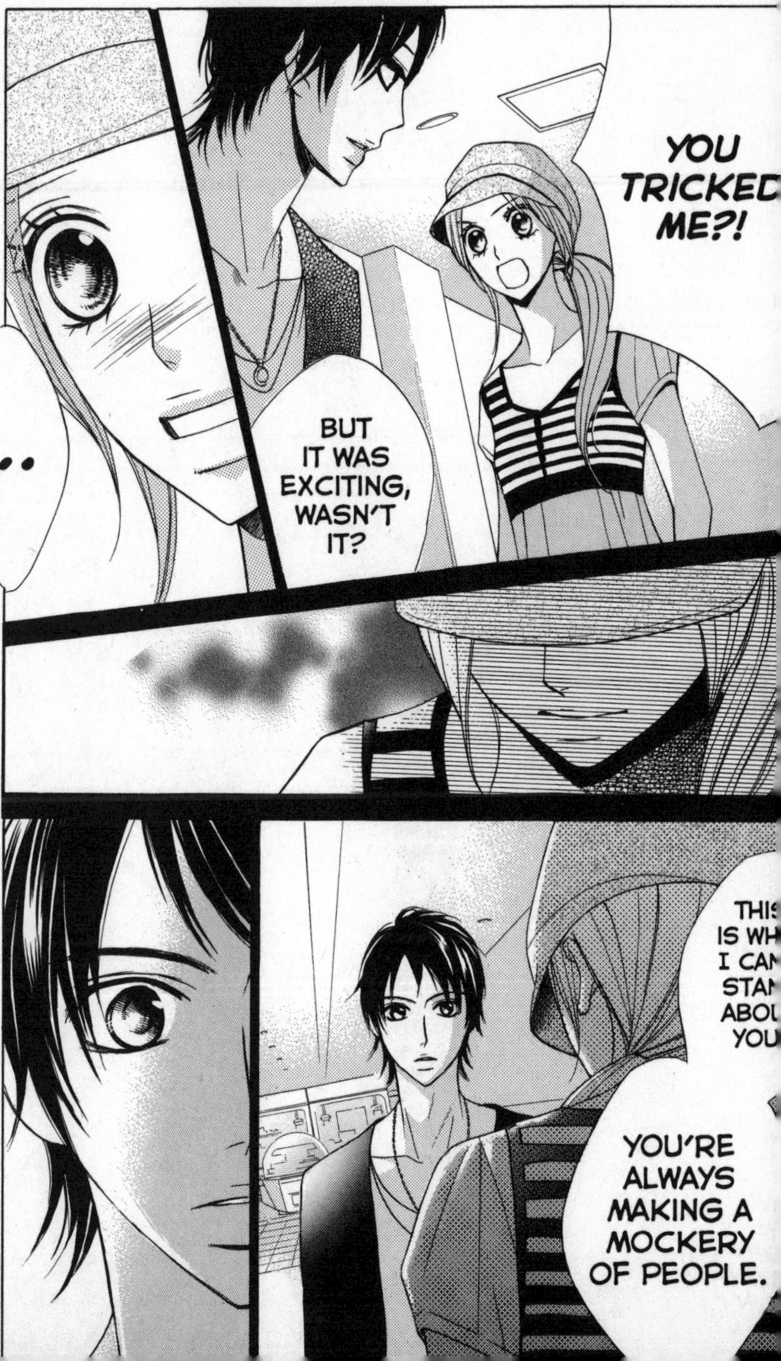
YOU TRICKED ME?!
BUT IT WAS EXCITING, WASN'T IT?
...
THIS IS WH I CAN STAN ABOU YOU
YOU'RE ALWAYS MAKING A MOCKERY OF PEOPLE.

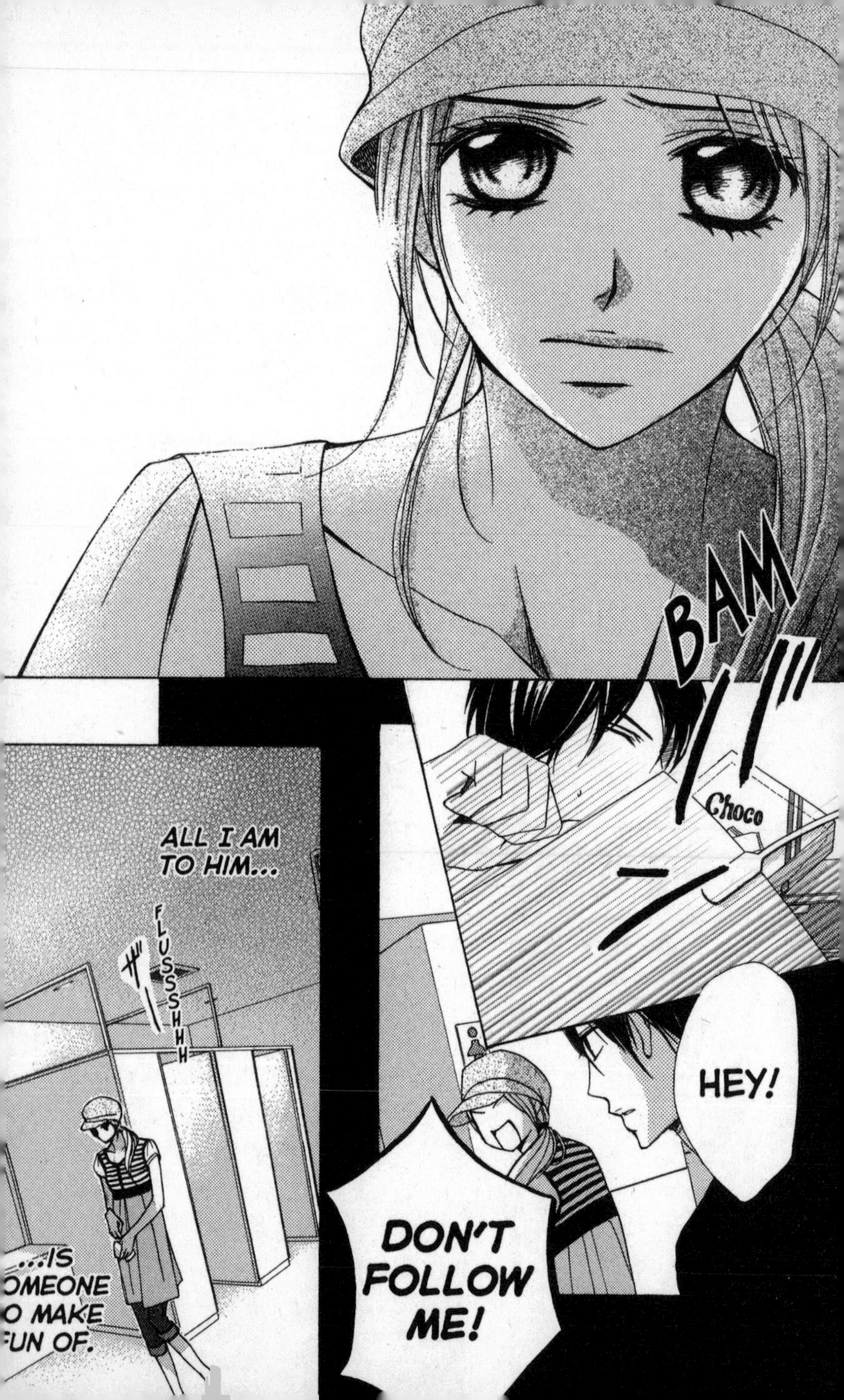
BAM
Choco
HEY!
DON'T FOLLOW ME!
ALL I AM TO HIM...
FLUSSSHHH
...IS
OMEONE
O MAKE
FUN OF.

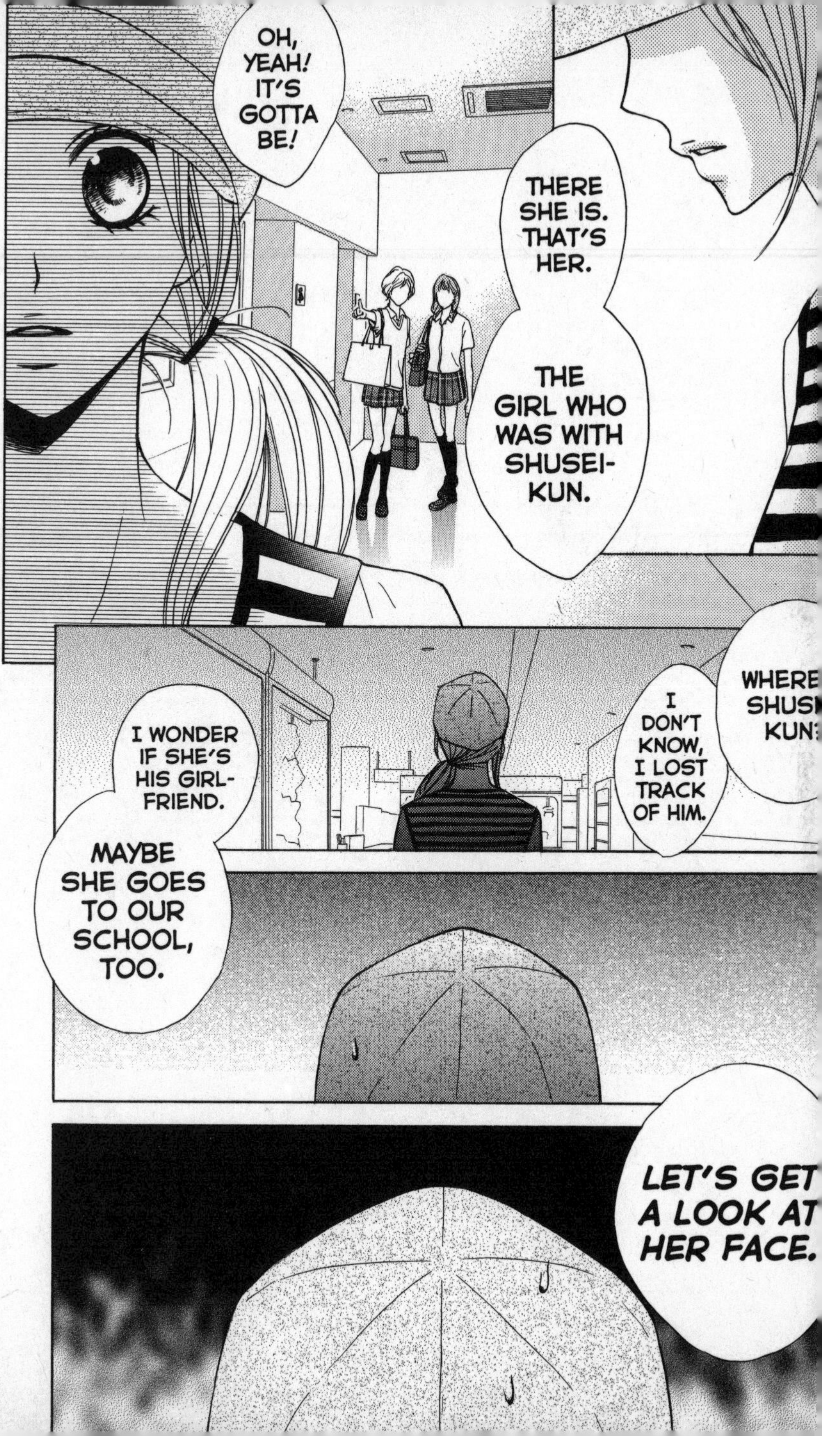
THERE SHE IS. THAT'S HER.
THE GIRL WHO WAS WITH SHUSEI-KUN.
OH, YEAH! IT'S GOTTA BE!
WHERE SHUS KUN
I DON'T KNOW, I LOST TRACK OF HIM.
I WONDER IF SHE'S HIS GIRL-FRIEND.
MAYBE SHE GOES TO OUR SCHOOL, TOO.
LET'S GET A LOOK AT HER FACE.

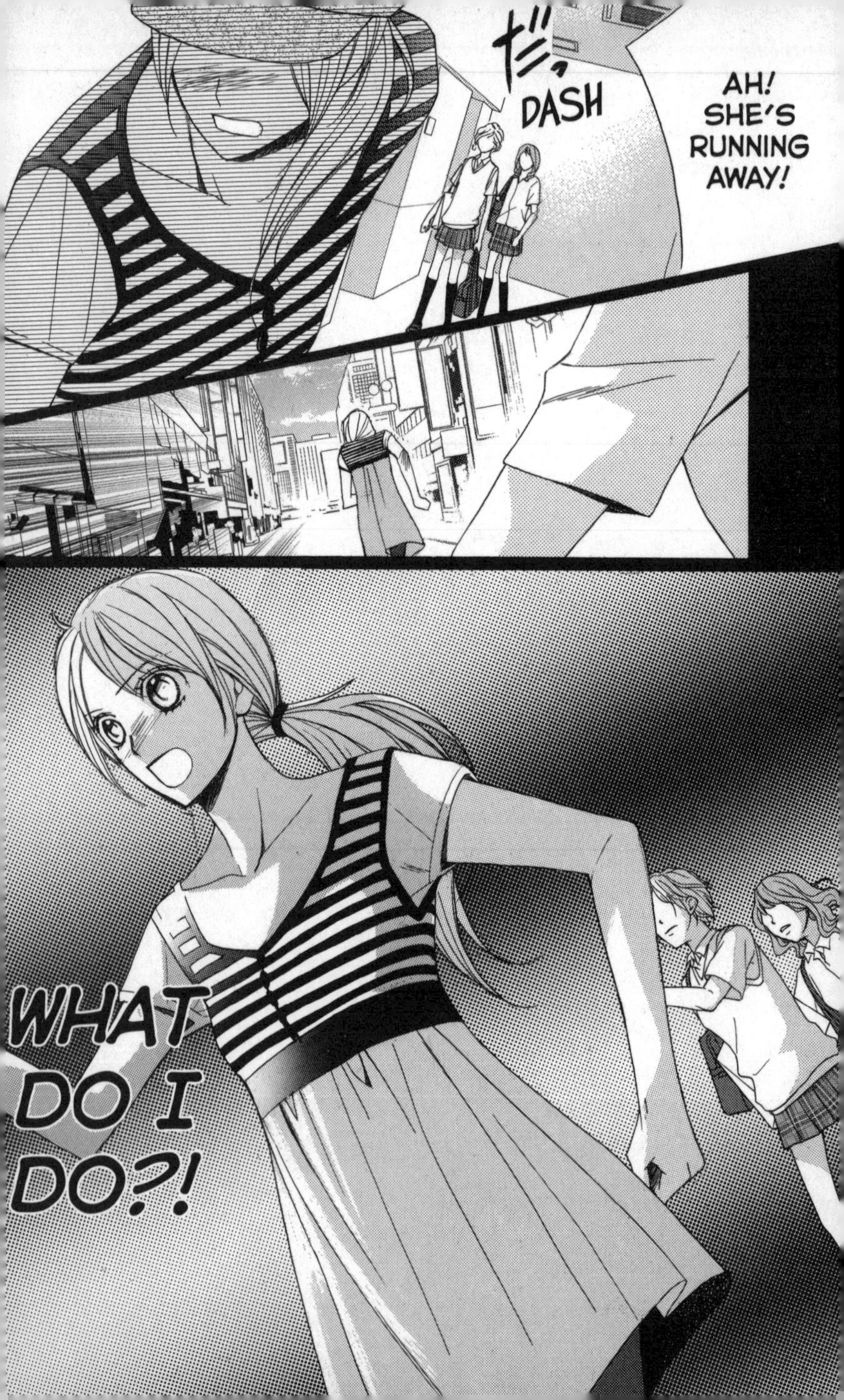
DASH
AH! SHE'S RUNNING AWAY!
WHAT DO I DO?!

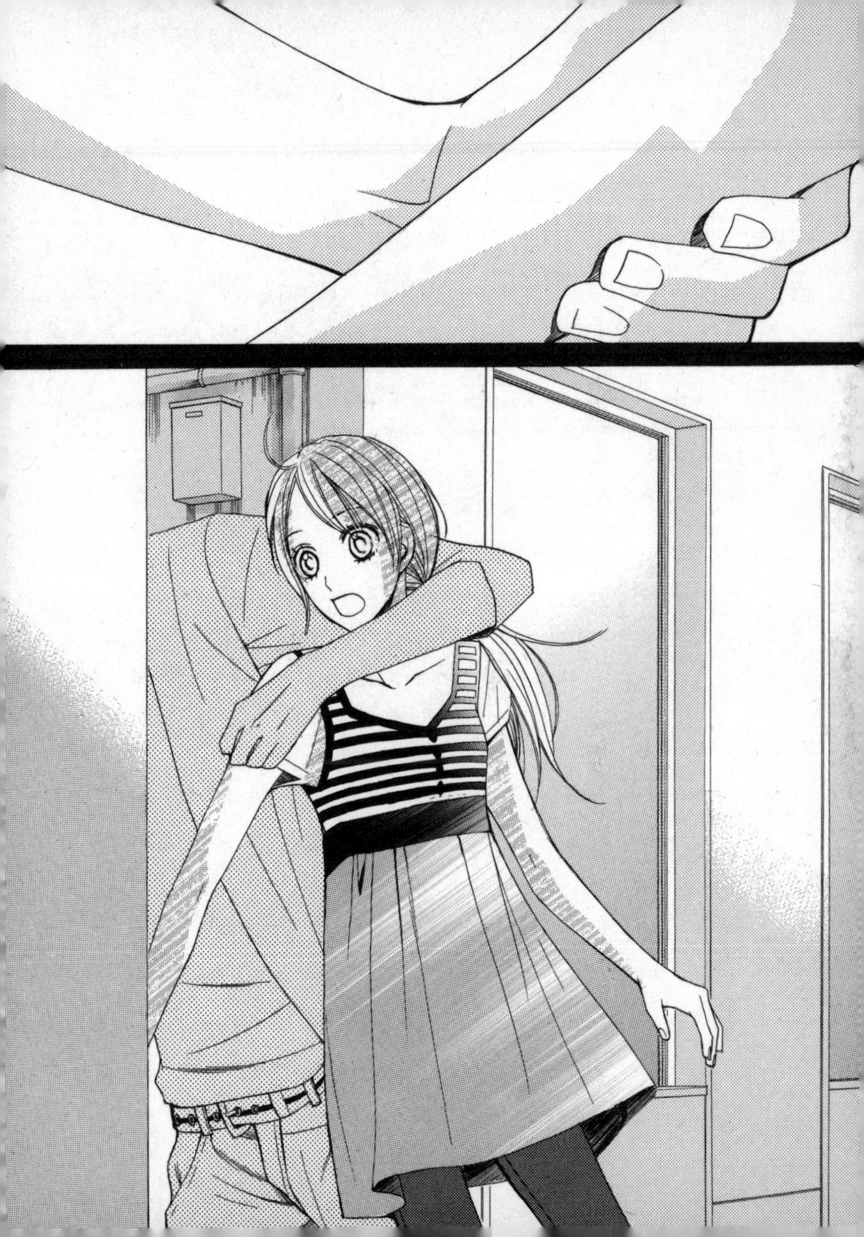

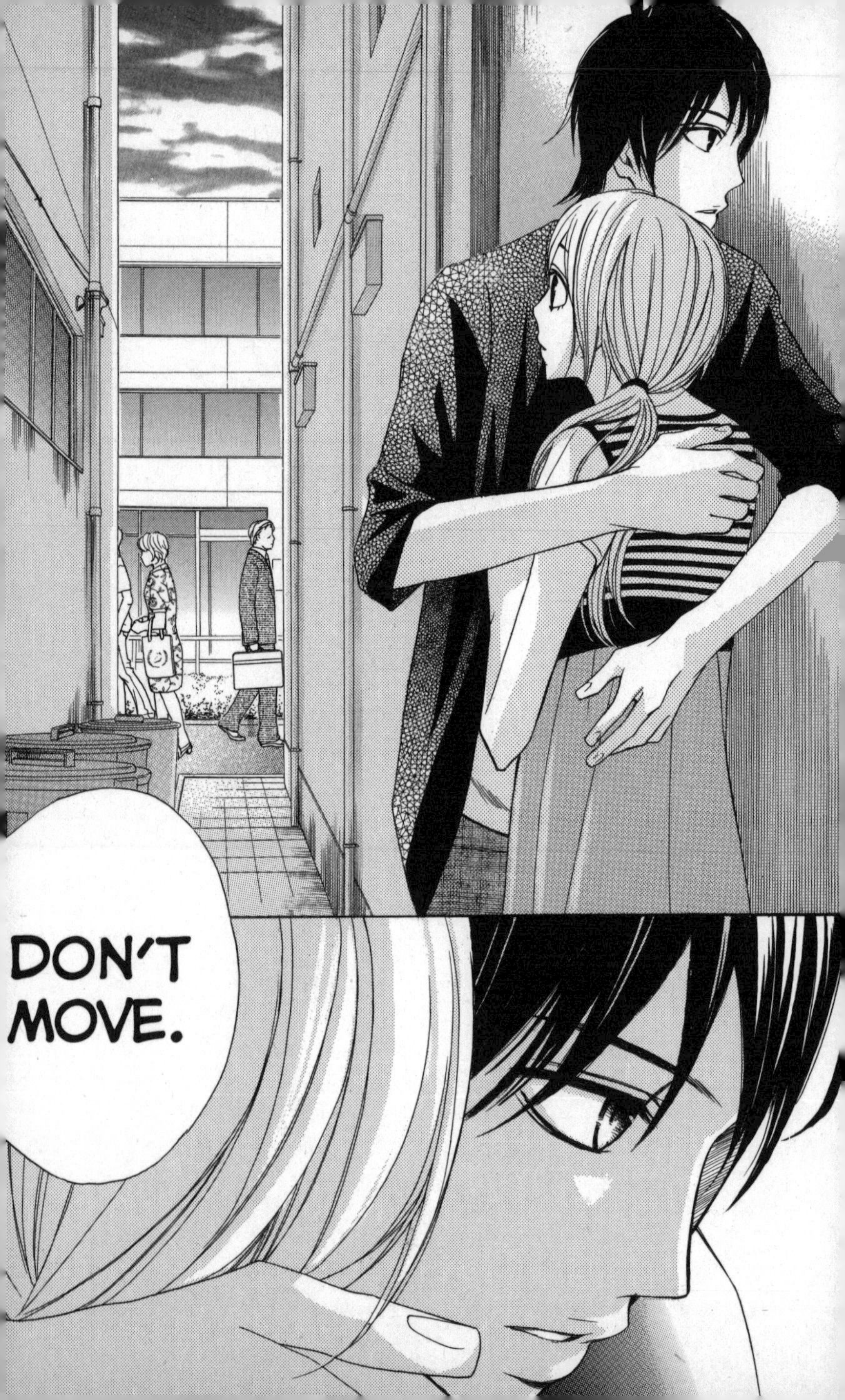
DON'T MOVE.

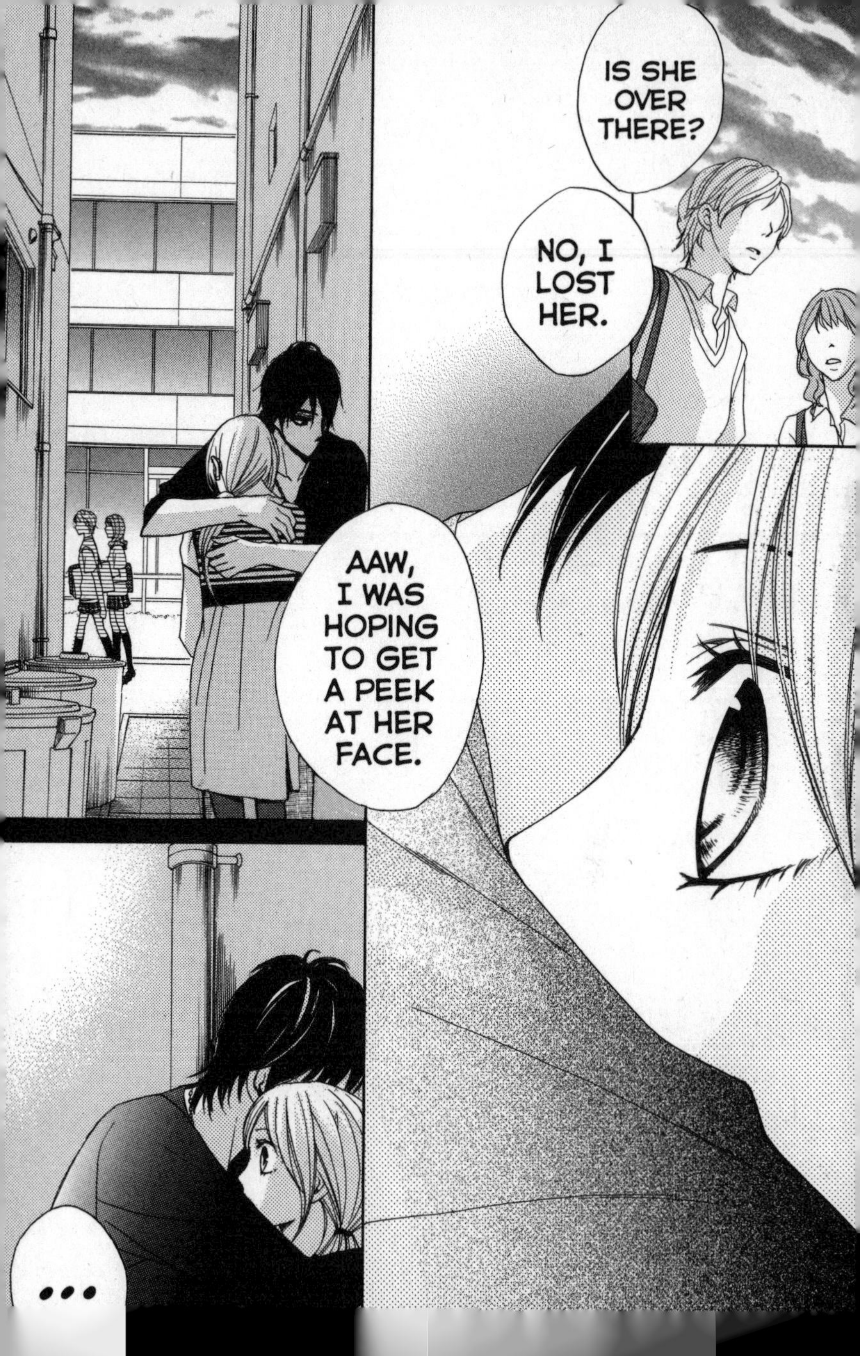
IS SHE OVER THERE?
NO, I LOST HER.
AAW, I WAS HOPING TO GET A PEEK AT HER FACE.
...

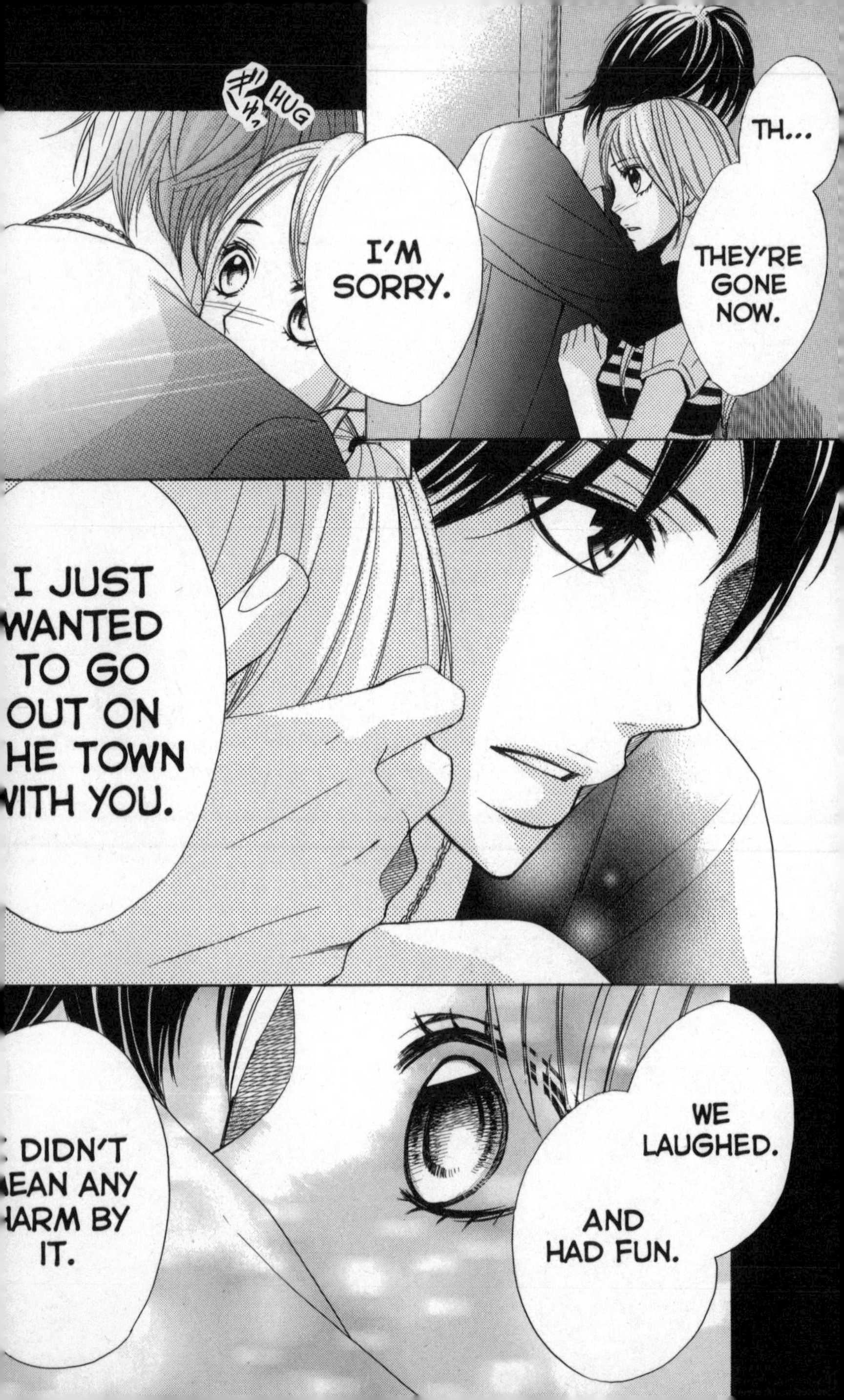
TH...
THEY'RE GONE NOW.
ぎゅっ HUG
I'M SORRY.
I JUST WANTED TO GO OUT ON HE TOWN ITH YOU.
WE LAUGHED.
AND HAD FUN.
DIDN'T EAN ANY ARM BY IT.

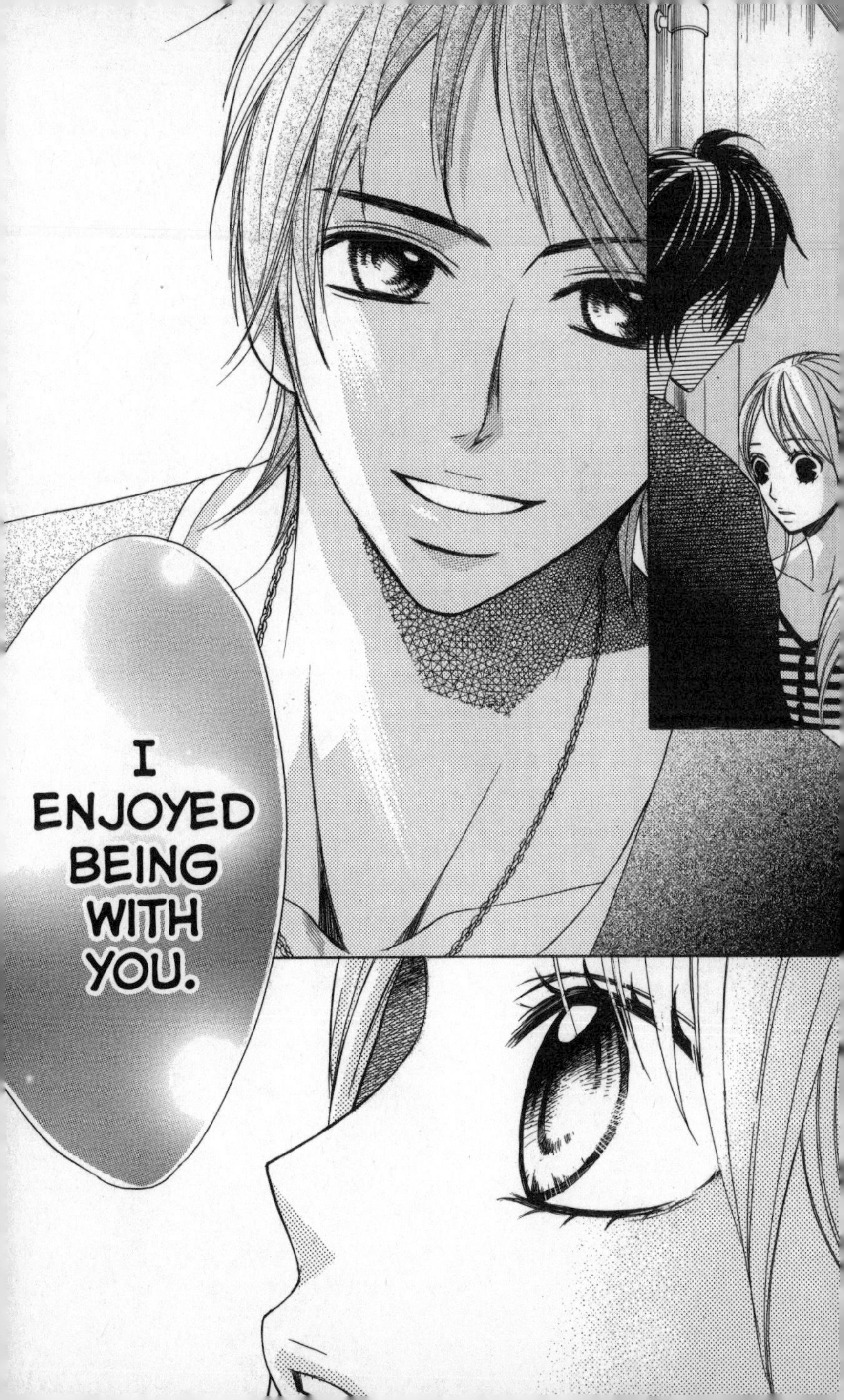
I ENJOYED BEING WITH YOU.

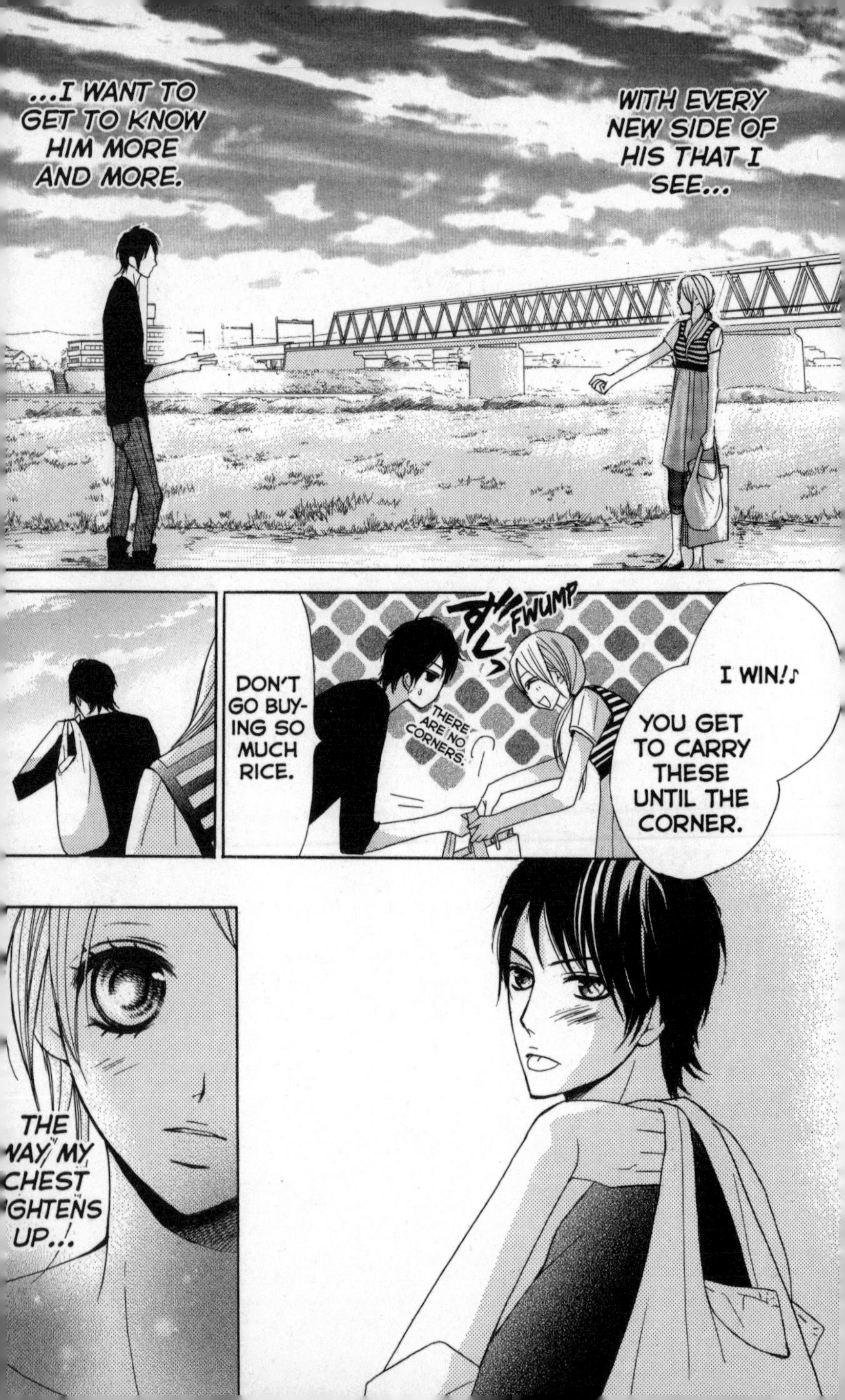
WITH EVERY NEW SIDE OF HIS THAT I SEE...
...I WANT TO GET TO KNOW HIM MORE AND MORE.
I WIN!♪
YOU GET TO CARRY THESE UNTIL THE CORNER.
FWUMP
THERE ARE NO CORNERS.
DON'T GO BUY-ING SO MUCH RICE.
THE WAY MY CHEST GHTENS UP..!

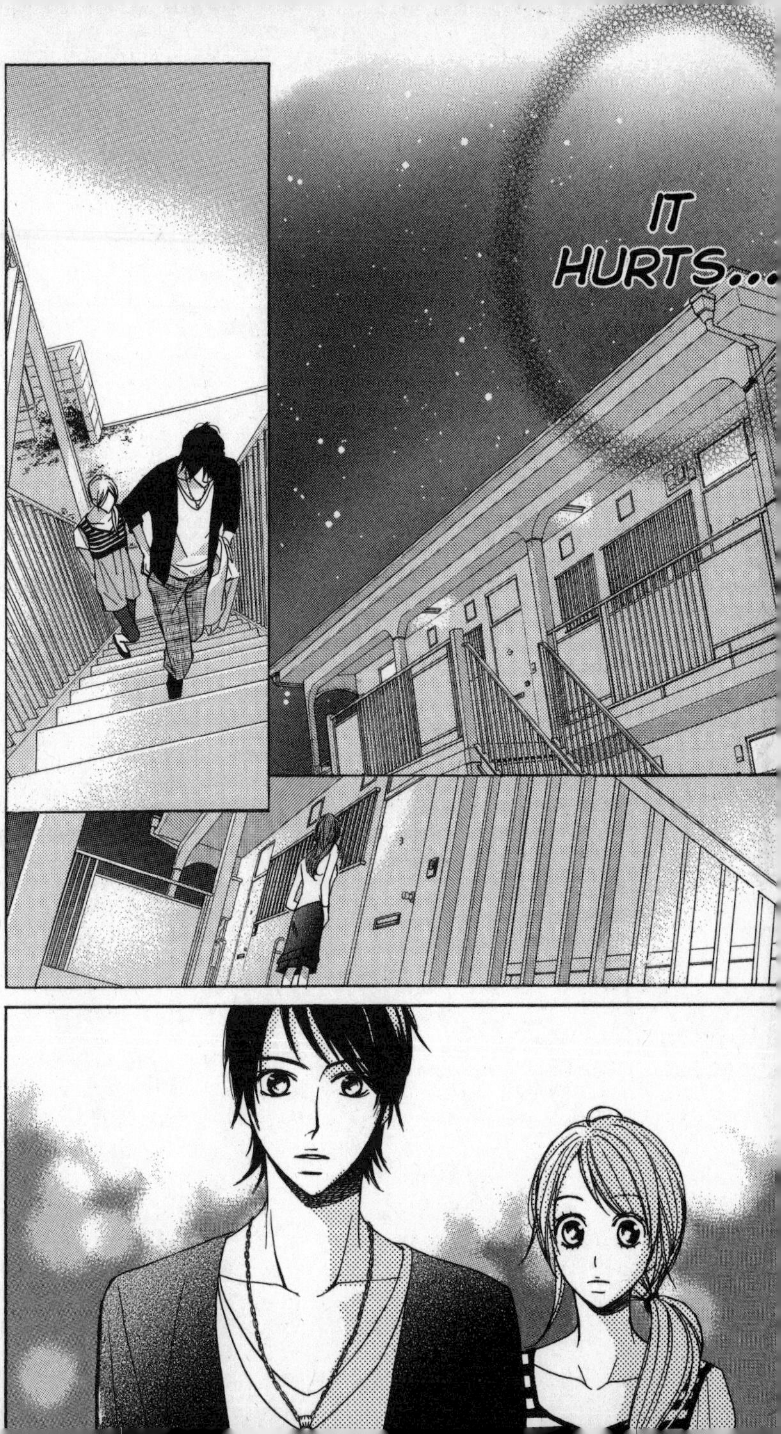
IT HURTS...

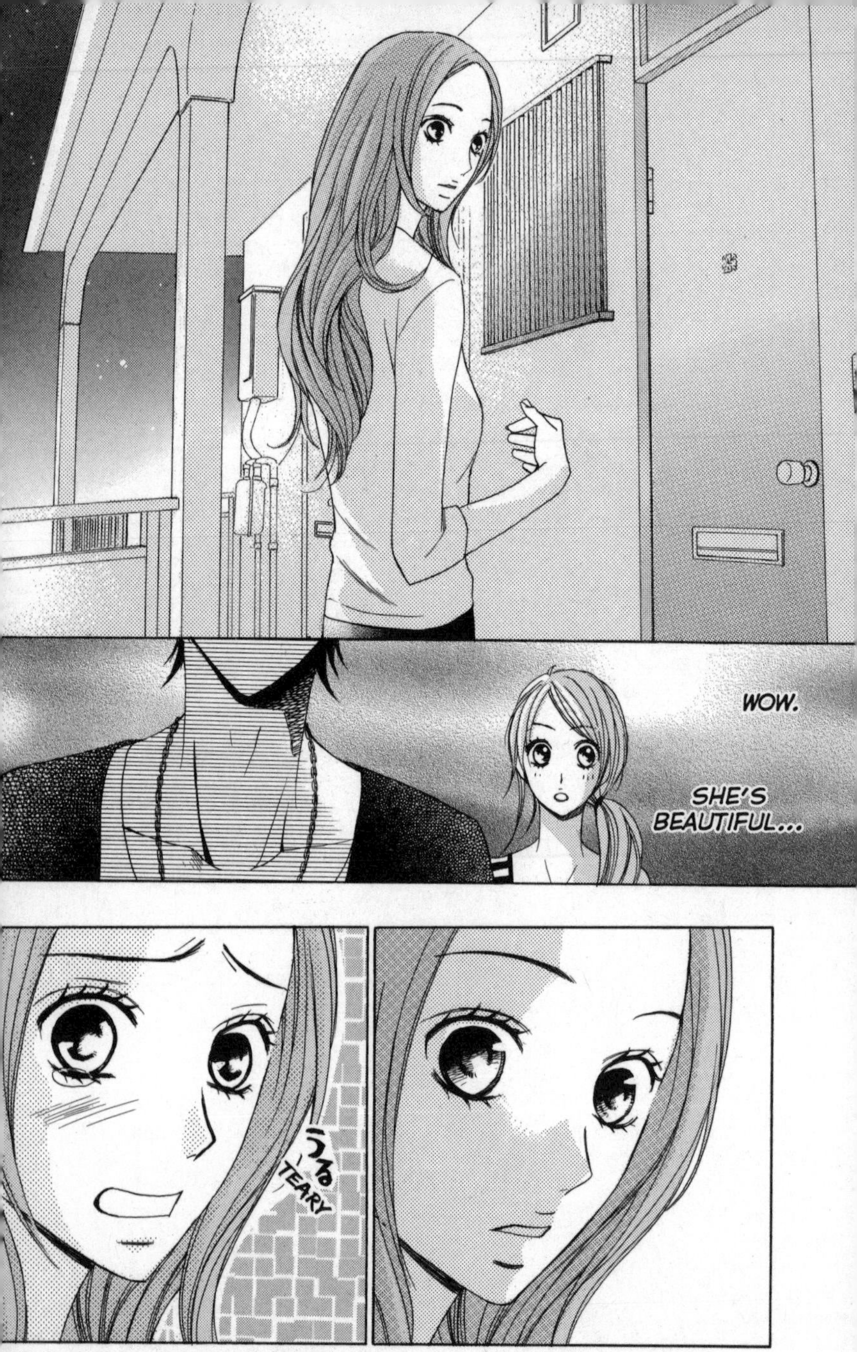
WOW.
SHE'S BEAUTIFUL...
うる
TEARY

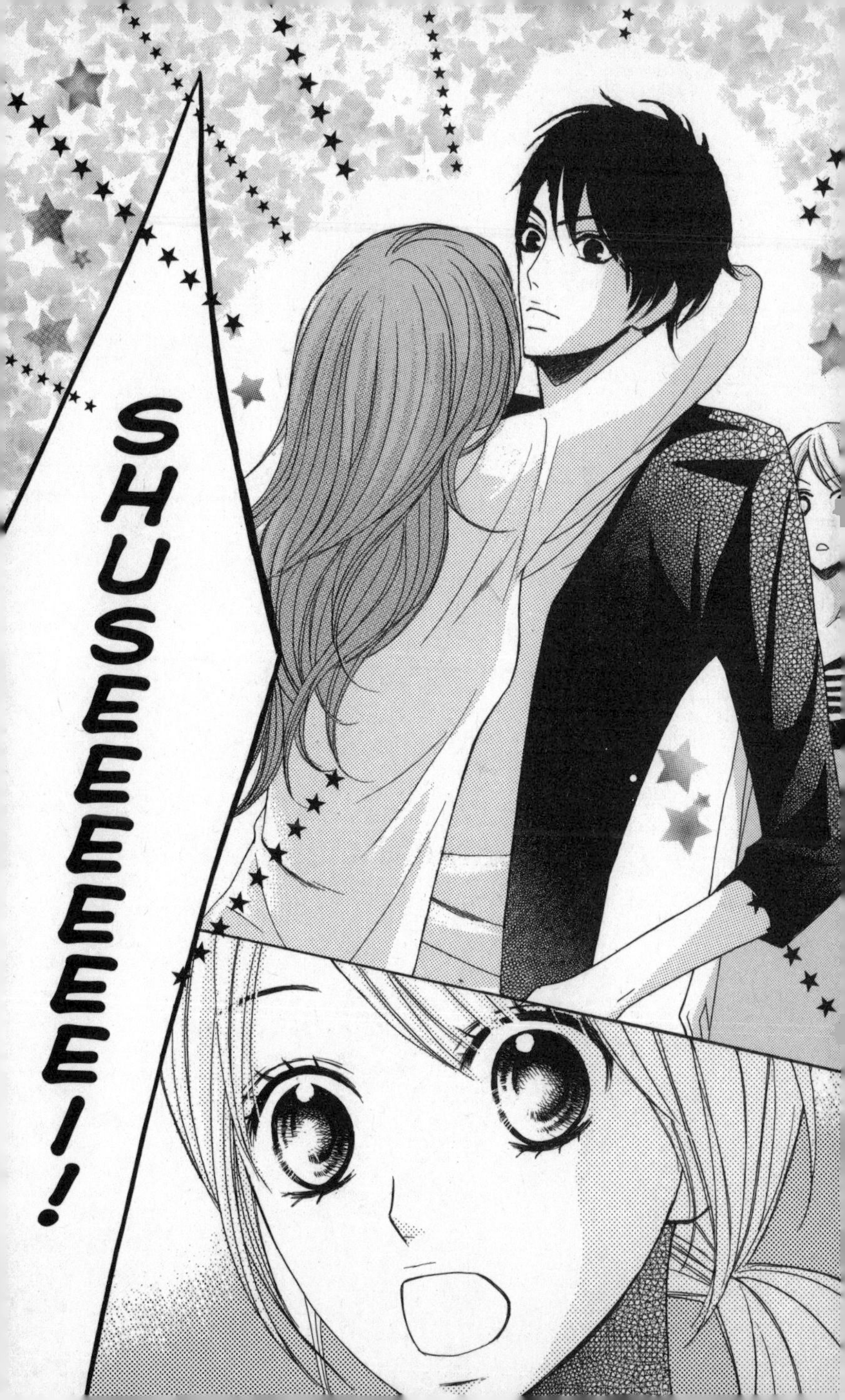
SHUSEEEEEI!!

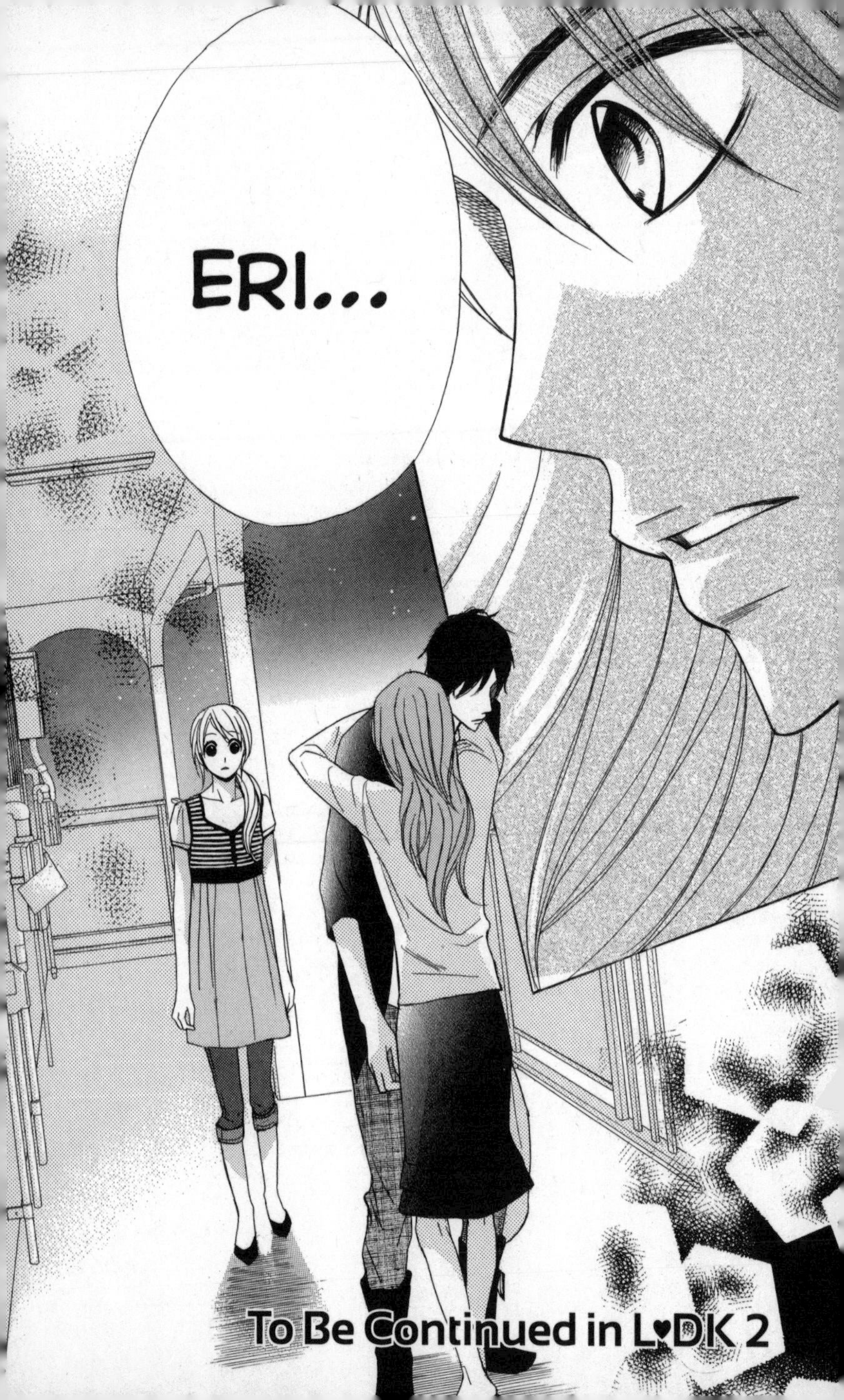
ERI...
To Be Continued in L♥DK 2

L♥DK

Hello, everyone! This is Ayu Watanabe. Thank you very much for picking up Volume 1 of L♥DK. How did you like it? I hope you enjoyed it. This makes my fifteenth compiled publication ever. When I was making my debut, I would never have been able to even imagine such a high number... Even now, it's hard to believe it's real. This is thanks to all of you who have supported me throughout my career. I truly savor the joy that I get when my friends tell me that they're reading my works, or when I receive warm encouragement from my readers. And while enjoying all that, I still pull my pen across the page every day to bring you the best work possible! Having come this far, I have even higher goals now! I want to see if I can reach twenty, or maybe even thirty volumes! And so, with an energy drink in one hand, I will persevere! Sorry for making this sound like a big speech. Oh yeah!!

Let's see, what recent news do I have to share... hmm...
Well, I'm staying in my home and focusing on my work. I rarely go out, so my wardrobe is two seasons behind the times... **As a girl,** this is very bad, so I at least try to regularly do my nails, and participate in a boot camp. Though it never lasts long (heh).
Also, maybe it's because I have sensitive skin, but my hands get super rough – it's not normal. Every month, when I work on my tones, my hands are already messed up... If anyone knows of a really good hand cream, please let me know!!

And with that, I hope you'll read volume 2, too!

Okay, so I believe there are some people who wonder what my process is when I draw my manga, so although this is just my way of doing things, I thought I'd take this time to showcase the workflow that brings you these pages.

---

① Plot Creation

After meeting with my editor, I write a summary of how the story will be constructed. Among mangaka, this is called the "plot." In my case, I type it on the computer, and include even the dialogue, as well as specific details. In a way, it's a bit like a novel. For 40-page installments, I fill up about five to six sheets of regular printer paper. I also write sentences that will describe the highlighted scenes.

When I write it on the computer, it's easier to polish it.

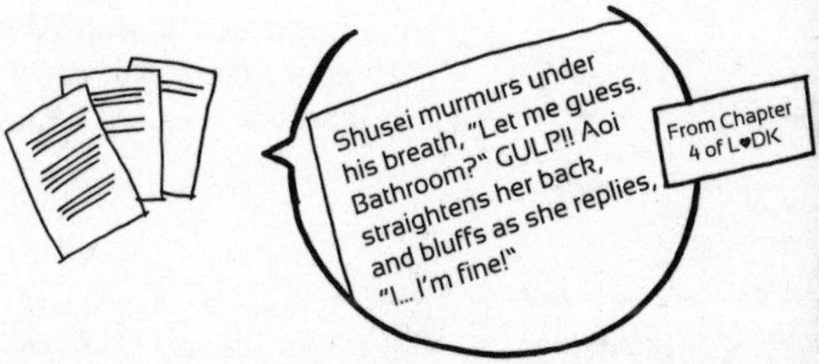
Shusei murmurs under his breath, "Let me guess. Bathroom?" GULP!! Aoi straightens her back, and bluffs as she replies, "I... I'm fine!"
From Chapter 4 of L♥DK

---

② Storyboard

After the editor and chief editor have checked the plot, and I get the okay, I move onto the storyboard. It's the stage where I decide the layout of the panels, the dialogue, and what pictures I'll be putting in. It's sort of like the blueprint of the manga, so it's one of the most important steps in the process. This is my favorite part. (Even though it's also a storm of rejections).

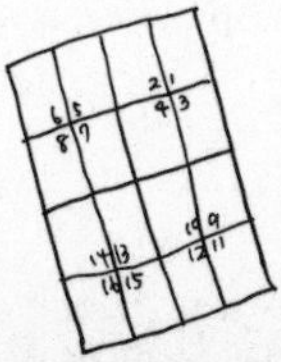

I split a size-B4 sheet of paper in sixteen parts, and construct the storyboard from that. This is where I decide where the highlight scenes will go, how many pages a scene will last, etc. It's very handy because it allows me to see the entire flow of the story. →

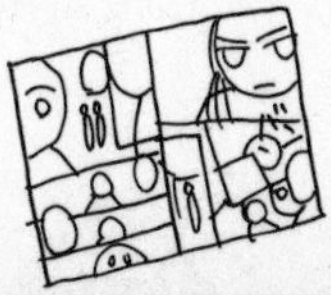

I then make a clean copy of it. I split a B4-size sheet of pap into two so that I ca see what the two-pa spreads will look lik

③ Rough Sketches

Once I've had the storyboard checked and I receive the okay on them, I can finally move onto the part where I draw the rough sketches onto draft paper. Since the completion of the storyboards makes it feel like the manga itself is in the bag, I can be rather slow about getting to work on this part (heh). I'm particularly meticulous about the designs and expressions, so I'm not very good at this part. I'd be thrilled if I could draw a decent picture on the first try. I'm sure that day will come... someday...

I get sleepy pretty quickly.

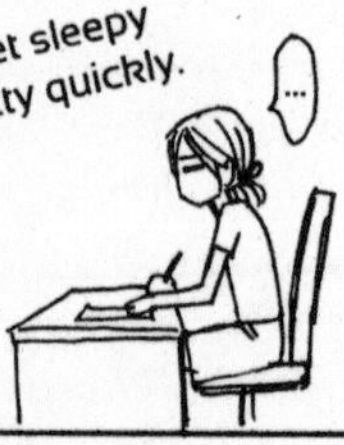
...

④ Inking

When the hellacious roughs are done, it's then time to trace my roughs with a pen and ink them in. The pictures that everyone sees in the magazines are the end product of this inking stage. I'm also not very good at this part... It's around this time that my shoulders clench up and become as hard as steel. Hot compresses are a must.

The ink I use is Kaimei Drawing Sol.

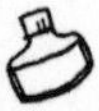

My pen nib is a Nikko mapping pen.

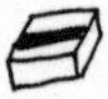

⑤ Completion

The oasis for my soul. My assistants come to help me erase my pencil marks, fill-in blacks, apply tones, and then voilà! It's complete!!

And this is how I dizzyingly spend a month. Every time, the pages are only completed when it's down to the wire and I feel battered and bruised all over. This is how a manga is born, folks. I'm so happy to deliver the results for your viewing and to receive your cheers. I'll continue to keep working just as hard from here on out!

special thanks

K.Hamano
N.Imai
S.Sato

my family
my friends

M.Morita
M.Horiuchi
Y.Innami

AND YOU

Ayu Watanabe
May.2009

Translation Notes

L♥DK

The title of this series has two meanings. In Japan, LDK is typically an abbreviation of "Living, Dining, Kitchen," which is used to describe the layout of an apartment. This is usually preceded by a number to denote the amount of bedrooms, so 1LDK means that there is one bedroom in addition to everything else. The other meaning, which is specific to this series, is "Love Doukyo" which means, "Love Cohabitation."

Afternoon special, page 9

It is typical for super markets to run a limited-time sale daily at around three in the afternoon to make sure they can get rid of perishable items, as well as try to attract customers at a usually slow time of the day.

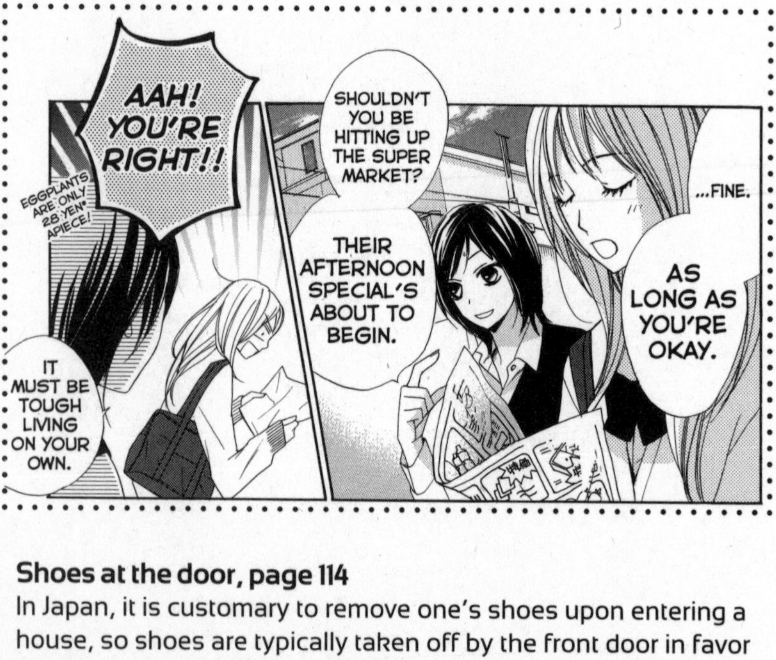

SHOULDN'T YOU BE HITTING UP THE SUPER MARKET?
THEIR AFTERNOON SPECIAL'S ABOUT TO BEGIN.
...FINE.
AS LONG AS YOU'RE OKAY.
AAH! YOU'RE RIGHT!!
EGGPLANTS ARE ONLY 28 YEN* APIECE!
IT MUST BE TOUGH LIVING ON YOUR OWN.

Shoes at the door, page 114

In Japan, it is customary to remove one's shoes upon entering a house, so shoes are typically taken off by the front door in favor of either going barefoot or wearing indoor-specific slippers.

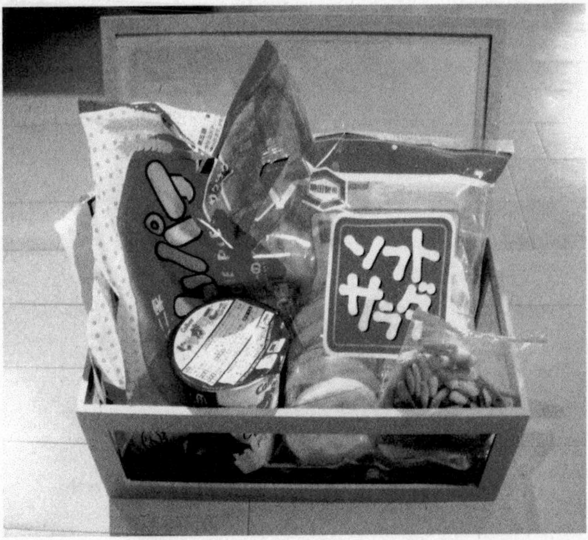
ソフト
サラダ

Everyday Essentials, Item 1
Snack Box

Crammed with all sorts of snacks, I nibble on these while working on my roughs. Actually, make that all day long. I buy so many I can't close the lid on it. It's packed with my dreams and hopes. But I have to be careful I don't overeat.

A Kodansha Comics Trade Paperback Original.

LDK volume 1 copyright © 2009 Ayu Watanabe
English translation copyright © 2015 Ayu Watanabe

Published in the United States by Kodansha Comics, an imprint of Kodansha USA Publishing, LLC, New York.

Publication rights for this English edition arranged through Kodansha Ltd., Tokyo.

First published in Japan in 2009 by Kodansha Ltd., Tokyo, as L♡DK, volume 1.

ISBN 978-1-63236-122-6

Printed in the United States of America.

www.kodanshacomics.com

8 7 6 5 4 3 2 1

Translator: Christine Dashiell
Lettering: Sara Linsley
Editing: Ajani Oloye
Kodansha Comics Edition Cover Design: Phil Balsman